The Politics of Domestic Consumption

Critical Readings

Edited by

STEVI JACKSON

and

SHAUN MOORES

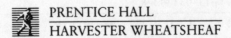

PRENTICE HALL

HARVESTER WHEATSHEAF

London New York Toronto Sydney Tokyo Singapore
Madrid Mexico City Munich

First published 1995 by
Prentice Hall/Harvester Wheatsheaf
Campus 400, Maylands Avenue
Hemel Hempstead
Hertfordshire, HP2 7EZ
A division of
Simon & Schuster International Group

Typeset in 10/12 pt Sabon by
Mathematical Composition Setters Ltd, Salisbury
Printed and bound in Great Britain by
T J Press (Padstow) Ltd, Padstow, Cornwall

Library of Congress Cataloging in Publication Data

The politics of domestic consumption: critical readings/
edited by Stevi Jackson and Shaun Moores.
    p.   cm.
Includes bibliographical references and index.
ISBN 0–13–433343–8
1.   Consumption (Economics)   2.   Households.
3.   Family.
I.   Jackson, Stevi.   II.   Moores, Shaun.
HC79.C6P63 1995
339.4'7—dc20   95–6416
                                                        CIP

British Library Cataloguing in Publication Data

A catalogue record for this book is available from
the British Library

ISBN 0–13–433343–8

1   2   3   4   5   99   98   97   96   95

WITHDRAWN

The Politics of Domestic Consumption

Introduction

Stevi Jackson and Shaun Moores

Our reader pulls together a previously dispersed range of work on various aspects of domestic consumption – and the extracts we have chosen to include in this volume come, like us, from rather different academic backgrounds. On the one hand, then, there are pieces drawn from a growing body of critical – principally feminist – sociological writings on 'the family'[1] and household life. On the other, there is a series of pieces here which can be located within the emerging interdisciplinary field of cultural studies – work which has also focused its attention on everyday practices in the home, such as those associated with the use of media technologies. Although no clear dividing line separates these two areas of academic endeavour, which we would argue share many of the same basic concerns, it is nevertheless the case that researchers in those different fields tend to carry out their investigations in relative isolation from each other. So a central aim of ours in editing the book has been to make connections and thereby demonstrate shared interests. In doing so, we hope this reader will constitute more than simply the sum of its several parts – and that it might help to open up a new, enlarged space for common teaching and research programmes around the theme of domestic consumption.

In one way or another, the contributions to this collection – whether they have their roots in sociology, women's studies or media and cultural studies – approach households with a strong emphasis on relations of power and social inequality. It is in this sense that we speak broadly about a 'politics of domestic consumption', because readings reprinted in the book raise important questions about the gendered and generational dynamics of family life – or about relations between households of different types, across divisions of class and ethnic culture. However, the necessary emphasis on power and structures of constraint does not blind all contributors to the frequently creative dimensions of domestic consumption: the active appropriation of consumer goods in everyday contexts and the construction of places called home. Our own perspective is one which recognizes a dialectic of creativity and constraint – of agency and structure – in the making of modern household cultures.[2]

A further, closely related connection which we hope to highlight by assembling this book is that between the material and symbolic aspects of daily domestic life. Whilst our intention is certainly not to propose a reductionist model of the household – in which the latter is seen only as a pale reflection of the former – we do believe that investigations into the cultural significance of objects and practices in the home need to be grounded in an understanding of economic resource distribution. They must also consider social patterns in the division of domestic labour and leisure. This is because opportunities for consumption in families are not equally available to all their members – and there will be significant differences in the amount of time, space and money that family members have access to. Indeed, the physical environment of the home itself marks an important intersection of the material and the symbolic, for it is both a bounded spatial area and a place that is lived in and made meaningful by its inhabitants. A crucial point for us, though, is that the cultural meanings they produce will inevitably vary as a consequence of their positions within hierarchies of power.

Given our view of the need to ground consumption studies in debates about household resource distribution, we have organized the collection so that it begins with a section on the economics of the domestic sphere. This is followed by writings on food and clothing practices, patterns of leisure and media reception, and the interpretation of household technologies – before the book is concluded with a more general look at symbolic constructions of the modern home. The reader's five section headings provide us with subtitles for this introductory essay, in which we now discuss our chosen pieces and situate them within their respective intellectual and political traditions – charting the interrelationship between them in greater detail. Finally, we assess the prospects for future developments in the study of domestic consumption, indicating gaps in the existing research literature.

The economics of domestic consumption

Contrary to the common ideals of modern household life – in which the family is represented as a cosy private haven in the heartless public world of work and commerce – we understand households to be fundamentally economic entities, underpinned by economic relations and embedded in wider socioeconomic structures. Within the home, then, resources are managed, services are performed and some goods may be produced as well as consumed.[3] This can certainly involve co-operation between family members, but it also entails the exercise of, and resistance to, forms of economic power. Sociologists have not always recognized this basic fact. Writing in the 1950s, before the major impact of feminist academic work on the discipline, functionalist Talcott Parsons was able to assert quite confidently that the family is a unit where the communal principle of 'each according to his [sic] needs' prevails.[4] Even today, in government statistics or in the models constructed by market researchers, households tend to be treated as undifferentiated units. Such a view is called into question by every piece in Part 1 of our reader, all of which point to a conclusion very much at odds with the one reached by Parsons – an important realization that 'while sharing a common address, family members do not necessarily share a common standard of living'.[5]

French materialist feminist, Christine Delphy, was among the first to challenge this conception of the family as an undifferentiated unit – preferring to see households as 'distribution centres' (Reading 1.1). She does not assume domestic consumption to be communal or egalitarian. Instead, her principal focus is on hierarchical, patriarchal relations in the home, and the argument is illustrated by data on small family farms in rural France. Here, the man's place as head of both household and business entitles him, socially at least, to the best of whatever is available. His entitlement is maintained through women's self-denial and by children being forbidden specific items. It is Delphy's claim, however, that the specific pattern she observes in these peasant households derives more generally from the dominant marital arrangement in modern Western societies where husbands exploit their wives' domestic labour and control economic resources.[6]

Male power is a pervasive feature of most traditional and non-Western societies too. In a cross-cultural study, Ann Whitehead has compared domestic budgeting practices among the Kusasi in Ghana with those typically found in British urban families (Reading 1.2).[7] Understandably, there are quite significant differences in how their household economies are structured and organized. So whereas consumption in British families is financed primarily through wages, the Kusasi supply basic household needs through their own system of agricultural production – although they do raise some cash crops and engage in trade. The 'conjugal contract' – terms on which husbands and wives exchange money, goods and services – also varies considerably. Where many British women perform housework in return for financial support, Kusasi wives play a major part in agricultural labour, as well as providing such services as cooking and childcare. Nevertheless, it is significant that in both cases men still exert greater control over resources than women and enjoy privileged rights to consumption. Husbands' economic authority rests either on their effective ownership of staple and cash crops or on the wage of a male 'breadwinner'.

Of course, over the last half century, women in industrial societies have been entering the paid labour force in ever increasing numbers – and this has led some feminists to ask whether 'the male breadwinner' is now just a myth.[8] Only about a quarter of women in Britain are engaged in full-time housework and childcare, with female earnings proving essential to the survival of many families. Having said that, women's wages are generally lower than men's and the majority of married women in waged work are employed on a part-time basis, so it is unusual for wives to earn as much as their husbands. A number of recent studies find that even where wives do make a substantial contribution to household income, the importance of that contribution is not properly recognized.[9] It is often understood to pay for 'added extras' rather than for the core items of family expenditure. Men's ideological claim to breadwinner status is thereby reaffirmed.

The precise ways in which couples manage the money coming into a household do vary, however, and Jan Pahl's pioneering investigations of family finances help us to comprehend this variation (Reading 1.3).[10] She outlines four systems of financial control in her piece here on patterns of spending within marriage. The first two systems are forms of 'pooling' where both partners have equal access in theory to a common fund – but which in practice is controlled by only one of them. The third is 'husband-controlled' where men typically allocate their wives a fixed housekeeping allowance. In these circumstances a woman need not always know exactly how much her spouse earns. A fourth system is 'wife-controlled'. Here, women both control and manage the household finances, although this is far from saying they have ultimate power – because it can still involve a relationship of economic dependency. There is a great deal of difference, then, between proper financial independence and being responsible for disposing of a partner's income. Another significant feature of Pahl's sample is that the husbands actually had more money allocated to them for personal, as opposed to collective, expenditure: for example, spending larger amounts than women on leisure activities.

Pahl's are not isolated findings – being backed up by further research reported in the work of Gail Wilson (Reading 1.4) or Sallie Westwood (Reading 1.5). In addition, the self-denial which Delphy noted is very much in evidence again. It would appear that women rarely spend guiltlessly on themselves yet regularly assume men have both a right and a need to do so. This denial is most marked when the man is the sole earner or else when his partner's earnings are significantly lower. In such a situation, a couple may talk of the husband's wage as jointly 'theirs' – but the wife does not see herself as having an equal right to spend it. An undoubted attraction of paid work for married women is that it provides them with a source of money over which they have some limited control. For instance, women in Westwood's study used various strategies – including catalogue or club purchases made in the workplace context – to dispose of their income directly before it all went into the common household pot. Strategies of this sort were particularly valued by those of the Asian factory workers who lived in extended families, where they tended to have even less individual control of common funds than women in nuclear family units. The so-called 'extras' which are bought in this way will typically be goods for the children or for the household as a whole rather than purely personal purchases.

Furthermore, Wilson and Westwood both highlight the fact that it is women who show greater responsibility in the management of money – compared with their partners' frequent irresponsibility – with the women here being responsible in a double sense. The day-to-day care, feeding and clothing of family members generally falls to them, and hence the expenditure this entails. They therefore remain constantly alert to the needs of others and to how those requirements go unmet if they fail to budget sensibly. As Wilson argues, where men are particularly insensitive to the needs of others and family income is low the net result is often real hardship for women and children. In fact, feminist researchers have found that lone mothers dependent on state benefit and living on or near the poverty line can still feel economically better off without a spouse. The greater freedom which they experience might only be what Hilary Graham[11] has called the freedom to go without – but these single parents at least retain control over the total household budget.

So if women's standard of living is commonly lower than that of other family members, it clearly helps to illustrate the relationship we have identified between differential consumption and differential economic power. It also reveals the way in which women's patterns of domestic consumption are inextricably bound up with the work they do as wives and mothers. However, this should not necessarily lead us to view them as passive victims of oppression. There are certainly examples in Wilson's sample where women appear to be cowed into submission – and yet Westwood's study points to evidence of resistance to male authority. She adds, though, that as long as the majority of women are denied a decent living wage, they have little alternative to financial dependence on individual men. Once again, the structural or material basis of gendered inequalities in household consumption is underlined by her research findings.

The significance of food and clothing in family life

We suggested earlier in our introduction that practices of domestic consumption are shaped by dual forces of creativity and constraint, and this general observation might now help us to comprehend the everyday meanings of food and clothing in particular. In both instances, consumers combine and transform commodities which they have bought in order actively to produce something – a meal or a style, an occasion or an identity – but they always do so in circumstances where various social determinations press down upon their routine cultural activity. Whilst paying attention to the creative practices of cooking or dressing in families, it is important to bear these constraining factors in mind. As signalled in the discussion above, the most immediate structural limitations are obviously financial – the amount and distribution of money available to be spent – yet these are not the only determinations.

For example, in the case of diet, it is possible to identify culturally specific 'food ideologies':[12] ideas about what constitutes a so-called 'proper meal', and what different dishes are appropriate for men, women and children. The notion of a proper meal is explored here by Anne Murcott (Reading 2.1)[13] and also by Nickie Charles (Reading 2.2). They each refer to research projects in which their interviewees employed this term spontaneously, and in which the idea was clearly located within wider ideologies of family life. So in Murcott's South Wales valley community, the proper meal is known as a 'cooked dinner' consisting of meat, potatoes and vegetables. Anything else, even when cooked and served at home, does not enter into the same category – a distinction that seems confusing at first for those coming to live in the region. That it is highly specific to white working-class communities can be demonstrated by travelling just a few miles down the road to inner-city Cardiff, where the range of cooking smells attests to a more diverse conception of good food and a balanced diet.

Proper meals are quintessentially family meals, to be eaten with all co-resident household members present at the table. In their elaborated forms – Sunday or Christmas dinner – they are frequently shared with other kin from outside the household group. Such occasions have a high symbolic value, representing home comforts and family unity. The women in Murcott's study referred to cooking for their husbands' return from work: hence the evening meal signified his reinclusion in the domestic context. In Charles's research, carried out in Yorkshire, it was often men who enforced high standards of table manners and insisted that children ate what they were given. Children thereby learn the appropriate dining behaviour; but just as importantly, says Charles, they learn about the power relations of families as social institutions.

Both Murcott and Charles point to another constraining factor, which is the dominance of men's culinary tastes. If the cooked family meal is not entirely for his benefit, then the food that gets served up will almost certainly have been prepared according to a husband's dietary preferences.[14] The extent to which wives actually consulted their partners on the precise content of meals varied. However, a man's known likes and dislikes were respected and women interviewed in these research projects counted themselves 'lucky' if their husbands' tastes were easy to please. Men exerted a strong pressure to keep to 'traditional cooking', so any experimentation with more exotic or adventurous dishes was usually abandoned in the face of discouraging responses. It seems that the deference to male desires is a product of the complex interplay between power and love in marital relations. Husbands may get what they want because of their position as head of household with greater economic authority or control, but it can also be a matter of wives demonstrating affection through cooking. When a man explicitly rejects something which his spouse has prepared for him, his displeasure therefore serves as a potent emotional weapon.

One important part of Charles's essay – and of the larger research project which she and Marion Kerr conducted – is what it has to report about generational as well as gender differences in domestic food consumption. There are two issues to consider here. To begin with, we need to note that some types of food have a far higher social status than others, with young children's dishes such as canned spaghetti and fish fingers generally being classed as low status meals. Meanwhile, red meat – the main staple of fathers' diets in the Yorkshire study – has much greater symbolic value. Secondly, though, it is necessary for us to acknowledge the fact that children do not consume freely. Their dependent, subordinate position within the household means they are largely subject to their parents' food choices – as when they are obliged to share the family meal. Still, they can and do resist this situation on certain occasions. So Charles suggests that a possible reason for children's difficult behaviour at meal times is precisely their reluctance to eat foods which are effectively being forced upon them and which they do not always want.

Indeed, the process of growing up and gaining greater independence from parents is typically marked by young people's insistence on making their own consumer choices. They might try to achieve this by acquiring pocket money through part-time work, or by negotiating with parents for more opportunities to express their personal tastes. Perhaps the area of consumption where that process is most evident would be the buying and wearing of clothes. In cultural studies, for instance, it has long been recognized that style can serve as a public statement of youthful independence and 'subcultural' identity.[15] Clothing is thus a potential arena for the expression of individual or peer group aesthetics – a space for teenagers to put a significant distance between their own preferences and those of an older generation. Our final piece in Part Two, by Peter Corrigan, explores these issues in an innovative way because it focuses on the significance and exchange of clothing within the private sphere, drawing particular attention to mother–daughter relationships in which clothes are symbolic of the latter's relative autonomy (Reading 2.3).

Corrigan adopts an alternative approach to those we have discussed up to now. Although several of the preceding readings in our volume deal with the symbolic aspects of domestic consumption, they all seek to relate this to the material or structural parameters within which consumers operate and meanings are made. Corrigan, in contrast, presents a micro-sociological, ethnomethodological analysis focusing more narrowly on how people make sense of intrafamilial exchanges of clothing. In doing so, he employs the concept of 'theoreticity' to explore the dynamics of mother–daughter relations.[16] A theoretic action, then, is one that can be accounted for in terms of known rules or criteria. Hence when Corrigan talks of daughters' emerging 'sartorial theoreticity', his reference is to the following of particular dress codes for which they know the rules – which may be quite distinct from the codes followed by their mothers. These young women's sartorial theoreticity undermines their mothers' attempts to continue buying clothes for them; the parent does not understand the conventions by which her child puts a style together – and is likely to have her purchases disparaged, dismissed and discarded.

As a general explanation of the ways in which young women in families establish some independent control over their personal consumption, Corrigan's analysis is convincing. It also has to be said that, from our point of view, other specific elements of the argument are rather less convincing because he neglects the structural context in which exchanges of clothing take place. This is most notably the case in the emphasis that he puts on gift-giving activities – a means by which clothes are circulated in the family economy. Here he includes not just the presents that are offered on special occasions such as birthdays but additionally the routine items of clothing bought, for example, by mothers for daughters. Whether these ordinary purchases are best seen by us as gifts is questionable. After all, the provision of clothes for children is part and parcel of routine maternal care. Similarly, if a wife buys her husband a new pair of socks because his old ones are worn out, is this necessarily a gift or merely an expression of wifely service? The anthropological dictum that giving gifts is an expression of power[17] hardly seems to apply to these forms of exchange, yet Corrigan insists on it. Observing that active participation in the 'family clothing economy' is chiefly the preserve of women, he sees men as the losers in this area of domestic distribution – as wives buy more for their husbands than vice versa – but by failing to recognize the material relationships of dependency which underpin the transactions, he turns domestic power relations on their head. Women's purchase of clothing for other household members is not simply an expression of power but of their domestic responsibilities as carers. It must also be remembered that clothes have to be maintained once they enter the private sphere, and no doubt there will be many daughters keen to demonstrate sartorial theoreticity who still expect their mothers to wash and iron for them!

The power relations of leisure and media reception

Rosemary Deem, in the opening contribution to Part 3, usefully sets the scene for the extracts which directly follow hers – because she advances a fundamental point about understanding domestic leisure in relation to household labour, and about the differential meanings of 'home' for men and women in families (Reading 3.1). For men, the home is primarily a space and time for relaxation: traditionally defined in relation to an external workplace and a fixed working day. For women, meanwhile, it usually signifies a place of work[18] – whether they are unpaid full-time housewives or have some paid employment outside the domestic context – and housework, as the popular saying goes, is 'never done'. There are always unfinished chores, and responsibilities to be fulfilled. Deem explains that women in this situation find it hard to then redefine their living spaces as settings for leisure, or to put aside time for undistracted cultural activity.[19] Nevertheless, she reports on how women in a British town manage to make do with the situational resources they have to hand, creating their own pleasures within these spatio-temporal and social constraints.

Media consumption, in its various forms, is perhaps the major domestic leisure pursuit in late modern society. Over recent years, critical audience researchers within the field of cultural studies have begun to address the household uses of media such as television, radio and popular fiction, and in doing so, they also inevitably engage with the kind of issues raised by a leisure sociologist like Deem. So reception analysts, employing qualitative research methods in their investigations, have posed a series of related questions to do with the gender politics of home entertainment. Are there distinctive masculine and feminine modes of reception as a result of the different socially constructed positions which men and women tend to occupy within the household? Have particular gendered patterns of pleasure and preference formed in response to a range of media genres? How might those differences in taste be negotiated within the power dynamics of domestic life? The pieces we reprint here from work by Dorothy Hobson (Reading 3.2), Janice Radway (Reading 3.3) and David Morley (Reading 3.4) each provide us with answers to some or all of these questions.

In the course of carrying out an ethnography of young working-class housewives in Birmingham during the 1970s, Hobson came to realize that broadcasting played a fundamental role in the organization of these women's everyday experiences.[20] Her essay in this collection deals first with daytime radio listening, and secondly with TV viewing practices and preferences. So in the mornings, pop music radio was used as a background accompaniment to the performance of domestic chores and childcare – helping to give shape or structure to a highly fragmented working routine, and to relieve at least some of the frustrations of being isolated in the home. The medium offered a kind of 'lifeline' which connected them to a social space beyond the front door, and the music played on air supplied them with a poignant reminder of leisure time before they were married. When she turned to consider patterns of television consumption in her women's lives, Hobson found that they spoke about 'two worlds' of TV. A gendered demarcation line appeared to be drawn in between the types of programme which were actively enjoyed and those genres that they avoided watching or that failed to interest them. While they could relate to a culturally constructed feminine realm of fictional output[21] which articulated the personal and emotional concerns of family life – or promised a fantasy alternative to their own daily experience – they disliked content which was thought to constitute a masculine domain, associated mainly with the factual reporting of current affairs or with action and adventure fiction.

If Hobson had begun by exploring broader experiences of household labour before concentrating on media reception, then roughly the same route was taken by Radway's research – but in the opposite direction. Her study of romantic fiction readers in an American Midwestern town she calls 'Smithton' was originally conceived as an investigation of how texts in this genre are interpreted by a particular reading community. She was surprised to find, though, that when they were asked about the meanings of the stories in question, her respondents tended to talk principally about the significance of the act of consumption itself: 'the meaning of romance reading as a social event in a familial context'.[22] She saw that the significance of this routine domestic act was just as important for the women in her study as the sense they made of the narratives. It provided them with an opportunity to mark out a time and space of their own in a day which, as wives and mothers, they devoted largely to the care and support of others – transporting them, temporarily at least, from the emotionally and physically draining job of attending to their families' needs.

Radway is thereby persuaded to unpack the notion of 'escapism', a term which previously had negative connotations for many cultural critics. Re-evaluating the pleasures of reading the romance, she contends that – in the precise circumstances which her interviewees find themselves – the desire to be transported elsewhere through the medium of fantasy literature is quite understandable. Of course, we also have to return to the structure of the narrative fiction because it is necessary for us to explain why such readers choose to escape via romance rather than through any other genre of popular literature. Here, Radway draws on the feminist psychoanalytical theory of Nancy Chodorow.[23] She borrows from it in order to argue that the Smithton readers are actively identifying with a heroine who, in the end, is nurtured, for in their own day-to-day lives they are destined only to nurture others. This fictional character is finally united with a male hero who shows himself to be capable of caring, producing compensatory yet contradictory reading pleasures. The imaginative excursions on offer are ones which promise to release those women from their immediate domestic surroundings, while ultimately confining them to the discourses of heterosexual romance which put them there in the first place.

With the parallel aim of analyzing TV consumption as a social event in a familial context,[24] Morley conducted informal conversational interviews in domestic settings: talking to household members about their viewing habits and preferences. His findings suggest that the home's different meanings for wives and husbands can lead to a marked cultural division of feminine and masculine styles of viewing. So for the women with whom he spoke, watching television was an activity which they were obliged to perform distractedly, often in tandem with other tasks such as ironing or cleaning. The men, however, expressed a preference for engaging with TV in a more concentrated and attentive way, something that they were far better placed to do because of their unproblematic definition of the home as a site of leisure.

Pursuing Hobson's earlier assertions about the two 'worlds' of television, Morley also identifies a gendered patterning of programme tastes, but goes on to emphasize the power relations and interpersonal negotiations which surround control of viewing choices in domestic life. In what we might call the 'politics of the sitting room', there is a struggle for possession of the remote control device – a struggle that, in Morley's households, is usually won by the father. Indeed, the researcher has even referred to this gadget as a 'descendant of the medieval mace':[25] a condensed symbol of power which sits 'on the arm of Daddy's chair'. An interesting exception to that general rule is in situations when, during the daytime or early on weekend mornings, mothers manage to find opportunities for undistracted 'solo viewing'. These stolen moments of guilty pleasure could be compared with the reading practices of women in Radway's project discussed above.

Two further papers in this section focus rather less on the gendered significance of domestic leisure and media reception than on cultural constructions of meaning which are shaped by ethnic, generational or class divisions. Marie Gillespie's discussions with teenagers from South Asian families living in West London reveal variant uses and interpretations of so-called 'Bombay films' – hired on video and watched in the privacy of the home (Reading 3.5). She discovers that whereas these texts are salient to parents and grandparents as a nostalgic link with their country of origin – helping to create a kind of 'imagined community' across space and time – second generation children position themselves differently and use the viewing occasion to debate with adults about the customs, values and beliefs of traditional Indian culture. Their responses to representations of tradition tend to be more critical and contradictory. Derek Wynne's article, meanwhile, describes frictions caused by the divergence of cultural tastes and lifestyles on a private housing estate in Northern England (Reading 3.6). He usefully situates domestic practices such as home decoration and furnishing within the wider context of public leisure pursuits: sport, drinking, nights out, holidaymaking, and so on. The neighbourhood setting which provides the focus for his study is inhabited by two distinct middle-class fractions. One has invested importance primarily in economic capital, the other in what Pierre Bourdieu would term 'cultural capital'.[26]

The uses and interpretations of household technologies

Domestic technologies offer us a good example of intersections between the material and the symbolic in everyday life. They appear in the home as material things: for instance, as washing machines, electric drills, TV sets or hi-fi systems. Their presence is itself consequent on material factors such as household income – and reflects prior decisions, and disputes, over expenditure. Yet those artefacts also acquire specific symbolic meanings for family members as they are incorporated into the household's hierarchical relations. Much of this machinery has become a taken-for-granted part of the furniture in affluent Western societies. Items unknown to, or outside the financial reach of, previous generations are now regarded more as necessities than luxuries. In Britain, then, 99 per cent of households possess a television, while some 89 per cent have a telephone and 88 per cent a washing machine.[27] Newer technologies, too, are constantly entering domestic culture: recent cases include the microwave oven and satellite TV.[28] Of course, certain meanings will already have been 'encoded' in the product at the stages of its design and marketing, but others are added as consumers 'decode' the object in contexts of use. Those meanings may occasionally be subject to change as the significance of a domestic technology shifts historically.[29]

The range of readings collected in this section of the book covers both work and leisure technologies, although we begin with extracts from Cynthia Cockburn (Reading 4.1) and Judy Wajcman (Reading 4.2) which concentrate on the machinery of household labour. Consumer appliances that are closely associated with women's work in the home often serve as a means of producing further things to be consumed: cooked food, clean clothes, and so on. They are the fundamental tools of a housewife's trade. Many men also have equipment for jobs in and around the house – these, however, are typically connected with traditional masculine tasks like car maintenance or putting up shelves. Men's tools differ from those routinely used by women in that they cannot be defined so straightforwardly as work-related objects. So various 'do-it-yourself' (DIY) tasks might just as easily be considered a spare time hobby or leisure interest.

Cockburn's key concern is with the exclusion of women from certain forms of gendered 'technological competence', an exclusion which arises from and perpetuates a particular division of activities in the domestic environment. In her research, she found that even where partners share tasks, they still retain a separation of 'women's jobs' from 'men's jobs' – with the latter depending on specialized masculine skills. For example, they may do the gardening together, but she weeds the flower beds while he wields the hedge trimmer. Tools associated with, say, electrical repairs and DIY require technical knowledge which men can guard quite jealously. Indeed, women themselves will accept that they are incompetent with such gadgets, only learning how to operate them when their partners show no interest in these traditionally masculine practices. The necessary skills are passed on from father to son, so reproducing women's exclusion from the male domain of the toolshed or workshop. Similarly, although women use advanced technical appliances in the performance of housework, they rarely know how to fix them when they break down. Cockburn argues that this situation puts men in control of women's domestic machinery – and creates a dependency on husbands or tradesmen to keep them running.

Conventional wisdom tells us that the standard equipment of modern housework – cookers, fridges, washing machines, irons and vacuum cleaners[30] – is labour-saving technology which has reduced the burden of domestic chores for women. This common assumption is strongly challenged by the feminist writings reviewed in Wajcman's contribution. The idea that technology, in and of itself, reduces the time housework takes is seen to be naïve. Such 'technological determinism'[31] ignores the wider social and historical processes which have surrounded the development and deployment of particular technologies. Available evidence suggests the hours full-time housewives spend on their work have declined very little, if at all, during the past century. Where innovations relieve some of the physical drudgery of domestic labour, this has been compensated for by factors such as the rising standards of personal and household cleanliness.[32] Wajcman argues that the main determinants affecting the hours women work in the private sphere are not to do with technologies themselves, but with the availability and cost of public or commercial services, changing ideals of home comfort and childcare, and whether they are also employed in a paid job elsewhere.

Cultural studies researcher, Ann Gray (Reading 4.3), examines the 'gendering' of a domestic leisure technology – the video cassette recorder (VCR) – following its widespread entry into household life in Britain during the 1980s.[33] In doing so, she returns to precisely those issues of technological competence raised earlier by Cockburn, and her discussions with women in West Yorkshire were consciously designed to consider the VCR's position within a wider 'ensemble' of work and leisure technologies in the home. Trying to make explicit the implicit – largely unconscious – gendered meanings of domestic tasks and artefacts, Gray invited the women she spoke with to code the various activities and technologies around their houses on a symbolic scale from pink to blue. She found that this 'produces almost uniformly pink irons and blue electric drills, with many interesting mixtures along the spectrum'.[34] In the specific case of the VCR, several parts of the machine were coded as lilac – but the timer switch was almost always blue, signifying dependence on male partners or children to set this device. Furthermore, Gray continues by noting that the 'blueness of the timer is exceeded only by the deep indigo of the remote control'. Her observations therefore tie in neatly with Morley's in the preceding section of our reader.

In the extract we reproduce here, Gray quotes the words of her interviewees at length, revealing a deep sense of inadequacy or self-deprecation on the part of many women in her qualitative project as they talk about the technicalities of operating the video machine. Certain things do need to be stressed, though, when considering this interview material. First of all, the researcher is careful to explain any lack of competence in relation to particular social contexts and subject positions. VCRs should in no way be thought of as inherently masculine or feminine objects. Rather, they can become gendered in given cultural and historical circumstances, within definite material constraints and relations of power. Secondly, there may in fact be subtle shades of resistance in the refusal of these women to learn how to use a gadget like the VCR timer switch. As Gray points out, on occasion there is a cunning display of 'calculated ignorance'. So those who have recognized a latent servicing element in the technical know-how avoid accepting responsibility for yet another household chore.

A home computing boom was also taking place during roughly the same period as the 'video revolution', and a British study of computer users, carried out by Graham Murdock, Paul Hartmann and Peggy Gray, has mapped out shifting meanings and competing definitions of the technology over a four-year period in the mid-1980s (Reading 4.4). In an earlier phase of the object's social history, computer manufacturers had chosen to target a specialist market of committed male hobbyists or gadgeteers.[35] Then came the introduction of a new generation of machines – aimed at a much wider audience, but still advertised as having serious applications and educational values.

However, parents who purchased this technology with a view to their children's schooling soon found the home computer being redefined – by many young users and manufacturers alike – primarily as a games machine.

Ann Moyal's piece, the last in Part 4, addresses women's uses of the telephone[36] – a surprisingly neglected medium in the critical literature on culture and communications (Reading 4.5). In this investigation, her research team asked Australian women in different social situations to distinguish between their 'instrumental' and 'intrinsic' calls: between phone calls made, say, for specific information-seeking purposes and those maintaining close interpersonal contact with sometimes distant friends or relatives. The second type was found to be more frequent and of longer duration – helping to construct a kind of 'psychological neighbourhood' which served as a valued substitute for regular face-to-face meetings with these absent others. For instance, there are intimate exchanges between mothers and daughters living far apart, or women in immigrant communities using the telephone to speak with others in their native language. Evidently, there are links here with what Gillespie says about video viewing and senses of imagined community. This is because domestic media technologies like the telephone and television set are not just significant as household objects: they also have the potential to stretch social relationships over vast geographical distances, mediating between the home and various outside worlds.[37]

The cultural construction of home

Home is far more than merely the physical space that household members occupy, or simply the site of domestic consumption. It signifies a place with powerful emotional resonances: a strong sense of belonging or attachment. The English language contains several well-known sayings which convey this deep sense of belonging – for example, 'home is where the heart is', or 'there's no place like home' – so that being at home means being where we feel most 'ourselves', where identity is confirmed.[38] Furthermore, home always gets defined in relation to an elsewhere. In symbolic terms, it is a place apart. Practices of consumption are one of the key ways in which home is culturally produced and sustained. Houses and apartments, whether owned or rented, are transformed into homes and made habitable largely via an appropriation and display of consumer goods.[39]

Underlining the historical and cultural specificity of modern ideas about the home, Leonore Davidoff and Catherine Hall (Reading 5.1) chart the formation of such conceptions in their piece on middle-class households in late eighteenth- and early nineteenth-century England. For the rising class of manufacturers and retailers in that period, home became spatially and symbolically separated from the sphere of industry and commerce. The trend was associated with an emerging 'domestic ideology',[40] within which the home was understood to be an intimate private haven of family, morality and security away from the public realm of business, vice and squalor. This division was gendered, of course, and at the centre of the domestic haven was positioned a wife and mother, the 'angel in the house'. Davidoff and Hall explain how suburban villas gave concrete shape to the new domestic ideology. These residences were situated at some distance from the business enterprises that funded an often affluent lifestyle. Garden hedges and gates provided a boundary behind which privacy could be maintained, while interior space was ordered in such a way as to preserve peace and create leisure. Work areas, and in particular the kitchen, were segregated from those parts of the house where the family relaxed and entertained guests. Rising standards of comfort and gentility were also manifested in increasingly elaborate furnishings, and became a means of demonstrating the family's prosperity and social status. All this necessarily expanded the work to be done in women's new domain, and although that labour was accomplished with the help of hired servants, only the wealthiest middle-class wives did no housework whatsoever.

Poverty and overcrowded housing conditions long prevented working-class people from achieving those standards of comfort and privacy attained by the middle classes. The domestic ideology had undoubtedly influenced aspirations among more prosperous groups of workers, but it was not until after the Second World War – with major slum clearance and housebuilding programmes – that most ordinary citizens in Britain were able to realize the ambition of a secure and private family home.[41] Using an oral history method, Judy Attfield seeks to recover the experiences of young working-class women in the 1950s moving from inner-city London to Harlow in Essex, and thereby reveals some of the struggles and contradictions of life in a post-war new town (Reading 5.2). Her essay explains how moving to 'Pram Town', whilst it meant having a home to call your own, was initially a disorienting experience for these women. They were leaving behind the familiar environment of their urban communities and coming to a place which, far from being a rural idyll, led many to feel isolated and depressed.

However, through their household decoration practices – embodying a specific popular aesthetic of 'pride and polish' – inhabitants of this new town tried hard to turn houses into homes, to produce a lived sense of place. In doing so, they were brought into direct conflict with the tastes and values of middle-class architects and designers.[42] Alongside the spoken accounts of the tenants, then, Attfield juxtaposes written accounts drawn from the official design discourses of the day: criticisms of so-called 'cosy clutter', of open plan housing being closed up behind net curtains and heavy drapes. The functional, modernist aesthetic of the planners was met by an altogether different domestic value system expressed by many of Attfield's interviewees.

A contrast between the competing taste cultures of different social classes is also an important theme running through the final three contributions to our reader: those by Pauline Hunt (Reading 5.3), Ondina Fachel Leal (Reading 5.4) and Marianne Gullestad (Reading 5.5). The case study examples which they discuss are taken from varying national and geographical contexts – from the North of England, from urban Brazil and from Bergen in Norway – and yet there are evidently links which can be made across these pieces in terms of what Bourdieu has referred to as distinct forms of class 'habitus'.[43] For Hunt and Gullestad, too, there is an added interest here in how class cultures and gender relations in the household intersect. Like Attfield, they each emphasize the physical and imaginative work done by women in creating a home environment for the family group.

Hunt observes, both in her middle- and working-class settings, that it is women who have to negotiate a tension between the home as a place of comfort and the home as a potential arena for display – open to scrutiny by visitors, including the researcher herself. The home must appear clean and tidy, but still be experienced as free and easy – a problem which most tackle by regularly tidying rather than by preventing any disorder from arising in the first place. Still, they manage to organize this labour so that it is accomplished when others are not around, for while it is being done, the house is unlikely to be homely. Hunt also points to the ways in which women's self-identities are bound up with their homes, and with the standards of style and comfort they achieve. This is exemplified in the ritual of giving them gifts for the house, whether practical or decorative, rather than for strictly personal use. Homes therefore become a vehicle for women's self-expression. They exert considerable influence over decor and furnishings, the choice of which is markedly class differentiated. So the ambience of a typical working-class home is cosy and warm whilst the middle classes construct a domestic sphere that is usually more spacious and uncluttered. Hunt explains the divergence of styles by specifying what each class distances itself from. Members of one are attempting to banish coldness and want from their private lives. Members of the other, meanwhile, are demonstrating their good taste as defined in relation to 'vulgar' proletarian aesthetics.

As cultural anthropologists, Leal and Gullestad pay careful attention to the precise arrangement of household artefacts and to the systems of meaning which are articulated by those social practices and material things – presenting 'thick' ethnographic descriptions[44] of the various domestic interiors they have observed. Leal's chief concern is with what she names in her piece an 'entourage' of decorative objects that were displayed close to the TV set in working-class Brazilian living rooms. She noticed how, even when the television was moved for some reason, these objects would follow it 'as interconnected pieces of one coherent set'. A cracked laboratory glass, plastic flowers, snapshots of family members, as well as images depicting religious scenes – are all understood in her reading to have a particular cultural significance. For instance, the lab glass is seen to be bound up with oppositions between tradition and modernity, or between the country and the city. Similarly, the photos form 'a bricolage of lost kinship webs' which serve to connect city dwellers with the memories of relatives left behind in rural areas. The positioning of TV in those middle-class homes that she visits is very different. Here, the technology is less valued socially and less central physically – hidden within spacious domestic surroundings, or else confined to the bedroom in slightly smaller apartments.

Gullestad's work considers home decoration as a continuous project which evolves over time: an ongoing expressive enterprise in the domestic lives of her research subjects. The ethnography she presents looks predominantly at the consumer preferences of 'ordinary' Norwegian couples – their label, not hers – although she goes on to compare their tastes with those of educated middle-class households. Just as Leal paints interpretative portraits of the home's internal organization, so Gullestad accounts for the fine detail of living room and kitchen layouts. A key requirement of life in these ordinary household cultures is being ready to receive guests who drop in without

warning – and this gives rise to some of the same basic tensions which Hunt has identified between a need for relaxed comfort and a desire to display the home to visitors.

Future developments?

It will be clear from our selection of material and from the introductory discussion
thus far that we privilege certain themes and perspectives over others, and that our
agenda is set in terms of a particular series of analytical pairings or oppositions. So,
to sum up, what we are advocating is an interpretative, interdisciplinary approach to
the study of domestic consumption which employs primarily qualitative methods of
enquiry, and which combines many of the diverse critical insights of existing work in
this area. Such an approach foregrounds relationships between the material and the
symbolic, and between agency and structure – or creativity and constraint – in everyday
consumer cultures. It also examines the spatio-temporal arrangements of the modern
home, explores connections between private lives and public worlds and situates the
social dynamics of the household within broader historical and geographical trans-
formations.

Despite the richness and variety of the 24 readings extracted below, we believe there
is still considerable scope for expansion in this developing field of study. In and across
each of our five main topic areas – economics, food and clothing, media reception,
household technologies and the home – further investigations are now called for. For
example, it seems to us that new research projects might productively look at the links
between cultural practices currently separated out under these section headings. How,
then, do conflicts over culinary preferences connect with different viewing and reading
habits, or with the possession and deployment of specific technical competences? How
do struggles around domestic budgeting serve to limit imaginative plans for home decoration? Posing questions of that sort will enable us to map out fuller consumer 'profiles'
for households and their members – showing up the complex articulations of consumption, domesticity and power.

In addition, we want to suggest that there are at least two significant absences from
our edited book – both demanding greater attention from qualitative researchers over
future years. The first of these gaps concerns that range of public discourses which
are addressed to consumers in the private realm, and which play an important part in
defining and reproducing 'the family' as a cultural category. What we have in mind
here are the disparate discourses of state, commercial and media institutions: for
instance, in the domain of economic policy or health and social welfare provision, in
the world of advertising or in the wider output of broadcast and print media. The focus
might be on matters of representation: how families and households are pictured and
spoken of. Equally, though, it is necessary to ask about the changing ways in which
domestic consumers are being spoken to by institutional authorities: the shifting modes
of address used to bridge divisions between the public and the private.[45]

Broadcasting provides us with many good examples of institutional discourse which
is consciously oriented towards viewers and listeners in the home environment. To

borrow a phrase from Paddy Scannell,[46] we could say that its distinctive 'communicative ethos' has evolved as a direct consequence of the domestic reception context. This ethos involves a stitching of programme output into the daily routines of audiences – and incorporates those relaxed, familiar modes of address or forms of talk which are more usually associated with private interpersonal encounters in everyday life. So television personalities will frequently engage us in a type of 'para-social interaction'[47] – facing the camera and speaking as if they were conversing personally and privately. Indeed, their skilled performances of 'intimacy at a distance' are getting increasingly informal in style and tone, as new programmes and genres emerge and old ones are transformed by a conversationalization of public discourse.

TV output has traditionally addressed its viewers as members of families, and the broadcasting schedules have long been built on assumptions about a typical 'family audience' – the supposedly classic nuclear unit – yet only a minority of households in Britain actually conform to that model.[48] This leads us neatly into discussing a second gap in our current collection, another area where more work would be welcome in the future: literature on the variability of family forms. Variations are generated by differences of class, ethnicity and sexuality, changes in household structure over the life course, and the effects of high divorce rates or single parenthood. Several of our chosen readings consider class divisions or class-specific consumer practices. We have also tried to include a number of studies which take ethnic minorities into account, or ones which feature non-Western societies. Even so, the reader's representativeness is ultimately hampered by the fact that much research on domestic consumption still focuses on white Western heterosexual families.

Many of the pieces reproduced below are informed by contemporary feminism, and white feminists evidently identify the household as a major site of oppression – although their perspective has been challenged, or modified at least, by black feminists who draw our attention to the alternative meanings which family life can have for them. In a very real sense, black families often serve as havens from a racist society, a source of solidarity and positive identity for their members.[49] At the same time, nobody is claiming that black households are necessarily more egalitarian, or that hierarchies of gender and generation are absent. There is some published material which looks at economic inequalities within ethnic minority families,[50] but little as yet on other aspects of their consumer practices in the home. Of course, it is hardly surprising that those researching such communities have had other priorities. Given the impact of racism on housing and labour markets, academic work has understandably placed emphasis on these areas rather than on black people's household arrangements and patterns of domestic consumption.

There is still less material available on those consumers who do not reside in heterosexual families. Research on gay and lesbian homes remains scarce, and that which exists tends to deal with issues such as relations with wider kin and the problems of parenting.[51] Same-sex couples will presumably have a far higher chance of achieving egalitarian divisions of labour, leisure and consumption in their private lives, and they therefore deserve much closer analytical scrutiny. Recently, the so-called 'pink pound' or 'pink dollar' has been the subject of some press interest – particularly the combined spending power of gay couples with household incomes based on two male salaries. The double accumulation of women's wages is usually somewhat smaller, hence the thinner lesbian slice of any growing 'pink economy'. Marketing opportunities which this provides are certainly being recognized by a few advertisers and retailers in the 1990s. Where academics have offered comments on the pink economy, they concentrate on extra-domestic consumption: as in David Evans's writings on the economic aspects of sexual citizenship.[52]

Finally, we cannot safely assume that all heterosexual couples are equally implicated in gendered patterns of consumption and power. Those consciously resisting conventional gender arrangements, or choosing to live in 'alternative' households, might constitute only a small subsection of the population – but they do nevertheless exist, and it is important for us to find out more about these groups. It may turn out that institutional hierarchies are so well established that even the very people engaged in challenging them discover how hard it is to form genuinely egalitarian relationships.[53] In addition, there are heterosexuals living outside nuclear families by necessity rather than by positive choice. Single parents, for instance, can fall into either category – being in their specific position as a result of divorce, accidental single parenthood or else actively choosing to rear children alone – and they now head around a fifth of families with dependent children in Britain. Here, research has been done on the consequences of poverty – which includes valuable data on household resource distribution[54] – although the dynamics of consumption in single parent families still require fuller investigation in the future.

Notes

1. We place the singular term in inverted commas here, noting the plurality of actual family forms. For further discussion, see S. Jackson, 'Women and the family', in D. Richardson and V. Robinson, eds, *Introducing Women's Studies: Feminist theory and practice*, Basingstoke: Macmillan, 1993.
2. One of us has developed this argument at greater length elsewhere: see S. Moores, *Interpreting Audiences: The ethnography of media consumption*, London: Sage, 1993.
3. It is sometimes said that the work women do within households is not productive since it does not produce commodities for exchange – or that it involves reproduction, of the labour force, rather than production. We see these distinctions as unhelpful. The idea that baking a cake in a bakery is production whilst doing the same thing at home is not adds little to our understanding of the economics of domestic life. In support of our case, see S. Walby, *Patriarchy at Work: Patriarchal and capitalist relations in employment*, Cambridge: Polity, 1986.
4. T. Parsons and R. Bales, *Family Socialisation and Interaction Process*, New York: Free Press, 1956, p. 11.
5. H. Graham, 'Women's poverty and caring', in C. Glendinning and J. Millar, eds, *Women and Poverty in Britain*, Hemel Hempstead: Harvester Wheatsheaf, 1987, p. 221.
6. For detailed expositions of this perspective, see C. Delphy and D. Leonard, *Familiar Exploitation: A new analysis of marriage in contemporary Western societies*, Cambridge: Polity, 1992; S. Jackson, *Christine Delphy*, London: Sage, forthcoming.
7. A more general discussion of cross-cultural, comparative studies can be found in H. Moore, *Feminism and Anthropology*, Cambridge: Polity, 1988.

8. See, for instance, L. Morris, *The Workings of the Household*, Cambridge: Polity, 1990.

9. For example, P. Mansfield and J. Collard, *The Beginning of the Rest of Your Life*: *A portrait of newly-wed marriage*, Basingstoke: Macmillan, 1988; J. Brannen and P. Moss, *Managing Mothers*: *Dual earner households after maternity leave*, London: Unwin Hyman, 1991.

10. Also J. Pahl, *Money and Marriage*, Basingstoke: Macmillan, 1989.

11. H. Graham, 'Women's Poverty and Caring', op. cit.

12. N. Charles and M. Kerr, *Women, Food and Families*, Manchester: Manchester University Press, 1988.

13. In addition, see S. Mennell, A. Murcott and A. van Otterloo, *The Sociology of Food*: *Eating, diet and culture*, London: Sage, 1992.

14. Similar findings are reported in a recent American study of food consumption: see M. De Vault, *Feeding the Family*: *The social organisation of caring as gendered work*, Chicago: University of Chicago Press, 1991.

15. Among the classic studies in this field are S. Hall and T. Jefferson, eds, *Resistance Through Rituals*: *Youth subcultures in post-war Britain*, London: Hutchinson, 1976; D. Hebdige, *Subculture*: *The meaning of style*, London: Methuen, 1979; P. Willis, *Common Culture*: *Symbolic work at play in the everyday cultures of the young*, Milton Keynes: Open University Press, 1990.

16. A concept drawn from P. McHugh, 'A common sense perception of deviance', in H. Dreitzel, ed., *Recent Sociology No. 2*, New York: Macmillan, 1970.

17. See M. Mauss, *The Gift*: *The form and reason for exchange in archaic societies*, London: Routledge, 1990.

18. Indeed, some feminist researchers have argued that men's leisure is dependent upon women's work: for instance, see L. Imray and A. Middleton, 'Public and private: Marking the boundaries', in E. Gamarnikow, D. Morgan, J. Purvis and D. Taylorson, eds, *The Public and the Private*, Aldershot: Gower, 1983.

19. For a valuable investigation of women's leisure and use of time – which focuses on the experiences of shift workers: see D. Chambers, 'The constraints of work and domestic schedules on women's leisure', *Leisure Studies*, 5: 309–25, 1986.

20. See D. Hobson, 'Housewives: Isolation as oppression', in Women's Studies Group CCCS, eds, *Women Take Issue*: *Aspects of women's subordination*, London: Hutchinson, 1978.

21. There is a body of literature in feminist media studies on soap opera as a genre and the gendered competences of its viewers. For example, see C. Brunsdon, '"Crossroads": Notes on soap opera', *Screen*, 22: 32–7, 1981; D. Hobson, *'Crossroads': The drama of a soap opera*, London: Methuen, 1982; I. Ang, *Watching 'Dallas'*: *Soap opera and the melodramatic imagination*, London: Methuen, 1985; I. Ang, 'Melodramatic identifications: Television fiction and women's fantasy', in M. Brown, ed., *Television and Women's Culture*: *The politics of the popular*, London: Sage, 1990.

22. J. Radway, *Reading the Romance*: *Women, patriarchy and popular literature*, London: Verso, 1987, p. 7.

23. N. Chodorow, 'Family structure and feminine personality', in M. Rosaldo and L. Lamphere, eds, *Woman, Culture and Society*, Stanford: Stanford University Press, 1974; N. Chodorow, *The Reproduction of Mothering*: *Psychoanalysis and the sociology of gender*, Berkeley: University of California Press, 1978.

24. See also J. Lull, *Inside Family Viewing*: *Ethnographic research on television's audiences*, London: Routledge, 1990.

25. D. Morley, *Family Television*: *Cultural power and domestic leisure*, London: Comedia, 1986, p. 148.

26. P. Bourdieu, *Distinction*: *A social critique of the judgement of taste*, London: Routledge and Kegan Paul, 1984.

27. Central Statistical Office, *Social Trends*, London: HMSO, 1994.

28. On the former, see C. Cockburn and S. Ormrod, *Gender and Technology in the Making*,

London: Sage, 1993. On the latter, see S. Moores, 'Satellite TV as cultural sign: Consumption, embedding and articulation', *Media, Culture and Society*, 15: 621–39, 1993.

29. For a case study, see S. Moores, '"The box on the dresser": Memories of early radio and everyday life', *Media, Culture and Society*, 10: 23–40, 1988. Also useful here is the idea that technologies have biographies – as discussed by R. Silverstone, E. Hirsch and D. Morley, 'Information and communication technologies and the moral economy of the household', in R. Silverstone and E. Hirsch, eds, *Consuming Technologies: Media and information in domestic spaces*, London: Routledge, 1992.

30. Accounts of the development of domestic labour technologies are available in S. Strasser, *Never Done: A history of the American housewife*, New York: Pantheon, 1982; C. Davidson, *A Woman's Work is Never Done: A history of housework in the British Isles, 1650–1950*, London: Chatto and Windus, 1982; C. Hardyment, *From Mangle to Microwave: The mechanisation of household work*, Cambridge: Polity, 1988; R. Schwartz Cowan, *More Work for Mother: The ironies of domestic technology from the open hearth to the microwave*, London: Free Association, 1989; S. Jackson, 'Towards a historical sociology of housework: A materialist feminist analysis', *Women's Studies International Forum*, 15: 153–72, 1992.

31. For a fuller critique of technological determinist perspectives, see D. MacKenzie and J. Wajcman, eds, *The Social Shaping of Technology: How the refrigerator got its hum*, Milton Keynes: Open University Press, 1985.

32. See 'Three kinds of dirt', in J. Williamson, *Consuming Passions: The dynamics of popular culture*, London: Marion Boyars, 1986.

33. By the mid-1980s, well over a third of households in Britain had already installed a VCR, a figure reported by A. Tomlinson, 'Home fixtures: Doing-it-yourself in a privatised world', in A. Tomlinson, ed., *Consumption, Identity and Style: Marketing, meanings and the packaging of pleasure*, London: Routledge, 1990.

34. A. Gray, 'Behind closed doors: Video recorders in the home', in H. Baehr and G. Dyer, eds, *Boxed In: Women and television*, London: Pandora, 1987, p. 42.

35. This phase in the object's biography is outlined in L. Haddon, 'The home computer: The making of a consumer electronic', *Science as Culture*, 2: 7–51, 1988.

36. See also A. Moyal, 'The feminine culture of the telephone: People, patterns and policy', *Prometheus*, 7: 5–31, 1989; L. Rakow, *Gender on the Line: Women, the telephone and community life*, Urbana: University of Illinois Press, 1992.

37. S. Moores, 'Television, geography and "mobile privatisation"', *European Journal of Communication*, 8: 365–79, 1993.

38. B. Martin and C. Mohanty, 'Feminist politics: What's home got to do with it?', in T. De Lauretis, *Feminist Studies/Critical Studies*, Basingstoke: Macmillan, 1988.

39. For perspectives on appropriation and display, see M. De Certeau, *The Practice of Everyday Life*, Berkeley: University of California Press, 1984; T. Putnam and C. Newton, eds, *Household Choices*, London: Futures, 1990.

40. That concept had been developed by Hall in earlier writings – especially C. Hall, 'The early formation of the domestic ideology', in S. Burstyn, ed., *Fit Work for Women*, London: Croom Helm, 1979.

41. J. Parker and C. Mirrlees, 'Housing', in A. Halsey, ed., *British Social Trends Since 1900*, Basingstoke: Macmillan, 1988.

42. Other instances of taste warfare being fought out between suburban inhabitants and modern architects are reported in P. Oliver, I. Davis and I. Bentley, *Dunroamin: The suburban semi and its enemies*, London: Pimlico, 1994.

43. By habitus, Bourdieu means a set of embodied cultural dispositions which are inculcated in the subject from the early years of socialization within the family. See P. Bourdieu, *Outline of a Theory of Practice*, Cambridge: Cambridge University Press, 1977; P. Bourdieu, 1984, op. cit.

44. A well-known term in the anthropological literature, first adopted by C. Geertz, *The Interpretation of Cultures: Selected essays*, New York: Basic Books, 1973.

45. Some of these shifting modes of address are analyzed in N. Fairclough, 'Conversationalisation of public discourse and the authority of the consumer', in R. Keat, N. Whiteley and N. Abercrombie, eds, *The Authority of the Consumer*, London: Routledge, 1994.
46. P. Scannell, 'Public service broadcasting and modern public life', *Media, Culture and Society*, 11: 135–66, 1989. See also the essays collected in P. Scannell, ed., *Broadcast Talk*, London: Sage, 1991.
47. A phrase coined by D. Horton and R. Wohl, 'Mass communication and para-social interaction: Observations on intimacy at a distance', in G. Gumpert and R. Cathcart, eds, *Inter/Media: Interpersonal communication in a media world*, New York: Oxford University Press, 1986.
48. J. Ellis, *Visible Fictions: Cinema, television, video*, London: Routledge and Kegan Paul, 1982, p. 114.
49. This case is argued, for example, in H. Carby, 'White woman listen!: Black feminism and the boundaries of sisterhood', in CCCS, ed., *The Empire Strikes Back: Race and racism in 70s Britain*, London: Hutchinson, 1982; K. Bhavnani and M. Coulson, 'Transforming socialist feminism: The challenge of racism', *Feminist Review*, 23: 81–92, 1986.
50. See S. Westwood and P. Bhachu, eds, *Enterprising Women: Ethnicity, economy and gender relations*, London: Routledge, 1988; H. Afshar, 'Gender rules and the "moral economy of kin" among Pakistani women in West Yorkshire', *New Community*, 15: 211–25, 1989.
51. For instance, K. Weston, *Families We Choose: Lesbians, gays, kinship*, New York: Columbia University Press, 1991.
52. D. Evans, *Sexual Citizenship: The material construction of sexualities*, London: Routledge, 1993.
53. Some interesting portraits of couples in this situation appear in J. Van Every, *Refusing to Be a Wife!: Heterosexual women's strategies for liberation*, London: Taylor and Francis, 1995.
54. D. Marsden, *Mothers Alone: Poverty and the fatherless family*, Harmondsworth: Penguin, 1973; H. Graham, op. cit.; M. Maclean, *Surviving Divorce: Women's resources after separation*, Basingstoke: Macmillan, 1991.

1 □ *The Economics of Domestic Consumption*

1.1 □ *Christine Delphy*

In challenging the dominant conceptualization of families as units of consumption, Christine Delphy contends that domestic consumption is neither unitary nor undifferentiated. Her use of food as an illustrative example anticipates material in the next section of our reader, but it is her theoretical position which is of primary importance here: the argument that families are based fundamentally upon relations of economic power and exploitation. She wrote this essay in the early 1970s.

Sharing the same table: consumption and the family

If there is one universally recognized function of the family it is 'consumption'. It would be tedious to list all the books and articles which mention this, because there is no sociologist, and more generally no author dealing with the family, who does not at least allude to it. It is presented as one of the principal functions of 'the modern family'.

If it is granted that the family is the institution (or one of the institutions) which fulfils this function, we might have expected that the next step would have been to study the ways in which the family satisfies what are undoubtedly seen as some basic biological needs of its individual members. But despite the social and theoretical importance of both the family and the 'function' of consumption, there is a strikingly poor literature on the topic. Not a single known study of the family takes consumption as its theme of research, or even sets out the ground for such research.

If consumption and the family were not the object of specific investigations, we might at least have expected to see it discussed in general theoretical introductions. But, after its obligatory and quasi-ritual mention, it is little developed. Indeed, the assertion of the existence of a consumption function is often put in the form of a negatively phrased sentence. That is to say, the function of consumption is presented as the *only remaining* function of the family within the economic order: what remains to it of a glorious past, of the global economic role it used to play. Its mention is an integral part of the – often advanced, never substantiated – thesis that the family in general (and not certain forms of the family) has recently been excluded from any role in production whatsoever (and not only from production for the market). It is as if consumption was put forward to give credit to the thesis of the loss of the family's role in production, and at the same time to affirm that – despite this vicissitude – the family continues to be necessary within the economic order. Hence, even at a theoretical level, the function of consumption is not treated in and of itself by those who study the family. E. M. Duvall's sentence[1] 'Families have shifted from production to consumption' is exemplary of this kind of thinking. It is considered only in a general historical perspective: from the point of view of the evolution of the family and its gains and losses of 'functionality'.

When we look at past work on family consumption, it rapidly becomes clear that the term 'consumption' is used to designate market demand. The titles of articles and journals lead us to think that what is being studied is individual consumption, but the consumption they describe is not that of any actual person, but is rather the purchase of goods and services on the market by households (generally in the person of the housewife). Such studies let it be thought that the family, which is a collective agent on the market, is equally a collective agent in consumption.[2] An INSEE study (the French equivalent of the Government Social Survey's *Family Expenditure Survey*) says explicitly:

> The field covered by this enquiry is that of expenditure on goods and services: purchase of products, consumption taking place outside the home, and payment for loans and services.

It is clear here that all consumption by members of the household (and this includes children at boarding school for instance), wherever it occurs, is taken into account in evaluating the standard of living of *households*.

Thus the use of the term consumption implies that individual consumption is being studied, while the way in which consumption is observed in practice – the relating of all consumption to the household – requires that distribution within the family should be studied. But not only do studies of individual consumption or sharing within the family not exist, the themes are not so much as broached, even theoretically, and it is precisely the choice of the household as the unit of observation which prevents such studies being possible using existing data. Taking the family as a unit does not allow family consumption to be studied – only the consumption of aggregates of families. What is studied is no longer the families themselves, but the way in which they differ from each other, or form groups. Moreover, the only difference between families which these studies are explicitly interested in studying, is that of 'the comparative standard of living of different socio-economic groups.'[3]

This comparison *itself* actually also suffers from the definition of the household, e.g. servants (waged and apprenticed) lodging in a household are held to be part of it from the point of view of consumption. The result is that studies of the standard of living of farm workers' households, for example, do not include those who lodge with – and who are consequently trapped by – the household of their boss. And these are those whose standard of living is lowest. Excluding them from farm workers' households has the effect of raising the average standard of living of the latter, while their being 'captive' has the effect of lowering the average standard of living of the households to which they are attached, i.e. those of the class of their masters. These two effects together lead to a not inconsiderable diminution of the economic distance between the two classes.

But distortions brought about in comparisons of social categories are a minor defect compared to the major sin of considering the very place – the household – where certain class relations are exercised (e.g. those of servant and master) as the place where they are annulled.

The absence of studies of distribution has a positive meaning. It means that the only pertinent perspective is how the family is a unit within a larger whole, because this is the only perspective considered. Above all, it lets it be thought that the family, a unity *vis-à-vis* the outside, is also one within itself. One of the images which the term 'unit of consumption' evokes is that of common – i.e. homogeneous – consumption. It connotes at one and the same time *common consumption*, and *undifferentiated consumption*.

Differences of consumption within families

However, such connotations of common and undifferentiated consumption are contradicted by the facts of everyday experience. Here the disparities of consumption between family members are not only visible, but recognized as *constitutive* of family structure. Differences in consumption are seen as correlated with the existence of different family statuses. Differential consumption plays a major role both in the perception of these statuses by outsiders and in the appreciation of their particular statuses by those involved.

Existing studies of consumption are, however, based on the opposite assumption. And they do not rest content with ignoring individual consumption: they pretend to know about it without having studied it. Thus:

> The average annual consumption *per head* . . . is obtained simply [sic] by dividing the values entered in the table . . . by the number of persons.[4]

It should be remembered, however, that among the individuals whom we are thus invited to consider as benefiting in equal shares from all the goods consumed in the household to which they are attributed, are not only children in boarding schools, and soldiers on military service, but also servants, waged employees and apprentices. Thus, while pretending to ignore the whole topic, existing studies of consumption in fact assume (impose) a theory of distribution – an egalitarian theory.

It is likely that the processes described above are no chance effects and that their convergence is no coincidence. The use of the term 'unit of consumption' – which in denoting a simple unit of reckoning connotes a unitas (union and communion) – tends to make the study of distribution seem pointless; and statistical practice, for its part, by always taking the household as the only unit of observation, makes any empirical research impossible. All these processes converge to prevent any study of real distribution, for on the one hand such a study would risk undermining the whole basis of existing research by showing it to be founded on an implicit postulate – that of

egalitarian distribution; while on the other hand it could not but confirm what is appre-
hended impressionistically by everyday experience – the existence of differential
consumption.[5]

Study of the consumption function of the family should consist of studying the role
of the family as the distribution centre for its members, and research should take as
its object the effect of family status on individual consumption. But, as has been noted
above, not one of the studies which refers to the family as a unit of consumption so
much as outlines the limits of what does or does not enter into this unit, so the very
framework of the research has still to be defined. Does individual consumption within
the family involve consumption effected collectively, with all the members of the family
present, regardless of place? Or is it consumption that occurs at home, whichever
members may be present? Or is it consumption by members of the family, whatever
the place and whichever individuals are present? Among the criteria which could be
envisaged, besides the place (at home or outside) and the presence or absence of the
family as a collective, must be the nature of the consumption. Would specific consumption (e.g. connected with a job) be opposed to common consumption, or
consumption of the same sort of thing (e.g. consumption of food) – these latter alone
being considered familial?

If the subject of research is the role of the family as a distribution point, it seems
obvious that all individual consumption should be considered as familial since it is based
on the status of the individual in the family whatever the place, the modalities, or the
form it may take. But in the absence of even elementary reflections and investigation
in this area we must proceed empirically and cautiously. In fact it is much more a matter
of using examples to set out the directing hypothesis for a new approach to family
consumption than of stating the methodological outlines for a systematic study.

I shall try to set out the outlines of such an approach in the remainder of this article,
using examples chosen from the area of non-specific consumption, effected mainly at
home, even if not in the presence of the whole family, since such consumption, and
particularly the consumption of food, is the most evidently familial. It is the family
seated around the table which most approximates the image of a really communist
community, of a really equitable distribution, and which seems most sheltered from
the effects of hierarchy.

I shall also deal with families on very low incomes, since there is a sentiment that
inequality is less cruel when it is a case of individuals getting more or less of what is
already a surplus, rather than when it is a question of individuals getting more or less
than the minimum needed for a healthy life. It tends to be thought that families on
the breadline must and do share what little they have.[6]

Both experts and the uninitiated like to situate the western version of 'subsistence'
within rural, and above all within peasant, families. Here production for self-consumption is relatively important compared to that destined for the market, and this suggests
a self-sufficiency, especially in food, which though far from existing in reality, is close
to the golden age of the popular imagination (which is curiously situated in the nineteenth century).

It is in this type of family that some of the lowest incomes within industrial society are to be found and here that the standard of living is at its lowest. It is also here that it is most recognized that *all* family members do hard physical work. It is thus the last place where one would expect to find differential consumption of food. Therefore, if it can be shown that such differential consumption does exist, there seem good grounds for expecting it to exist in *all* families: that it is part and parcel of the *structure* of the family. That is to say, the stress given here to the rural family, and to the consumption of food, is not due to a particular interest in these areas as such, but rather to a belief that once the fact of differential consumption is established and established here (for the reasons evoked above), it will require further research into its principles and functioning, i.e. its existence as an institution. It will involve, in sum, the freeing of a problematic which will allow us to return to new concrete studies since future research will no longer be aimless: its problematic will have been constructed.

The distribution of food in peasant families

There is, needless to say, no scientifically collected information which can be used in considering whether there is or is not differential consumption in poor farm families. On the contrary, so called scientific data have been collected in just such a way as to mask it. But, as was said earlier, the point of this essay is not to present new facts, but to look at facts, which are universally known to the social actors, from a new angle.[7] So I shall therefore draw on descriptive studies and personal knowledge.

In the traditional rural family (of the eighteenth and early nineteenth centuries in Britain, and still today in marginal family smallholdings of the type that predominate in south-west France and much of southern Europe), consumption of food varies greatly according to the individual's status in the family. This variation concerns the quantity of food and sets apart primarily children and adults, and women and men. But among the adults the old eat less than those who are mature, and the junior members eat less than the head of the family. It is he who takes the biggest pieces. He also takes the best: variation concerns quality as much as quantity.

Children are fed exclusively on milk, flour and sugar until two or three years old. The old, particularly the infirm elderly, return to a similar regime based on cereals and milk, bread-soups (*panade*) and broths.

Meat is rarely on the menu, and even more rarely on the menu for everyone. It often appears on the table to be consumed only by the head of the family, especially if it is butcher's meat. Less expensive meat – chickens reared on the farm, preserves made at home – are not subject to such exclusive privilege. However, women and children will never have the choice piece, which is reserved for the father (or, on social occasions, for distinguished guests). Thus according to Cazaurang,[8] the prime pieces of ham, a prime food in itself, fall to the future son-in-law. Infants and the elderly never touch it. Alcohol is another food whose consumption is strongly differentiated. It is for adult men, to the exclusion of women and children.

Respect for food prohibitions is obtained by both coercion and the internalization of these prohibitions. The physical infirmity of young children and the old makes coercion so easy that it becomes not useless but invisible. It is mainly necessary, and becomes visible, in relation to children during the period when they are 'thieves': i.e. when they have not yet internalized the prohibitions.

Hence many types of food which are kept in the kitchen are put in high-up places, on hanging shelves (*planches à pain*) or on the tops of cupboards, where only people of adult height can reach them. This coercion by height is so classic that many folk tales have as their hero a child who has decided to outmanoeuvre it. The tale generally tells of the confident solution of the problem by the hero using a stool, and of the unhappy outcome in a punishment, either mediated (inflicted by an adult hand) or immediate (coming from the sky in the shape of indigestion). A brand of jam has even chosen for its trademark the picture of a little girl dipping her fingers into a jar: she is perched on a chair.

But if certain foodstuffs are physically protected only from children, others are protected from the whole family:

> Provisions which it is thought should not be allowed into the kitchen are put in the bedroom, especially in the master's bedroom. For pieces of pork meat, such as sausages, the stay in the upper storey enables them to finish drying out. Further, it shields them from the temptation of the young, who are always hungry. The same line of thought leads to the week's supply of bread being put on a shelf from which it is only given out as needed.[9]

Some of the measures which back up prohibitions with physical obstacles apply to the whole household – except for the women, or rather except for the mistress of the house. These measures would in fact be inconvenient if applied to her because it is she who prepares all the food. She therefore has access to all the foodstuffs, even to those which she does not eat. But this access is clearly tied to her operations as preparer. Alcohol escapes her operations because its preparation is a masculine prerogative. The physical taboo to which it is subject may extend to the mistress of the house: often the 'master's' bottle is touched only by his hand.

Repression in all its aspects – punishments and threats, verbal injunctions, physical obstacles and taboos on contact – play only a security role, except with regard to children, or perhaps even (as in the case of the bottle of alcohol) only a symbolic role in founding and maintaining differential consumption. For this is essentially a customary act (i.e. the constraints are internalized and reproduced as spontaneous behaviour by those involved). A whole corpus of proverbs, sayings and beliefs are both tokens of the content of the roles and the justification for these roles.

Sometimes these precepts seem like observations from experience – 'women eat less than men'. Sometimes they are in the shape of advice on hygiene – 'such food is "bad" or "good"' – with the prescriptive aspect on differential consumption only appearing in the second part of the phrase, where it is revealed that this 'goodness' or 'badness' strikes the organs in a selective manner according to the status of their possessors. Thus 'jam spoils (*only*) *children's* teeth', 'wine gives (*only*) *men* strength', etc. The waiter in the restaurant where the young David Copperfield was stranded when he was travelling alone explained to him in the same vein that the beer which had been served to the youth would be fatal for him, and he saved David from death by gulping it down

for him. At other times the norm is prescribed under the guise of aesthetic considerations – 'There's nothing more ugly than a drunken woman' – or moral – 'a woman
who drinks is worthless' (*femme de vin, femme de rien*) – which completely masks the
repressive aspect, since it leaves those concerned free to be 'ugly' or 'worthless' and
passes in silence over the anticipated benefit of such repression, i.e. the monopoly of
a prized commodity.

[. . .]

The total absence of proteins from the diet of infants and the elderly leads to food
deficiencies which have serious repercussions on the development of the former and
the ageing of the latter, and the life expectancy of everyone. Their relative absence in
the diet of women leads to consequences for their general state of health, whose effects
are doubled by the physiological burden of pregnancies, as was previously evidenced
by the very high rates of maternal and infant mortality in rural areas. Nevertheless, it
is held that babies and children do not need meat, and that women have 'less need'
of it. Men, however, 'need' such noble food. Vegetables which do not 'hold to the body'
and do not 'sustain a man', apparently nourish women and children.

Indigenous theory suggests a relationship between the stature of the individual and
the quantity of food necessary for his or her constitution.[10] That this is a rationalization and not a principle of distribution is evident from the number of exceptions it
suffers: a husband, a master, a father, or an eldest son, however puny he may be, does
not give up his privileged share to a wife, a worker, a child, or a younger sibling,
however heavily built or tall.

The theory of differential needs allows a third level of argument – that of differential expenditure of energy. This form of argument does not rest on the measure of
energy really expended by the individual, but establishes an impersonal relationship
between an activity and the expenditure of energy. This relationship is based on clas-
sifying activities into 'heavy' and 'light' work, but the classification is not based on
the actual expenditure of energy required by the activity considered, but rather by the
nature of the activities. It is not the technical operation itself which is the real criterion of the classification (carrying water is considered to be 'light work', carrying
manure is 'heavy'), nor is it the labour of the task (cutting corn with a scythe is 'heavy
work', gathering it into bundles and binding it is seen as 'light work'). Rather,
throughout France, carrying water and gathering are, or were, exclusively work for
women, while other sorts of carrying and harvesting were men's work. The criteria
of classification of work into 'heavy' and 'light' rests, in fact, on the status of those
who usually do it.

Certain work, reserved for men and hence supposedly 'heavy' in some regions, is
reserved for women in others and there changes its qualifications. This applies, to give
just a couple of examples from among many sex-related tasks, to earthing up potatoes and driving draught animals. When women do supposedly 'heavy' work in one
particular region – either in an exceptional way, at certain times of year, or in an ordinary way, as in Brittany or in the Alps where they do all agricultural work – the
evaluation of the energy they expend and need is not thereby modified. This is not

surprising since this expenditure and their real needs are never measured nor compared. The simple counting of hours of physical activity per day (more than a third higher on average for women than for men) would lead one to think that, contrary to indigenous belief, women's expenditure and hence need for energy would be greater than men's. But the theory of 'needs', while invoking explicitly or referring itself implicitly to objective physiological imperatives, in fact ignores them totally.

Does it, then, take into account subjective needs and desires? Still less. It is clear that in determining the 'needs' of a given individual, the evaluation of those 'concerned' does not enter into it. The feeling of hunger experienced by children and adolescents does not lead to a conclusion that they need food. On the contrary, in reply to requests there is a set response: 'you don't need it', which suggests that need is different from, external to, and even antinomic to desire. The theory of needs thus calls on objectivity as against subjectivity, albeit (as we have seen) refusing any objective measurement.

This double contradiction is well expressed in the previously cited passage by Cazaurang:

> It shields them (the pieces of meat) from the temptation of the young, *who are always hungry* . . . the week's supply of bread . . . is only given out *as needed*.

The needs to which he alludes are thus not those of the youngsters. Their present hunger will not be satisfied, and had their previous needs been covered, they would not be 'hungry'.

This quotation shows that a state of hunger is considered to be normal among the young, or rather that satiation does not form part of the needs which are recognized for them. 'To eat one's fill' is one of the pleasures of life and this objective always runs the risk of not being achieved. Nonetheless, a chronic feeling of hunger is not considered an attribute of adults as an age class, although it is attributed as a distinctive characteristic to adolescents in rural society. 'Hunger' as concerning, not specific cases, but a whole category of individuals, 'the young', is considered not a characteristic of their social condition but an irremediable physiological fact. In other societies, such as that of North America or even urban France, a state of perpetual non-satiation appears as just as subjectively undesirable and objectively injurious among the young as among adults.[11]

When peasant farmers say – and most do concede it – that 'we live better than before', it is often primarily to evoke those changes which have occurred in everyday experience. In this regard, today is compared advantageously to yesterday. This 'before' is repeatedly evoked with bitterness, as a period of deprivation of food, and in all cases this relates to childhood.

> I remember, when I was a kid, I went out in the morning with the sheep. I went out with a 'drubbing' and that's all I had till evening (from an interview in the Lot Region).

The maintenance of differentials in consumption

If coercion is primarily used to make up for the lack of internalization of prohibitions among the young, and to create them, this is never so perfect that some slackening is not to be found. Between pure coercion and pure internalization, gossip plays a role, calling in the last resort on the presence of others and on shame, or its inverse, honour.

As Cazaurang again says:

> A small gesture of an earlier mistress of the house is worth pointing out. She used to profit by the absence of other family members to yield to her gluttony. She would make herself some separate small dishes or simply coffee. If an intruder arrived unexpectedly, the *sinful* object was swiftly slid into the unlit oven near the hearth.[12]

If for the young, food prohibitions – even when internalized – remain as constraints, especially since they are linked to a necessarily transitory status, for women they are integrated into a wider repressive system which allows a greater flexibility in its details. This system is the ideology of the role of wife and mother.

Women are in practice managers of the home and like all overseers they find themselves confronting situations for which no instructions exist. At such times a general principle takes over from the precise prohibitions which have become inappropriate. This general principle is simple: the wife and mother should always preserve the privileges of the husband and father, and 'sacrifice' herself.

Different modalities are used to this end in different societies. In Tunisia, for example, differential consumption is effected in a radically different way. Men have two or three meals a day while women have only one or two, and these meals never coincide. The women eat foodstuffs prepared once a year and obtained from second quality produce. The meals they make for men on the other hand use fresh and best quality ingredients. The rigorous separation of time, place and the basic substance of the meals makes any competition for the food between men and women impossible.[13]

In France today, except for a few specific prohibitions – such as alcohol and tobacco – men and women eat 'from the same table' (*au même pain et pot*). Differential consumption derives essentially not from prohibition on this or that food, but from attributing women the smallest and most mediocre share of each food. It is difficult to say if it is the circumstances – sharing the same meal – which make necessary the creation and application of a general principle, or whether it is the existence of this principle which makes possible the preparation of but one meal. Perhaps it would be more appropriate to say that only such a principle could give an account of the variability of content of differential consumption.

In a particular social situation, in a given family and at a given standard of living, the content is not so flexible: the same dishes appear regularly on the table each week and it is not necessary to work out a new evaluation and a new distribution each time. The shares are fixed once and for all: in each family and in each chicken there is 'father's bit'.

Here again restrictions are experienced differently according to the degree of internalization and the transitory character or definitive status to which they are attached. For children, especially male children, they are persecutions on which they are revenged from the first occasion when they have access to the 'father's bit' which they have coveted for years. Women, however, think that they have chosen the piece to which they are entitled.

[...]

But there is absolutely no need for sacrifice to be liked: it becomes second nature. The mistress of the house takes the smallest steak without thinking, and will not take one at all if by chance there are not enough for everyone. She will say 'I don't want any'; and nobody is surprised, she least of all, that it should always be the same person who 'doesn't want any'. There is also no need at all for her to refer to the ideology of sacrifice as an integral part of feminine nature, nor that she be aware of her generosity or abnegation. Recourse to a universal principle supposes an out of the ordinary situation where the purely mechanical conduct of everyday life no longer suffices to guide action.

When one moves from the country to the town, and from low income sectors to higher sectors, consumption of food increases and differential consumption becomes less marked in this area. Since the level of food consumption is higher, it might be expected that basic needs are better covered and that differences of consumption would more and more concern less visible qualities and modalities. Indeed, food being sufficiently abundant, it might be expected that differences in food consumption would tend to disappear completely and be replaced by, or only exist in, other areas.

However, the flexible character of differential consumption, the fact (discussed above) that it is not the specific content but the principles of attribution which are defined, allows other expressions of subordination when for one reason or another the household's scale of relative values is modified. One example can illustrate this move back to using food to express status differences, and this also illustrates the flexibility of the system.

In [. . . the 1970s] France, and Paris in particular, experienced a shortage of potatoes which lasted for a fortnight. Since the demand for this basic commodity is relatively inelastic, prices rose and queues formed in front of the greengrocers. When questioned in one of these queues by a radio interviewer, a woman replied: 'I'll keep the potatoes for my husband. The children and I will eat pasta or rice.' [. . .] The solution adopted seems to be explained neither by the physiological impossibility for the husband to absorb products (replacements in this particular situation) which were in any case consumed in almost as regular a way as potatoes, nor by the economic situation of the family, but rather by the symbolic necessity of marking privileged and statutory access to goods which are rare (or become rare) – this access being both the sign and at the same time the reason for the hierarchy of consumption.

If differentiation were studied in all sectors of consumption it is likely that the following principle and its corollaries would be confirmed:

1 The rarest goods in each sector, and the most prestigious sectors of consumption, are subject to privileged access.
2 The relative difference between the standard of living of different family members stays more or less constant in all social situations (and increases in absolute value as the privileged access concerns more and more costly goods and/or the differentiation is exercised on an enlarged global volume).

Indeed, with growth in the part of the budget which is available for spending on things other than food, forms of consumption develop which were previously of little importance or non-existent. The raising of the general standard of living may thus allow the development of differentiation in certain existing areas. In addition, it allows the emergence of new areas of consumption which are fresh fields for the exercise of differentiation. For example, the acquisition of a car by a household in which previously everybody travelled by public transport, not only considerably increases the global difference in consumption – variance in the standard of living – between the user of the car and other family members, but above all it introduces differentiation into an area – transport – which up till then was undifferentiated.

The study of differential consumption cannot be reduced to the study of quantitative differences in access to particular goods, however, it is also qualitative. Does a child being taken for a Sunday outing consume the family car in the same way as the father who drives it? Above all, does it consume the same outing? The problems which are currently being put forcefully in rural areas when two generations live together, reveal – if one listens to those concerned – that the conflicts experienced divide not 'the generations', but rather concern the 'freely chosen' consumption which the 'invited' children want, and the 'compelled' consumption which is 'given' them (imposed) by their parent-hosts.

These examples seem to indicate that ways of consuming are perhaps more important than quantities consumed. But up to now the study of consumption has always been preoccupied with – has always meant exclusively – volumes, and the very existence of modes of consumption has not even been hinted at.

Yet consumption after all concerns not only goods but also services, and if the classical economic studies sometimes include under the rubric of 'self-consumption' goods which are made at home, they always ignore the services produced in the household. However, despite what the titles of research on household budgets may lead us to think, household consumption does not only involve what is bought on the market: we do not eat raw steaks or unpeeled potatoes at our family tables. We consume not only primary materials but also their preparation: the housework of the 'mistress of the house' (work of which the preparation of food constitutes only a part). The provider of these services does not consume them in equal manner with the non-providers, for diverse reasons (of which some are obvious: e.g. you cannot serve at table and be served at the same time). [. . .]

Taking these services into consideration overturns not only the existing accounted evaluation of family consumption, it overturns at the same stroke the evaluation of family production, because these services are also 'self-produced'. Above all, it re-poses, at the level of production, the problems of the meaning of the very term 'unit' when applied to the family – i.e. the problem of the internal functioning of the family as an economic institution.

Notes

1 E. M. Duvall, *Family Development*, New York: Lippincott, 1957, p. 58.
2. Galbraith shares this critique of the household. See J. Galbraith, *Economics and the Public Purpose*, London: André Deutsch, 1973.

3. B. Jousselin, 'Les Choix de consommation et les budgets des menages', in *Consommation*, 1972, p. 141.

4. INSEE (National Institute for Statistics and Economic Studies), 1973.

5. See M. Perrot, *Le Mode de vie des familles bourgeoises*, Paris: Colin, 1961, pp. 21–40. The history of the creation and construction of 'consumption scales' recounted by Perrot is very instructive. In these studies, differential consumption is dissembled . . . by the act of bringing it to light. Three types of studies can be distinguished which, with apparently different methods, all lead to surprisingly similar scales. In the first (Engels) 'the increase of weight and height represents the progression of expenditure of consumption'; it suggests lower coefficients of consumption of food for women and children. Others ('budgetists') cling to the actual behaviour of households and 'discover' that consumption is indeed differentiated by age and sex (thus 'confirming' the initial assumptions of the first school). Lastly, the nutritionists try to evaluate the calorific needs of family members, but by 'considering that the expenditure on food of a family is proportional to the needs in calories of the people of whom it is composed' (i.e. by taking the actual consumption as the indicator of 'needs'). In corroborating the coefficients of the 'budgetists', those of the 'nutritionists' carry the guarantee that the actual expenditure well covers the 'calorific needs', and that differential expenditures are justified by different needs. In addition, they give the impression that no consideration whatsoever, other than the provision of calories, enters into the consumption of food. It is implicit that differentiation of food intake cannot relate to quality but exclusively to calorific values. Quantities being adapted to needs, distribution is hence – in the full sense of the word – just.

6. This tendency to find what is morally unacceptable and also theoretically unthinkable – or at least not to think about it – overflows the restricted area of consumption. Thus Engels (followed by Simone de Beauvoir) could see nothing in the hierarchy of the proletarian family other than a dulling 'remnant of brutality' which did not profoundly debase the essential 'equality in misfortune'. . .

7. I feel authorized by an illustrious mentor to choose 'homely facts', 'drawn from everyday life' when handling 'phenomena whose intimate place in men's life has sometimes shielded them from the impact of economic discussion'. T. Veblen, *Theory of the Leisure Class*, New York: Mentor, 1953, pp. xx.

8. J. Cazaurang, *Pasteurs et paysans Béarnais*, Pau: Marimpouey, 1968.

9. Ibid., p. 97.

10. The similarity between this indigenous theory and the basic postulates of consumption scales is striking. The latter 'scientifically' confirm the former. Thus the 'nutritional' scales (the most 'scientific') of 1918 are closer to the 'budgetary' scales of 1918 than to the 'nutritional' scales of 1970. The evaluation of the calorific needs of the individual thus vary with the allocation of food considered as 'normal' for that individual by the society (and the sociology) of his or her time.

11. Consumption scales give many indications on this subject, but since they cannot be analyzed in detail here, let us simply stress the coincidence of the relative share of adolescents in food consumption – a coefficient of 84 in the USA in 1917 and 60 in France in 1965 – and the existence or absence of a theory of adolescent hunger.

12. J. Cazaurang, op. cit., p. 124.

13. S. Ferchiou, 'Différenciation sexuelle de l'alimentation au Djerid (Sud Tunisien)', *L'Homme*, Premier Trimestre, 1968.

1.2 □ *Ann Whitehead*

Ann Whitehead's work introduces a valuable cross-cultural dimension into the study of domestic consumption, identifying both commonalities and differences in the lives of British and Kusasi women. She adopts a theoretical stance which is more traditionally Marxist than Delphy's – although her conclusions are not dissimilar. She, too, emphasizes the impact of men's power on the distribution of resources within households.

'I'm hungry, mum': the politics of domestic budgeting

This article considers aspects of relations between men and women within households in economies which are very different in the way in which consumption goods are acquired – in the first case mainly through direct production (rural Ghana), and in the second case mainly through the purchase of wage goods (industrial Britain). I examine both some of the processes by which household members gain unequal access to, and control over, the resources which are available to the household as a whole, and the forms of sharing that occur between husband and wife. I shall use the term *conjugal contract*[1] to refer to the terms on which husbands and wives exchange[2] goods, incomes, and services, including labour, within the household. The paper draws attention both to the necessary existence of such conjugal contracts as the basis both for marriage and the household as a collectivity concerned with the daily maintenance of its members, and to the changing terms and nature of such contracts according to the location of the household in the wider economy. The paper also draws attention to the conflicts of interest between husbands and wives which different forms of conjugal contract entail.

In demonstrating observable and institutional arrangements by which women lose access to the resources they have produced themselves, or to equal shares in the household resources, I have treated husband and wife relations at a relatively low level of abstraction. It should therefore be emphasised that the major underpinning of the discussion is an interest in power as an aspect of gender relations. These institutional arrangements are one important battleground in the establishment of male domination in the sphere of marital and family relations. At the same time, they have a relationship to the other bases of husbands' and men's power over wives and women. As the descriptions of the two empirical situations reveal, however, the relationship between the position of the genders in the sexual division of labour outside the family, and the power relationships within it, are complex and indirect.

[. . .]

In household-based production the household is the locus within which men and women cooperate as members of a single productive enterprise in which some production for own use goes on. There is a marked division of labour between men's tasks and women's tasks, including, but not confined to the work of childbearing, and the more arduous work of childcare and domestic service and maintenance. By the sexual division of labour is meant not merely a list of men's jobs and women's jobs, nor indeed a set of cultural values about the suitability of various activities to the gender categories, but rather a system of allocating the labour of the sexes to activities, and highly importantly, a system of distributing the products of these activities. Edholm et al.[3] stress that the sexual division of labour within household-based productive enterprises renders the work that men and women do non-comparable. The allocation of different tasks to men and women has implications for the organisation of productive processes in that it involves issues of command and control. It also creates the necessity of exchanging and distributing between the sexes goods which their joint or separate labour has produced.

In these economies, the conjugal contract includes the exchange of labour in production as well as the exchanges in which personal and collective consumption needs, including the feeding and maintenance of children, are met. Here the arrangements within the conjugal contract are not separate from the way in which labour is rewarded, or from the distribution of the products of work, which in market economies by contrast take place outside the household and in the market. Edholm et al. make this comment about the problem of analysing these relations:

> . . . it is hard to analyse the relations which obtain within the unit; they are usually spoken of as relations of distribution: the product of the household is distributed according to local cultural criteria of need after outside obligations have been met. The assumption is generally made that an equal distribution is made between all active members of the household.[4]

These comments about the sexual division of labour in household production need however to be modified in so far as the rural economies of the third world are not based entirely on self-provisioning. Production for own use occurs side by side with the production of goods and services (including labour or labour power) which are exchanged or appropriated. This production for own use may go towards provisioning a member who is in wage labour – be this rural wage labour, plantation labour or migrant wage labour; it may occur side by side with peasant production for exchange; or part of the household produce or labour may be yielded up as sharecropping rent.

But if we turn to the literature on capitalist economies to illuminate these situations we find a strong tendency for there to be relatively separate discussions of the sexual division of labour within the family and outside it. [. . .]

The perspective taken in this paper is that, although in market economies the sexual division of labour separates men and women outside the family-based household, they come together within it, and in doing so, arrangements for personal and collective consumption needs have to be met out of total household income. Thus the relations of exchange, distribution and consumption which comprise the conjugal contract characterise household relations even where the household is not a unit of production. They thus constitute a significant area of comparison. It is for this reason that I have juxtaposed two case histories whose economic determinations take such very different forms, and indeed whose conjugal contracts are very different. One is marked by the idea of a common household subsistence fund, and the other by the family wage and the housekeeping allowance. Although in some senses the basis for making this comparison is a shaky one, my purpose is to demonstrate areas of theoretical continuity in one aspect of gender relations. It is not to deny differences in economic determination, nor to imply homologies in the sexual division of labour, in the forms of gender subordination or in the nature of the family-based household in the two cases.

Nevertheless one form of similarity does provide food for thought. What family-based households have in common is that they are small residential units, which, if not themselves biologically reproductive, are derived from biologically reproductive units. Some of their members sell their labour-power to purchase or produce by direct production the goods and services vital to the maintenance and well-being of the members of the unit. The producing and consuming collectivity is normally surrounded by ideologies of sharing and self-sufficiency. Many writers characterise the exchange and distribution of products between members of any family or kin group as governed by social definitions of need – as in Marx's description of relations within the primitive communist mode. The implication is of an absence of exploitation within such units, and this together with the folk ideologies of sharing between family kin, seems to be the source of the view that the family based household is an intrinsically democratic and cooperative unit operating in the interests of all its members. In so far as the household has an important connection with the family,[5] then the feminist literature on the family in the last fifteen years can be seen as an elaboration of precisely the opposite of this view. It is an analysis of the family as a site of subordination and domination, of sexual hierarchies of many kinds, and of conflicts of interests between its members, especially between husbands and wives.

The household common fund in North-East Ghana

In this section I shall discuss the way the conjugal contract operates in a savannah farming community in North-East Ghana. Exchanges between husbands and wives will be discussed both as a way in which production is organised, and a way in which members of the household are maintained and gain access to consumption goods on a household basis. The household productive enterprise, while family based, is not based on the conjugal core, nor on the nuclear family, but on a relatively large and complex extended family household. So, for the Kusasi who inhabit this area, the terms under which husband and wife exchange goods and services including labour are embedded in the set of social relations of the extended family unit. In these circumstances, the budgeting for both individuals and for the collectivity has to allow for substantial variations in household membership. The basic model is of each household having a common fund, shared by all, but I shall show that individual household members have differential access to this fund, and differing degrees of dependence on it. I shall argue that commoditisation of the economy has lessened men's dependence on the household common fund while reinforcing the dependence of women on it.

[. . .] Today Kusasi are self-provisioning farmers who aim in a relatively short farming season to produce enough food for a whole year's consumption. They also aim to sell enough crops for cash or to get cash from other sources to obtain a range of consumption necessities (including clothes) which they cannot provide for themselves, and also a few agricultural inputs. The staple crop is millet, with ground nuts and to a lesser extent rice, grown for cash. Many households own a handful of cattle, which are used for bridewealth payments and in a number of other ceremonial and debt relationships, as well as for ploughing. Agriculture is largely non-mechanised and uses mainly locally produced inputs although about one-fifth of households own a plough which is the major non-local agricultural input.

The farming system is still sufficiently based on self-provisioning for it to be considered extremely wrong to sell millet; no-one would admit doing so. All the households in the community farm; and the majority build and repair their own houses and provide for themselves a wide range of other consumption goods. Virtually all men, women and children over 10 have some form of money income, whether this is the miniscule income of a young boy or girl from selling biscuits or oranges; the petty income of some adults from selling vegetables or hens; or the substantial incomes of adult men (or, more rarely, adult women) from hoarding and speculating in staple crops, from trading in cattle or occasionally from wage employment.

Although this kind of society is best described as communal, in that there are no classes or strata which have different relationships to productive resources, nor is there a hierarchy of associated status, this is not to say there are no differences in income, wealth and subsistence life styles amongst the various households. A proportion of the households rarely produce all the food they need to consume in a year, while other households, regularly produce a good surplus. Individual men farm acreages which range from less than 5 acres to over 40. Land is allocated by the chief and elders; it is not in any simple sense individually owned, nor can it be bought or sold. [. . .] The major factor affecting a household's resource base is where its head stands in the power relations within clan and community.

At this level of technology, and without absolute land scarcity in the region, an important determinant of successful rural livelihood is command over labour. Labour is provided on a permanent basis by household members, or more intermittently by communal or exchange work parties, where a farmer 'begs' household heads who are his kinsmen, neighbours or in-laws to provide labour for a particular farming activity, on a particular farm, on a particular day. Although an ideology of reciprocity surrounds these work parties ('I beg my neighbour and then I go to help him when he calls') surplus producing households in fact call work parties most often, and poorer households work a disproportionate number of labour days for others.

[. . .]

For Kusasi the cliche that the household is the basic unit of social structure is very appropriate. The Kusasi word for house – *yim* – means both the house (compound) and the people who occupy it. The household is a well defined system of statuses, authority and decision making; it is the primary locus of consumption and despite the importance of labour exchanges between other households in the community, its members form a significant production unit.

[. . .]

Households in the community vary from those consisting of a man and his wife and children, through a simple polygamous household where the head has more than one wife, to complete households containing more than one married man each of whom may have more than one wife. It is probably helpful to bear in mind that the ideal Kusasi household is composed of male head, his junior brother, both of whom are married with two wives each, an unmarried adult male (brother or son) and able-bodied daughter or daughters, a woman given in pawn and one or more 'mothers'.

The Kusasi household is a complex social institution in which various forms of hierarchy coalesce to give clear lines of superordination and subordination, with the basic status markers being age, gender and marital status. Every household has a male head who is called the 'owner' of the compound or its 'landlord' and all others within it are collectively referred to as 'dependants' even when the household includes a middle-aged married brother who may be wealthy in his own right. In terms of household composition, relations between household members, and relations between the constituent households of a community, the male head forms a pivotal point. The proper behaviour of inferiors to superiors is deference. The women always kneel when they present food and water and other things to men. All dependants crouch with their heads turned away when they have to greet or speak to a head. The 'owner' of the compound juridically mediates between household members and members of other households and ritually represents them at, for example, the sacrifices at harvest time. The hierarchy within the household is reflected in its spatial arrangements, which are conventionally uniform with arrangements in huts, yards, and kraals reflecting the division of social space within the unit.

The way in which production is organised within the household depends on a number of factors, including the sexual division of labour. North-East Ghana, unlike many parts of Anglophone West Africa, is predominantly a male farming area. The staple crop (millet) requires a large amount of male labour input, although women's labour is important. Women in fact do not grow the staple crop. Only men have land on which millet is grown and Kusasi men argue that a woman will starve if she is not living in a household containing a male farmer, be he her husband, father or son. And despite the fact both men and women produce agricultural products, women are not really regarded as farmers at all. Although virtually all Kusasi women do some cultivation of food crops other than vegetable, the acreages they farm as their own are pitifully small (less than one acre). Women do nonetheless contribute to the agricultural cycle as the schematic outline of the gender typification of certain agricultural tasks below indicates.

While the sexual division of labour is an important factor affecting the work done by household members, the primary distinction which orders the production relations of the compound is the distinction between private farms and household farms. The household farm/farms are the most important acreages of the compound. [. . .] They are always planted with millet which, once harvested, is stored in large granaries immediately outside the entrance to the house, and in the area where men sit and talk to one another and to visitors. The millet produced on these farms is supposed to feed the household for the year. It is a primary obligation of all household members to work to fill these granaries. It is also a primary obligation of the household head to see that they are filled. These farms are to be contrasted with the 'private' farms which both male and female members of the household also have. On them men grow millet, guinea corn, rice and groundnuts, while women grow rice and groundnuts. In direct contrast to the disposal of crops from household farms, the products from private farms, regardless of the labour which produced them, are owned by the individual farmer, and may be disposed of as he or she wishes.[6] Rice and groundnuts are conventionally regarded as cash crops (groundnuts having been introduced by the colonial government precisely in the drive to commoditise the indigenous economy), while the millet and guinea corn may be used to supplement the subsistence of their own wives and children. 'Surplus' grain is also required for the copious beer supplied to exchange work parties. Other cash crops include cotton, kenaf fibres and dry season vegetable gardening. These all come into the category of private farming, as does the management of small livestock (poultry, goats and sheep, pigs), but not of cattle.

The Kusasi household is a very important labour unit; one measure of the hierarchy within it is the command that individuals have over the labour of other household members. The farms which require labour are both communal and private; the private farms may belong to the household head or his dependants, and to either men or to

Input of men and women to agricultural tasks

Crop:		Millet	Groundnuts			Rice	
Sex of Farmer:		Men	Men	Women		Men	Women
Task:	Clearing	M	M	M+W		M	M+W
	Planting	M+W	W	W		W	W
	Weeding	M	M	M/W		M	M/W
	Harvesting	M+W	M+W	M/W		M/W	M+W

Key: M+W Men and women cooperatively.
M/W Men and women on separate farms: either on own farms or as all male or female work parties.

women. The labour available includes own labour, the labour of other household members and reciprocal exchange labour. Utilising these categories the pattern of labour use is as follows: household farms are worked by all members of the household, and by exchange labour, according to gender type of activity, under the direction of the household head. Indeed, the ploughing, weeding and harvesting of the household fields, using compound labour and exchange are the mainstay of the agricultural round. The work of household members on household farms is not directly rewarded, while that of exchange labour is rewarded with food and drink. However neither the use of unremunerated household labour, nor of exchange labour is confined to work on household fields. Household heads, especially the more wealthy farmers, rely heavily on both male and female exchange labour and unremunerated household labour for the labour input to their private farms. Among dependants, however, labour provided for the private farms shows an interesting difference between men and women, the crucial point of which is that whereas men can use the unremunerated labour of their wives (and often of all the women in the household), the only way a woman can use the labour of household men is by calling small exchange working parties which are remunerated in the sense that she provides food and beer. In other words, men only work for women of the household if this work is conceptually and materially turned into another form of work ('exchange'-type).

To summarise, the Kusasi household is conceptually, and in practice, an important use-value producing enterprise in which the labour of all members contributes to the production of subsistence goods. Through the organisation of so-called reciprocal links between household heads, household members also contribute to the annual grain product of other households. 'The household' also produces goods for sale, but these crops are grown under a different form of organisation, being mainly grown on private farms, for which all men, but household heads especially, utilise the unremunerated labour of household members. The cash from products sold from these farms is owned by the private farmer, as are other forms of cash income. Some of the content of the exchanges between husband and wife are subsumed in the obligations of each male and female member in the communal production of the agricultural cycle, and in the obligations to provide labour for private farms. Similarly, the terms under which husband and wife exchange other goods, services and income are embedded in the complex organisation of consumption and distribution within the whole household. For example, a Kusasi married woman has rights and obligations both with respect to the male household head to whom she may or may not be married, and to her own husband. It is proper to think of all of these obligations in terms of her conjugal status, in so far as she is referred to as 'wife' by the household head, and by all married men in the household.

Like the British ideology of the male breadwinner, the responsibility of the household head to provide the staple crop for all members of his household, and secondarily of a married man to ensure the staple food supply of his wives and children, are basic to Kusasi concepts of male gender identity. No other member of the household, except the head, may look inside or reach inside the granary. Each married woman in the compound receives a basket of millet from the granary every ten days or so, from which she is responsible for providing her husband and children with meals. She is also obliged to provide other food substances as soup ingredients, such as salt, fat, vegetables and dried fish powder.

Work by dependants carries with it rights other than basic subsistence which are a call on household income. For men, household labour builds up a right to the 5 cows of the marriage payment paid to the bride's male agnates. The obligation to provide the brideprice coincides with the younger men's compound labour obligations; they obtain the brideprice from the older men (compound heads) for whom they have worked, usually their father, father's brother, or their own senior brother. Work in the household also carries the rights to medical and ritual attention should this become necessary. Visits to the clinic and the diviner, or the performance of sacrifices, may be withheld if the head feels that a household member is not pulling his/her weight. Wives have a right to be clothed, as have young children who are also, in principle, entitled to be educated, although few children attend the village school. It is important to understand that these conventional claims on the common fund are subject to cultural evaluation of need and to competition made inevitable by scarcity. In both of these processes men have an undeniable, and often openly acknowledged, advantage over women.

Arguably a more significant aspect of gender differentiation than these commonly found sexual inequalities in the assessment of needs or in the power to command joint resources is the implications for men and women of the conceptual and material distinctions between the collectivity and the individual mentioned above. It is various features of this which I now wish to elaborate.

I described earlier the distinction between household farms and private farms. In part this becomes overlaid with the distinction between the staple crop and all other crops, implied in the linguistic equation of millet and food. Household farms grow the staple crop, and the staple crop is treated differently from all others in the sense that it ought not to be sold. Its production and distribution symbolise the common interests of household members, yet remain under the real and symbolic control of the household head at the same time. In contrast, the groundnuts and rice grown on private farms are potential food crops and cash crops. However, once private farm produce is sold, it becomes lost to any claims of household members, since, although attempts can be made to cajole or claim privileges, no other person has rights over an individual's cash income. In particular this applies to husbands and wives, in so far as, in common with many parts of sub-Saharan Africa, husband and wife do not pool resources, and do not have a common housekeeping or childrearing budget. This means both that buying and selling occur across the marital bond, and that their common responsibilities are ordered through stated conventional divisions (as in the responsibilities for different categories of food supply for meals described above), or through running accounts of who has provided what (as for example for children's education).

However, within this essential set of rules which ostensibly treats men and women equally, the potentialities for substantial gender differences arise. In the first place, despite the fact that both men and women have private farms, women's farms average less than one acre in size, so it is only men who have substantial cash incomes from private farms. There are also significant differences in the ways that men and women are supposed to dispose of their crops. Women, Kusasi say, grow groundnuts to feed to their children in the hungry season. Men farm to get cash. It is for men then, that an effectual and highly important conceptual boundary is drawn between money and subsistence. Men do not use cash income for the staple food which is part and parcel of their obligations as household head or as husband, nor normally for many other subsistence items. This boundary, while it enables individuals to retain control over their cash income, has to be seen in the light of two things: firstly the extremely poor development of the local market in such subsistence items as food, pots, baskets and building materials, all of which are rarely bought, and of the scarcity of cash in relation to compulsory expenditure (such as taxes and school fees) and desirable consumption goods (such as trousers and bottled beer), and secondly, in the light of the household's most powerful members' ability to claim that they have important duties in reconciling the competing claims of their dependants in assessing the best ways of distributing scarce resources.

The right of individuals to spend their money how they like is tempered by at least two ideologies and practices, and these also relate to men and women differently. The first is that of 'helping others'. However, there is an observable differential capability to keep control over one's own income. It is much easier for a household head, married man, senior wife, unmarried son or brother and junior wives and daughter (in that descending order) to hold on to their income. There is an ideological elision between this 'helping' and 'begging' with the responsibility of the household head and/or married man to clothe wives and clothe and educate children, since they must now be provided by cash whereas before they were provided in kind. The second ideology applies particularly to mothers and is of the mother's care for her children, and especially that she will not let them starve. As I pointed out above, a woman's groundnut harvest is described often as food for her children. Kusasi say that at the beginning of the hungry season when millet hand-outs by the household head get more infrequent, mothers give their children groundnuts to prevent them from being hungry. A 'strong' woman is a wife or mother who can provide independently of her husband and/or household head during the hungry season. In households where women have other income sources throughout the year from brewing and speculating in grain, this ideology leads to *their income* being used to provide staple food during the hungry season.

In summary, in North-East Ghana, the sexes have a different relationship to different areas of the commoditised economy. Discussions of the changing sexual division of labour in commoditised rural production systems in Africa frequently find an intensification of women's work in food subsistence production, and the use of her unremunerated labour for male cash crop production.[7] In the situation I am describing there is a marked asymmetry in the relation of the sexes to the commoditised sector – women (except in relatively few cases) earn relatively small cash incomes from trade, from petty commodity production or from agricultural cash cropping, but the form of farming system precludes massive intensification of women's work in subsistence crops. However, commoditisation in this form has increased the comparative dependency of women on the household common fund compared to men, since women lack the cash to purchase alternatives. This throws new light on the trends in regional agricultural production. Such statistics as are available show a decline in regional millet production, which is probably the result of men's decisions to concentrate on the cash crop to the neglect of the subsistence crop.

Men and women obviously experience any decline in subsistence crop production quite differently, insofar as men have access to much more substantial alternative forms of income, but they are not, in the last analysis, responsible for the sustenance of their children. Married women, while they are wholly dependent on either a husband or a household head for staple, have little effective control over how much staple is produced, or over how it is disposed of. The introduction of cash cropping may not have altered the sexual division of labour in agriculture very substantially, but it has led to an intensification of women's work. Women are working harder to produce income from sources additional to food production, in order to purchase alternatives to make up for the shortfall in household production.

The family wage and household budgeting in industrial Britain

Let us turn now to an entirely different situation, that of intrahousehold exchanges between husband and wife within the family based household of industrial capitalism. There are several theoretical themes which underlie the material presented here but are not discussed fully themselves. These include the nature of the characteristic working-class family under capitalism, especially features of the wage form, and of domestic labour; the sexual division of labour within the labour market and within the home; and contrasts between the normative expectations and legal obligations of husband and wife in relation to their mutual support and patterns of behaviour.

If female headed households are excluded completely from the discussion, it is most common in working-class families in Britain for both husband and wife to be in wage work. [...] Proletarian women most commonly resume work when their youngest child goes to school and are more likely to work part-time than full-time. They thus participate in what is conventionally regarded as social production although they have different activity rates from their husbands and their work takes place in only certain sectors of employment. In addition these jobs are low paid. Women's employment occurs in a climate of opinion that considers that the family's income should be earned by the husband while the housework, which is unpaid, should be performed by the wife. This is not simply folk ideology: as Land[8] has shown, while the income support part of the social security system decisively allocates bureaucratic and legal responsibilities to a husband for the economic support of his wife and children, it equally decisively allocates to a wife the care of her husband and of their home and children.

The basic model of the conjugal contract in this context derives from the exchanges made necessary by this family wage earned by the husband in the labour market, and the performance of unpaid domestic labour by the wife. In general form it consists of the idea that the husband contributes his income and some services, while the wife contributes the wide ranging services making up housework and childcare, to a mutually beneficial collectivity. It has been a common assumption that the family based household operates a single budget, enshrined in the census category of common housekeeping. As Pahl[9] points out it is a corner stone of social policy that the income which comes into the household is available to all its members, according to their needs. Indeed historically the move to such a sharing unit, in which some members, regardless of sex, age or physical condition could be kept by others, is rightly regarded as a considerable advance from the early period of proletarianisation when families could only afford to retain those members who were independent earners. Nevertheless these assumptions about the equal availability of resources within households have been periodically questioned by feminists and others.[10] [. . .]

Pahl has reviewed the data and discussions on household income allocation flows that do exist with special reference to the working-class family of a married couple and two dependent children.[11] [. . .]

Pahl distinguishes three actual household allocational forms in situations where there is a single male breadwinner or social security claimant – the whole wage system, the allowance system and the pooling system. The whole wage and allowance system appear to be most common among working class couples. [. . .]

However as Pahl's survey makes clear, in both allocational systems, the relation of the spouses to what is left after . . . compulsory expenditure has been accounted for is asymmetrical. Men take a sum of money, often called their pocket money, for their personal expenditure in both systems. Ideological justifications for this are that he has to have money when he goes out to work or to the pub. Working class wives' personal expenditure by contrast often comes out of what she can scrape out of 'her' housekeeping, or she may ask her husband for the money for specific items. Occasionally she may have her own allowance! Pahl reports that in those few cases where women had full 'control' of the family income, these women still expected to give the husband money for his own use. This state of affairs is sometimes justified by the fetishisation of the wage, as the authors quoted below indicate:

> The wages are paid to the wage labourer and as such they are seen as the individual property of that individual. So that whereas men can often separate two areas of expenditure (personal and family) women, for ideological reasons, tend to merge their interests with those of the family and hence we can see that the division of wages within the family very often works against women in favour of men.[12]

The non-comparability of housework and wage labour has been much discussed in the literature on the subordination of women in advanced capitalist societies. [. . .] Where the sexual division of labour is such that only the husband's labour power enters the market, and the wife's work is domestic labour, it is difficult for there to be any commensurability in the exchanges between husband and wife. Thus we have the familiar problem of how to measure housework, and how it should be rewarded. Similarly, in bourgeois society, the appearance that the wage is individually earned by the labour of the employed worker alone, combined with the dominant concept of private possession, create the basis for the power of the (male) employed worker to compel a sum for individual consumption. The domestic worker cannot compel such a sum and her needs (and desires) are merged with those of other dependants, such as children.

The important case then becomes when wives enter wage work, for, under these circumstances, although it is true that the terms on which they enter the labour market are disadvantageous compared with their husbands, nevertheless they now sell their labour power in return for a cash wage, just like their husbands. They receive the wage as persons in their own right. As husband and wife are paid in money, all sums of which are equivalent and exchangeable, the only difference between them should stem from the difference in the power conferred by the different amounts of wages they receive. Potentially both husbands and wives are empowered to buy goods to the amount of their respective wages on the market outside the household, and potentially both husband and wife contribute a highly divisible object into the common budget. The form which intrahousehold economic transactions take under these circumstances is of some significance.

Hunt[13] examined the financial arrangements between couples in a mining village in the North Midlands where both husband and wife were working. She notes the importance of the man as the breadwinner. Almost all couples thought that it demeaned men if, as in some cases, his wife was earning more than he was. [. . .] She also reported that it was common for a two-income married couple to spend that income of husband and wife on different categories of consumption spending. All necessary expenditure, e.g. rent, heating, normal food bills, weekly outgoings, which cannot easily be reduced, are taken out of the husband's income, while the wife's income is used for extras, e.g. consumer durables, holidays, clothes for all family members etc. The justification for this is if the wife's income disappears then the family does not have a level of compulsory expenditure which it cannot keep up. It is not simply at the ideological level that distinctions are made between what the husband earns and what the wife earns, but also at a material level, in so far as sums of money are *concretely set aside* for different purposes.

If some of a wife's income is distinguished from her husband's by ideology and by concrete processes which set aside her wages to pay for different kinds of expenditure, what can we say about her power over its disposal as a whole, that is to say her capacity to hold on to part of her income for her own use as against her husband's? The crucial question is the extent of the benefits to women of their independent access to part of the surplus income. Women frequently report satisfaction at having a source of income of their own but their relation to its disposal is quite different from that of men in many ways.

There is little evidence of any folk category of women's pocket money similar to that of men. This despite the much vaunted category of pin money, which I think expresses the view that a woman's earnings from waged work, or from petty business, are minor, and are also her own, to be spent on items for her own use; that these are neither essential to her subsistence or normal maintenance; nor are they to be spent on routine family maintenance (despite the evidence to the contrary given above). 'Pin money' supports the model of wifely 'dependence' while implying that she has control of her own income. But in decisions about spending her own income she is subject to powerful sets of values. One of these I term 'the ideology of maternal altruism'. By this the mother and wife always put the family or the children first. In another form, no less pernicious, but more morally complex to comment upon, the altruistic mother has to deny herself resources to make scarce resources go round. As well as better and more food to the manual workers, she ensures food for the children before she eats herself.[14] An early study by Jephcott[15] suggested that the power of married women vis-à-vis their husbands could decrease when they acquired earnings of their own, because this meant that their husbands could keep more of their earnings for personal expenditure, while the women's earnings went to pay for collective family expenditure. To this must be added the evidence that, however the decisions are arrived at, husbands consume more of the household's surplus for their personal needs than do wives. Maher,[16] Delphy[17] and Pahl[18] all make this general assessment although the evidence is scattered, and often has to be read off indirectly, as for example from the fact that men's leisure time pursuits outside the home tend to be more costly than women's.

[. . .]

The evidence suggests that money wages earned by men and women, in a continuous, though possibly sectored, labour market, are rendered non-comparable when they are brought into the household by wage earners who are respectively husband and wife. Essentially I am arguing that a wife's wage enters the household and she loses control of it. This seems to me to illustrate fairly clearly hierarchies of super-subordination in operation in the household. The conjugal contract, including the ideology of maternal altruism, effectively creates barriers to women disposing of their income freely on the market, even where this income takes the money form, with the implications of personal control implied by ownership of money, and despite the free flowing character of money.

The treatment of the wife's income in this way may be a rational response to the sexual division in the labour market. As a woman she cannot command very high earnings, she is less well protected by legislation and union organisation and is liable to be forced out of wage employment at the vagaries of the market. It should not need to be pointed out that any view that the wife's income is used for holidays and non-essentials is in many families untrue. Apart from poor proletarian households, which have been specifically excluded from the discussion and for whom the two incomes cover at most only essential expenditure, many of the items purchased by the wife's wage are simply lumpy consumption goods and items of domestic technology which have to be saved for. The particular form of joint income division that I have outlined is a powerful reinforcement of male gender stereotypes. At the point where the husband's gender identity is threatened – when his wife may be about to enter the breadwinner role – the mode of dealing with her income into the household reinstates him into this role. All such ideologies of the male wage as being different from the female wage serve to maintain the general characteristics of the sexual division of labour under capitalism.

Conclusion

This article has a deliberately narrow focus on some of the distributional aspects of intrahousehold relations. I have described as the conjugal contract the terms on which products and income, produced by the labour of both husband and wife, are divided to meet their personal and collective needs, and given details of this in two very different circumstances. In them the basis for the material maintenance of the co-residential members of the household are very different, but nevertheless I have argued in each case that inequalities of power between husband and wife become manifest in the various arrangements by which the goods, services and/or income of husband and wife are allocated and distributed. Overall a woman's effective possession of the resources she has either produced, or earned, within the family-based household is determined by her relative power vis-à-vis other household members, especially her husband. This relative power is *not* simply dependent on the relative wages commanded in the labour market, or on the relative labour input into agricultural production. In both cases women are closely attached to the collective or family aspects of consumption, in one case in the form of the subsistence common fund, and in the other in the form of the housekeeping allowance, while men are much more individuated in relation to their control over resources and in their own consumption. [. . .]

The major undiscussed perspective in this paper is what is the significance and meaning, if any, of finding such similarities between wholly different economic forms, and wholly different types of sexual division of labour. I have hardly speculated at all on the various factors which may affect the relative powers of husbands and wives over the disposal of income and produce: an important area for more substantial theoretical elaboration is the link between the differential position of the genders with respect to relations of production, and the ability to influence disposal and distribution. Similarly, although it emerges in each case that the sharing and caring which dispossess women take place in family and kinship ties, it is clear that the nature of family and kinship relations in the two circumstances are markedly different, because of their differing relationship to the production system as a whole.

Nevertheless, stress should be placed on the finding that the relative power of husbands and wives does not simply reflect relative wages commanded in the labour market. A major theme in discussions of the sexual division of labour in non wage-labour economies is that the sexual division of labour effectively renders the work that men and women do as non-comparable. And as a consequence, products are not distributed on the basis of the relative labour input into production. I have argued that both the treatment of income from waged work as being available for different categories of expenditure, and the sexual division of responsibility for specific consumption needs, are further aspects of non-comparability.

Finally both situations serve to remind us that the conjugal contract implies specific material conflicts of interest between husbands and wives. Conflicts of interest between men and women are not generic conflicts of interest, or natural antagonisms; they are, like other conflicts of interest, rooted in the nature of social relationships. In a rural area in Britain, I found that marital disputes and quarrels were often about how much time was spent outside the house by the husband, about his drinking in the pub, about his performance of domestic chores and about contraception.[19] Although these could be described in terms of behavioural conflict or of differences in role expectations, many of them are, in essence, about the forms of expenditure of ostensibly 'shared' resources. I also found, as have many other studies, that financial matters are directly the subject of many other crises and disputes. Whatever the form that the material conflicts of interest between men and women in the household take, they are an expression of the extent to which, despite ideology, the household is not a collectivity of mutually reciprocal interests.

Notes

1. The origin of this term is now a little uncertain to me. I think I coined it to describe the area discussed, although I was clearly influenced by the conjugal fund: see W. Goode, *World Revolution and Family Patterns,* New York: Free Press, 1963; and for the conjugal contract, see J. Goody, *Production and Reproduction*, Cambridge: Cambridge University Press, 1976; as well as by the description of the Hausa marriage contract, see R. Longhurst, *The Provision of Basic Needs for Women: A case study of a Hausa village in Nigeria*, Draft Report for the ILO, Geneva, and MOD, UK.
2. I am using exchange in its general sociological sense, and not in the more technical sense in which it is used by economists.
3. F. Edholm, O. Harris and K. Young, 'Conceptualising women', *Critique of Anthropology*, 3: 101–30, 1977.
4. Ibid.
5. See R. Rapp, E. Ross and R. Bridenthal, 'Examining family history', *Feminist Studies*, 5, 1979; A. Whitehead, 'The intervention of capital in rural production systems: Some aspects of the household', Paper to Conference on the Continuing Subordination of Women in the Development Process, University of Sussex, 1978.
6. This situation is not uncommon in West Africa. Roberts's description of the Niger version of 'gandu' organised farming is of a similar sexual division of labour and a similar form of collective household farm: see P. Roberts, 'The integration of women into the development process: Some conceptual problems', *IDS Bulletin*, 10, 1979. Dey describes a similar household/private farm distinction within an agricultural system with a somewhat different sexual division of labour: see J. Dey, 'Women farmers in the Gambia: The effects of irrigated rice development programmes on their role in rice production', Unpublished Paper, University of Reading, 1979.
7. B. Rogers, *The Domestication of Women: Discrimination in developing societies*, London: Routledge and Kegan Paul, 1980.
8. H. Land, 'Social security and the division of unpaid work in the home and paid employment in the labour market', Department of Health and Social Security, 1977.
9. J. Pahl, 'Patterns of money management in marriage', *Journal of Social Policy*, 9: 313–35, 1980.
10. H. Land, 'The family wage', *Feminist Review*, 6: 55–77, 1980.
11. J. Pahl, op. cit.
12. Women's Studies Group, 1976, quoted in P. Hunt, 'The parlour and the pit', Unpublished MSc Thesis, University of Keele, 1977.
13. P. Hunt, 'The parlour and the pit', Unpublished MSc Thesis, University of Keele, 1977.
14. Rather than a string of academic references the reader is recommended to consult the following interesting collections of self-written experiences of British working women:

M. Llewellyn Davies, *Life as We Have Known It, By Cooperative Working Women*, London: Virago, 1977; M. Llewellyn Davies, *Maternity: Letters from working women*, London: Virago, 1977.

15. Cited in J. Pahl, op. cit.
16. V. Maher, 'Work, consumption and authority within the household: A Moroccan case', in K. Young, C. Walkowitz and R. McCulloch, eds, *Of Marriage and the Market*: *Women's subordination in international perspective*, London: CSE Books, 1981.
17. C. Delphy, Reading 1.1, this volume.
18. J. Pahl, op. cit.
19. A. Whitehead, 'Sexual antagonism in Herefordshire', in D. Barker and S. Allen, eds, *Dependence and Exploitation in Work and Marriage*, London: Tavistock, 1976.

1.3 □ *Jan Pahl*

Jan Pahl has been at the forefront of empirical research on domestic budgeting in Britain, and has developed a classification of marital financial arrangements which is now widely used by others in the field. In this article, she summarizes some of her findings, paying particular attention to degrees of male and female control over money. Pahl points out that, whatever system of control and management a couple adopts, men still tend to enjoy greater freedom in personal spending than do women.

Household spending, personal spending and the control of money in marriage

The aim of this article is to examine the extent to which money is shared within marriage and to consider the implications of this for patterns of spending. The article draws on my own study of the control and allocation of money within marriage.[1] Two sets of quotations from the interviews carried out in the course of the study may serve to set the scene: in both cases it is the husband who is speaking.

> My wife is totally dependent on me. We are basically traditional: she has a set amount of housekeeping money and I pay the bills as they come in. I wouldn't want a joint account: I like to feel I'm in control of the family scene and I feel more in control this way.

> Marriage is a joint partnership: the money is there for both of us. I wouldn't want to keep our incomes separate. I earn more than my wife and it equalises incomes putting them in a joint account. My wife controls the money and decides how much she needs to spend on housekeeping.

These quotations raise complicated issues about the transfer of resources within households and about responsibility for spending. Where one partner is the main earner and the other the main spender, what social and economic processes shape the transfer of resources from earner to spender? We know that household spending patterns reflect household income levels: do they also reflect the control and allocation of money *within* the household? The working hypothesis which underpins the article is summarised in Figure 1.

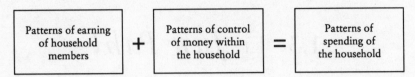

Figure 1   Earning, sharing, spending

Traditionally economists have treated the household as though it were an individual and have assumed that the same economic theories apply. In terms of Figure 1 they have created a black box in the space between earning and spending. There is room for only one example:

> A typical household sells, or attempts to sell, its labour services to employers and receives as proceeds of the sale, labour income. Moreover, the household may own financial assets (such as savings certificates, shares, *etc.*) and non-financial assets (such as property) from which it also derives income. The household's income may also include payments from the government in the form of social security payments, old age pensions *etc*. With this income the household purchases goods and services, pays taxes, and, perhaps, saves.[2]

In reality, of course, income is earned by individuals, not households, and goods and services are purchased not by households but by individuals. However, 'by a heroic simplification the separate identities of men and women are merged into the concept of the household. The inner conflicts and compromises of the household are not explored.'[3]

By treating it as though it were an individual the household has become a sort of black box, within which the transfer of resources between earners and spenders has been rendered invisible. This has had three important effects. First, it has blurred distinctions between controlling, managing, spending and consuming. The person who decides that a particular item should be bought is often not the person who investigates where the best bargain is to be found and makes the purchase; the purchaser may not consume what he or she has bought. Thus, for example, a child may have no real control over the family finances and may manage and spend only her own pocket money, but may still be a privileged consumer. A non-earning wife who receives a housekeeping allowance from her husband is likely to play a major role as a manager but may still not feel able to spend money on herself; her husband's role as an earner and controller of income enables him to hand over the work of spending to someone who will protect his interests as a consumer.

Secondly, the black box model of the household has blurred distinctions between different sorts of spending. These differences may reflect the fact that money for spending may have different sources: it may come, for example, from one's own wages, from a common kitty or from money given to one by another member of the household. Additionally, spending can have different claims on those sources of money according to the item being bought. The distinction between *household spending* and *personal spending* is an important one here. For example, household spending may be seen as a legitimate claim on the household budget, so that items under this heading are paid for by the main earner or out of the common kitty. On the other hand, personal spending may have to come out of the individual's own income, if any. [. . .]

Thirdly, the black box approach has led to a neglect of all the issues which surround the sharing of resources within households. The disparities in income between men and women, especially when there are young children to be cared for, mean that there has to be some sharing of incomes if women and children are not to live at a lower standard of living than men. Traditionally policies related to income tax and income maintenance have assumed that married couples do share their resources. However, in the field of taxation there is currently a move towards making the individual the main unit rather than the couple. [. . .] The move away from joint taxation and towards the independent taxation of married people is an international phenomenon.[4] It is often presented as an ideological shift towards greater equality between men and women and away from the inequality associated with the financial dependence of wives on husbands. However, assuming that all the adult members of a household are financially independent of each other does not make them so, especially when the household is located within social and economic structures which offer unequal opportunities for becoming financially independent. [. . .]

This article examines these issues in the light of data drawn from a study of the control and allocation of money within the household. The study focused on households containing two adults, who were married in all but one case, and at least one dependent child. The words 'household', 'family' and 'couple' may be used interchangeably in the pages which follow. However, it is important to remember that both households and families can take many different forms. The extent to which money is shared within other social groups offers a rich field for further research.

The study

The main aim of the study was to gain a better knowledge of patterns of allocation of money within households and to investigate the significance of different allocative systems for individual members of households. Husband and wife were interviewed first together and then separately, and interviews were completed with 102 couples. The small number of respondents means that it would be rash to claim that they were representative of a wider population of families; it is likely that unhappy marriages and couples with money problems were under-represented. However, in many respects the study couples had characteristics which one would have hoped to see in a representative sample. At the time 48 per cent of married women with children in Britain were in employment, while the proportion in the sample was 50 per cent. In Britain as a whole 88 per cent of married men with children were employed, while the proportion among the men who took part in the study was exactly the same.[5] Nearly three quarters of the couples owned their own homes, a proportion very similar to the figure for married couples in England as a whole.[6] In terms of the Registrar General's social class classification and of the ownership of consumer durables the study couples were again like the total population of households with children in Britain at the time. All the women were in receipt of child benefit, since all had at least one child under sixteen, and all the men who were not in employment received either unemployment benefit, invalidity benefit or supplementary benefit (now income support). Thus every individual who took part in the study had some form of income, whether as wages, salary or social security benefit.

Four patterns of control

There are many different criteria which might be used to create a classification of household financial arrangements. However, for the purpose of this analysis it seemed important to focus on the extent to which income was pooled and on the control of the pool, if there was one. The existence of joint and separate bank accounts offered a relatively objective way in which to assess the jointness or otherwise of a couple's financial arrangements. Having a joint bank account suggested some degree of pooling, so couples with a joint account were divided from those without.

Next the couples were sorted according to the wife's answer to the question 'Who really controls the money that comes into this house?' The possible answers to this question were 'wife', 'husband', and 'both'. However, where 'both' were said to control finances, the analysis showed that husbands were likely to be responsible for paying major bills, checking the bank statement and making financial decisions. So couples where 'both' controlled the money had financial arrangements which most closely resembled those where husbands controlled finances. In the analysis which follows 'both' and 'husband' have been combined in order to reduce the number of categories. Support for the choice of the wife's answer came from the interviewers, who at the end of the joint interview noted discreetly which partner had been the most authoritative in talking about money. A very significant correlation existed between the husband appearing authoritative in the joint interview and his being described by his wife in her separate interview as controlling the money: conversely wives who appeared authoritative were likely to control the money.

Sorting in this way the 102 couples in the sample produced four categories. The first category contained couples where there was a joint bank account and where the wife described herself as controlling the money. There were 27 of these and they were described as 'wife-controlled pooling'. Among these couples it was usually the wife who paid the bills for rates, fuel, telephone, insurance, and mortgage or rent. In the majority of cases, neither partner had a separate bank account and all finances were handled from the joint account.

The second category was described as 'husband-controlled pooling'. This contained couples where there was a joint bank account, but where the wife considered either that the husband controlled the finances or that they were jointly controlled. There were 39 couples in this category. Among this group husbands were typically responsible for the bills for rates, fuel, telephone and insurance and for paying the mortgage or rent.

Lack of a joint account implied one of two things. Either the couple were paid in cash and were too poor ever to need a bank, or one or both partners rejected the idea of a joint account. The third category contained couples where there was no joint account and where the wife considered that control was in the husband's hands. There were 22 couples in this category, which was described as 'husband-controlled'. Typically the husband had his own personal bank account and he was responsible for all the main bills.

Finally, there was a small group where there was no joint bank account and the wife considered that she controlled the finances. This category contained 14 couples and was described as 'wife-controlled'. These couples typically had no bank accounts at all and operated in cash, with the wife controlling and managing the finances and taking responsibility for the major bills.

Wife control of finances was particularly common in low income, working-class households where neither partner had any qualifications. Wife control was associated with the payment of wages in cash and with the absence of any bank accounts. Typically the wife also managed the money, paying for food and for rent, fuel, insurance and so on, while the husband had a set sum for his personal spending money. Thus in many respects wife control was synonymous with wife management.

Husband control was associated with relatively high income levels. Typically these couples had a set amount of housekeeping, which was given by the husband to the wife as an allowance: she paid for food and daily living expenses, while he paid the main bills. Most of these couples kept their money separate. When the wife was earning her wages typically went into the housekeeping purse, while the husband was responsible for larger bills. Husband control was characteristic of couples where the husband was the main or sole earner, and there was a tendency for it to be associated with marital unhappiness for both partners.[7]

There were interesting differences between wife-controlled pooling and husband-controlled pooling. Wife-controlled pooling was associated with medium income levels, while husband-controlled pooling was more typical of higher income levels. Wife-controlled pooling was associated with the employment of both partners; when only the husband was in employment he was likely to control the pool. Table 1 shows that

Table 1 Control of finances by wife's earnings as a proportion of husband's earnings

	Wife's earnings		
	Over 30% of husband's earnings	Under 30% of husband's earnings	Wife had no earnings
Wife control	6	—	8
Wife-controlled pooling	12	8	7
Husband-controlled pooling	5	14	20
Husband control	5	5	12
Total number	28	27	47

the more the wife contributed to the household income the more likely it was that she would control household finances; this effect was particularly marked among pooling couples. Where wives' earnings were 30 per cent or more of their husbands' earnings, wives were twice as likely as husbands to control the pool; where wives had no earnings, husbands were three times more likely than wives to control the pool. When neither partner was employed there was a tendency for wives to control finances; however, the term 'wife control' of finances seems a misleading way to describe what was essentially a struggle to make ends meet in very poor households.

The effect of social class was particularly marked among pooling couples, especially where husband and wife were of different classes. Social class was defined according to the Registrar General's classification. Where the husband was classified as middle class and the wife as working class, the husband always controlled the pool, or joint account. Where the wife was middle class and the husband working class, she controlled the pool in all but one instance. The same pattern occurred for qualifications. If one partner had more qualifications than the other he or she was likely to control finances: where both partners had gained some qualifications after leaving school there was a tendency for the husband to control finances.

To sum up this section, then, where a wife controls finances she will usually also be responsible for money management; where a husband controls finances he will usually delegate parts of money management to his wife. Thus where a wife controls finances she will usually be responsible for paying the main bills and for making sure that ends meet, as well as for buying food and day-to-day necessities. Where a husband controls finances he will typically delegate to his wife the responsibility for housekeeping expenses, sometimes giving her a housekeeping allowance for this purpose. Marriages where the wife controls the money and the husband manages it are rare. There were no examples of this pattern in the study sample, nor were there examples of the small number of marriages where the husband both controls and manages the money. Evidence from other studies suggests that in these circumstances there is likely to be extreme inequality between husband and wife and deprivation on the part of the wife and children.[8]

Who spends on what?

What is the relationship between the control of money within the household and patterns of spending by individual household members? Patterns of spending were investigated in the joint interview, when each couple was asked who was responsible for spending on each item in a long list. They were asked 'who actually buys each item or pays each bill?' As Table 2 shows, patterns of spending were differentiated by gender. Wives were likely to pay for food, clothing for themselves and their children, presents, and school expenses such as dinner money. Husbands were likely to be responsible for paying for their own clothing, the car, repairs and decorating, meals taken away from home, and alcohol. Joint responsibilities, paid for by either partner or by both together, included consumer durables, donations to charity and Christmas expenses. This pattern is similar to that found by Todd and Jones:[9] the main difference between the two studies lies in the increase in goods purchased by 'either or both', a change which reflects the spread of joint bank accounts.

Responsibility for spending varied significantly according to the control of finances within the household, but only for some items of expenditure. In general the person who controlled finances, whether or not there was a joint account, was also responsible for the major bills. This applied in the case of the bills for mortgage or rent, rates, fuel, phone and insurance. However, the pattern for consumer goods was rather different: where there was a joint account, whether it was controlled by husband or wife, it was likely that they would both be responsible for buying the washing machine, refrigerator or other household item. However, where there was no joint account, husbands were likely to be responsible for spending on consumer goods.

In the rest of this article we shall examine [two] different areas of spending. These are, first, spending on food, since this clearly comes into the category of household spending and represents a major claim on most household budgets. Secondly, we shall consider expenditure on leisure, as an example of an area where spending and consumption are most individualised. [. . .]

Table 2   Household spending patterns (all percentages of total 102)

	Person responsible for spending on each item			
	Wife	Either/both	Husband	Not applicable other answers
Food	74	18	9	—
Mortgage/rent	31	23	35	11
Rates	33	19	36	12
Fuel	30	27	41	2
Telephone	28	10	41	21
Insurance	28	24	40	9
Clothes (wife)	78	15	7	—
Clothes (husband)	24	27	50	—
Clothes (children)	69	24	7	1
Car or motor bike	4	14	51	31
School expenses	63	13	10	15
Repairs and decorating	14	28	58	1
Consumer goods	12	42	41	5
Children's pocket money	27	27	16	31
Presents	61	36	2	1
Meals out/trips out	4	23	60	13
Holiday expenses	10	35	38	17
Charities	43	48	4	5
Christmas expenses	44	50	5	1
Drinks in house	13	15	36	37
Drinks in pub	2	9	55	34

Spending on food

Recent research in Africa, Asia and Latin America has suggested that the proportion of household income spent on food and daily living expenses varies according to the extent to which women have control of household finances.[10] Is the same pattern true in Britain? What affects how much a couple spends on housekeeping? Both husband and wife were asked 'Do you have a set amount that you budget for housekeeping expenses/for food and day-to-day expenses?' Half the couples who took part in the study said that they had a specific sum which they earmarked in this way, while most of the rest could name an approximate amount. Two wives and fifteen husbands said that they did not know how much was spent on housekeeping, so for these couples the other partner's answer was used for the analysis. A comparison between the answers given by husbands and wives showed that the two were closely related and that when there was a discrepancy the wife was likely to give a higher figure than the husband.

On average, the sum spent on housekeeping represented 26 per cent of household income. However, the proportion of total income going to housekeeping varied from 6 per cent to 75 per cent: this enormous range suggested that there might be some cases where either 'income' or 'housekeeping' had been misrepresented. Looking at the extreme cases showed that this was indeed so. Some were self-employed people whose official incomes were very low, so that practically all their earnings appeared to go as housekeeping. Others were affluent couples with substantial incomes who, in giving a sum for weekly housekeeping, forgot to include the butcher's monthly bill or the cheques which they wrote at the end of bulk shopping expeditions to the supermarket: this made the sum given for housekeeping appear a ludicrously small proportion of their total income. These exceptional cases contorted the results in a misleading way, so eight couples were removed from the sample for this analysis.

Among the remaining 94 couples the average amount spent on housekeeping was £41 and the amounts spent varied from £20 to £81; these figures are very similar to those found in a study carried out in London at about the same date.[11] Other comparable figures come from two national surveys carried out by market research firms. The Birds Eye Housekeeping Monitor for 1983 gave £53.94 as the average amount spent on housekeeping by British families, while in a survey by Millward Brown the average housekeeping was £48.70.[12] The lower average figures given by the couples in Kent may reflect the wording of the questions on this topic. They were asked about 'housekeeping', but the interviewers went on to clarify what was meant by this by adding 'food and day-to-day living expenses'. This may have led some respondents to omit some bills from the figure they gave in the interview. The couples in the study spent on average 26 per cent of their income on housekeeping; this can be compared with the average British household, which spent 23 per cent of its income on food in 1980.[13]

What was the relationship between a couple's total income and the amount they spent on housekeeping? Since wives were responsible for shopping for food their estimate of housekeeping seemed to provide the most reliable figure [. . .]. As household income rose the amount spent on housekeeping increased. However, the ratio between housekeeping and income was not the same at every income level. That is to say, though the average household spent 26 per cent of its income on housekeeping, poorer households spent a higher proportion than this, while richer households spent a lower proportion. The proportion of income spent on housekeeping varied from 48 per cent in a very poor household with numerous children to 14 per cent in an affluent household with low living costs.

[. . .] At any one income level the housekeeping-to-income ratio varied considerably: some households were spending a much higher proportion of their income on housekeeping than others. Up to this point we have been concerned only with the total income of each household. But the total income was made up of contributions from both husband and wife, coming to them either as wages and salaries, or as child benefit or other social security payments. Did the variations in the housekeeping depend in any way on the proportion contributed by each partner?

This question was examined statistically by means of a linear regression analysis. The analysis explored the relationship between, on the one hand, the husband's income, the wife's income and their joint income and, on the other hand, the amount spent on housekeeping.

[. . .]

The regression analysis suggested that

(a) the husband contributed most absolutely to housekeeping since on average his income was four times as great as that of his wife.
(b) the wife contributed most relatively to housekeeping; this meant that if the incomes of wife and husband rose by the same amount 28 per cent of her increase would go to housekeeping compared with 16 per cent of his.

Put simply, if an additional pound entered the household economy through the mother's hands more of it would be spent on food for the family than would be the case if the pound had been brought into the household by the father.

We have seen that the amount spent on housekeeping was likely to differ depending on who earned the money: did it also differ according to who controlled the family's finances? Table 3 suggests that the way in which household finances were organised, and the person who controlled the money, had a powerful influence on the proportion of total income spent as housekeeping. Where wives controlled finances the proportion spent on housekeeping was likely to be higher than in households where husbands controlled finances. Thus at one extreme, in wife-controlled systems, two thirds of couples spent over a quarter of total household income on housekeeping; at the other extreme, in husband-controlled systems, only two fifths of couples spent more than a quarter of their total income on housekeeping. This difference was statistically significant.

The same pattern existed for the average proportion of income going to housekeeping. As Table 3 shows, the proportion was nearly a third in households where women controlled finances but only one quarter where men were in control. However, some of this difference probably reflected differences in income levels. As we have seen,

Table 3   Spending on housekeeping by control of household finances

Housekeeping as proportion of total household income	Wife control	Wife-controlled pooling	Husband-controlled pooling	Husband control
Low (less than 25%)	5	9	21	11
High (25% and over)	9	18	15	8
Mean % spent on housekeeping	32	29	26	26
Mean household income in £ per week	124	157	165	173

the proportion spent on housekeeping is lower at higher income levels and Table 3 shows mean incomes increasing from £124 per week, where wives controlled finances, to £173 where husbands were in control.

The conclusion of this analysis is that the amount spent on housekeeping is related, first, to the level of household income, secondly, to the sources of that income and thirdly, to the control of income within the household. In recent years a number of researchers working in developing countries have investigated the relative contribution which men and women make to household budgets; their work has drawn attention to the significance of financial arrangements within households for family living standards. The results of these studies have been drawn together by Dwyer and Bruce.[14] Their conclusion is very important. Though in absolute terms men may contribute more to the household economy than do women, in relative terms women typically contribute a higher proportion of their income to the household's basic needs, and especially to the needs of children. Compared with men, women hold less back, both absolutely and relatively, for their personal use. Since the goal of many development planners is to raise the standard of living of children it follows that the best way to do this is to direct economic aid to women.

It is interesting that the research described in this paper produced a similar result: though husbands typically contributed more absolutely to housekeeping, wives typically contributed a larger proportion of their income. The implications for policy are also similar. The best way to raise the living standards of poor children is to increase the amount of money over which their mothers have control. It is becoming clear that the financial dependence of women and children, far from protecting them, constitutes a major cause of their poverty.[15] The results reported in this paper are therefore very relevant to current debates about poverty, about the future of child benefit and about changing patterns of female employment. Giving additional money to mothers, whether in the form of wages or social security payments, is likely to produce bigger increases in family living standards than giving the same sums of money to fathers.

Spending on leisure

A number of studies have shown that, compared with men, women have less 'free' time to give to leisure, see leisure and sport as much less central to their identity, are involved in fewer activities outside the home, and belong to fewer clubs and organisations; these differences are particularly pronounced among the working class and among couples with young children.[16] A study of leisure and gender in Sheffield showed that lack of money, and not liking to go out alone after dark, were major constraints on women's activities.[17] The different lifestyles of married men and married women are a reflection of the ways in which gender differences structure daily life. For women, participation in activities outside the home is often limited by the expense involved, by the disapproval of husbands, by the embarrassment and possible danger involved in going out alone at night, or by the sexism of those who provide leisure and sports facilities. On the other hand, men's leisure tends to be seen as a well-earned reward for paid work and there are few barriers to going out to participate in organised leisure activities. A study of redundancy showed that when wives become unemployed their first economy was to give up spending on themselves, while husbands typically continued to have some personal spending money, even though the amount might be reduced.[18]

In this study the question of spending on leisure was approached in various different ways. In the joint interview each individual was asked to identify a source of money for personal things 'like cigarettes, tights, a drink out with friends, a present for your spouse'. In the separate interviews each was asked about their personal spending money, the sums involved and the items it had to cover; each was asked what leisure activities he or she pursued and how much was spent on each activity. Each was then asked to describe their partner's leisure pursuits and to estimate how much he or she spent on them.

Husbands were more likely to have money for personal spending and for leisure than were wives. Thus 12 husbands said that they had an identified allowance for personal spending, compared with only 2 wives, and 86 per cent of the men said they spent money on leisure activities compared with 67 per cent of the women. Husbands were also likely to have more money to spend on themselves than wives. Among the 102 couples who took part in the study seven either spent nothing on leisure or had no set amounts for this, while 23 couples spent approximately the same amounts. Seventeen wives spent more than their husbands on leisure activities, while 55 husbands spent more than their wives. Estimating spending on leisure is difficult because it is often spasmodic, with subscriptions payable yearly, fees for classes payable termly, sports equipment bought when needed and so on. Nevertheless, the problem of estimating the amount spent on leisure applied to both husbands and wives, since they were asked identical sets of questions, so it may be assumed that comparisons between the two sets of answers are justified, even if the total amounts spent are likely to be inaccurate. In addition, it is important to remember that drinking and gambling were the most common leisure activities on which men spent money and that sums spent on these are notoriously underestimated. Thus, if anything men were spending even more on leisure than they admitted to the interviewers.

Typically, husbands over-estimated the amounts wives spent on leisure, while wives under-estimated how much their husbands spent. They also had rather different attitudes to each others' leisure activities. Both husbands and wives tended to give precedence to the husband's right to leisure: as a nurse said of her milkman husband:

'You can't deny a man when he's earning'. By contrast wives' rights to leisure seemed less secure and 'leisure' sometimes involved domestic work. Thus when one husband was asked what leisure activities his wife had, he replied, 'ironing, sewing, reading'.

Employment status had both financial and ideological implications. Unemployment could drastically alter leisure patterns. One couple said:

Husband: I used to spend money on the garden when I was at work but I can't now. There's a twenty foot greenhouse in the garden and it's empty. No money for seeds or anything like that.
Wife: I used to play bingo, but we can't afford it. I like to read but now I borrow books from friends. I like a Mills and Boon in bed.

Wives who were earning had more money to spend and more money over which they had a degree of control, and they also felt they had a right to pursue leisure activities of which their husbands disapproved, such as going to the pub with women friends or taking independent holidays. However, the fact that a wife managed or controlled the money did not necessarily give her more to spend on herself. A secretary who had given up paid work to look after their two small children, said

I feel guilty if I buy something for myself. My husband says I shouldn't have to, but I do. As he brings in the money I do need to justify how I spend it.

The ideological construction of the relationship between earner and dependant, which expresses itself in the dependant's deference and subordination, is seen particularly clearly in the case of spending on personal needs and leisure.

What determined the amount of money which each person felt they could spend on leisure and personal needs? Table 4 shows from what part of the household budgeting system each person drew her or his personal spending money. Husbands were more likely than wives to take their personal spending money from their earnings, while wives were likely to use housekeeping money for their personal needs especially if they were not earning. The source of personal spending money varied according to how the couple organised their finances. Where there was a joint account and money management was shared, both partners tended to get their own spending money from the pool. When money was managed independently both partners took their personal spending money from their earnings. Where there was an allowance system the

Table 4   Sources of personal spending money

Personal spending money taken from	Wives	Husbands
Pool or joint account	40	39
Own earnings	17	39
Housekeeping money	38	7
Separate amount for this purpose	2	12
None/other answers	5	5
Total number	102	102

Table 5 Control of finances by relative amounts spent on leisure

	Wife spent more than husband	Similar amounts spent	Husband spent more than wife
Wife control	1	5	8
Wife-controlled pooling	3	11	13
Husband-controlled pooling	10	7	22
Husband control	3	7	12
Total number	17	30	55

husband's personal spending money tended to come from his earnings, while the wife's money came from the housekeeping money, a situation which was particularly likely to make a woman feel that she had no right to spend on herself.

Table 5 shows how spending on leisure varied depending on the control of money within the household. In the sample as a whole husbands were likely to spend more than their wives, but this was especially so when there was no joint account. Husbands were particularly likely to spend more on leisure than wives in those households where wives controlled finances, that is, in households with the lowest incomes. A rather unexpected result was found, however, when wife-controlled pooling couples were compared with husband-controlled pooling couples. It was among the latter category that wives who spent more on leisure than their husbands were most commonly found. Of the 17 women who spent more on leisure than their husbands, 10 were found in those households where the husband controlled finances and there was a joint account. Perhaps these were the households where a larger than average income was combined with an ideology of financial sharing?

[. . .]

Conclusion

The evidence presented in this article demonstrates the value of opening up the black box of the household in order to understand the social and economic processes which lie between earning and spending. The field offers many possibilities for future research. There are two important principles to bear in mind. First, it is important to see financial arrangements in terms of social processes, as dynamic rather than static. Secondly, it is important not to separate financial arrangements within the household from the social and economic context in which the household is located. [. . .] The amounts spent on leisure activities and on food reflect both the total income of the household and the control of money within it. Thus inequalities in the wider society are translated into inequalities within the household and *vice versa*. Money, as one of the most fundamental measures of equality, provides a fruitful route to exploring the social and economic processes involved.

Notes

1. J. Pahl, *Money and Marriage*, London: Macmillan, 1989.
2. H. Jones, 'Consumer behaviour', in D. Morris, ed., *The Economic System in the UK*, Oxford: Oxford University Press, 1985.
3. Galbraith, quoted in H. Land, 'Poverty and gender: The distribution of resources within the family', in M. Brown, ed., *The Structure of Disadvantage*, London: Heinemann, 1983, p. 49.
4. J. Hills, *Changing Tax: How the tax system works and how to change it*, London: Child Poverty Action Group, 1988.
5. Office of Population Census and Surveys, 1985.
6. Department of the Environment, 1981.
7. J. Pahl, op. cit.
8. G. Wilson, *Money in the Family*, Aldershot: Avebury, 1987. See also Reading 1.4, this volume.
9. J. Todd and L. Jones, *Matrimonial Property*, London: HMSO, 1972.
10. D. Dwyer and J. Bruce, *A Home Divided: Women and income in the third world*, Palo Alto: Stanford University Press, 1988.
11. G. Wilson, op. cit., p. 121.
12. Birds Eye, *Housekeeping Monitor 1983*, Public Relations Department, 1983; J. Nelson, 'What it costs – and where it goes', *Women's Realm*, March: 27–30, 1983.
13. Office of Population Census and Surveys, 1984.
14. D. Dwyer and J. Bruce, op. cit.
15. C. Glendinning and J. Millar, eds, *Women and Poverty in Britain*, Hemel Hempstead: Harvester Wheatsheaf, 1987.
16. R. Rapoport and R. Rapoport, *Leisure and the Family Life Cycle*, London: Routledge and Kegan Paul, 1975; E. Wimbush and M. Talbot, eds, *Relative Freedoms: Women and leisure*, Milton Keynes: Open University Press, 1988; R. Deem, *All Work and No Play: The sociology of women and leisure*, Milton Keynes: Open University Press, 1986.
17. E. Green, S. Hebron and D. Woodward, 'Leisure and gender: A study of Sheffield women's leisure experiences', Sheffield City Polytechnic, 1986.
18. C. Callendar, 'Redundancy, unemployment and poverty', in C. Glendinning and J. Millar, eds, op. cit., p. 151.

1.4 □ *Gail Wilson*

Choosing not to use Pahl's approach to money management, Gail Wilson focuses instead on the consequences of financial inequalities between spouses at various income levels. Like Pahl, though, she does highlight the issue of men's personal spending – and her research material reveals the hardship this can cause within poorer households.

Money: patterns of responsibility and irresponsibility in marriage

This chapter attempts to look at financial organization within the household from the point of view of women. The first part discusses some of the practical and theoretical difficulties encountered in interviewing a group of women in inner London. The second outlines some patterns of financial organization and looks at their consequences in terms of women's responsibility for the standard of living of the household.

Money, so far as it has been considered at all by social researchers, is usually looked at from a masculine point of view. Studies of poverty concentrate on inequalities in male earning power. Work on family finance has taken the male wage as a starting point.[1]

[. . .]

This long standing inability to see the interests of women and children as anything other than subsumed by those of their partners has a number of practical consequences. The first [. . .] has been the difficulty of conceptualizing the subject at all. This has led to a lack of research in the area. The second is that the dominant ideology, which sees women as peripheral to the economic system, is widely accepted by both men and women. This acceptance influences the replies which will be given to surveys on the subject. The third is that there is an inevitable conflict between the dominant ideology and the actual experience of women, and this also affects the replies that women give when they are interviewed on the subject of money.

However, once it is accepted that the distribution of money within the household is a subject for research, then it is essential to look at it from different points of view. For women with children, as Mavis Maclean has said, money is not *primarily* a reward for work or a source of personal satisfaction. It is more commonly seen as a means to an end and that end is the fulfilment of women's responsibilities.[2] These are the maintenance of the standard of living of the family, particularly the children, the maintenance of family health and the maintenance of family respectability.[3] As far as women are concerned, therefore, the amount of money available for fulfilling these aims becomes more important than total household income. Furthermore, once it is no longer assumed that men as 'breadwinners' are also in charge of spending and saving, it becomes important to consider financial organization in terms of who has to find lump sums and pay the bills. This may seem obvious but previous writers (for example, Berthoud on fuel bills) have often managed to ignore the fact that it is women who have to make ends meet in most low income families.[4]

Financial organization

If we are to try to look at financial organization from women's point of view, any theoretical interpretation has to take account of the great variety of financial arrangements liable to be encountered in the field. If the object of the study is to find out what actually goes on, rather than to fit households into predefined categories, it is unlikely that the raw data will look very manageable. Pahl has dealt with this problem by seeing the four categories she chose as 'points on a continuum of allocative systems'.[5] This approach was not adopted for the project reported on here.

A theoretical framework

A theoretical framework which can cope both with variety in financial organization and with many of the methodological problems which interviewers encounter when talking to women about money (see below) has been put forward by Sen. He says we need a clear 'analysis of the existence of both co-operating and conflicting elements in family relations . . . The essence of the problem is that there are many co-operative outcomes – beneficial to all the parties compared with non-co-operation – but the different parties have strictly conflicting interests in the choice among the set of efficient co-operative arrangements'.[6]

Sen was concerned with what happens to households in times of famine. However, his model holds well in less extreme circumstances. As far as we are concerned he states that a couple stays together because each partner perceives herself or himself as being better off with the partner than without. It is important to stress that the definition of 'better off' can vary and will not be confined simply to material well-being, but will include a wide range of emotional, social and economic considerations as well. For example, the fact that men normally earn so much more than women with dependent children[7] means that women have a much stronger financial incentive than men to put up with poor conditions in marriage. [. . .]

Fieldwork

The fieldwork on which this chapter is based was not conducted with Sen's theory in mind.[8] The basic assumption was that women's lives were important and were often ignored. However, at the stage of analysis Sen's model seemed to fit the methodology adopted and to explain the findings. A major problem was that while marriage is popularly assumed to be women's best chance of financial well-being, this did not always appear to be the case. However, it did not make sense, either from the point of view of the women interviewed or of the research data, to take the opposite extreme feminist view that all women are exploited in marriage. Nor did exploitation, where it was identified, take the same form at different income levels and under different methods of financial organization. Sen's model is able to accommodate the different perceptions of benefit and exploitation which women, men and researchers of both sexes have of marriage.

A total, taking the pilot and the main project, of 90 women and 24 of their husbands were interviewed. All lived in an inner city area and the main interviews were done in 1983/4. Not all were white or born in Britain, but the dominant patterns described here held for all but the four Afro-Caribbean and Asian women seen in the pilot. The 61 women on the main project were all married or cohabiting, though three were without a resident partner at the time of the interview, and all had at least one dependent child. Their household incomes ranged from £27 a week, plus £25 rent and rates paid by the local authority, to over £500 a week including expense allowances, but excluding two cars paid for entirely by the employer.

[. . .]

What follows is therefore based on two different types of data. Firstly, quantitative information on sources and levels of income was collected and analysed in the same way as in most other income surveys, notably the Family Expenditure Survey and Townsend,[9] and suffers from the same limitations on accuracy. These are, most notably, some women's ignorance of total household income, and occasions of deliberate concealment. Secondly, the qualitative data on financial organization are the result of a content analysis of transcribed interviews. The interviews lasted from two to four hours and usually took two visits. The women were representative of attenders at the inner city health centre where they were first encountered. [. . .]

Barriers to talking about money

As far as research based on interviews is concerned, the power of money makes some aspects of it difficult and dangerous to talk about. There are few households which have enough money to satisfy their every want. Objectively speaking therefore, money is a source of competition for scarce resources. However, competition implies conflict and most women are unwilling to consider their financial arrangements in these terms. (There were a very few exceptions.)[10] There is, therefore, very often a gap between what women say, and what they would say if they started by acknowledging that there was competition for money.

However, it is important to distinguish between talking about money in the context of the daily or weekly chore of getting in the food and shopping within a budget, and talking about the financial arrangements within a marriage and the power structure that goes with them. Very few women minded talking about their everyday budgeting. Women who had to subsist on state income support were usually only too glad to draw attention to the impossibility of trying to feed and clothe a family on the money allowed. Difficulties came in two main areas. The first was the broad question of financial organization and its relationship to power. The second was one specific aspect of the wider issue of power – the division between money for collective domestic consumption and personal spending.

Financial power

Financial power was an area that many women preferred to avoid. The commonest description of financial organization was a variant of 'We share', as of course they did. The trouble is that, as Comer has pointed out, sharing can mean many things:

> Loyalty and self-abnegation are powerful agents of economic oppression. If any sociologist or interested person had inquired into the financial arrangements in my marriage, I would have lain my hand on my heart and sworn that we shared money equally. And, in theory, I would have been telling the truth. In fact, it would no more have occurred to me to spend money on anything else but housekeeping than it would have occurred to him not to.[11]

One basic consideration of the distribution of financial power within marriage is that for most women it is so obviously unequal that it does not need mentioning.[12] [. . .]

For most of the women interviewed, men had the money and they had a share of it – how much or how that share was arrived at was something they preferred not to think about. In the cases where women earned as much or nearly as much as their husbands [. . .] women played down their own role in family finance and if anything placed even more emphasis on sharing. Stamp also found that her breadwinning wives were reluctant to emphasize their financial power.[13]

Personal spending money

It was quite simply impossible, given the type of co-operation requested from participants and the methodological constraints outlined above, to get *believable* figures for personal spending money. Others, in particular Edwards and Stamp,[14] have encountered this problem. Women were often able to explain that for a variety of reasons they felt guilty about spending on themselves, for example: 'If ever I want anything, the children *need* something', but very few could give detailed accounts of what they bought for themselves. Even fewer could say much about what their husbands spent on themselves. This silence covered the amount that husbands spent, what they spent it on and whether their wives approved or disapproved. It appeared that very few, if any, husbands took or kept a *regular* amount of money each week, though many were described as having a basic amount. If they needed more they took more, for example: 'Well, if he's going up to his mum's he just takes the fare out of my purse. And he likes a drink.' Some husbands paid back what they took and some did not. In either case husband's money was not only what Morris has called 'a highly protected category'[15] but also it was unpredictable. For women in low income households this unpredictability could be a serious practical problem. In higher income households the material consequences of husband's spending were usually less severe but the subject was still something most women preferred to avoid.

In terms of Sen's model, men were either able to claim as much spending money as they needed or, even if income was low, they had first call on the available money. For many men therefore, money was not a source of conflict in marriage and they were able to redefine it as an area of co-operation (sharing). Women also subscribed to this dominant view as we have seen above.

A nice example of collusion over husband's spending money was given by one woman who was on the verge of breaking what appeared to be the important ground rules of avoidance and 'not knowing', but carefully drew back:

> We were having a sort of joking argument, or I was. I was getting at him a bit the other week, because he was away on a course for a week and that week I had money left over from the week's money, you see. And I said 'Well interesting, interesting that I have money left over when the two of us are home', and in fact my mother was staying here so I wasn't actually buying any less food really, and I was saying 'That's because of you', but I mean he doesn't. You know, his spending money might amount to, you know, some flower pots or he needs some fertiliser, he'll get that sort of thing. But for himself, he might buy a salad or something at the canteen. I can't think of anything else much he'd buy for himself.

[. . .]

In the context of household finance we are not dealing with deliberate secrecy but with what could be termed unconscious concealment, which breaks down only when the marriage is under threat or ended. Support for this interpretation comes from the women in this study who were not cohabiting at the time of interview, or who were contemplating leaving their partners. They were all much more open about the financial power of their husbands. Sharma, working in a different society, found the same subconscious avoidance of the issue: 'It is only in the rather unusual situation in which a woman's relationship with her husband and his kin had deteriorated to the point where she no longer identified herself with the interests of his household, that she would realise subjectively the true extent of her economic dependence'.[16] And Pahl noted that women who left their husbands for a refuge were surprised to find that they had more money as claimants than when they were married.[17]

Factors affecting financial organization

The factors that were identified as influencing financial organization in the families studied were: level of household income; sources of income; who spends on bills and rent; who spends on food and sundries; and who saves.

As far as women were concerned the most important factors were source, i.e. whether they had an *income of their own*, and their ability to save. Saving in this context means saving for *collective* domestic consumption, not personal savings, though many women found it hard to make the distinction since they thought of all 'their' money as being for collective consumption.

Saving also had different meanings at different income levels. In low income households it was essential to save if bills were to be paid. This was saving for current consumption. However, where there was more money, saving became a matter of generating lump sums which could be used in different ways but for the benefit of the whole family – for holidays, consumer durables, or for doing up the house, for example.

There were three other factors which did appear important: age, life stage and whether earnings were paid in cash or not. They could not be considered because the numbers in the study were too small. [. . .]

Since it was important to relate total income to household needs, even if this could be done only in a relatively crude way, incomes were standardized as a percentage of each household's Supplementary Benefit entitlement, as modified by Piachaud to take account of the cost of children.[18] The households were then divided into three groups: low (up to 139 per cent of SB entitlement); middle (140–239 per cent); and high (over 240 per cent of SB entitlement). In the low income group (24) 7 men were low paid and the remaining households were dependent on state support of one kind or another. Two wives had part-time work. The 22 households in the middle income group were skilled manual workers (7 with working wives), or lower paid professionals. The higher income group (15) were dual career couples (6), other households where the wife had a source of income (2) or highly paid professionals.

Financial patterns

Although the numbers of families involved are small, it was possible to discern certain dominant patterns in the ways the factors affecting financial organization interacted, and to identify deviant or negative cases. Given Sen's theoretical model, we would expect that the diversity of financial arrangements would be least at low income levels where there is little scope for negotiation because the sources of income are fewest, choices are limited and surpluses are small or non-existent. We might then expect diversity to increase as income and the possibilities for choice or negotiation go up. However, it is here argued that diversity is greatest at middle income levels. This, briefly, is because at low income levels the economic forces of the labour market act as prime constraints on family finance. In high income households the much greater financial and social power of husbands, as compared with their wives, has a similarly constricting effect on the type of financial arrangements that evolves within a marriage. At middle income levels both these two forces are reduced and diversity is greater.

Financial organization in low income households

Other writers have pointed out that at low income levels it is easier to make ends meet if one person is in control of family finance. The findings from the present survey bear this out. In 18 out of 24 low income households one member was responsible for all spending on collective consumption, including saving. Seventeen were women and one was a man. This illustrates yet again the very great importance of women in maintaining family living standards, particularly at low income levels.

In the 4 of the 6 households where husbands took some responsibility for collective consumption, the women bought the food. In the remaining 2 households husbands bought food as well as everything else. This pattern, with the husband in control of all expenditure including food, was deviant as far as British families were concerned and in all cases (2 in the low income group and 3 in the middle), where it was observed wives appeared to be unhappy with the arrangement. Two were suffering from lack of food, one was ill, one severely depressed and one clearly very frightened of her husband. This finding – that women whose husbands would not allow them sufficient control of resources to ensure an adequate standard of living for their children were depressed or ill – can only be described as tentative, given the numbers. However, it is an area that would repay further investigation.

In both the low income households where the husbands took primary responsibility for collective consumption, there was no saving. Both husbands were long term unemployed. One was reported as trying to save 'but of course he doesn't get very much' and he apparently took the Child Benefit when a bill came. The other couple were still running down the savings from the wife's former job.

It is important to note that nearly all the women in this group would have been *financially* better off without their husbands. In 1983 the difference between Supplementary Benefit entitlement with a husband in residence and without was £16 a week. Husbands in this group were reported as spending between £5 and £10 a week *on themselves* and this was clearly an under-estimate in most cases (see above). It was impossible to provide a husband with food, heat and sometimes clothing on the remaining £6–£10 a week and women clearly cut back on their own, and sometimes their children's, consumption in order to pay for their husbands. In some households where the husband was in work but low paid the situation was better, but in others, since a working husband usually expected more personal spending money than one on state support, there was little improvement.[19] Women in these households were unlikely to benefit financially from marriage until they were able to get paid work of their own. For them marriage at the childbearing stage was best seen as a long term investment.

Financial arrangements in middle income households

Nearly half the families in this group had two earners and a quarter would certainly have been assigned to the lower income group were it not for the wife's earnings. This once again illustrates the importance of employment for women even if it is only part-time (as it was in 9 out of 11 cases).

At middle income level financial pressures were generally fewer than for the previous group and one partner had sole responsibility for finance in only 9 out of 22 cases. Once again 8 of these were women and one was a man. In one other case the wife was responsible for everything including some saving, but her husband also saved.

As might be expected in households where there was more money, the surplus available over and above basic needs was greater and the chore of making ends meet less onerous. There was a greater possibility of exercising financial control within the family, rather than simply responding to outside pressures or controls, and more men took responsibility for family finances and behaved in a more responsible way when they did.

The importance of women's financial contribution may account for the fact that at this income level women in dual earner households were more likely to have financial responsibilities than they were in single earner households. Women were solely responsible for the standard of living in 6 out of the 9 families where they were joint earners but in only 2 out of the 13 families where they made no monetary contribution. As to the division of responsibilities in families where financial management was shared (13), husbands were solely responsible for the bills and rent or mortgage in 9 cases. In 5, wives who had their own income paid one or more bills.

As at other income levels, women were generally responsible for food and sundries but a relatively high proportion of families shared the shopping (8 out of 22). Shared shopping carried different meanings. In 2 cases husbands controlled nearly all the money and part of this control was that they wrote the cheques at the supermarket. There was not, however, at this income level the suggestion that they were restricting spending on food. In other cases young married couples shopped together because they did most things together and presumably because they had not fully established food preferences and budget control.

Shared shopping could also mean that husbands were taking some responsibility for household food consumption. This was an area which was difficult to define. A husband who chose vegetables and paid for them with his own money on the way home from work was clearly responsible, particularly if he then cooked them upon getting home. The husband who took a list to Sainsbury's and expected to be given the money or have it paid back when he returned was equally clearly participating in division of labour but was not taking responsibility for the standard of living of his family. The line was more difficult to draw when a husband took a basic list, added to it as he thought fit and paid from a joint account, a common pattern at higher income levels.

Although 'shared shopping' could take different forms which were more or less disadvantageous for the general standard of living of the family, there was one very important aspect which was common to all forms. This was that the husband who shopped had some idea of prices and of the effects of inflation. Husbands who never shopped were characterized as having 'no idea' of prices and this could make life difficult for women, even in high income families.

Saving once again presented the most complicated picture. Only 3 households were recorded as not saving. Two were newly-weds and the other was one where the husband controlled all the money. All but one of the women who had a source of income of their own were able to save, which again illustrates the importance that outside work has for women and the well-being of the family – since saving is here defined as being for collective consumption only.

Saving for women who had no income of their own (that is, they relied on housekeeping money) was much more problematic. In the two cases which followed the low income pattern of giving complete financial responsibility for collective consumption to the wife, both were able to save. However, these were in fact atypical households. One was a professional household at the top of this income group and the other was one in which the husband took a very high proportion of his income in personal spending money but since the joint account was managed by the wife she was able to restrict her consumption when a bill was due. As she said, 'When they read the meter we know there'll be a bill soon and we start saving'. In this case 'we' appeared to be a euphemism for a drop in consumption by wife and children. Only 2 other wives who had no income of their own were able to save at this income level.

As the theoretical model predicted, financial arrangements were more complicated at middle income levels. Husbands had more money and expected to take more responsibility for collective consumption. Once again there was only one case of a husband who took complete control of family consumption, though 2 came very close, and only the fact that the women had some freedom to choose what to buy in the supermarket because there was enough money prevented them from being classed as households for which the husband took complete responsibility.

Although 8 women still managed all family finance at middle income level, the pattern of joint financial responsibility was more common. Jointness did however have different meanings. Professional women expected to help pay the bills if they were earning. Others earned in order to have a modicum of financial independence, either on principle or because their husbands were mean. They used their earnings mainly for collective expenditure and felt that they acted as a hedge against inflation. As one woman who had not had an increase in her share of her husband's earnings for two years said, 'I think it's because I go to work that he hasn't had to put my money up. If I didn't work I'd have had to ask him.'

Financial arrangements in high income households

The main difference between financial arrangements at high income level and the rest was that nearly all the women, with the usual exception of the newly-weds, were able to save. Only 2 other women did not. Of these, one saw it as her responsibility to economize on fuel and to shop sensibly but, since all the money came out of the joint account and she had no control of overall financial matters, she has not been counted as responsible for saving. The other woman preferred to spend and refused to have her own account and manage it herself. Although 4 out of 15 women were solely responsible for paying bills and buying food, none was solely responsible for saving. It is also worth noting that women's savings (which were included because they were used to finance general household consumption as well as their own personal expenditure), were in all cases less than their husbands. With two exceptions, their role, particularly at the level of seeing to the bills and the mortgage, was strictly executive and could not be described as responsible or managerial, whereas at lower income levels their responsibilities were very great.

The high income pattern of the wife as responsible, only in the sense that someone has physically to pay the bill, was normal in those households where the husband was the sole earner but expenditure on collective items was shared. Sharing usually meant that the husband was seen as paying the mortgage and perhaps the rates by standing order from his own account or the joint account, but bills were looked after by the wife. The contrast in degrees of responsibility is expressed in the following quotations, the first from a middle income woman with problems: 'Bills? Well I have to do all that. I have to juggle the money, take from Peter to pay Paul'; and the second from a non-earning wife in a high income household: 'Oh you mean who actually writes the cheque and puts it in the post. Well that's usually me.'

Women who earned were in a different position. Only 2 earned much less than their husbands. Two who earned more took virtually complete financial responsibility for all aspects of daily life, while one husband restrained himself to long term saving and investment and the other paid out as directed: 'I just ask him how much he's got and tell him what we can do with it.'

All the women who earned in this income group had their own bank accounts and all took responsibility for paying at least one bill.[20] Only one, a part-time worker, received an allowance from her husband. This she added to her earnings and used to pay for food and sundries, the gas bill, her own personal consumption and to save. One couple transferred half their respective incomes, which were the same, to a joint account and used it to finance all collective consumption including holidays. Only 2 husbands with earning wives took responsibility for any shopping for food.

There were, therefore, two very distinct groups of financial arrangements at high income level. Women who earned usually had the type of financial responsibility that was confined to husbands in other income groups. They were either solely responsible for all aspects of daily consumption *and* able to finance their activities largely from their own earnings, or they managed their own money and had at least the potential to share in financial decisions and responsibilities on a basis that approached equality.

Women who did not earn, on the other hand, had relatively little financial responsibility. They paid bills and went shopping but often said that they did not know much about family finances and left all that to their husbands. This lack of financial power and responsibility would have had serious consequences in terms of general living standards if it had been at all widespread in low income families. However, at the high income level it did not result in actual hardship and wives not only spent more on food but also were usually able to save as well.

Ways of talking about breadwinners

There were two different views of men's financial role in the family, though of course not all men could be so easily categorized. At lower income levels men were typically seen as being good or bad providers. No one actually described a *resident* partner as a bad provider, but the unemployed and the low paid were by definition unable to bring in enough money to allow their families to take part in the normal life of the community. Most were categorized as 'trying hard to find work' or 'to save money'.

However, a very important difference between women in the lower income groups and women in high income households was that most low income men were not expected to be good managers even if they were good providers. The pervasive idea was that men earned the money, but that was all they did. Financially they were not to be trusted further. Their priorities were wrong and they did not understand about keeping out of debt, paying the bills on time and making sure the children came first. At low income levels if the women could keep control or, as income rose, as much control as she wished, of financial management then she had a fair chance of diverting extra income to her own spending priorities. These priorities were clearly articulated in terms of home and family.

At high income levels the view of men was very different. Their ability to provide the basics was assumed and most high earning husbands were characterized as being good with money and as understanding more about it than their wives. Some high earning wives or those who had held very responsible jobs connected with money did see things differently, but even in these cases men were not the problem they were at low income levels. For example, one woman said of her husband, who would not have his own account and just took cheques from her when he needed them, 'He has never quite got over the feeling that money's basically dirty. Not that he doesn't like to spend it, of course'. His conduct was inconvenient but not a threat to family living standards.

These two different ways of looking at men were related to two different strategies or distributions of financial responsibility. At low income levels women were up against the financial irresponsibility of men as well as the economic system which limited their earning power. Their solidarity expressed itself most of all in terms of close relationships between mothers and daughters but also between sisters and other female kin.[21] Mothers, particularly those who worked, often gave considerable financial help to their daughters. They sent money, paid the hire purchase on washing machines and furniture and provided grandchildren with shoes, clothes, cheese, yoghurts and sweets.

At high income level men were powerful financially and socially and the benefits of being married to them came in kind, not in usable cash. Nice houses, varied leisure, private schools for the children and a high housekeeping allowance had to be consumed on the spot (shared). The surplus was there but it was not managed by the wife. It was the subject of joint decisions or husband's decisions. Similarly, it was not mothers who were reported as helping the young professional families so much as 'parents', that is fathers, who provided holiday cottages or paid hotel bills. The economic focus was the man in both generations.

Conclusion

The preceding discussion has suggested that at low levels of income men's lack of earning power severely restricted the choices that were available to a household. Women were normally responsible for the family standard of living but they did not feel that they were in control. They usually saw themselves as responding to intense pressures from outside (final demands for bills, rising food prices, the need to keep the children looking respectable, and so on). Most women could cope with these pressures provided their husbands did not keep too much money for themselves and provided the women were in control of the money that was left.[22]

At middle income level responsibilities were much less clearly defined. More men were involved in paying bills and buying food and sundries than at the upper and lower levels. The women in this group were all low earners but even so their earning power gave them the ability to save, that is, to divert some of the household surplus to their own collective consumption priorities. They remained largely in control of expenditure on food and sundries but in nearly half the cases had been able to devolve all or part of the responsibility for bills onto their partners. Women who had no income of their own also had less responsibility for bills than in low income households but were less often solely responsible for food. In some cases this was a benefit but in others it deprived them of some ability to buy according to their perception of priorities.

The high income group was most notable for the presence of surplus income over and above basic needs. This gave both husbands and wives more choice than was available for most at lower income levels. However, the group was divided between households where women had incomes that were high enough to enable them to spend more or less as they wished, and households where women had no income and took relatively little financial responsibility. Both groups had more freedom to spend money according to their own priorities than most women in lower income groups, but in the case of non-earning women this freedom was limited because the proportion of total income to which they had access was relatively small.

The conclusion is that economic and social forces translate themselves into financial arrangements within the household. As far as women were concerned, money management on a low income was nearly always a source of hardship, but the indications were that the hardship for themselves and their children increased as they lost control of financial management. At middle income level outside economic pressures were fewer and women who managed the money or who could rely on responsible husbands to pay the bills had a relatively good chance of implementing their own spending priorities. At high income level all the women had more choice about how to spend than low income women but they were faced with two problems. If they earned a 'man's wage' they usually felt that they had to play down their financial power. If they had no earnings they usually had a high standard of living but were heavily dependent on their husbands. Small problems perhaps, but ones that seemed to need a complicated structure of denial and avoidance.

The dominant ideology of man as the arbiter of family living standards was thus in force at all income levels, but among low income women it *co-existed* with women's ideology which recognized that women were responsible for the well-being of the family.

Notes

1. See J. Pahl, 'Patterns of money management within marriage', *Journal of Social Policy*, 9: 313–35, 1980; J. Pahl, 'The allocation of money and the structuring of inequality within marriage', *Sociological Review*, 31: 237–62, 1983; L. Morris, 'Redundancy and patterns of household finance', *Sociological Review*, 32: 492–523, 1984; and L. Morris, 'Local social networks and domestic organisation: A study of redundant steelworkers and their wives', *Sociological Review*, 33: 327–42, 1985. This is true to a lesser extent of M. Edwards, *The Income Unit in the Australian Tax and Social Security Systems*, Melbourne: Institute of Family Studies, 1984.
2. M. Maclean, 'The financial consequences of divorce for children', Paper to Study Group for the Distribution of Resources within Households, Institute of Education, University of London, 1983.
3. R. Frankenburg, 'In the production of their lives men . . . ?: Sex and gender in British community studies', in D. Barker and S. Allen, eds, *Sexual Divisions and Society: Process and change*, London: Tavistock, 1976.
4. R. Berthoud, *Fuel Debts and Hardship*, London: Policy Studies Institute, 1981.
5. Pahl, 1983, op. cit., p. 244.
6. A. Sen, *Resources, Values and Development*, Oxford: Basil Blackwell, 1984.
7. M. Maclean, 'Households after divorce: The availability of resources and their impact on children', in J. Brannen and G. Wilson, eds, *Give and Take in Families: Studies of resource distribution*, London: Allen and Unwin, 1987.
8. A. Sen, op. cit.
9. P. Townsend, *Poverty in the United Kingdom*, Harmondsworth: Penguin, 1979.
10. H. Graham, 'Being poor: Perceptions and coping strategies of lone mothers', in J. Brannen and G. Wilson, eds, op. cit.
11. L. Comer, *Wedlocked Women*, Leeds: Feminist Books, 1974, p. 124.
12. C. Delphy, Reading 1.1, this volume.
13. P. Stamp, 'Balance of financial power in marriage: An exploratory study of breadwinning wives', *Sociological Review*, 33: 546–57, 1985, p. 554; J. Brannen and P. Moss, 'Dual earner households: Women's financial contributions after the birth of the first child', in J. Brannen and G. Wilson, eds, op. cit.
14. M. Edwards, op. cit., p. 138; P. Stamp, op. cit., p. 551.
15. L. Morris, 1984, op. cit.
16. U. Sharma, 'Segregation and its consequences in India', in P. Caplan and J. Bujra, eds, *Women United, Women Divided*, London: Tavistock, 1978, p. 266.
17. J. Pahl, 1980, op. cit.; H. Graham, op. cit.
18. D. Piachaud, *The Cost of a Child*, Poverty Pamphlet 43, London: CPAG, 1979; D. Piachaud, *Children and Poverty*, Poverty Research Series 9, London: CPAG, 1981; K. Lovering, *The Cost of a Child*, Melbourne: Institute of Family Studies, 1984.

19. For a parallel with food distribution see N. Charles and M. Kerr, 'Just the way it is: Gender and age differences in family food consumption', in J. Brannen and G. Wilson, eds, op. cit. See also N. Charles, Reading 2.2, this volume.
20. See also J. Brannen and P. Moss, op. cit.
21. See L. McKee, 'Households during unemployment: The resourcefulness of the unemployed', in J. Brannen and G. Wilson, eds, op. cit.; H. Qureshi and K. Simons, 'Resources within families: Caring for elderly people', in ibid. See also G. Wilson, *Money in the Family*, Aldershot: Avebury, 1987.
22. See H. Graham, op. cit., for examples of women whose husbands did take too much.

1.5 □ *Sallie Westwood*

Sallie Westwood spent a year doing participant observation in the hosiery factory which she refers to in this extract. She explored the interconnections between work and family for the women employed there – about two-thirds of whom were white and one-third Asian. Here, she gives us a lively account of how these factory workers talked about financial tensions in their relationships with men.

Money, money, money

Households, as Rayna Rapp has reminded us, are concerned with the pooling of resources and effort as part of the general process of reproduction.[1] This work turns consumption decisions into a specific standard of living through cooking and cleaning. [. . .] Reproduction is made possible under capitalism through the wage form: wages are turned into goods and services through the efforts of wives and mothers. Generally, it is women who have control over the domestic economy and the household's resources on a day-to-day basis, while men may control the public world of mortgages and bills – a division which reasserts the traditional view of women in the home, the private sphere, and men in the public sphere. In effect, it means that men do not have to worry about the day-to-day details of life which sap the energies and fill the minds of women.

It was often at tea-time on Fridays before they went home, but after they had been paid, that the women discussed the ways in which they managed their money. I joined in with the groups, rotating between them, asking for advice and information. One Friday I asked Pat and Michelle how they managed their money, and the latter replied:

I do it. We bring in £130 a week between us and he gives it all to me, and I look after the shopping and the bills. On a Friday we go shopping so he can carry all the heavy stuff and we go and fill up with petrol. I buy me fags for the week. He doesn't need much money because I make his sandwiches, he's got petrol and he doesn't smoke, so it's just me. I have some spending money for here, just a few quid which includes fares. I budget for the bills by putting a bit away every week for each one, then we put the rest in the bank. Where we are going it's really cheap so I reckon we can easily live on £50 a week and go out one night a week. So we can save the other £80 and we'll soon have £1,000, it won't take long.

In this case, Michelle controlled the household income and joint decisions were made in relation to major purchases and savings. She was very frugal; a model, she said, that had come from her mum who always controlled the money at home. This has been a common pattern among sections of the working class and it was reproduced by some of the other women in the factory. A common alternative was expressed in Pat's life:

> Well, Bob gets paid on Wednesday which helps so his money goes in the bank to draw on for bills and things we want to buy. Every week I put some of mine in the building society to add up for the mortgage. I have another account for savings and I try to put some in there. Then I spend my money on shopping or whatever Bob and I need through the week. We just budget it out, like.

Gracie and Tula, who were also at the table, joined in at this point:

> *Gracie* Well, you've got to [budget], otherwise you never keep it straight, do you?
> *Tula* That's right, you get in a mess if you don't plan it out right.
> *Sallie* So, Pat, do you share the expenses or do you look after everything?
> *Pat* No, Bob pays the bills from our account, that's what we do. I keep an eye on the food.
> *Tula* That's like me, 'cept I really see to it all. His money goes in the bank from work so it's there. I buy the food and things we need and he draws out what more we want and pays the bills, when I remind him! Ha ha!
> *Gracie* You've got to pool it, you can't manage on one wage these days.
> *Maria* That's what we've always done. We put our money together and put bits away for the bills every week.
> *Gracie* Well, you've got to plan it out, it's the only way everything gets paid and you can save a bit.
> *Tula* Yes, I have my savings taken out here so that's one lot and then we try to save some more on the side, out of his money in the bank.
> *Michelle* I know what happens to every penny and I keep accounts. He can look at them, but he doesn't seem bothered. But it's for my peace of mind. I have to know what's happening. It took me a while to get straight, but I never borrowed off me Mam. She said I would, but because she said that, I said I never would and I haven't needed to.

The income that the women had available to them varied according to the age and skill of their husbands and children. Gracie's husband was a toolmaker earning £130, close to the average male wage for the area in 1980. Tula's husband was a bus driver and he earned less than this. Most of the women lived on the council estates which ringed the city, and a few were already involved in buying the houses they had lived in for a while, from the council. Even those women who were married to knitters – the aristocrats of the hosiery industry who were earning £150 a week – were not living in households where there was much spare cash. Because of this, all the women took great pride in their ability to manage the resources they had as well as possible. They operated with strict budgets which allowed them to save some of their income every week. A week in which there was no saving was considered a disaster and everyone would be very upset. Most women spent their wages on food and cleaning materials, and not on goods for themselves. They took care of the day-to-day matters and most of their money was, in fact, eaten because it bought food which they transformed into meals.

The women were in no doubt that two wage packets were necessary for a minimum standard of living; this recognition reinforces my earlier conclusions on the economic importance of marriage to working-class people. It is a way in which they can generate sufficient income for a reasonable, but definitely not extravagant or elaborate standard of living. But there was more to it than just pooling resources, these had to be managed and they were managed by women who tried to stretch the household income as far as possible. The current generation of home managers showed a remarkable continuity with the women studied by the Fabian group in Lambeth in the early part of the twentieth century.[2] The women in Maud Pember Reeves' study also emphasised budgets and tried to save; they also endeavoured to provide the best possible food and clothing for the man of the house, the breadwinner.

The situation of Indian women varied according to the type of household they lived within. If it was a joint household, then money was pooled and traditionally controlled by the father of the family. In changed circumstances, many fathers had lost this role and economic affairs were controlled by brothers. Parents often had little say in decisions, except in relation to their daughters-in-law, and because their power had waned in other areas they have tried to exercise it more virulently in relation to the women of the household – not always with success. Some women lived with their husbands and children, like Lata and Amina, or with their husband, brothers-in-law and sisters-in-law, like Taruna. In these cases, there was often more pooling of resources and discussion surrounding the way in which money was to be used. Some women were the main wage earners, but they handed their money over to their husbands who gave them housekeeping and pocket money in return.

There was no doubt that for some women the money they were allocated was insufficient, and the union reps and the welfare officer commented on this. Annie said:

> You know, Sallie, these Indian women are so malnourished and mostly it's because they haven't got money to buy a meal at lunch-time. Their husbands or their mothers-in-law take their money and give them five bob a day to eat and have drinks. We have men in here boasting about the fact that they give their wives £5 a week for housekeeping. I'm not kidding.

Annie's indignation was fired by what she saw as a major injustice. Indian women did not seem to have any access to their own earnings because they were handed over to the male members of the family and became part of the 'family pot'. But this was not so far removed from the situation of English women who spent their earnings on the well-being of everyone else. However, there were Indian women I knew who would have liked more control over their own earnings. One of the great bonuses of a Western-style marriage commented upon by women like Lata, Shanta and Geeta, was that they could control more of their earnings in the home. Money became even more important when the women had children, who, in a joint family, would have to compete with other members for resources; whereas in a nuclear family, resources, if available, could be used by them. Young women controlled resources in a way that their mothers did, but they did not have to wait until their sons were grown and they became mothers-in-law to do this. It added to their status and sense of power in much the same way as it did among the young brides like Michelle and Pat.

Indian men could, and sometimes did, appropriate the earnings of their wives. But they were not alone in this. There were plenty of non-Indian examples on the shopfloor, including Tessa and Julie. However, the difference was that the twins were less likely to accept this as legitimate or normal because, of course, it conflicted with the ideologies surrounding the notion of the male breadwinner and the family wage.

Julie was scrounging a fag from a friend and, as she took it, she waved it at me and said angrily:

> We've got no bloody money because Dave hasn't been paying the HP on his car and they sent the law around. He's got to go to court over it. Huh! He thought he'd pay up some of the instalments, and it means no money from him and he's living off me! I'm payin' the rent and buying all the food. Well, I'm not doin' it this weekend. I'm not going through another week where I have no fags again. Men are stupid; they never grow up. Well, he and Carl are gonna have to grow up real quick because soon he's going to have me at home and a baby. It makes me sick!

Julie's twin sister was no less sanguine about her own financial affairs, which seemed to deteriorate week by week. Carl had been sacked and because of this he faced problems getting his dole money.

> *Tessa* At the moment I've got to pay for most things and we've got an electricity bill that I can't pay. Normally we share the price of the shopping and we go together to get it and that's about it. He won't cook anything and he won't clean. Still, he'll have to learn when the baby comes.
> *Sallie* What will happen when you aren't earning, Tess?
> *Tessa* Well, he'll have to cough up for housekeeping and expenses, won't he? Then he'll find out what it's like to have a family. I hope he goes back to work soon, I'm fed up with paying for him.

One response to this reversal of the notion of the male breadwinner which both Julie and Tessa made, was to insist upon male responsibilities in relation to them as wives and future mothers. They did not regard it as legitimate that their wages should be keeping their husbands, but it was a growing pattern among the women as their husbands lost their jobs in the engineering and hosiery industries locally. At the same time, women with youngsters ready to leave school looked pessimistically at their job opportunities, and resigned themselves to the ongoing burden of young adults. Previously, they would have expected them to be working and contributing to the family income.

The older women emphasised budgets and savings because they had grown up with the insecurities surrounding manual work under capitalism, while their daughters took these models from them into the current recession. Indian women, as part of an immigrant community, knew the importance of savings against hardships, to send money to poorer relatives or help new arrivals, or, as they became more settled, for the education and future of their children, for the chance to go back to India or to renovate the terraced houses they had bought. Savings, in all these cases, were being used as the year wore on for the shortfalls created in the homes where unemployment had struck.

More generally, the lives of the women at StitchCo demonstrated the deep contradictions apparent in the situation of women wage earners who were also wives and mothers. As wage earners, women have the possibility of greater economic independence and, therefore, of autonomy in their own lives – but they do not earn living wages. Their subordination in the labour market encourages women to marry and join hands with higher male wages; it also means that their wages are conceived of as secondary wages, adding to the main wage supplied by the male breadwinner which, in turn, means that their status in the family unit will not be greatly enhanced by their economic contribution. The equation 'money equals power' is a gross oversimplification in relation to the lives of women.

As a wife and a mother, a woman might have a great deal of control over the management of the household's budget and this could give her power in the domestic unit. But it may be that a woman controls nothing more than her own wages because what used to be housekeeping money paid from male wages has been replaced by money from women's wages – which again poses problems for the notion of the family wage and the male breadwinner. It suggests that women are subject to even greater levels of exploitation: not only do they carry the burden of domestic labour and home management, but also pay for the immediate reproduction needs of family members. While a man's wages are transformed into cars and housing through mortgage repayments or rents, a woman's wages are used to buy food which she transforms into meals that are eaten. I do not want to suggest that housing and food are not equally necessary. The important point is that men have access to both; women have to fight for rights to housing if they separate themselves from men.

Notes

1. R. Rapp, 'Family and class in contemporary America: Notes towards an understanding of ideology', in B. Thorne and M. Yalom, eds, *Rethinking the Family: Some feminist questions*, London: Longman, 1982.
2. M. Pember Reeves, *Round About a Pound a Week*, London: Virago, 1979.

2 □ *The Significance of Food and Clothing in Family Life*

2.1 □ *Anne Murcott*

In this essay, Anne Murcott discusses both the importance of meals in sustaining definitions of home life and the place of cooking within domestic gender divisions. She puts particular emphasis upon the symbolic meaning of the cooked dinner in these South Wales households.

'It's a pleasure to cook for him': food, mealtimes and gender in some South Wales households

Introduction

> I think it lets him know that I am thinking about him – as if he knows that I am expecting him. But it's not as if 'oh I haven't got anything ready' . . . Fair play, he's out all day . . . he doesn't ask for that much . . . you know it's not as if he's been very demanding or – he doesn't come home and say 'oh, we've got chops again', it's really a pleasure to cook for him, because whatever you . . . oh I'll give him something and I think well, he'll like this, he'll like that. And he'll always take his plate out . . . and he'll wash the dishes without me even asking, if I'm busy with the children. Mind, perhaps his method is not mine.

Every now and then an informant puts precisely into words the results of the researcher's analytic efforts – providing in the process a quotation suitable for the title! The extract reproduced above, explaining the importance of having the meal ready when her husband arrives home, comes from one of a series of interviews on which this paper is based.[1] The discussion starts by remembering that 'everyone knows' that women do the cooking: all the women interviewed – and the few husbands/boyfriends or mothers who came in and out – took it for granted that cooking was women's work. Informants may not enjoy cooking, or claim not to be good at it; they may not like the arrangement that it is women's work, or hanker after modifying it. But all recognise that this is conventional, some volunteer a measure of approval, most appeared automatically to accept it, a few resigned themselves and got on with it.

Studies of the organisation of domestic labour and marital role relationships confirm that cooking continues to be a task done more by women than men; this is also the case cross-culturally.[2] Emphasis in the literature has shifted from Young and Willmott's[3] symmetrical view of sharing and marital democracy. Now rather more thoroughgoing empirical study suggests their assessment is little more than unwarranted optimism.[4] This work improves on earlier studies of the domestic division of labour by going beyond behaviourist enquiry about 'who does which tasks' to consider the meanings attached to them by marital partners.

[. . .]

Recent commentary has [. . .] proposed that the view of the family as stripped of all but the residual economic function of consumption is ill-conceived and over-simplified. Domestic labourers refresh and sustain the existing labour force and play a key part in reproducing that of the future – as well as providing a reserve of labour themselves. The precise manner in which the political economy is to be accounted continues to be debated.[5] For the moment, however, the general drift of that discussion can be borne in mind by recalling the everyday terminology of eating; food is consumed, meals have to be produced. The language favoured in cookbooks echoes that of industry and the factory.[6] Home-cooking may nicely embody the terms in which the family and household's place in the division of labour has to be seen. [. . .]

This paper [. . .] brings together informants' ideas about the importance of cooking, their notions of propriety of household eating and indicates their relation to gender. It starts with views of the significance of good cooking for home life, and goes on to deal with the place of cooking in the domestic division of labour. The familiar presumption that women are the cooks is extended to show that their responsibility in this sphere is tempered with reference to their husband's, not their own, choice. The paper concludes with brief comment on possible ways these data may illuminate some of the questions already raised.

Home cooking

Aside from love, good food is the cornerstone of a happy household . . . (Opening lines of a 1957 cookbook called *The Well Fed Bridegroom*).

Right through the series of interviews three topics kept cropping up; the idea of a proper meal, reference to what informants call a 'cooked dinner' and the notion that somehow home is where proper eating is ensured. Moreover, mention of one like as not involved mention of another, sometimes all three. The composite picture that emerges from the whole series suggests that these are not merely related to one another in some way, but virtually equated.

It first needs to be said that informants seemed quite comfortable with a conception of a proper meal – indeed the very phrase was used spontaneously – and were able to talk about what it meant to them. Effectively a proper meal is a cooked dinner.

This is one which women feel is necessary to their family's health, welfare and, indeed, happiness. It is a meal to come home to, a meal which should figure two, three or four times in the week, and especially on Sundays. A cooked dinner is easily identified – meat, potatoes, vegetables and gravy. It turns out that informants displayed considerable unanimity as to what defines such a dinner, contrasting it to, say, a 'snack' or 'fried'. In so doing they made apparent remarkably clear rules not only for its composition but also its preparation and taking. I have dealt with their detail and discussed their implications in full elsewhere.[7] But in essence these rules can be understood as forming part of the equation between proper eating and home cooking. And, as will be noted in the next section, they also provide for the symbolic expression of the relationship between husband and wife and for each partner's obligation to their home.

The meal for a return home is, in any case, given particular emphasis – a matter which cropped up in various contexts during the interviews. Thus, for some the very importance of cooking itself is to be expressed in terms of homecoming. Or it can provide the rationale for turning to and making a meal, one to be well cooked and substantial – not just 'beans on toast . . . thrown in front of you'.

The actual expression 'home cooking' – as distinct from 'cooking for homecoming' – received less insistent reference. Informants were straightforward, regarding it as self-evident that people preferred the food that they had at home, liked what they were used to and enjoyed what they were brought up on. Perhaps untypically nostalgic, one sums up the point:

> When my husband comes home . . . there's nothing more he likes I think than coming in the door and smelling a nice meal cooking. I think it's awful when someone doesn't make the effort . . . I think well if I was a man I'd think I'd get really fed up if my wife never bothered . . .

What was prepared at home could be trusted – one or two regarded the hygiene of restaurant kitchens with suspicion, most simply knew their chips were better than those from the local Chinese take-away or chippy. Convenience foods had their place, but were firmly outlawed when it came to a cooked dinner. In the ideal, commercially prepared items were ranged alongside snacks, and light, quick meals: lunches and suppers in contrast to proper dinners. Informants talked about home cooking, but used this or some such phrase infrequently; the following is an exception:

> I'd like to be able to make home-made soups and things, it's just finding the time and getting organised, but at the moment I'm just not organised . . . I think it would probably be more good for us than buying . . . I suppose it's only – I'd like to be – the image of the ideal housewife is somebody who cooks her own food and keeps the household clean and tidy.

The sentiments surrounding her valuation of home-made food are not, however, an exception. Time and again informants linked not only a view of a proper meal for homecoming, but a view of the proper parts husband and wife are to play on this occasion. So cooking is important when you are married.

you must think of your husband . . . it's a long day for him at work, usually, . . . even if they have got a canteen at work, their cooking is not the same as coming home to your wife's cooking . . . I think every working man should have a cooked meal when he comes in from work . . .

Cooking is important – though not perhaps for everybody 'like men who don't cook' – for women whose 'place [it is] to see the family are well fed'.

In this section, I have indicated that informants virtually treat notions of proper meals, home-based eating and a cooked dinner, as equivalents. The stress laid on the homecoming not only underlines the symbolic significance attached to both the meal and the return home. It simultaneously serves as a reminder of the world beyond the home being left behind for that day. Put another way, the cooked dinner marks the threshold between the public domains of school or work and the private sphere behind the closed front door. In the process of describing these notions of the importance of cooking in the home, it becomes apparent that the familiar division of labour is assumed.

Cooking in the domestic division of labour

As noted in an earlier section, all those interviewed took it for granted that it is the women who cook. What they had to say refers both to conventions in general, and themselves and their circumstances in particular.[8] There are two important features of their general presumption that women are the cooks; one indicates the terms in which it is modifiable, the other locates it firmly as a matter of marital justice and obligation. The upshot of each of these is to underline the manner in which the domestic preparation of meals is securely anchored to complementary concepts of conduct proper to wife and husband.

To say that women cook is not to say that it is only women who ever do so. It is, however, to say that it is always women who daily, routinely, and as a matter of course are to do the cooking. Men neither in the conventional stereotype nor in informants' experience ever cook on a regular basis in the way women do.[9] Husband/ boyfriends/fathers are 'very good really'; they help informants/their mothers with carrying the heavy shopping, preparing the vegetables, switching the oven on when told, doing the dishes afterwards.[10] Such help may be offered on a regular enough basis, notably it is available when the women are pregnant, dealing with a very young infant, unwell or unusually tired. But none of this is regarded as men doing the cooking.

More significantly, it is not the case that men do not cook – in the strict sense of taking charge of the transformation of foodstuffs to some version of a meal. They may make breakfast on a Sunday, cook only 'bacon-y' things, can do chips or 'his' curries: all examples, incidentally, of foods that do *not* figure in the proper cooked dinner.[11]

For some, however, competence in the kitchen (and at the shops) is suspect: he'll 'turn the potatoes on at such and such a time . . . but leave him he's hopeless' and another just 'bungs everything in'. For others, it is men who make better domestic cooks than women, are more methodical, less moody. Another couple jokingly disagree: she 'not taken in' by Robert Carrier on TV, he claiming that 'the best chefs are men'. The point is that either way, of course, informants do regard gender as relevant to the question of who is to cook.

It is not even the case that all men cannot cook the proper, homecoming meal. One or two, when out of work for a while, but his wife still earning (this only applied to those having a first baby) might start the meal or even have it ready for her return. But once he is employed again he does not continue to take this degree of responsibility, reverting either to 'helping' or waiting for her to do it. Now and again, wives have learned to cook not at school or from their mothers, but from their husbands. But it was still assumed that it was for the woman to learn. This was even so in one instance where the informant made a 'confession . . . my husband does the cooking'. But now that she was pregnant and had quit paid work she would take over; 'it would be a bit lazy not to'. Like others for whom the cooking may have been shared while both were employed, cooking once again became the home-based wife's task.[12]

The issue is, however, more subtle than an account of who does what, or who takes over doing what. Men and women's place involve mutual obligation. 'I think a woman from the time she can remember is brought up to cook . . . Whereas most men are brought up to be the breadwinner.' The question of who does the cooking is explicitly a matter of justice and marital responsibility. A woman talks of the guilt she feels if she does not, despite the greater tiredness of late pregnancy, get up to make her husband's breakfast and something for lunch – 'he's working all day'. Another insists that her husband come shopping with her so he knows the price of things – he's 'hopeless' on his own – but she has a clear idea of the limits of each person's responsibility: each should cook only if the wife *has* to earn rather than chooses to do so.

Here, then, I have sought to show that informants subscribed in one way or another to the convention that it is women who cook. In the process it transpired that it is certain sorts of cooking, i.e. routine, homecoming cooking, which are perennially women's work. The meal that typically represents 'proper' cooking is, of course, the cooked dinner. Its composition and prescribed cooking techniques involve prolonged work and attention; its timing, for homecoming, prescribes when that work shall be done. To do so demands the cook be working at it, doing wifely work, in time that corresponds to time spent by her husband earning for the family.[13] This is mirrored in Eric Batstone's[14] account of the way a car worker's lunch box prepared by his wife the evening before is symbolic of the domestic relationship which constitutes the rationale for his presence in the workplace; he endures the tedium of the line in order to provide for his wife and family. It transpired also that men do cook in certain circumstances, but such modification seems to reveal more clearly the basis for accounting cooking as part of a wife's responsibility (to the family) at home corresponding to the husband's obligation (to the family) at work, i.e. their mutual responsibilities to each other as marriage partners.

Who cooks for whom?

At this point I introduce additional data which bear on cooking's relation to the question of marital responsibility. Repeatedly informants indicated that people do not cook for themselves; evidently it is not worth the time and effort.[15] But the data suggest implications beyond such matters of economy. Two interrelated features are involved: one is the distinction already alluded to in the previous section, between cooking in the strict sense of the word and cooking as preparation of a particular sort of meal. The other enlarges on the following nicety. To observe that people do not cook for themselves can mean two things. First it can imply that a solitary person does not prepare something for themselves to eat while on their own. But it can also imply that someone does not do the cooking on their own behalf, but in the service of some other(s). Examination of the transcripts to date suggests that not only could informants mean either or both of these, but also that each becomes elided in a way that underlines the nuances and connotations of the term cooking.

The question of a lone person not cooking themselves a meal unsurprisingly cropped up most frequently with reference to women themselves, but men, or the elderly were also thought not to bother.

Informants are clear, however, that not cooking when alone does not necessarily mean going without. Women 'pick' at something that happens to be in the house, have a bar of chocolate or packet of crisps later in the evening or a 'snack'. Men will fry something, an egg or make chips. No one said that a man would go without altogether (though they may not know), whereas for themselves – and women and girls in general – skipping a meal was thought common enough. Men – and occasionally women – on their own also go back to their mother's or over to their sister's for a meal. One informant was (the day of my interview with her) due to go to her mother's for the evening meal, but fearful of being alone in the house at night, she was also due to stay there for the next few days while her husband was away on business.

The suggestion is, then, that if a person is by themselves, but is to have a proper meal, as distinct from 'fried' or a 'snack' then they join a (close) relation's household. The point that it is women who cook such meals receives further emphasis. Indeed, when women cook this particular meal, it is expressly *for* others. In addition to the temporary lone adults just noted who return to mothers or sisters, women in turn may cook for the older generation, as well as routinely cooking for children or for men home at 'unusual' times if unemployed or temporarily on a different shift.

This conventional requirement that women cook for others is not always straightforward in practice. At certain stages in an infant's life the logistics of producing meals for husband *and* child(ren) there as well meant the woman felt difficulties in adequately meeting the obligations involved. And not all informants enjoyed cooking; most just accepted that it needed doing, though there were also those who took positive, creative pleasure in it.[16] Part of this is expressed in the very satisfaction of providing for others something they should be getting, and in turn will enjoy.

More generally cooking can become tiresome simply because it has to be done day-in, day-out. The pleasure in having a meal prepared for you becomes all the more pointed if routinely you are cooking for others.[17] In the absence of any data for men, it can only be a guess that going out for a meal is thus specially enjoyable for women. But for those who on occasion did eat out this clearly figures in their pleasure. Even if it rarely happened, just the idea of having it put in front of you meant a treat: 'it's nice being spoiled'.

The question 'who cooks for whom?' can now begin to be answered. Apparently it is women who cook for others – effectively, husbands and children. If husbands and children are absent, women alone will not 'cook', indeed many may not even eat. It is the others' presence which provides the rationale for women's turning to and making a proper meal – that is what the family should have and to provide it is her obligation. Men – and children – have meals made for them as a matter of routine: but for women it is a treat. That solitary men do not 'cook' for themselves either, and may go to a relative's for meals,[18] or that a woman on her own may also do so does not detract from the main proposal that it is women who cook for others. For it is not only that informants or their husbands will go temporarily back to their mother's, not their father's, home-cooking. It is also that both men and women revert to the status of a child for whom a woman, a mother, cooks. The mother may actually be the adult's parent, but they – and I with them – may stretch the point and see that she may be mother to the adult's nieces or nephews or indeed, as in the case of cooking for the elderly, she may be mother to the adult's grandchildren.

The appreciation that it is women who cook for others elaborates the more familiar convention, discussed above, that in the domestic division of labour cooking is women's work. First of all it indicates that this work is service work. Cooking looks increasingly like a task quite particularly done for others. Second, when cooking for others women are performing a service to those who are specifically related (sic) rather than for a more generalised clientele known only by virtue of their becoming customers. The marital – and parental – relationship defines who is server, who served.

That said, there remains the question of deciding what the server shall serve. As already discussed in an earlier section, the conventional expectation shared, it seems, by both woman and man, is that meals shall be of a certain sort – a cooked dinner for a certain occasion, most commonly the return home from work, or the celebration of Sunday, a work-free day. The 'rules' involved are not entirely hard and fast, or precisely detailed. Cooked dinners are neither daily nor invariable affairs.[19] And the cooked dinner itself can properly comprise a number of alternative meats (and cuts) and range of different vegetables. What, then, determines the choice of meat and vegetables served on any particular day? Some of the factors involved, as will be seen in the next section, once again echo ideas of responsibility and mutual obligation.

Deciding what to have

A number of factors feature in deciding what to have for a particular day's meal.[20] First, a question of cost was taken for granted. This does not necessarily mean keeping expenditure to a minimum – eating in the customary manner despite hard times was highly and expressly valued by some. Second, the conventional provision of proper dinners itself contributed to the determination of choice. These two factors present themselves as marking the limits within which the finer decisions about what the precise components of the day's dinner are to be. Here reference to their husband's – and, to a lesser extent, children's – preferences was prominent in informants' discussion of such detailed choices.

It was indicated earlier that in an important sense women's cooking is service work. This sort of work has two notable and interrelated aspects affecting decisions and choice: is it the server or served who decides what the recipient is to want? Exploring the mandate for professionals' work, Everett Hughes[21] highlights a key question: 'professionals do not merely serve: they define the very wants they serve'. Servants, and service workers such as waitresses[22] compliantly provide for the wants identified by the served. On the face of it, then, the professional has total and the waitress nil autonomy. Examples reflecting this sort of range occurred among informants varying from one woman apparently always deciding, through to another always making what he wants for tea. But in the same way that the maximum autonomy of the professional is continually, to a certain degree, a matter of negotiation and renegotiation with clients, and that, similarly, the apparent absence of autonomy is modified by a variety of more or less effective devices waitresses use to exert some control over customers, so a simple report of how meal decisions are reached can, I propose, either conceal negotiations already complete, or reveal their workings.

Thus informants interested in trying new recipes still ended up sticking to what they usually made because their husbands were not keen. Others reported that 'he's very good' or 'never complains' while some always asked what he wanted. A non-committal reply however did not necessarily settle the matter, for some discovered that being presented with a meal she had then decided on could provoke adverse and discouraging remarks. But it was clear that even those who claimed not to give their husbands a choice were still concerned to ensure that he agreed to her suggestion. It is almost as if they already knew what he would like, needed to check out a specific possibility every now and then but otherwise continued to prepare meals within known limits. Deciding what to have already implicitly took account of his preferences so that the day-to-day decision *seemed* to be hers.

The material presented in this section provides only a glimpse of this area of domestic decision-making. Other aspects need consideration in future work. For instance, what degree of importance do people attach to the matter?[23] Attention also needs to be paid to wider views of the legitimacy of choice in what one eats. In what sense do restaurant customers choose and mentally subnormal patients not? Does a child that spits out what it is fed succeed in claiming a choice or not? And in apparently acquiescing to their husband's choice, are wives circumscribing their own? But it looks as if deciding what to have is of a piece with a shared view of marital responsibility whereby he works and so deserves, somehow, the right to choose what she is to cook for him.

Gender and the production of meals

I know a cousin of mine eats nothing but chips, in fact his mother-in-law had to cook him chips for his Christmas dinner and she went berserk. . .

This 'atrocity story' recapitulates various elements of the preceding discussion. Such unreasonableness is, no doubt, unusual but its artless reporting emphasises a number of points already made. Not only do chips break the rules of what should properly figure in a Christmas meal, superior even to the Sunday variant of a cooked dinner, but it remains, however irksome, up to the woman to prepare what a man wants. The burden of this paper, then, may be summarised as revealing allegiance to the propriety of occasion such that a certain sort of meal is to mark home (male) leisure versus (male) work-time, and that such meals are cooked by women for others, notably husbands, in deference, not to the woman's own, but to men's taste.

This examination of cooking, mealtimes and gender within the household has implications for the continuing analysis of domestic work as work. While it does not shed light on why such work is women's, only reasserting that conventionally this is so, it clearly casts the work of meal provision as service work.

The everyday way of describing dishing up a meal as serving food is embedded in a set of practices that prescribe the associated social relationships as of server and served. As already observed this involves two interrelated matters: control over the work, and decisions as to what are the 'wants' the worker shall serve, what the work shall be. Each is considered in turn.

Oakley[24] reports that one of the features of housewifery that women value is the feeling of autonomy. Care is needed, though, not to treat such attitudes as tantamount to their analysis. Just because housewives express their experiences in terms of enjoying being their own boss does not mean that their conditions of work can be analysed in terms of a high degree of autonomy. The material presented in this paper suggests that doing the cooking is not directed by the woman herself, but is subject to various sorts of control.

First of these is the prescription for certain kinds of food for certain occasions. The idea of the cooked dinner for a homecoming is just such an example of cultural propriety. Related to this is a second control, namely that the food is to be ready for a specific time. Mealtimes construed in this way may exert just the same sort of pressure on the cook as any other production deadline in industry. Third, control is also exerted via the shared understanding that it is the preferences of the consumer which are to dictate the exact variant of the dinner to be served. What he fancies for tea constrains the cook to provide it. These kinds of control in the domestic provision of meals find their counterpart in the industrial concerns of quality control, timekeeping and market satisfaction. A woman cooking at home may not have a chargehand 'breathing down her neck' which is understandably a source of relief to her. But this does not mean to say that she enjoys autonomy – simply perhaps that other controls make this sort of oversight redundant. [. . .]

Linked to the issue of control of domestic cooking is the question of decision-making. [. . .] Reports such as Edgell's that food spending, cooking or whatever is regarded as the wife's responsibility, cannot, of itself, be seen as evidence of her power and freedom from control in those areas. For as Jan Pahl[25] has so cogently observed, 'being able to offload certain decisions and certain money-handling chores on to the other spouse can itself be a sign of power'. The delegatee may be responsible for execution of tasks, but they are answerable to the person in whom the power to delegate is originally vested.

The preliminary analysis offered in this paper has theoretical and political implications concerning power and authority in marriage and the relation between domestic and paid work. The exploration of ideas about cooking and mealtimes starts to provide additional approaches to detailing the means of domestic production. And the sort of work women are to do to ensure the homecoming meal provides a critical instance of the juncture between the control of a worker and the (his) control of his wife. The meal provides one illustration not only of a point where the public world of employment and the private world of the home meet one another; it also shows how features of the public take precedence within the private. For the stress informants lay on this mealtime offers an interesting way of understanding how the industrial rhythms which circumscribe workers are linked to the rhythms which limit women's domestic work.[26] And women's continual accommodation to men's taste can also be seen as a literal expression of wives' deference to husbands' authority.[27] This acquiescence to his choice provides the cultural gloss to the underlying economic relationship whereby industry produces amongst other things both the wage, and the raw materials it buys, for the domestic to produce what is needed to keep the industrial worker going. Part of the conjugal contract that each in their own way provide for the other, it does indeed become 'a pleasure to cook for him'.

Notes

1. I conducted a single-handed exploratory study . . . holding interviews with a group of 37 expectant-mothers attending a health centre in a South Wales valley for antenatal care (22 pregnant for the first time), 20 of whom were interviewed again after the baby's birth. No claim is made for their representativeness in any hard and fast sense, though they represent a cross-section of socio-economic groups . . . The data are treated as a composite picture. The prime concern is to indicate the range and variety of the evidence gathered. An instance that occurs only once thus becomes as interesting as one occurring 30 times. This is reflected in the discussion by the deliberate use of phrases such as 'some informants' rather than '6 out of 37'. In any case, reference to numbers of instances is no more exact, and risks implying a spurious representativeness. These qualifications are most important . . . [and] do actively have to be taken as read.
2. W. Stephens, *The Family in Cross Cultural Perspective*, New York: Holt, Rinehart and Winston, 1963; G. Murdock and C. Provost, 'Factors in the division of labour by sex: A cross-cultural analysis', *Ethnology*, 12: 203–25, 1973.
3. M. Young and P. Wilmott, *The Symmetrical Family*, Harmondsworth: Penguin, 1975.
4. A. Oakley, *The Sociology of Housework*, Oxford: Martin Robertson, 1974; A. Oakley, *Housewife*, Harmondsworth: Penguin, 1974; S. Edgell, *Middle Class Couples: A study of segregation, domination and inequality in marriage*, London: Allen and Unwin, 1980; D. Leonard, *Sex and Generation*, London: Tavistock, 1980; A. Tolson, *The Limits of Masculinity*, London: Tavistock, 1977.
5. J. West, 'A political economy of the family in capitalism: Women, reproduction and wage labour', in T. Nichols, ed., *Capital and Labour: A Marxist primer*, London: Fontana. 1980; B. Fox, ed., *Hidden in the Household*, Toronto: Women's Press, 1980; J. Wajcman, 'Work

and the family: Who gets "the best of both worlds"?', in Cambridge Women's Studies Group, ed., *Women in Society*, London: Virago, 1981.

6. A. Murcott, 'Women's place: Cookbooks' images of technique and technology in the British kitchen', *Women's Studies International Forum*, 6: 33–9, 1983.
7. A. Murcott, 'On the social significance of the "cooked dinner" in South Wales', *Social Science Information*, 21: 677–95, 1982.
8. Informants referred not only to themselves but also to mothers, sisters, sisters-in-law and women friends doing cooking.
9. No informant who had children old enough to cook currently shared the household with them.
10. See D. Leonard, op. cit.
11. A. Murcott, 'Cooking and the cooked', in A. Murcott, ed., *The Sociology of Food and Eating*, Aldershot: Gower, 1983.
12. See E. Bott, *Family and Social Network*, London: Tavistock, 1957, p. 225; A. Oakley, *Women Confined: Towards a sociology of childbirth*, Oxford: Martin Robertson, 1980, p. 132.
13. A. Murcott, 1982, op. cit.
14. E. Batstone, 'The hierarchy of maintenance and the maintenance of hierarchy: Notes on food and industry', in A. Murcott, ed., op. cit.
15. Market researchers know how to trade on such reports. During the period of interviewing a TV commercial was running which sought to persuade busy housewives not to neglect themselves but have a frozen ready-cooked meal at lunchtime.
16. See A. Oakley, *The Sociology of Housework*, Oxford: Blackwell, 1974.
17. Interestingly, no one talked of hospital meals put in front of them as a treat. (None had a home delivery.) Rather it was the quality of the food provided which informants concentrated on. Institutional cooking could not be home cooking.
18. See C. Rosser and C. Harris, *The Family and Social Change*, London: Routledge and Kegan Paul, 1965; D. Barker, 'Keeping close and spoiling', *Sociological Review*, 20: 569–90, 1972.
19. A. Murcott, 1982, op. cit.
20. It might have been expected that nutritional criteria would figure in these decisions. Analysis so far suggests that cultural prescriptions for proper eating at home override what is known about healthy eating. See A. Murcott, 'Menus, meals and platefuls', *International Journal of Sociology and Social Policy*, 1983.
21. E. Hughes, 'The humble and the proud', in *The Sociological Eye: Selected Papers*, Chicago: Aldine-Atherton, 1971, p. 424.
22. W. Whyte, *Human Relations in the Restaurant Industry*, New York: McGraw Hill, 1948; J. Spradley and B. Mann, *The Cocktail Waitress: Women's work in a man's world*, New York: John Wiley, 1975.
23. See S. Edgell, op. cit., pp. 58–9.
24. A. Oakley, *The Sociology of Housework*, Oxford: Martin Robertson, 1974; A. Oakley, *Housewife*, Harmondsworth: Penguin, 1974.
25. J. Pahl, 'The allocation of money and the structuring of inequality within marriage', University of Kent at Canterbury, mimeo, 1982, p. 24.
26. See R. Rotenburg, 'The impact of industrialisation on meal patterns in Vienna, Austria', *Ecology of Food and Nutrition*, 11: 25–35. 1981.
27. C. Bell and H. Newby, 'Husbands and wives: The dynamics of the deferential dialectic', in D. Barker and S. Allen, eds, *Dependence and Exploitation in Work and Marriage*, London: Longman, 1976; S. Edgell, op. cit.

2.2 □ *Nickie Charles*

Nickie Charles's findings echo many of Murcott's, confirming the influence that men exert over the form and content of family meals. Examining generational as well as gender hierarchies, this research deepens our understanding of the domestic power relations which underpin food consumption.

Food and family ideology

> At an ideological level the bourgeoisie has certainly secured a hegemonic definition of family life: as 'naturally' based on close kinship, properly organised through a male bread-winner with financially dependent wife and children, and as a haven of privacy beyond the public realm of commerce and industry.[1]

The ideology to which Michele Barrett refers is one which defines women as child-rearers and home-makers and men as bread-winners; it assumes women's dependence on men within the family and their different, and less permanent, attachment to the labour market; it is an ideology which is historically bounded and class specific; it disadvantages women of all social classes, resulting, for instance, in their greater vulnerability to poverty than men; it stabilizes capitalism both socially and politically. It does not, however, exist unchallenged. This challenge comes from conflicting egalitarian ideologies emanating from various social movements, most recently the Women's Liberation Movement, and taking concrete form in contradictory public policies and private unease over divisions of labour based on gender. For instance, numerous policies, from social security legislation to employment policies, are predicated upon the assumption of women's financial dependence upon men within marriage (or marriage-like relationships) and their prime responsibility for child rearing. Others however, such as the Equal Pay Act (1970) and Sex Discrimination Act (1975), seek to assert women's right to equality with men. Gender equality is profoundly at odds with the ideology of the family as defined above. This has been apparent in the conflicts within the trade union movement over demands for equal pay and support for a 'family wage' to be paid to men. The ideology of the family has been used to justify women's low pay – they only work for pin-money after all – and at times to justify women's exclusion from certain areas of work altogether. Family ideology has, in effect, come to structure the divisions within the labour market and other areas of 'public' life as well as structuring divisions within the home. It therefore has a material as well as an ideal existence. [. . .] The way we live our daily lives, what we do, the way in which we do it and the choices we make therefore shape, as well as being shaped by, ideology.

Much has been heard recently of 'the new man' and the 'post-feminist' era. It is assumed in this sort of discourse (or ideology) that women and men are free to assume the roles they wish and to negotiate a division of labour which is satisfying to them. External constraints have gone, free choice and individual fulfilment are the order of the day. However, studies show that the aggregate outcome of individual choice is startlingly similar to the outcome during the so-called 'pre-feminist' era.[2] It seems that individual choices are in conformity with an inegalitarian family ideology rather than an ideology of gender equality. Perhaps this has something to do with the embeddedness of this ideology in the material reality of our daily lives; a material reality which means that most women earn less than most men and that if a person has child-care responsibilities their labour market participation is severely curtailed. The reality within which choices have to be made therefore reflects family ideology and makes it difficult and potentially disruptive for people to make choices which do not conform to this ideology.

The focus of this chapter however is not on the 'public' domain of state and economy which provides the context for choice, but on the 'private' domain of the household or family where many such choices are made. Its purpose is to explore the relationship between family ideology and food provision and consumption within households. The central question to be addressed is whether the practices surrounding food and eating bear any relation to family ideology and, if so, what is the nature of this relationship.

Sharing food is an important part of family life and is a symbol of community.[3] It seems (at least as far as the Department of Social Security is concerned) that it is also a symbol of the existence of a relationship of financial dependence between a woman and man. If a woman and man are thought to be cohabiting, evidence of this relationship is sought not only through ascertaining whether their relationship is sexual, but also by enquiring as to their eating arrangements. If meals are shared, cohabitation is assumed and the woman forfeits her independent access to support from the state.[4] Clearly, for the state, the sharing of food is seen as indicating a close relationship and it is one of the characteristics of family life that food is regularly shared among co-resident family members. Conversely, when petitioning for divorce one of the indications of separation is that meals are no longer being shared by marital partners.[5] The sharing of food is therefore something that happens within family households and is an indication of their existence. However, this sharing, although symbolizing a community, is not necessarily equal. On the contrary, it has been found that the distribution of food within families is dependent upon age and gender with adult men consuming food in larger quantities and of a higher social status than other family members.[6] The suggestion is that the way in which food is distributed within families is dependent upon family ideology with the male bread-winner getting the lion's share and, if the household is in poverty, women going without in order to ensure that the wage earner and then the children get enough to eat.[7] However, the distribution of food within families is not equal even when resources are adequate to ensure that food is available to all.[8] It seems, therefore, that the inegalitarian ideology of the family structures the distribution of food within family households and affects the type of food that is eaten by women, children and men.

This is not surprising. Mrs Beeton recommended that snipe 'may be given whole to a gentleman, but in helping a lady, it will be better to cut them quite through the centre, completely dividing them into equal and like portions, and put only one half on the plate.'[9] Women, particularly 'ladies', are supposed to eat less than men, indeed they are seen as 'needing' to eat less than men. Explanations of the way in which food is distributed between family members are often couched in terms of 'needs' which are perceived as 'natural'. Further exploration of these explanations, however, reveals that far from being based on nature or biological difference they are rooted in family ideology, and have often been consciously constructed, as with Mrs Beeton's strictures on proper household management.

Distribution of food within households, as the distribution of other resources, is unequal and reflects relations of power and authority which appear to conform to family ideology. Much recent research has focused upon this aspect of family life and highlighted women's lesser access to resources within households throughout British society.[10] Here, however, I want to discuss not only the ways in which family ideology shapes families' eating patterns, but the ways in which it is used as a means of understanding and justifying practices within families, the ways in which it structures the process of socialization of children and defines socially acceptable eating patterns and behaviour, and the ways in which it *unites* households from different classes.

The research

The study on which this chapter is based was carried out between 1981 and 1985 with Marion Kerr in the Department of Sociology of the University of York. It was funded by the then Health Education Council. Two hundred women with children of pre-school age were interviewed twice about all aspects of feeding their families. The interviews were separated by a fortnight and during that time the women were asked to keep a record of what was eaten by everyone in their household. They were not asked to weigh amounts but were asked to give an indication of the size of the portions. The assumption was made that it would be women who were mainly responsible for food provision and cooking and this was in fact the case. In 177 (88.5%) of the families it was the women who were responsible for daily cooking and in only two cases was cooking shared equally between partners. These figures in themselves testify to the strength of family ideology, at least at this stage in the life cycle. The women were selected for interview on the basis of the age of one of their children: the study was focusing on the formation of eating habits in young children and the sample was therefore stratified according to the age of the sample child; their ages ranged from six months to five years. The women were initially sent a letter from the Health Authority giving them some information about the research and asking them if they would be prepared to participate in it. This was followed by a visit from one of the researchers to arrange a time when it would be convenient for the first interview to take place. Most of the women approached agreed to participate in the study.

The research took place in the north of England in a prosperous manufacturing and marketing town and its surrounding villages. It may be that the findings are therefore peculiar to that region but there is as yet no evidence to indicate that this is the case. In fact, the only other research on food and families in Britain indicates that the findings are not geographically specific.[11] The interviews covered all aspects of food provision within households and were not confined to feeding children. Many of the questions were open ended and the women were encouraged to talk freely about the issues that concerned them. The interviews were tape recorded and transcribed making a qualitative as well as a quantitative analysis possible. The former is what I shall concentrate on here as I am concerned to uncover the meanings attached to food and its provision within households.

Gender and food provision

As has already been noted, the ideology of the family is profoundly inegalitarian. Men are defined as the bread-winners, women the home-makers and women are dependent upon men. Figures are frequently produced to show that at any one time only a certain proportion of British households actually conform to this pattern.[12] However, the evidence from our study and from an increasing focus on the life cycle indicates that most individual women and men will experience living in this type of household at some stage in their lives, usually when their children are very young.[13] Of the 200 women we interviewed 119 were not working in paid employment and were, therefore, totally financially dependent upon their partners. Only five women were in full-time employment, most of the others were working part time and part-time work has been seen by governments, trade unions and women themselves as a way of enabling women to combine paid employment with domestic responsibilities, particularly child care.[14] Women's participation in part-time employment does not, therefore, challenge the gender division of labour assumed by family ideology. Those women who were in full-time employment were in jobs that enabled them to pay nannies or obtain other help with their child care; class in these cases enables some women to overcome the constraints of gender. In fact, as far as cooking was concerned, women's part-time employment outside the home seemed to have no impact on the gender division of labour; most of the women working part-time along with most of the women who were full-time housewives were always responsible for cooking. Interestingly, the partners of the women in full-time employment were not involved in cooking at all, two of the five women were wholly responsible for cooking and three had help with cooking from nannies. Women's full-time employment outside the home did not, therefore, mean that there was a transformation of the gender division of labour within the home. In the two households where cooking was equally shared the women were full-time housewives. This is significant in the light of the explanations advanced by other women for a gender division of labour which assigned to them the main responsibility for cooking; this is explored below.

Cooking and preparing meals for men and children is, according to family ideology, a central part of a woman's role within the home; it is fundamental to her role as wife and mother. This view was clearly expressed by many of the women we spoke to and they linked cooking to the importance of sharing meals as a family. They were asked how important they thought it was for a woman to be able to cook. One replied:

> Very important, it's part of the family existence, it's one of the main occasions in the day when everybody gets together to eat and chat and if you've got rubbish in front of you, you're miserable, aren't you?

This view was common:

> To me, very, I think. Because I think mealtimes are important, I mean it's the only time we're together as a family really. Yes, I do think it's important, even if you're working . . .

Another woman said it was very important for a woman to be able to cook and clearly linked it to the gender division of labour defined within family ideology:

> Well, to me it's the basic history of the woman doing all that sort of thing and the man going out to work, you know, he's the bread-winner and the wives – I wouldn't say I agree with it – that the wife should be at home to look after the children, housekeep and cook, but I think it's just the way of the world . . .

Women cooking is therefore seen as central in terms of creating a family and is justified with reference to a gender division of labour which defines men as bread-winners and women as home-makers.

Although most of the women we spoke to were the ones who were responsible for meal preparation, this had not always been the case. The arrival of children and women's withdrawal from the labour market often pushed women into accepting a more rigid gender division of labour. This is not to say that domestic tasks had previously been equally shared – this had only been the case in seven households.

[. . .]

Conformity with ideological definitions of gender divisions appropriate to the family was reinforced by several factors, among them men's perceived incompetence in the kitchen but, perhaps more importantly, by the fact that men were out at work all day.

[. . .]

Whether women accepted this division of labour without question or reluctantly made no difference, all except two of them conformed to it. And this conformity was itself sometimes conceptualized in terms of free choice:

> I think each relationship, whether married or not, finds it own level. *I don't believe* a woman's role is to be at home and cook and look after the children and her man. Having said that, that is what I *do*, but *purely* because it works out that way.

Ideologies can seemingly be adhered to and reinforced without having to be believed in; this emphasizes the importance of the notion that ideologies are embedded in material practices and reproduced by them.[15] Belief does not have to enter into the process of ideological reproduction; indeed at the individual level conformity may be perceived as free choice or as being forced into a situation not of your own choosing as well as many gradations of willing or unwilling conformity between these two extremes. Whatever the individual process the end result is that the gender division of labour within the households of the women we spoke to closely conformed to the gender division of labour defined within family ideology.

Part also of the ideology of the family is that cooking for others is seen as part of a woman's caring role. She cooks for her family in order to show that they are cared for by her and in order to ensure that they are healthy and able to participate in the required activities outside the home. Associated with caring for others is a lack of care for yourself and this is expressed in the way in which women's own tastes and preferences are subordinated to those of their partners, first, and their children, second. This process often starts from day one of the relationship.

> I think I used to try to introduce a lot of new things when I first got married and over the years it just caused arguments so I just tend to not buy the things he doesn't like, you know. He'll just say 'No I don't like it' and I think if he keeps saying that in front of the kids it's bad for them. I tend not to buy the things that he doesn't like so I only cook the things that the three of us like when he's away and at lunchtime.

What was cooked for the family was therefore shaped by men's and, to a lesser extent, children's preferences:

> The main thing is something that we all like, which is difficult because Karen is choosy. I must admit we always have meat because Tony likes meat more than anything . . . [What about your own likes and dislikes, do you think of those when you are making something?] Mine tend to get pushed into the background I must admit . . . I tend to get what the majority like which ten out of ten it's not my favourite.

Women's preferences did not enter into the picture. Indeed, if men were 'easy to please' women considered themselves lucky.

> There is very very little that Don doesn't like which does tend to make it very easy for me to feed him.

The enjoyment of cooking was very much bound up with whether the end product was appreciated, not by the women but by those for whom they were cooking, particularly their partner. As one woman put it:

> I try to make every meal for Ian a nice meal – whereas for myself I maybe wouldn't eat as much. I could eat it but I put weight on easily and he doesn't like me fat.

She later commented that if her husband was away:

> I don't enjoy it. I don't enjoy cooking it as much or eating it – I don't really enjoy it without him. I enjoy putting a nice meal in front of the family and seeing them enjoy it. I've always got pleasure out of that.

And another woman said that preparing food was 'a loving gesture'. She continued:

> So what I would hope for myself is that I could hold his heart through his recognition that what I was doing for him was prepared in a loving spirit.

Clearly the provision of food for a man by a woman can be seen as an expression of caring, and this caring involves putting his needs and preferences first. Women's position as 'servers and providers' therefore involves a systematic subordination of their own preferences to those of their partners.[16] It would be interesting to explore whether this happens when men are the ones who take on the role usually assigned to women, that is whether it is a result simply of cooking for others, or whether it is linked to the way in which relations between women and men are structured such that women are carers and dependants at one and the same time.[17]

Family meals

This subordination of women's own likes and dislikes clearly reinforces the domination of men's tastes over the whole family. Nowhere is this clearer than in the provision of the main meal of the day, often the only meal which all family members shared. This was seen as being a very important occasion in the life of the family:

> It's the only time that we all get together really, catching up on news and William is telling us what he's been doing at school or something like that. It's a bit of a family gathering I suppose.

Many of the women mentioned that mealtimes were the only times that they came together as a family – this was seen to be important even though it may not happen very often. One woman told us:

> I've been brought up on a family meal every day . . . I believe that the children should experience a family meal, that's why I sometimes have a meal so at least twice a week they sit down and they have a family meal, in the kitchen.

And another said:

> It's very rare that the family unit is broken up. Even if Brian has a staff meeting or something like that then we will generally wait until he's home and we'll all eat as a family.

Although most of the women felt it was important that the family ate the main meal of the day together, on weekdays this happened in only 124 (62%) of households, on Saturdays 142 (71%) of the families shared their main meal and on Sundays the main meal was shared by 162 (81%) of the families. There is a slight difference in practice in terms of class with fewer households in occupational classes I and II sharing the main meal on weekdays than those in other social classes. This can partly be explained by the practice of feeding children their main meal at midday while the adults ate theirs in the evening which, although not widespread, tended to be more likely amongst I/II households. It may also reflect the fact that men with professional occupations sometimes worked late and children had to be fed and got to bed before they arrived home in the evening. However, at weekends these class differences disappeared and in most households all family members shared their main meal together.

We have discussed at length elsewhere the women's views on the nature of the main, family meal: that it should be a 'proper' meal consisting of meat and two veg shared by all members of the family.[18] Here I wish to concentrate on the relations of power and authority that structure the 'proper' meal and the ways in which they are symbolized in the food that is consumed. However, before doing so it is interesting to look at some of the women's descriptions of the ways in which meals are organized as it brings together the ideological importance of family meals and the daily organizational considerations involved in feeding a collection of individuals involved in various activities, occupying the same household.

> I'm afraid they [meals] have to fit in with what everybody happens to be doing at the time except I do like for us to sit down together when possible. It annoys Martin dreadfully if they say 'Oh, I haven't got time for lunch today, can you put dinner in the oven', or 'they'll eat when they get back from so and so' – he much prefers them to sit down together. During the week he would hardly ever see them to talk to. [Is that something important to you?] Yes, I get a good feeling seeing them all sat down together, it satisfies me, I don't know what it is.

The following description underlines the importance of Sunday dinner as a family occasion, often in contrast to meals during the rest of the week:

> [Where do you eat meals?] All over the house. It's terrible. Sometimes I get annoyed and say we must sit round the table. We eat in here [sitting room], we eat it next door [dining room] round the table, or we eat standing up in the kitchen. If there's something on television that we want to watch we'll have it in here even though I don't particularly like it as we seem to fall over one another. Depends on what it is – if it's something sloppy we'd have it in the dining room. We always have Sunday dinner in the dining room, though. I do like us to all sit round together when we are eating at the same time . . . I don't like to see people picking plates up and rushing off.

Eating a meal together as a family usually involved sitting at table and talking to one another. During the week 147 (73%) families ate their main meal at the table and this increased to 167 (83%) on a Sunday. However, togetherness did not always mean that families sat round a table to eat. In one household the table was so small that there was only room for the two children and their mother to eat at table, their father ate his meal in the armchair in front of the television. Similar arrangements were made in other households. What is interesting, though, is that if there was not room at the table for all the family it was usually the father who sat elsewhere; women and children, especially if the children were young, sat at the table. This can partly be seen as arising from the need to control young children while they are eating and to teach them acceptable patterns of mealtime behaviour; it is therefore regarded as important that they, at least, eat at table. Men do not necessarily need to be part of this socialization process and can eat their meals without the added stress of participating in this aspect of their children's initiation into proper family life. However, in most households mealtimes were shared by the whole family and men's presence at table enabled the children to learn not only what behaviour was appropriate at mealtimes, but also the social relations which structure the provision of proper, family meals. This is apparent in the type of food that is provided for this meal. Children were often allowed to choose what food they ate for non-main meals, but for the main meal of the day they had to eat what they were given. Of course, in the preparation of the meal their likes and dislikes were taken into account, but women very often characterized their children's food preferences as being changeable and inconsistent and therefore not to be taken too seriously. Men's likes and dislikes, however, *were* taken seriously and, as we have already seen, meals were usually prepared with their preferences in mind. In addition to this, 'proper' meals were often not prepared if men were not present for the main meal:

> If Bob's been away I've not bothered to cook proper meals – proper meals inasmuch as a cooked meal. I probably wouldn't go to the trouble of cooking myself meat, vegetables and potatoes.

> I do a simpler meal if Dave's not there, I'll do something on toast for me and the kids, cheese on toast or eggs on toast, but if he's here then I would never give him anything like that for his tea. He has something like that maybe lunchtime.

The main meal of the day was also eaten at a time which fitted in with men's hours of work, usually in the evening when they arrived home. This again reinforces the importance of the position of bread-winner as well as making sense in terms of women's cooking arrangements. Thus the presence of men and, to a lesser extent, children is an important precondition for the preparation of a 'proper' meal. In addition, children were expected to eat a 'proper' meal without having any say over its content. It can be argued, therefore, that the provision of a 'proper' meal, prepared by the woman and consumed by the family together, symbolizes the gender division of labour and relations of dependence which are constitutive of a specific ideology of the family.

Talking is also viewed as an important part of the 'proper' family meal. This is often linked to the fact that the main meal is the only time during the day when the family are all together. Women were asked whether they thought it important to talk together at mealtimes, and 127 of them felt that it was. This view was linked to class with a higher proportion (81%) of women in occupational classes I and II attaching importance to talking at mealtimes compared with 56 per cent of women in classes IV and V. There was also a class difference in eating at table: it was most common in classes I and II and least common in classes IV and V, but having said that the majority of households in all occupational classes ate their main meals at table.[19] However, this may be taken as an indication of the disjunction between ideology and reality which relates to the material conditions within which households are placed. These material conditions may make it more difficult for working class families to conform to ideological definitions of family life than it is for middle class families. For instance, there may simply not be enough space for everyone to eat at a table and this was certainly the case in several of the working class households we visited. And eating in cramped conditions is not conducive to a relaxed mealtime where talking can be indulged in. In these circumstances eating and getting the meal over and done with may assume greater importance than taking part in an exchange of news and views with members of the family who have not been seen all day. One woman explained the way she organized meals:

> Well, I think in a way everything fits round them, I think they are very, very important because I think it's the time when the family come together, and its really the only time they come together as a family. Which is why we all sit down and have a chance to talk . . . I think it's the most important part of the day apart from cooking.

A different view is expressed by another woman for whom meals are more about eating than about talking. She was one of the women who had no space for the whole family to sit at table and eat together so it seems that for her mealtimes are primarily about controlling the children and ensuring they eat. Talking in this context may be a distraction:

> I've played pop with the kids because sometimes they're talking more often than they're eating. When I was young I wasn't allowed to speak at table, which I wasn't. It was sit down, eat your meal and then 'Can I leave the table' when we were little. We could never speak unless we were spoken to. And I think now, I think well, I'm not going to be so strict with me kids but sometimes I will say to them, 'Now shut up and get on with your tea' or lunch or whatever, you see. But I don't stop them ever from speaking . . . sometimes I do – 'I think I've heard enough now and let's just get on with our tea, another word and you go off in the bedroom' – but more often than not we talk among ourselves.

Happy families

Thus far I have concentrated on women's views of family meals and the way in which they reflect a particular inegalitarian ideology of the family. According to this ideology the family is a 'haven in a heartless world'[20] and it is part of a woman's role to ensure that this is in fact the case. Providing a man with a 'proper' meal on his return from work, a meal which is shared by all the family, happily and peacefully, is part of this task. The reality of family meals, however, is often not one of peace and harmony. The provision of food which all the family can share is seen as important by women, but is often an ideal which they are aiming for rather than the reality they experience. Again, the disjuncture between family ideology and the actual organization of family life is apparent, and it is women who feel responsible for this disjuncture and who are constantly trying to ensure that their own family operates according to the ideology. It is hard to see how this can be the case, however, particularly when young children are involved and mealtimes are such an important area of socialization. Women are at one and the same time expected and expecting themselves to service men on their homecoming and to socialize their children. These two, often conflicting, expectations result in tension and friction rather than peace and harmony at mealtimes. The family is not necessarily a haven, even for the homecoming male.

According to family ideology then, mealtimes are congenial occasions. However, only 55 of the 200 women we spoke to said that mealtimes never gave rise to arguments; thus for 145 (72.5%) of women, mealtimes were often marked by conflict, usually conflict between parents and children (120) but it could also be conflict between marriage partners. This was reported by 39 of the women. These two sources of conflict will be looked at separately.

It is perhaps not surprising that mealtimes should give rise to conflict. As many of the women said, it was often the only time that family members came together and it might therefore be regarded as potentially hazardous. Indeed it has been noted that when family members are forced to be together, such as over Christmas or on holiday, conflicts which can at other times be contained often erupt and marital breakdown increases in frequency. Also, research into domestic violence has shown that the provision of food for men by women can often be the trigger for a violent incident.[21]

The women were often aware of the potential for conflict at mealtimes and tried to avoid it. One of the ways of doing this was to provide food that their partners liked. Of the 190 women we spoke to who were living with a partner, 60 said that at some stage the food they had prepared for them had been refused; for many of the women this had been a very upsetting experience and was clearly something that they tried to avoid. Women also tried to keep conversation to areas which were safe. One woman was discussing the importance of talking at mealtimes:

> I think it's important that Mike and I – when he comes in I try to shut the children up because I think you should talk if there's something you want to be told about. I like to have twenty minutes or so with him, generally, when we're eating. [Do mealtimes ever give rise to arguments?] I was brought up in a family in which it did and I was determined it never would. No, no, I never ever broach anything that's likely to cause disharmony at mealtimes.

And another woman in response to the same question said:

> It depends really how tired we are. It could do – I have known him to leave his food and go upstairs, yes. We don't encourage it. Usually it's a happy occasion. It just depends what's going on at the time.

One of the women was interviewed with her partner present and their combined response to the questions about talking and arguing at mealtimes is interesting. She was asked whether she thought it important to talk together at mealtimes, *he* replied:

> Not necessarily. Sometimes if you're having an enjoyable meal – 'cos I mean some meals are just refuelling sessions aren't they, whereas others are social occasions or happy times. Not necessarily. I think we talk when we have something interesting to say, we don't make small talk. . . . One of the reasons we get on so well is because Sally isn't a great talker, you know, that just is us.

His partner chipped in 'You make up for it'. At another stage in the interview they went on to recount how he had once thrown a meal at her which he had deemed 'unacceptable'. This sort of event highlights the unequal power relations which structure marriage and which allow men to assume they have a right to expect meals which they consider appropriate and which are served to meet their needs rather than the needs of other family members. One woman was asked if her partner had ever refused to eat anything that she had prepared:

> Oh yeah, many a time, yeah. We had stew and I'd forgotten what I was doing and I'd chipped the potatoes up so I thought I'll just do chips with it, 'cos I like chips with gravy, and he wouldn't eat it. . . . He said, 'You don't have gravy on chips', so he wouldn't eat it.

She added later that she did not usually cook things that he disliked. This response on the part of some men to food that does not meet their taste or expectations helps to explain why women quickly eliminate food that their partners dislike from the family menu.

The second major area of potential conflict at mealtimes is between parents and children. One woman put the problem very succinctly:

> [Do mealtimes ever give rise to arguments?] Oh, yes. Yes, I think inevitably because the children are learning about manners and learning about caring for each other and that's all very sticky territory. They are just learning things like passing things to other people before they take them themselves and each of those things involves a lot of arguments along the way. . . . I think the area of feeding is an opportunity for real training and consolidation of all sorts of social skills or it can become just a dreadful battleground.

This battleground can be with children, or between partners over the way that children are treated and what they are allowed to get away with.

> [Do mealtimes ever give rise to arguments?] Yes, but only since Darren has come along, because some days he'll eat his dinner no trouble at all and then other days he'll play and then another day he wants me to feed him, and another day he'll play up because we turn the television off and take him to the table. Or if he's out playing and you make him come. I would say that since he's been born we've had more arguments at the table. [So your husband and you have more arguments?] Well because I suppose we've got different ideas on exactly what he should do and what he should not do, I suppose. My husband likes him to sit at the table and behave himself but I mean a three year old, they do just play and you just can't expect them to be as interested in food as you are . . . Maybe I aren't as strict as I should be, I suppose that's it, but Andrew likes to sit and have his meal not with a lot of aggro I suppose you could say, yeah.

She related this difference in their attitudes to her experience of mealtimes as a child:

> When we were young and we didn't finish a meal we had to sit at that table until we'd finished that meal. Well, Andrew thinks that he should eat everything that's put in front of him 'cos he doesn't like waste you see. . . . I don't mind if he leaves a little bit, but Andrew doesn't like him to waste food.

Another woman described the conflict that could arise at mealtimes as follows:

> There are a few smacked bottoms and sent to bed . . . it's usually Laura the little one . . . she's messy, she messes you know, she doesn't like using a knife and fork and sometimes if she makes a mess and she doesn't do as she's told . . . she usually gets something . . . she gets sent up to bed, then he usually lets them come down when they're calm.

In both these accounts it is the men who are stricter than the women as regards mealtime behaviour. Children are expected to eat 'properly' and behave in ways that are appropriate to the family meal. Sometimes men were reported as having more patience with their children at the end of the day and therefore being more able to persuade them to eat – women would give in sooner. Thus, men seem to exert their authority through the children's enforced consumption of the proper, family meal. It is usually *their* views that prevail at this meal, even when women may not agree with their insistence that children eat what they have been given. Several of the women said that they did not voice their disagreement with men over these sorts of issues because it would only create further tension during what ought to be a happy, family occasion.

Clearly for young children to learn to eat a meal at table using the proper implements and behaving in an acceptable way is a process fraught with difficulty. They become bored if the meal takes too long, they are frustrated by their inability to manipulate knives and forks and their need for assistance with such things as cutting up meat, and they rebel against being made to eat a 'proper' meal which is not of their own choosing and which their parents expect them to eat because it is 'good' for them. As we have seen, at meals other than the main meal of the day children exercise a certain degree of choice, for the main meal they have to eat what's put in front of them. If children do not eat 'proper' meals regularly women become anxious. Eating a proper meal was viewed as important at two levels. Firstly, in the women's opinions, it ensured that the child was being adequately nourished and, secondly, it symbolized the child's incorporation into the life of the family. It is part of the 'civilizing process'.[22] [. . .]

Inculcating acceptable behaviour in children at mealtimes happened in all households although the standards thought appropriate varied. One woman said:

> I don't abolish speaking at mealtimes but I don't let them jump about and throw things or owt like that.

And another said:

> I don't allow them to stand on the table while we're eating. . . . I encourage Ben to use a knife and fork but usually he uses a fork and a finger to shovel it in. . . . If they've got a mouth stuffed full of food and try and talk then, you know, we will say 'Finish that off first', I don't allow them to spit and do things like that but I wouldn't say I was very strict.

Others, however, took a different view:

> We try to make them behave at the table. I suppose it's when you take them out anywhere really, they know how to behave then. . . . I don't allow them to read at the table . . . they've always used knives and forks, as soon as they are old enough I let them have a little knife and fork. I get them at the table as quickly as possible, even when they are in a high chair with their own little table I pull it up to the table so they can join in.

As she points out there are social pressures on women to ensure that their children know how to behave appropriately; it was around the age of eighteen months to two years that children started eating at the table with the rest of the family and that 'table manners' began to be seen as important. This was also the age at which children began to be perceived as difficult to feed and to have problems with eating. We would suggest that this is not coincidental and that it indicates that children are not so much rejecting the food as food – they will often eat the same food item later in their fingers out of the refrigerator – but that they are rejecting, or refusing to conform to, the social relations within which the food is consumed. If the women spoke about their children not eating they were referring to the 'proper' meal, the meal that they felt it important for children to eat; children were very rarely reported as being problematic eaters in relation to the other meals prepared during the day.

Children's refusal of food presented to them in the form of a proper meal is seen as problematic firstly, because if they do not eat it they may not be receiving adequate nutrition and, secondly, because of the symbolic importance of their participation in this 'family' meal. Women often capitulated to their children and ended up feeding them what they would eat rather than what they thought they ought to eat. This can partly be seen as a response to anxiety that their child is going to starve rather than eat the food in the form that it is presented, but it can also be seen as a way of reducing tension at mealtimes:

> I always said before I had a child that any child I had would eat what we ate but it hasn't worked out like that, unfortunately. We've been through the most *awful* year where Rebecca and I were always at loggerheads, we were always fighting over mealtimes and in the end a friend turned round to me and said, 'For heavens' sake, Carol, ask her what she wants for a meal and give it her 'cos you're getting nowhere the way you're going on . . . if she wants fish fingers and beans every day, let her have them 'till she's fed up of them'. And I tried what Joan said and it's worked 'cos she's starting to eat – every day she has a little bit different, you know.

Ultimately this child will adapt to the appropriate eating patterns, the process of negotiation having been rather fraught. This was not that unusual, however, and many women had capitulated to their children's refusal to eat a proper meal by providing them with food they would eat, such as chips and fish fingers, at least a few times a week. The desire to see them *eat* overcomes the socially felt necessity that they eat a proper, family meal.

> I do often have to do special meals for Kirsten which I vowed I would never do but which I ended up doing. I found it was easier to give her what she likes and for her to eat it than to give her a plateful of something she didn't like and end up putting it in the bin because she's so stubborn she'll starve before she'll eat something.

Ensuring that children eat proper meals is clearly not only about ensuring that they are well-nourished. It is also part of the process of socialization through which they learn not only behaviour that is socially acceptable but also about the social relations which constitute families. These relations are unequal in terms of power and the allocation of tasks, both power and tasks being differentiated along lines of gender and age. In consuming proper meals children are acquiescing to the social relations within which they are consumed and in teaching children to eat in this way women and men are teaching them about the social order. [. . .]

Conclusion

My co-researcher, Marion Kerr, and myself have shown elsewhere that food consumption within families differs according to age and gender and between families according to class. We have also shown that the social status of individuals is reflected in the food and drink that they consume.[23] The differences of consumption between women and men are often related to the 'fact' that men go out to work and women stay at home. Thus, the gender division of labour associated with family ideology is used as justification for women's and men's different access to the resource of food within the home.[24] Here I have explored further the relation between family ideology and food within households and contrasted this ideology, as it is expressed by women, with what actually happens within households at mealtimes. In certain important respects, practices within families conform to family ideology. This is particularly clear in the area of food preparation and cooking which is carried out mainly by women while full-time paid employment is largely undertaken by men. The gender division of labour, therefore, conforms to family ideology. Indeed we would expect families at this stage in the life cycle to conform more closely to this pattern than those at different stages. The expectations of women were also that their families would lead a 'normal' family life. Among other things this involves women cooking and caring for men and children and creating a loving and happy environment for men to come home to after a hard day's work. Part of this is to be achieved by the whole family sharing the main meal of the day and talking to each other about the day's events. This, however, is where the 'ideal' no longer fuses with the reality, harmony is not the norm and conflict can, and often does, erupt at mealtimes. However, although this may not accord with women's views of how meals ought to be conducted, it reveals the unequal relations of power and authority which are an integral part of family ideology and which structure every aspect of the family meal, from who does the cooking to what food is served, the form it takes and the time at which it is eaten. The process of socialization which takes place at mealtimes, therefore, is a process of learning not only about appropriate ways of behaving in terms of eating, but also about appropriate relations between fathers, mothers and children. Men's authority and women's subordination is symbolized in the provision of the proper meal and in learning to accept the meal children are also internalizing important lessons about the social relations which constitute families.

Notes

1. M. Barrett, *Women's Oppression Today*: *Problems in Marxist-feminist analysis*, London: Verso, 1980, p. 204.
2. M. Henwood, L. Rimmer and M. Wicks, *Inside the Family*: *Changing roles of men and women*, Occasional Paper 6, London: Family Policy Studies Centre, 1987; J. Brannen and G. Wilson, eds, *Give and Take in Families*: *Studies in resource distribution*, London: Allen and Unwin, 1987.
3. M. Douglas, ed., *Food in the Social Order*, New York: Rusell Sage Foundation, 1984.
4. DSS Form A6(LT), 1988.
5. Matrimonial Causes Act, 1973, cited in P. Bromley and N. Lowe, *Bromley's Family Law*, 7th edition, London: Butterworths, 1987.
6. N. Charles and M. Kerr, 'Just the way it is: Gender and age differences in family food consumption', in J. Brannen and G. Wilson, eds, op. cit.; N. Charles and M. Kerr, *Women*,

Food and Families, Manchester: Manchester University Press, 1988; C. Delphy, Reading 1.1, this volume; M. Kerr and N. Charles, 'Servers and providers: The distribution of food within the family', *Sociological Review*, 34: 115–57, 1986; M. Pember Reeves, *Round About a Pound a Week*, London: Virago, 1979; M. Spring Rice, *Working Class Wives: Their health and conditions*, London: Virago, 1981.

7. N. Charles and M. Kerr, 'Eating properly, the family and state benefit', *Sociology*, 20: 412–29, 1986; H. Land, 'Poverty and gender: The distribution of resources within the family', in M. Brown, ed., *The Structure of Disadvantage*, London: Heinemann, 1983; M. Pember Reeves, op. cit.

8. N. Charles and M. Kerr, 1987, op. cit.; N. Charles and M. Kerr, 1988, op. cit.

9. Beeton, 1906, quoted in M. Barrett, op. cit., p. 209.

10. J. Brannen and G. Wilson, eds, op. cit.; N. Charles and M. Kerr, 1988, op. cit.; C. Glendinning and J. Millar, eds, *Women and Poverty in Britain*, Hemel Hempstead: Harvester Wheatsheaf, 1987; M. Kerr and N. Charles, op. cit.; J. Pahl, 'The allocation of money and the structuring of inequality within marriage', *Sociological Review*, 31: 237–62, 1983.

11. M. Blaxter and E. Patterson, *Mothers and Daughters: A three generation study of health attitudes and behaviour*, London: Heinemann, 1982; A. Murcott, 'The social significance of the "cooked dinner" in South Wales', *Social Science Information*, 21: 677–95, 1982.

12. See, for example, C. Glendinning and J. Millar, eds, op. cit., p. 18.

13. V. Beechey and E. Whitelegg, eds, *Women In Britain Today*, Milton Keynes: Open University Press, 1986; M. Henwood, L. Rimmer and N. Wicks, op. cit.; J. Martin and C. Roberts, *Women and Employment: A lifetime perspective*, Department of Employment/Office of Population Census and Surveys, London: HMSO, 1984.

14. N. Charles, 'An analysis of the ideology of women's domestic role and its social effects in modern Britain', Unpublished PhD Thesis, University of Keele, 1979; J. Lewis, *Women In England, 1870–1950*, Hemel Hempstead: Harvester Wheatsheaf, 1984.

15. L. Althusser, 'Ideology and ideological state apparatuses: notes toward an investigation', in *Lenin and Philosophy*, London: New Left Books, 1971.

16. N. Charles and M. Kerr, 1988, op. cit.; M. Kerr and N. Charles, op. cit.

17. H. Graham, 'Women's poverty and caring', in C. Glendinning and J. Millar, eds, op. cit.

18. N. Charles and M. Kerr, 1986, op. cit.; N. Charles and M. Kerr, 1988, op. cit.

19. N. Charles and M. Kerr, 1988, op. cit.

20. C. Lasch, *Haven in a Heartless World*, New York: Basic Books, 1977.

21. R. Dobash and R. Dobash, *Violence Against Wives: The case against the patriarchy*, Shepton Mallet: Open Books, 1980.

22. N. Elias, *The Civilising Process: The history of manners*, Oxford: Blackwell, 1978.

23. M. Kerr and N. Charles, op. cit.; N. Charles and M. Kerr, 1987, op. cit.; N. Charles and M. Kerr. 1988, op. cit.

24. N. Charles and M. Kerr, 1988, op. cit.

2.3 □ *Peter Corrigan*

Unlike foodstuffs, clothes are thought of more as individual possessions – hence their circulation within the domestic economy helps to cast light on the relationships between familial and personal consumption. Peter Corrigan's investigation demonstrates gendered and generational dynamics in operation, particularly the ways in which teenage daughters' assertions of individual style are a means of signifying independence from their mothers.

Gender and the gift: the case of the family clothing economy

My interest in families grew from a prior concern with the sociology of dress. While investigating some wardrobe contents as part of a pilot study, I noticed that between a quarter and a third of all items present had not been self-purchased on the market by their owners, but obtained from other sources. These other sources turned out to be overwhelmingly family members. Clothes appeared to be used as a way of displaying family links through, for example, a gift of an item of clothing from mother to daughter. But a gift is just one form of the more general category of circulation. Consequently, it was decided to examine *all* forms of clothing circulation within families.

The research was carried out in Dublin in 1983–4, and the sample is depicted in Figure 1. Introduction to the Kennedy and Cash families was obtained through the intermediary of a cousin, who also happened to be a friend of the author. Items of clothing had been exchanged between these two families at various times in the past. When I discovered that Helena Cash regularly shopped for clothes with her friend Astrid Murphy, I asked for and obtained access to the Murphy family, and when it became clear that Lydia Murphy acted in the same way with her sisters, I also interviewed them. In this way, a sample based on kin and clothing was generated. I was introduced to the Robinsons through the daughter Kerstin, who frequently acted as baby-sitter for a friend of this writer, but failed to extend the sample from here. With the exception of the middle-class Robinsons, all the families were from a skilled working-class background. There were no instances of unemployment in the sample. Family members commented individually on photographs in the family album and on items of clothing in their wardrobes, as well as responding to a more structured interview. All talk was taped.

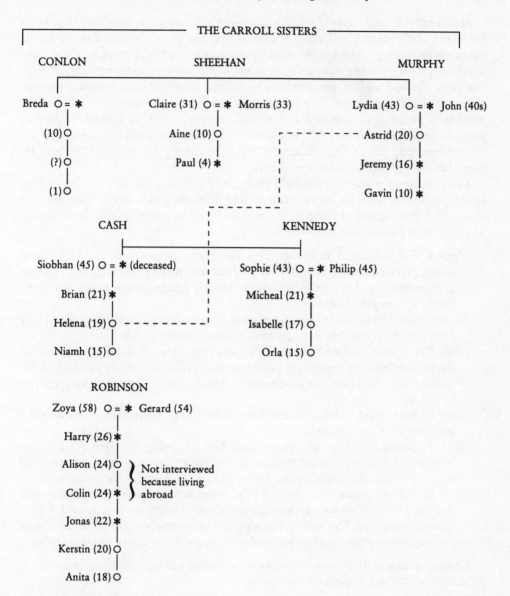

—————— THE CARROLL SISTERS ——————

CONLON   SHEEHAN   MURPHY

Breda O = *   Claire (31) O = * Morris (33)   Lydia (43) O = * John (40s)

(10) O   Aine (10) O   Astrid (20) O

(?) O   Paul (4) *   Jeremy (16) *

(1) O   Gavin (10) *

        CASH   KENNEDY

Siobhan (45) O = * (deceased)   Sophie (43) O = * Philip (45)

Brian (21) *   Micheal (21) *

Helena (19) O – – – – – – – –   Isabelle (17) O

Niamh (15) O   Orla (15) O

    ROBINSON

Zoya (58) O = * Gerard (54)

Harry (26) *

Alison (24) O   ⎫ Not interviewed
                  ⎬ because living
Colin (24) *   ⎭ abroad

Jonas (22) *

Kerstin (20) O

Anita (18) O

NOTE: Dashed line indicates
      friends who shopped for
      clothes together

        O = Female
        * = Male

Figure   1

At first sight, it might appear obvious that every individual has their 'own' wardrobe (by 'wardrobe' I mean a collection of clothes that any given individual in the family considers to 'belong' to them). We might expect, then, to find a number of exclusive wardrobes corresponding with given persons. It will be convenient to start out from this initial idea and see how the connection is upheld, modified or undermined through empirical clothing practices. The following are the individual to individual relations possible in the families researched, and we will consider each in the light of the clothing practices associated with them: (1) Husband–wife; (2) father–son; (3) father–daughter; (4) mother–son; (5) mother–daughter; (6) sister–sister; (7) brother–brother; (8) sister–brother; (9) family members–others.

The circulatory patterns discussed below are of course valid only for the current sample, and other samples may provide different forms. It is unlikely, however, that many other basic forms of circulation could be found in contemporary Irish society. The following modes were discovered:

Mode A: Gift purchased on market. This includes purchases made on special occasions (overwhelmingly birthdays and Christmas in the current sample) as well as more mundane buys, such as mothers regularly bringing home items of clothing for their younger children.

Mode B: Gift family made. This form includes any item of clothing made by any family member that has been given to another family member.

Mode C: Commodity family made. This quite rare category includes such cases as the paid ordering of items from family members who have clothes-making skills.

Mode D: Cast-offs. These comprise items of clothing originally, but no longer, worn by the donor.

Mode E: Borrowing. Taking an item for wearing on particular occasions with the permission of the 'owner'.

Mode F: Stealing. Taking an item *without* first obtaining the permission of the 'owner'. This does not imply *permanent* possession, but 'stealing' will be retained as it is the term the interviewees themselves use to describe the practice.

Mode G: Self-purchased. As a general rule, it has been assumed that all items *not* described by their 'owners' as having been obtained by methods A through F have been self-purchased. The *transition* to self-purchasing turns out to be one of the pivotal moments of mother–daughter sartorial relations, and this will be discussed below.

Let us now look at the flow patterns of the circulating garments in the separate family relationships. We will begin with the spouses.

(1) Husband–wife

The most remarkable thing about husband–wife sartorial relations is the fact that they take place exclusively in Mode A, with wife giving husband a much greater variety of clothing than the reverse. Shirts were the most frequent gift from wife to husband, but cardigans, jackets, sweaters, pants, pyjamas, socks, ties and underwear also figured. Only cardigans and sweaters flowed in the opposite direction.

Even when sharing the same physical closet space, there seemed to be no cases of one wearing an item belonging to the other. During the marriage, wife sometimes bought husband clothing on an everyday basis as well as on special occasions such as birthdays and Christmas, while husband bought wife gifts of clothing only on the latter two days. So while the woman's giving is at least sometimes a *mundane* event, the man's takes place only on *special* occasions. This may be linked to the fact that all the married women in the sample were housewives and all the married men employed outside the home, thus mapping domestic (including clothing matters) and non-domestic spheres onto women and men respectively. So strongly was clothing considered to belong to the female sphere that Morris Sheehan remarked that 'all the Carroll kids are well dressed' by their mothers – using the *original* family name of the three married sisters in the sample to characterize their dressed children.

Wife's mundane buying is best represented by the Sheehans. According to Claire, 'I bring home clothes for Morris so Morris'll have clothes, otherwise he wouldn't bother', and indeed Morris claimed to get presents of 'everything' from her. The Robinsons and the Murphys also saw a certain amount of mundane gifts although at a much lower level of intensity. As we will see below, mundane gifts are more typical of the mother/younger child relationships found in the sample, and engaging in this sort of relationship with a husband might not always be appreciated. So relations between spouses have a tendency to remain at the ceremonial level.

(2) Father–son

There was very little incidence of direct purchase of clothes by fathers for sons: a single example of football gear given to Gavin Murphy on his last birthday. Mode C was also extremely exceptional.[1] Mode D – the cast-off – being seemingly the closest to a 'typical' father–son sartorial relation. Cardigans, jackets, sweaters and ties flowed from older to younger here.

Sons' gifts to fathers were limited to shirts and ties, and tended only to happen in collaboration with the latter's sisters (i.e. *joint* gifts) and then only on birthdays or at Christmas: lone male sartorial gift-giving was quite rare in the sample, and usually met with resistance, as we will later discover. Compared to the relations discussed below, there was very little mutual borrowing or swopping of clothes between fathers and sons, whether their clothes tended to follow similar styles or not. Modes E and F were found only in the case of Jonas Robinson: on the rare occasions he wears a suit, he borrows his father's ties 'because I don't have any'. He might borrow a shirt of his father's 'an odd time' but would do so only secretly, never asking permission ('I'd keep it a big secret'). This is in contrast with 'open stealing' we will come across below.

(3) Father–daughter

There is also very little interaction between fathers and daughters in the area of clothing. Contemporary cases of fathers giving clothes to their daughters in Mode A (jumpers, a coat) were extremely rare, while there was only a single instance of Mode D (a shirt). *Money* tends to be provided, but this implies a different type of relationship. In the mother–daughter relation, there is a tendency for mothers to cease giving clothes and begin giving money, while fathers only ever give money.

Relations in the other direction were confined to Modes A and F. The former, consisting of shirts, socks and ties, took place only on birthdays and at Christmas, and only from the Robinson and Kennedy sisters. The more everyday Mode F (cardigans, jumpers) was confined to the same people, excepting Anita Robinson. No explanations of Mode F were offered, with Philip Kennedy wondering why they 'just take without permission' and his daughter Isabelle stating merely that 'he's well used to me taking his clothes'.

(4) Mother–son

Just two Modes are involved in this: to put it bluntly, mothers give and sons receive. Mode B (cardigans, jumpers) is more typical of mothers past making for children under 12, rarer for teenage boys or young men. Large numbers of knitted garments were made for small children: Sophie Kennedy claims to have knitted *all* her children's clothes 'when they were young' (confirmed by Philip and Isabelle), while Harry Robinson stated that his mother 'knitted a lot' for the children. The Carroll sisters had no clothes-making skills.

Where mothers cease to make direct purchases of clothing items for their daughters after a certain age (see below), most continue to do so in the case of their sons. With Brian Cash, Mode A is restricted to shirts and sweaters on birthdays and at Christmas, but a more everyday event with the Robinsons and the Murphys. Contrasting them with her daughters, Zoya Robinson said that 'the boys are different, I *have* bought them clothes'.

With the Murphys, Mode A relations take on a remarkably stable periodicity: every Friday, Lydia Murphy goes shopping with her sisters and *invariably* buys clothes for her sons (jumpers) – but never her daughter. I found such frequent buying difficult to believe at first, but the rest of her family (including two of her sisters) confirmed it.

In general, the evidence is that children of both genders receive clothes from the mother in the early years of life but it is only with sons that this initial relation is continued beyond the age of about 12 or 13. Michael Kennedy, according to his mother, 'wouldn't wear' what she might buy him. But this is much more typical of the mother–daughter relation, as we will now see.

(5) Mother–daughter

Broadly speaking, there are two phases to the mother–daughter relation: an earlier one where the mother, her direct family or friends act as more or less exclusive sources of clothes, and a later one (after about 13) where daughters *refuse* clothes bought or made by the mother, sometimes begin to take clothes the mother acquired for herself, and almost invariably begin to swop clothes with non-familial girlfriends of their own age. [. . .]

In all cases, a point came where the daughters would no longer accept clothes from the mother: 'They change completely after the confirmation' (which takes place at about 13 or 14 in Ireland) was how Sophie Kennedy put it on several occasions, while Zoya Robinson also stated that confirmation marked the last occasion she dressed her daughters. For most of the mothers in the sample, this transition point was the source of some problems. As this transition seems to be one of the central sartorial events in family life, it merits further illustration. Two examples follow, the first an extract from an interview with Siobhan Cash:

[. . .]

SC: I'd ( ) and yih see it started with me that, I'd ehm I'd buy something for them and I think, I'll ehm I'd bring it home and I'd surprise them and they'd look at me and say mam are yih mad? I wouldn't *wear* that and I'd be disappointed, I'd be expecting them to say that's great and I love it and kissing my hand for thinking about them and every-thing, but it didn't always *work* like that. They just had a different taste, they would, they would just have their own kind of thing about clothes and that's it, yih know.

Zoya Robinson had a very similar story to tell:

PC: What sorts of clothes do you give to your kids now as gifts, or would you at all?
ZR: Well I'll be honest and say that I am afraid to buy a handkerchief, for any of the girls, and I really mean that now because if you bought as much as a handkerchief you'd find that the hem would be too narrow, or, there was a blue dot in it and they really would have preferred a red dot, and. I hate not being able to buy them, like for Christmas now I like to go into town, buy the present, have it as a surprise for Christmas, but there's no way I'd do that, because I wouldn't run the risk of them not liking it and it's amazing what they don't like, little, what you think is lovely they can just, you know *by* them that they don't like it yih know. I remember buying a nightdress for Kerstin was it Kerstin? yes it was, just about two years ago now, and it was a grandfather style which she had said she would like and I bought this in Clery's and I thought it was very nice, and it was expensive for a nightdress and I gave it to her and I knew by her that, she wasn't so keen on it so I said to her well now if you don't like it, bring it back and you can get something instead of it. And eh, she went in to Clery's, and she didn't see anything she liked now even though Clery's is a big department store there was nothing in it, so I said to her well then I'll keep it and give it to somebody else and I'll give you the money and you can buy it for yourself. And she went off to town and she arrived home, full of enthusiasm, just got exactly what I wanted, and she opened the bag, what she took out was a shirt, a white shirt yih know with a sort of vaguely stiff in the front, which I think was second hand, that men used to wear them as dress shirts. And that's what she bought like, I'd say if I had got it for nothing I wouldn't've thought of buying it for her. So I never buy anything for the girls now, literally.

What sorts of mother–daughter sartorial relations are sketched in the above stories? It can be shown that the stories consider the problems mothers face in coming to terms with the emergence of independent daughterly sartorial theoreticity, to borrow a term ('theoreticity') from McHugh. For him,

Members generally make a distinction between knowing what they are doing (theoretic action) in the sense that the actor can be said to formulate what he is doing in terms of some rule or criterion; and not knowing what they are doing (practical action), in the sense that the actor is unable to so formulate what he is doing.[2]

He locates the transition from practical to theoretic action in the movement from younger to older children.[3] In terms of *sartorial* theoreticity, we can locate the same transition at about age 13 in Dublin families. For McHugh, theoreticity implies the possibility of deviance – one can only be deviant if one knows what one is doing and other choices were available ('conventionality'). Although they do not use the term, the mothers in the present sample were faced with 'deviant' teenage daughters whose *independent* sartorial theoreticities proved difficult to accept.

Siobhan's is the simpler narrative and speaks about her children in general terms, where Zoya's story concerns a specific incident which is used to illustrate her general point. Siobhan wishes to 'please them', but this is no longer possible. Her views on appropriate sartorial gifts to daughters are called into question in a most strong manner: 'mam are yih mad?'. Despite her disappointment, she *accepts* her children's different views.

Zoya's narrative was provoked by practically the same interviewer question, and begins with a statement of the general situation. Her inability to give her daughters appropriate – as they would see it – gifts is dramatized by the supposed rejection of a handkerchief because of some small details that were 'wrong'. The implication would seem to be that if fault could be found with even such a tiny gift then there would be no point in attempting a larger one. The example establishes different mother–daughter sartorial theoreticities in terms of disagreements over the appropriateness of small details such as narrow hems or blue dots: sophisticated theoreticities are thus implied for both sides. Zoya clearly has difficulty in understanding the clash of sartorial theoreticities between mother and daughters: 'it's amazing what they don't like'. She then illustrates this with a detailed example.

The story about Kerstin's nightdress begins with apparent coincidence of mother–daughter sartorial theoreticities: 'which she had said she would like'. The eventual gift is not appreciated, and Zoya suggests an exchange. This was unsuccessful, however. Not only was the gift of the mother rejected, but nothing suitable was found *anywhere* in the store the mother chose to visit to buy her gift. Here, there is a daughterly rejection not only of the original gift, but also of all possible gifts that could be obtained from the site the mother chose as repository of possible gifts. In the end, Zoya is forced to offer money. Kerstin's subsequent purchase – that into which she transformed the money-gift of the mother – was 'exactly what I (Kerstin) wanted'. Zoya's reaction to this indicates complete lack of understanding of her daughter's sartorial theoreticity: 'I'd say if I had got it for nothing I wouldn't 've thought of buying it for her'. This episode appears to mark the end of the mother's buying: 'So I never buy anything for the girls now, literally'.

Both Siobhan and Zoya have in no uncertain terms been prevented by their daughters from making sartorial purchases for the latter, and both, although clearly hurt and a little puzzled, accept the situation. It would seem that the independent attainment of daughterly sartorial theoreticity lies through the refusal of motherly gifts of clothing and the acceptance by the latter of their daughters' ways.

Sophie Kennedy now also gives her daughters money to buy clothes rather than giving them actual garments. So the shift to giving money rather than clothes seems to be a major component of the transition period.

The motherly difficulty in accepting that the sartorial theoreticities of their daughters are quite different to their own seems to be exacerbated by claims that their sartorial relations with their *own* mothers were quite unproblematic. Zoya Robinson maintained that there was 'no bone of contention' over apparel and that 'shopping for clothes with my mother was a pleasant experience', while Sophie Kennedy and Claire Sheehan made similar claims. There is a shift, then, from mother–daughter *consensus* to mother–daughter *conflict*. When the mothers interviewed were younger, mother–daughter sartorial theoreticity was *shared* (more accurately, the daughters would have been considered non-theoretical: only the mother would have exercised theoreticity). Now, mothers and daughters have different sartorial theoreticities and the latter clearly risk coming into conflict at certain times.[4]

What of the daughters' accounts of the above problems? Although considerably less expansive or articulate about the matter (from which one might deduce that the said matter caused few problems for them now), almost all confirmed that they did indeed now refuse to wear anything bought for them by their mothers. The refusal appears to have little or nothing to do with any concrete characteristic of the actual item that might be bought, so it would be reasonable to infer that the refusal is tied rather to the fact that the item of clothing was given by the mother. That is, the *source* of the gift and the subsequent relation between mother and daughter mediated by this gift – and not the gift itself as particular type of concretely existing object – lies at the base of the reason for refusal. This should be particularly clear after the analysis of Zoya's attempted nightdress-gift to Kerstin.

Mother–daughter relations in the other direction are generally quite restricted. Mode A relations take place only on birthdays and at Christmas and are frequently joint presents from two sisters. It may be noted that daughters tend to give accessories rather than clothing to their mothers, scarves and gloves being particularly good examples of this. The scarf can lay claim to being the most typical form Mode A relations take: Kerstin and Anita Robinson and Orla and Isabelle Kennedy each purchased them as joint gifts.

Mode E relations [. . .] are confined to the Cashs, and in fact veer between Modes E and F: if Siobhan is home they will ask her permission to borrow, if not they will just take. This is much more typical of sister–sister relations, as we will now see.

(6) Sister–sister

Sisterly clothing circulation patterns in the sample were found to fall into two quite distinct modes, each corresponding to a generational difference. Mode A relationships predominated among sisters who were themselves mothers, while teenage/young adult sisters – the daughters of these mothers – partook to a remarkably intense degree of Mode F. Furthermore, Mode A items were given only on birthdays or at Christmas, while Mode F characterizes the everyday relations of the younger generation of sisters.

Now it could be objected that the older generation of sisters did not live together in the same household while the younger generation did, and so naturally there would be more opportunity for the latter to engage in Mode F. In other words, Mode A relations would be characteristic of sisters who live apart, Mode F of those who live together. This is plausible, except that the older generation all stated quite clearly that Mode F relations were most atypical of *their* girlhood, whereas it is almost the defining characteristic of the younger sisters. Several of the mothers remarked that their daughters had far more clothes as teenagers now than they did at the same age, when the range of outfits included little more than the school uniform, an everyday dress and a Sunday outfit. Clearly, there was little opportunity for Mode F under such circumstances. Mode F is only possible when a sufficiently large wardrobe exists, as is now the case for most people, and presumably also only when the sisters are living under one roof.

Mode B was quite rare, and D of quite a low level compared to F.

The degree of stealing from each other's wardrobes was considerably higher among sisters than in any other relationship, and appeared to take place quite regularly: at least weekly, with Kerstin Robinson saying that 'we steal each other's clothes an awful lot' and Isabelle Kennedy claiming that 'every single day I wear something belonging to my sister'. Borrowing was quite rare in the sample, and sisters seemed almost never to ask each other's permission before taking an item of clothing. Stealing was in no case one-way, but always mutual: sisters, then, appear to engage in a *negative reciprocal gift relationship*. This was both balanced, with definite periods between theft and retaliation, and quite violent. In reply to my question about whether she ever failed to ask for her sister Niamh's permission before taking one of her garments, Helena Cash said:

HC: Yeh, and there's always war at the end of it, yih know.
PC: And would she do the same thing to you?
HC: Yeh just to get her own back. Like if I took this without asking her she'd give out to me, I could always say don't forget last week or something you took something belonging to me, so it's kind of.

Not asking permission led to 'fights with Helena' (Niamh Cash); 'causes most fights in this house' (Isabelle Kennedy); while Anita Robinson said that 'The worst rows in this house are over clothes'. Anita added that items were frequently taken 'in revenge'.

Another rather unexpected form of circulation was found among the older sisters in the sample. When sisters have children of their own, they sometimes create a new sartorial relation between themselves by a *collective* dressing of all their children, or at least those under the 'critical age'. This holds both for sisters who have clothes-making skills and those who do not. Sophie Kennedy's sisters, for example, made all the children's clothes when they were younger.[5] The Robinson children received a lot of cast-offs, from one of their aunts when they were small, a pattern also noted by

Humphries[6] in his earlier study of Dublin families, while the Carroll sisters still purchase items for their younger female offspring during a collective shopping expedition that takes place every Friday. There appears to be a very strong sense of sisterly 'collective motherhood'. As Claire Sheehan put it, 'When I say our children, I mean my sisters' children and my own children', while I have already quoted her husband's referring to 'the Carroll kids' collectively by their mothers' original family name.

(7) Brother–brother

Compared to other sartorial relationships, this one is not very intense, consisting only of Modes D and E (jackets, jumpers, shirts, ties). In general the flow of cast-off clothing tends to be age-based: from older to younger brother in the case of the Murphys, the Robinsons, and the young Morris Sheehan. It is a rare example of the non-occurrence of Mode A, the most widespread. I have much less data on fraternal sartorial relations because of the peculiarity of the sample, and none of it in elaborated form. Nevertheless, all indications are that they are not as intense as the sisterly relations described above. No incidence of joint purchase was discovered, and no 'collective fatherhood through clothes' seemed to be practised. Boys, indeed, do not appear ever to serve as the source of clothing gifts (although the instance of a 'failed' gift from brother to sister will be discussed below), except in alliance with sisters when buying for parents on birthdays or at Christmas, and their wardrobes are more closed to each other: where sisters are continually stealing one another's clothes, brothers seem only to touch clothes the other *no longer* wears or, at most, ask permission to borrow for special occasions. In the case of the Robinsons, the boys' wardrobes were 'fully interchangeable' (Harry Robinson) when they were very young, but such a typical sisterly relation seems to disappear completely.

(8) Sister–brother

In general there was very little active flow from brother to sister, while sisters gave (single or joint) gifts of clothes such as sweaters and shirts to brothers on the special occasions that are birthdays and Christmas.

[. . .]

It would appear that gifts from brothers either do not take place or are effectively refused (a 'failed gift').

(9) Family members–outsiders

Although my research design was very family-centred and little attempt was made to go outside family boundaries, all evidence from the data indicates that clothing remains very much a 'family affair'. A form of reverse proof can be found in the two cases (Cashs, Robinsons) where a non-kin friend of the mother made clothes for the children: in each instance she was called 'aunt' by the latter. In both cases the 'aunt' made clothes for her own daughters and the Cash and Robinson girls, Siobhan Cash describing the results as 'they were like sisters together' (i.e. the 'aunt's' daughters and Siobhan's). Such bestowal of fictive kinship would seem to be a way of overcoming the threat to the family implicit in a gift of clothing coming from the 'outside'.[7]

Apart from this, only daughters seem to have definite sartorial relations with non-kin. They may shop for clothes with their girlfriends and borrow items from their respective wardrobes, but we do not normally find the negative reciprocity we came across in the case of sisters. Such sartorial alliances can disrupt the family clothing economy we have identified by breaking its exclusivity.[8]

There is one case type of the family relating to a relatively anonymous external other or others, and that concerns the matter of clothing no longer worn. The Sheehans, Robinsons and Kennedys all regularly gave their old clothes to collectors from the St Vincent de Paul,[9] while the Murphys give theirs to 'an itinerant woman from Malahide' (Lydia Murphy).

General model

[. . .]

It is evident that the family clothing economy is organized along very clear gender lines. Women and girls are highly active (even though mother/daughter relations change over time), and men and boys highly passive: the latter, indeed, barely participate at all. The former are also highly active with respect to each other, and we can see very clearly that Mode F – stealing – is *the* typical sisterly mode. It is now time to consider our findings within a more general framework.

Gender and the gift relationship

Pahl[10] has written that:

> it is important that we cease to regard the household as a unit through which resources flow unimpededly; instead we need to look at particular points in the flow and at the social and economic relationships which structure the control which different members of the household have over the flow at each point.

As we have just seen, the flow turned out to be quite complex: family clothing circulation can be characterized in terms of six different modes, five of which can be classified as variant forms of the gift relationship. The exception, Mode C, occurred only once and concerned family-made commodities. How do our findings compare to earlier writings on the gift relationship? Many of them are in accord with the literature, but question the accepted status of negative reciprocity.

(i) Commodity relations

The rarity of commodity relations between kin has been remarked upon in the anthropological literature,[11] and the same seems to hold for the modern families in our sample. But why might this be so? Gregory[12] succinctly characterizes the gift/commodity distinction: 'commodity exchange establishes a relationship between the objects exchanged, whereas gift exchange establishes a relationship between the subjects'. Clearly, any attempt by a family member to engage in commodity relations with another family member amounts to replacing family-based intersubjective relations with market-based objective ones. Of course, this can be interpreted as a way of escaping from the subjective relations of the family by treating other members in the same way as any non-kin exchange partner: thus can family ties be loosened.

(ii) Buying gifts/making gifts

In an early statement, Emerson[13] distinguishes between two types of gifts in the following terms:

> The only gift is a portion of thyself. Thou must bleed for me. Therefore the poet brings his poem; the shepherd, his lamb; the farmer, corn; the miner, a gem; the sailor, coral and shells; the painter, his picture; the girl, a handkerchief of her own sewing. This is right and pleasing, for it restores society in so far to the primary basis, when a man's biography is conveyed in his gift, and every man's wealth is an index of his merit. But it is a cold, lifeless business when you go to the shops and buy me something, which does not represent your life and talent, but a goldsmith's.

This distinction is very similar to the difference between Mode A and Mode B forms of circulation, with the former referring to items obtained on the market and the latter to garments made by a family member. There is a difference, however. Emerson's categories of true gift givers refer to *professional* activities: his gifts are portions of a 'self' that is defined by particular competences. But there is nothing about, for example, 'brotherness' or 'sisterness' that would indicate the nature of gifts appropriate to these statuses. Emerson's true gifts display *social* standing and a tight fit between person and activity, but family gifts refer precisely to *family* relations and are therefore free of the person/activity coincidence. One could argue that family gifts *should* avoid the person/activity coincidence: giving a professional gift to a family member could be read as treating them as non-family. This would hold particularly on those occasions when the family (a) celebrates itself as 'the Family' (Christmas), and (b) celebrates the anniversary of individual members' arrival in the family (birthdays).[14] The same thing, however, does not hold for the case of mundane gifts, as these could be seen as part of the everyday professional activity of, say, the mother. This tends to be confirmed by the sample evidence: Mode B was quite rare at the time of the interviews, but was far more frequent when the children were young. Then, Zoya Robinson and Sophie Kennedy both knitted for their children on an everyday basis.

The transition of an object from a commodity purchased on the market to an object circulated as a gift (Mode A – the most frequent in our sample) is by no means unusual or odd, as Codere[15] and Cheal[16] point out in respect of industrial societies. But this also holds for 'primitive' societies:

> when *entering or leaving* these societies, precious objects provisionally took the form of bartered commodities at fixed, or barely fluctuating prices. *Within* each society they usually ceased to circulate as commodities, and became objects to *give or distribute* in the social process of social life, kinship relations, relations of production and power, etc.[17]

(iii) Gifts of money

We have seen that where gifts circulate *within* primitive societies[18] or families (our sample), money comes into operation at *boundaries*: those between societies[19] and between the family and the commodity economy (the sample). But money itself can become a gift, and indeed, according to Douglas and Isherwood,[20] acts as a gift in our modern societies only within the family. But giving money

> removes all traces of the persons upon whom the personal relationships of family networks depend. With the giving of money, one completely withdraws from the relationship; one has settled matters more completely than giving an object, which, by its contents, its selection, and its use maintains a wisp of the personality of the giver.

In this sense, it resembles the dangers to the family inherent in Mode C relations. If the giving of money sails uncomfortably close to the commodification of family relations, there is yet another factor at work. Schwartz[22] writes:

> the giver of the Hannukah *gelt* inevitably surrenders to the recipient a measure of control because money, unlike a particular commodity, does not presume a certain life system: it may be used in any way and thus becomes a more flexible instrument of the possessor's volition.

It is precisely this aspect of money-as-gift that daughters, in particular, turned to their advantage in the sample. By their refusal to accept gifts of clothing from the mother after the age of 13, they forced the mother to give money instead, thereby gaining autonomy in terms of their own choices. In other words, the peculiarity of money, the general equivalent of the commodity economy, as gift permits daughters to control their own clothing through making their own self-purchases on the market. But what is so undesirable about gifts of things other than the general equivalent?

(iv) The balance of indebtedness

The power relations inherent in gift-giving have often been remarked upon.[23] For Sahlins[24] 'The economic relation of giver–receiver is the political relation of leader–follower'. Yet much of the anthropological literature maintains that power aspects of the gift have no place in *family* relations.[25] Sahlins[26] refers to this as 'generalized reciprocity', and finds its ideal type in what Malinowski called 'pure' or 'free' gifts:

> an act, in which an individual gives an object or renders a service without expecting or getting any return. . . . The most important type of free gift are the presents characteristic of relations between husband and wife, and parents and children.[27]

But even if it is true that the person giving has no expectation of return, this does not rule out the power dimension: dominance is all the greater where no return can come. The latter certainly seems to play a part for the teenage daughters of the present sample: why else would they refuse gifts of clothing from the mother, if not to put an end to the motherly dominance of the clothing economy? The potlatch response – returning a greater gift – does not seem to be operative, as it implies an acceptance of the mutual relations implied in gift exchange. The teenage girls set up their *own* sartorial economies through the overthrow of the mother as source of clothing gifts and with the help of money.

Far from the family being free of the power struggle implied in the relationship, we can see the unilateral clothes gifts of the mother as one of its elementary forms. Sahlins[28] rather hesitantly seems to admit something like this:

> Often, in fact, high rank is only secured or sustained by o'ercrowning generosity: the material advantage is on the subordinate's side. Perhaps it is too much to see the relation of parent and child as the elemental form of kinship ranking and its economic ethic.

As this paper has tried to show, it is by no means 'too much'.

(v) Negative gifts

So far, we have treated the gift as positive. But gifts in negative form are also possible: Sahlins refers to this as 'negative reciprocity', and we can recognize it as the stealing – Mode F – we frequently met among the sisters in the sample. He discusses this form in detail:

> Reciprocity is inclined toward the generalized pole by close kinship, towards the negative extreme in proportion to kinship distance.
>   The reasoning is nearly syllogistic. The several reciprocities from freely bestowed gift to chicanery amount to a spectrum of sociability, from sacrifice in favor of another to self-interested gain at the expense of another . . . close kin tend to share, to enter into generalized exchanges, and distant or non-kin to deal in equivalents or in guile.[29]

But the 'nearly syllogistic' reasoning does not seem to be operative in the case of the family clothing economy: stealing does *not* correspond to increasing kinship distance. Indeed, it is hard to imagine a closer kinship relation than sister–sister, a relation characterized more than any of the others precisely by Mode F practices. Stealing among sisters, as we have seen, is not unilateral but reciprocal and thereby the exact negative image of the exchange of gifts familiar to anthropology. Where the latter is a means of binding persons (usually strangers to each other) but upholding their difference, the former is a means of binding persons (already kin-related, at least in the present case) through *abolishing* difference.

Conclusion

The parallels between primitive societies and the contemporary family appear to be quite striking in their frequency, and we can see that the family can usefully be considered in terms more usually associated with primitive exchange. Once a commodity crosses the border from the outside world to the family, it is susceptible to insertion into a gift-based economy. But why a *gift*-based economy? Why not, for example, a family economy based on individual consumption? Perhaps the answer can be found in the fact that 'the concept commodity, which presupposes reciprocal independence and alienability, is a mirror image of the concept gift, which presupposes reciprocal dependence and inalienability'.[30]

It would appear that the familial gift economy is also a *women's* economy, a point noted by Cheal[31] and many of the papers in the Brannen and Wilson[32] collection. Indeed, male passivity is striking. [. . .] But there would appear to be a difference between the circulation of food and the circulation of clothing: Delphy[33], Sen[34] and Charles and Kerr[35] all show how women tend to lose out in food distribution, but indications are that it is *men* who lose out in the clothing economy. It may be that this is linked to traditional notions of men as substance (food) and women as appearance (clothing), but I have no firm data on this point. Nevertheless, it seems as if there might be a number of economies at work in the contemporary household, each benefiting specific genders and ages in different ways.

Recognition by men that the family clothing economy *is* an overwhelmingly female area may explain mothers' continued, and generally uncontested, giving to sons. Recognition by *women* that this is so may account both for mother/daughter conflict and for the less obviously explicable mutual sisterly stealing. If this economy is feminine, then each woman would seem to need to attain her own independent control over it. I have shown elsewhere[36] that the content of mother and teenage daughter sartorial theoreticities is, despite initial appearances, identical: in the Dublin case, it consists of age-appropriate dressing. In this way, daughters reproduce their mothers' sartorial discourse. The conflict arises from daughters claiming/motherly denial of expertise in the area and from differing views on the *correct* match between age grade and clothing. This conflict seems to be the way in which daughters attain *independent* control over essentially the same schema. But where teenage/young adult sisters attempt to *differ* from their mothers, it would seem as if they lay claim to the *same* theoreticity as each other: hence, the other's clothing cannot be seen as entirely independent and stealing seems a perfectly 'natural' thing to do. That this is interpreted by sisters in conflictual terms may be due to the violation of notions of the individual wardrobe that this entails, but more evidence is needed on this point.

In conclusion, then, it would appear that this investigation of the family clothing economy confirms earlier work on the gendered aspects of resource distribution within households, but concentration on one particular good has shown that the circulatory patterns involved here are perhaps much more complex than at first supposed. Not only do men and women operate differently in this economy, but different categories of women – mothers, daughters, sisters – correspond to specific modes and directions of circulation which vary according to stages of the life course. Future research could apply itself to tracing the (presumably gendered) circulatory patterns of objects other than clothing, or begin with specific sets of social relations and account for the ways in which objects (which could include persons) circulate within them. The boundaries of object circulatory patterns are the boundaries of social worlds.

Notes

1. Mode C is quite anomalous. All other sartorial relations within the family are characterized by some variant of the gift relationship; even stealing can be reformulated as a negative gift. Commodity relations such as mode C appear to be so rare precisely because they do not quite fit into family clothing relations. The empirical instance referred to in the sample concerns Michael Kennedy's father, Philip, who brought a jumper home for his son from the clothing factory in which he worked. Michael had requested this, and given his father the money to cover the cost.
2. P. McHugh, 'A common-sense perception of deviance', in H. Dreitzel, ed., Recent Sociology No. 2, New York: Macmillan, 1970, pp. 165–6.
3. Ibid., p. 167.
4. These difficulties may be linked to the different implications for family relations implicit in the different technological states of clothing production and consumption today as compared with the time the mothers interviewed were themselves teenage girls. When the mothers were that age, a much greater proportion of clothing, at least in Ireland, originated in family-based production, and where clothing was not family-made each family generally had their 'own' dressmaker or tailor. Clothing, then, was much more under family control and mother–daughter disputes over the matter seemed rare. The much greater penetration of mass-produced items today allows for more autonomous action.
5. This seems hardly an exaggeration. Very nearly every photograph in the family album provoked comments such as 'this was made by my aunt' [mother's sister] (Isabelle and Orla Kennedy) or 'this was made by my sister' (Sophie Kennedy). The actual wardrobes contained a much lower number of aunt/sister made items, tending to confirm the idea that sartorial relations undergo a change at the age of 13 or so.
6. A. Humphries, New Dubliners: Urbanization and the Irish family, London: Routledge and Kegan Paul, 1966.
7. Fictive kinship can be seen as a way of solving the problems which arise when the relationship between A and B is characterized by practices that are seen as appropriate to a relationship between the two that is different to the 'officially' existing one. That is, the officially existing relationship is redefined: see J. Pitt-Rivers, 'Pseudo-kinship', in International Encyclopaedia of the Social Sciences, London: Macmillan, 1968, p. 409. So in the case of the

'aunt' in our sample, she is so addressed because her sartorial behaviour is appropriate to that of a mother's sister. The use of fictive kinship to overcome potentially threatening situations is mentioned by S. Mintz and E. Wolf, 'Ritual co-parenthood', in J. Goody, ed., *Kinship*, Harmondsworth: Penguin, 1971; Esther Goody sees it as a way of linking adults (the mothers and friends in the present case) and generations (the Robinson/Cash daughters and their 'aunts'). See E. Goody, 'Forms of pro-parenthood: The sharing and substitution of parental roles', in J. Goody, ed., op. cit.

8. P. Corrigan, 'Troublesome bodies and sartorial dopes: Motherly accounts of teenage daughter dress practices', *Semiotica*, 77: 393–413, 1989.

9. Again, A. Humphries, op. cit., noted the same tendency in his Dublin sample. Giving old clothes to the St Vincent de Paul seems to be a well-established Dublin tradition, and indeed the taunt 'Vincent's clothes' was used against some of the less well-dressed children at Jeremy Murphy's school.

10. J. Pahl, 'The allocation of money and the structuring of inequality within marriage', *Sociological Review*, 31: 237–62, 1983, p. 256.

11. G. Bateson, *Naven*, Stanford: Stanford University Press, 1958, p. 83; P. Bohannan and L. Bohannan, *Tiv Economy*, London: Longman, 1968, p. 147.

12. C. Gregory, *Gifts and Commodities*, London: Academic Press, 1982, p. 19.

13. R. Emerson, 'Gifts', in *Collected Works. Vol. 3*, Cambridge, MA: Harvard University Press, 1983, p. 94.

14. Cheal maintains that 'Christmas and birthdays are uniquely opportune times for staging the cult of the individual', but his analysis misses the familial dimension of these occasions. See D. Cheal, *The Gift Economy*, London: Routledge, 1988, p. 148.

15. H. Codere, 'Exchange and display', in *International Encyclopaedia of the Social Sciences*, London: Macmillan, 1968, pp. 239–40.

16. D. Cheal, '"Showing them you love them": Gift giving and the dialectic of intimacy', *Sociological Review*, 35: 150–69, 1987, p. 157.

17. M. Godelier, *Perspectives in Marxist Anthropology*, Cambridge: Cambridge University Press, 1973.

18. Ibid.

19. Ibid.

20. M. Douglas and B. Isherwood, *The World of Goods: Towards an anthropology of consumption*, Harmondsworth: Penguin, 1978, p. 59.

21. D. Cheal, 1987, op. cit., p. 165; G. Simmel, 'Prostitution', in *On Individuality and Social Forms*, Chicago: University of Chicago Press, 1971, p. 121.

22. B. Schwartz, 'The social psychology of the gift', *American Journal of Sociology*, 73: 1–11, 1967, p. 5.

23. For example, M. Mauss, *The Gift*, London: Routledge and Kegan Paul, 1969; A. Gouldner, 'The norm of reciprocity', *American Sociological Review*, 25: 161–78, 1960; G. Homans, *Social Behaviour: Its elementary forms*, London: Routledge and Kegan Paul, 1961; B. Schwartz, op. cit.

24. M. Sahlins, *Stone Age Economics*, London: Tavistock, 1974.

25. C. Gregory, op. cit.

26. M. Sahlins, op. cit.

27. B. Malinowski, *Argonauts of the Western Pacific: An account of native enterprise and adventure in the archipelagoes of Melanesian New Guinea*, London: Routledge and Kegan Paul, 1922, p. 177.

28. M. Sahlins, op. cit., p. 205.

29. Ibid., p. 196.

30. C. Gregory, op. cit., p. 24.

31. D. Cheal, 1987, op. cit.; D. Cheal, 1988, op. cit.

32. J. Brannen and G. Wilson, eds, *Give and Take in Families: Studies in resource distribution*, London: Allen and Unwin, 1987.

33. C. Delphy, Reading 1.1, this volume.
34. A. Sen, *Resources, Values and Development*, Oxford: Blackwell, 1984.
35. N. Charles and M. Kerr, 'Just the way it is: Gender and age differences in family food consumption', in J. Brannen and G. Wilson, eds, op. cit.
36. P. Corrigan, 'Backstage dressing: Clothing and the urban family, with special reference to mother/daughter relations', Unpublished PhD Thesis, Trinity College, Dublin.

3 □ *The Power Relations of Leisure and Media Reception*

3.1 □ *Rosemary Deem*

This is an extract from Rosemary Deem's larger study of women and leisure in which she draws principally on material from a two-stage research project carried out during the early 1980s in Milton Keynes. Her crucial point of departure is the obser-vation that, as a con-sequence of gendered divisions of labour, the home can have quite different meanings for men and for women.

Leisure and the household

Home leisure – the peaceful haven?

[. . .]

The home for most women, employed or not, is a workplace in a way that is true for few men, except those that do paid work from home and even in this case it is not the same thing as being a place for unpaid work. Workplaces do not convert easily into places for leisure. Especially for women who are at home all day, undone domestic chores and other aspects of housework are omnipresent. They cannot escape dirty dishes, grubby carpets and piles of dirty washing by going out of the door and escaping to another workplace as can many men; women with jobs often speak of the pleasure they take as did this one; 'in closing the door behind me when I go off to work where I can't see the dust or worry about the clutter' (school meals worker with two chil-dren, Sample B, Milton Keynes study).[1]

All members of a household are likely to see the home as a base for some leisure, but in order to make this possible it is often necessary for women to forfeit their leisure. The continued presence of household duties and obligations means that it is difficult for women to set aside time for leisure at times when others are relaxing which they can be sure will be uninterrupted. It is rare for women who live with others to have a space of their own for leisure, whereas men and frequently children too if they do not simply leave the house, often have special places to go even in cramped housing conditions – a room, a corner of the garden, a shed – where they are likely to remain undisturbed. Home-based leisure too, does not just involve those people who live in a particular household, but often involves other people, friends, acquaintances, relatives, coming into the house. Women may have little or no control over who their male partners bring to the house and indeed may have to sacrifice yet more time catering (often literally) for the needs of such visitors. Consequently women's home-based leisure and enjoyment is often based on or derives from, the same activities and tasks which form part of their work in the household, or is fitted into those tasks and activities sometimes simultaneously. Whilst men's leisure may also derive from work, it is usually from their paid rather than unpaid work and they are from the available evidence, much less likely to combine work and leisure activities simultaneously (how many men iron whilst watching TV or try to read a book whilst cooking the evening meal?). When the home is also a work place it is much more difficult to switch off from things which have to be done, to things which are chosen in their own right – you cannot easily shut up the kitchen or the undusted bedrooms or pretend that bored or hungry children are not there.

So leisure in the home is far from the idyll that some commentators (usually male) believe it to be and has to be fought for and struggled over by women in the same ways that leisure in the community has to be struggled over. No wonder then that much of women's household leisure consists of needlework, knitting, cooking, reading, TV watching, writing letters, day dreaming and snatching quick naps. All of these activities can be fitted into a fragmented time schedule, don't require large blocks of time, are cheap or free, require little space or equipment and can quickly be disposed of or stopped when work obligations intervene. Although [. . .] employment is a crucial variable in women's leisure, nevertheless within the home, almost all women whether old or young, with dependent children or adults are not, working or middle class, from an ethnic minority group or majority group, are subject to constraints and determinants on their leisure. These relate partly to male patriarchal power over women. As well as those constraints and determinants, there are further ones which result from living in a capitalist society, which is for example more interested in making a profit out of building houses than whether those houses provided a pleasurable and well-designed leisure and work environment for the people who live in them. Capitalism also invades the home in the form of consumerism; leisure at home often only *seems* private and uncommercialized (e.g. TV, video, records).

At-home leisure activities and perceptions of leisure

[. . .] Women themselves may find it difficult to decide what aspects of their lives at home are leisure, which are enjoyable through work, and which are definitely work and this has consequences for how and when they are able to relax. Men whose main employment is outside the home seem to have no such problems distinguishing between work, work related activities and obligations, and enjoyment and relaxation, nor do these categories often seem to overlap.[2] For women, however, the same activities and/or time periods may simultaneously provide both work and leisure. The context or degree of choice which enters into whether something is done or not can also help to determine whether it is seen as leisure or not. So ironing, which is mostly not seen as enjoyable, may enable some leisure because it can be combined with watching TV. Whilst cooking dinner for the household is not either seen as enjoyable or leisure, cooking a meal for friends can be both and is not regarded as work. Other activities which many women did, for example in the Milton Keynes study, such as writing letters, may not be regarded as leisure because they aren't seen as important or legitimate uses of time by other people in the household: letter-writing may also involve tasks (condolences, thank-yous) others won't undertake. Women who are in employment do seem, from the Milton Keynes research at least, more able to compartmentalize their time than women who are involved only in unpaid work, and thus exercise more control over their lives and perceive their leisure in a different way from women whose ability to control their lives [is] lessened by total financial dependence on a male income and whose unpaid work is not easily or at all compartmentalized.

The 1983 General Household Survey data on leisure activities[3] offers the gender related breakdown of home-based activities (see Table 1).

But of course this kind of data does not necessarily tell us whether all the DIY and gardening done by these individuals was enjoyable, nor whether some undertook these activities purely as work. *Social Trends* also tells us that women watch television more than men, according to research by the BBC in 1983–4, with women watching nearly four hours more than men a week in the first quarter of 1984, and nearly three hours more than men in the summer months. Women are less likely to read a daily newspaper than men but more likely to read weekly magazines (in 1983 46 per cent of women read a women's weekly magazine[4]). None of this information gives us any indication of the amount of time nor the *quality* of time that women are able to devote to these various activities. Also the GHS data is derived from prompted responses (that is, interviewees are offered certain activities and asked if they do them) which as a method is far from satisfactory. Nor of course does it tell us anything about the conditions under which home-based leisure takes place.

If we turn to the more detailed studies on women however there is only a slightly

Table 1   Home-based activities by gender, Great Britain 1983

Percentages in each group engaging in each activity in four weeks before interview	males	females
activity	%	%
listening to records and tapes	65	62
gardening	50	39
needlework, knitting	2	48
house repairs and DIY	51	24
reading books	50	61

Source: Table 10.3, *Social Trends 1985*, p. 149

greater variety of activities evident, although these are subject to all kinds of variation, including seasonality, ethnicity, social class, life cycle differences and household size. In the Milton Keynes study TV was the most popular home-based activity amongst Study A women, followed by sewing and embroidery, gardening and care of house-plants, knitting, reading and listening to the radio. In the Milton Keynes sample B, popular at-home activities during the day were reading, 'just relaxing', sitting down, watching TV, knitting, sewing, radio, sleeping and gardening. Unlike the GHS, none of these were prompted responses. Evening activities at home mostly consisted of TV and sitting down quietly when there was nothing pressing to do. But evenings [. . .] are often a busy time for women at home and such relaxation as did occur was often fleeting for the women in the Milton Keynes study. Where longer time-periods were available there was a clear preference for going out as this removed the likelihood that leisure would be interrupted by household tasks. I also asked in Study B what aspects of daily routine women found pleasurable and here playing with children emerged as an important part of pleasure in everyday life, alongside the more ubiquitous TV, reading, gardening, and relaxing, with cooking being a significant minority choice when it took the form of baking, jam making or any cookery *not* involving routine meal preparation.

In the Sheffield NOP study TV, knitting, sewing and other crafts plus reading, and sitting down 'doing nothing' were major evening and week day activities, with a preference for weekend activities to be out-of-home rather than in home, with the exception of TV viewing.[5] The Sheffield study also suggests that there are social class variations discernible in the pattern discovered, with middle class women more likely to enjoy gardening and less likely to watch TV, and working class women doing more TV watching than reading. Working class women, older women and those with dependent children were also more likely to spend evenings relaxing or doing nothing.[6] The Leeds study of Armley suggested that leisure for women there was about 'being with people, watching television, reading, drinking and playing bingo'.[7] The weekly evening time-tables of women of different backgrounds in this study reveal similar choices of at-home leisure to the Milton Keynes and Sheffield studies, although there are evident life cycle variations in the amount of leisure time spent on home-based leisure rather than out-of-home leisure. Wimbush's Scottish research[8] on well-being indicates that at-home leisure is often spent alone, with some encouragement of partners and children to go out, thus making solitude possible. On the other hand, Talbot and Dixey[9] found that women whose husbands were frequently absent from the house because of leisure involvement, rationalized this situation by developing their own home-based interests and were therefore able to contain any resentment they might otherwise have at their partners being out frequently. But Wimbush's research is worth pausing over because it stresses the extent to which what is done at home reflects the state of health and energy (or its absence) of individual women. Often tiredness limits the range of things done in the home, especially in the evenings, which may explain the lack of variation in the kinds of leisure women have at home. The Sheffield study findings confirm this view too. One of Hunt's[10] respondents in her study of a Staffordshire mining village sums up this tiredness and its effects thus:

Alan doesn't come in 'till twenty past or half past six at night. So by the time we've had tea we haven't got time to go out very far. We don't go out much. We watch the television and I do a bit of reading. *Woman* and *Woman's Own*, and I knit in between when I feel like it. Quarter past nine I feel that tired, l always have an hour and then my Ovaltine and go to bed.[11]

The lack of variety is not the only feature of home-based leisure for women. Whilst a high proportion of home-based activities or leisure involve a certain and very understandable degree of passivity (sitting down, TV, radio, cat-naps) which insofar as they are allowed to be uninterrupted are often a necessary recuperative strategy, others including gardening, sewing, knitting and embroidery actually involve production and creativity. As Delphy[12] points out, much of what is done in the household, but not remunerated, involves production as well as consumption, and indeed this applies to leisure as much as to housework (or as Delphy prefers to call it, familial work). Nor is it always the case that what is produced by home-based leisure is for the the benefit of the woman herself, although it *may* be in the case of dressmaking or sewing.

More often however it is others in the family who are recipients of things produced by women in their leisure time – garments, household items, a pleasant garden or beautiful houseplants, a cake. Just as Thompson[13] talks about the ways in which doing something creative in the form of adult education appeals to women, so does the same notion appeal to many women in the home. But this latter 'choice' is limited by many factors including the kinds of craft skills easily available to women in school, further and adult education, and the costs of materials and the way these are marketed, as well as available space and whether others in a household see these activities as a legitimate use of time.

Who does what in the household and how long does it take?

At one level this is a simple and easily answered question, but at another level it is extremely complicated because there is no straightforward definition of what constitutes household work. A lot of the current debates over the 'informal economy' (that is, the economy outside the formal one – casual work, DIY, voluntary work, etc.) have considered this question, but provided no more sophisticated answers than previously.[14] Pahl. R. talks of the various strategies adopted by households with regard to the work to be done and distinguishes between formal employment, informal employment (i.e. work for those *outside* the household, for example mending a friend's car or baking a cake for a friend) and communal/household work. But he found that the last two categories in particular presented great difficulties of definition, with the result that his Isle of Sheppey research concentrated on 'the labour that is done *for* households, including whether or not they do it themselves'.[15] Thus he drew up a list of forty-one tasks ranging from house maintenance, home improvement and routine housework to production, car maintenance and child-care. It was found that much of this work was done by the household and was not paid for, with house improvement and house extension tasks being those most frequently done and paid for in the formal market sector. Pahl also attempted a highly complicated system for exploring the division of labour between household partners. This included weighting according to whether the tasks were in practice and to what extent they are conventionally, male or female and how frequently a task is done (for example painting may be done bi-annually, making beer less that once every four months, cooking two or three times daily). Pahl's analysis of the Isle of Sheppey material, after all this, still allows him to say little more than that 'it is overwhelmingly obvious that women do most of the work in the household . . . the domestic division of labour is more unequally shared by women . . . they also do substantial *amounts* . . . there is very little variation between the classes'.[16] However Pahl did find that the employment status of women and their age far outweighed the importance of social class factors in determining the domestic division of labour, with the most asymmetrical division of labour occurring when women are not in employment and have young children. Hunt's smaller ethnographic study[17] is able to reach the same conclusion in a rather less obtuse way, but both Pahl and Hunt have done very relevant work which is not necessarily seen as being about leisure at all.

What such studies as these tell us is about the limited amount of time many women have available in the home for leisure, something which both my own research and the Sheffield study confirm, which helps to explain why women's at-home leisure activities are either those which are linked to domestic work, or are things which require no advanced preparation and can be done in short time-spells. Green, Hebron and Woodward[18] found in the Sheffield study that whilst most women in the NOP survey said that they had between two and four hours free every weekday evening, 15 per cent had under one hour per evening. Women with dependent children were found to have less free time that those without, and women under 25 and over 45 (those *least* likely to have dependent children) have most free time. Similar patterns (varying with age and dependants) were also found to be the case for weekend free time, with 65 per cent of women having five or more hours of free time, but women with dependent children having least.

Time budget studies also offer some insights into the tasks women have to do and the amount of time left over, although as Pahl. R.[19] and Wyatt[20] have pointed out, time budget studies do have limitations, not least of which is a failure on the part of respondents to include simultaneous activities in their time diaries and failure to record some activities at all. Time budget studies prior to 1975 show that although the amount of domestic work was decreasing over the post-war decades, women were still doing most of the work, and as Pahl. R.[21] says of these studies, 'while men are doing more non-routine work in terms of domestic maintenance and improvement, their contribution to the routine domestic tasks is still in the order of "helping" rather than any substantial shift to true role reversal'. Maynard[22] says also that 'More recent research shows women spending amounts of time on domestic tasks, to the extent that if it was paid employment it would certainly be regarded as full time'. All the time budget data suggests that the longest working week of any person is that of employed women, even though their absence outside the home ensures that they do fewer hours of housework than non-employed women. Finch's [23] perceptive study of the incorporation of women into their husbands' jobs, offers a nice illustration of this in the following extract from the diary of the wife of a clergyman, who (unusually for a cleric's wife) had a full-time job as a primary school teacher:

Day: Monday
   Got up at: 7.30

Morning:
   7.30 to 8.30   Prepared husband's lunch and pre-set it in cooker.
                               Breakfast
   8.30 to 12.00   At school
   Lunch at 12.30   On duty

Afternoon:
   1.00 to 4.00   At school
   4.00 to 4.30   Cup of tea and crossword
   4.30 to 5.30   Cleaned landing and stairs and washed down all the paint work.
                               Prepared tea.
   Evening meal at: 6.00

Evening:
   7.00 to 9.30   Weekly ironing
   9.30 to 10.30   Watched TV and discussed church cleaning for tomorrow
   Went to bed at   11.00[24]

This woman's free time thus consisted of half an hour after finishing teaching, and one hour much later in the evening, with the latter being interrupted by having also to discuss something connected with her husband's (but not her) job. For many women in similar situations, this is an all too familiar scene. As Delphy[25] argues, the problem of housework is not exhausted by looking at the tasks and duties which it consists of; it is 'a certain *work relationship*, a particular relationship of production, it is all the work done unpaid for others within the confines of the household'. Time budget studies can tell us about the tasks it involves, and something about the time that is thus taken up, but they offer only a limited insight into the kinds of relationships between women and men which underlie that work and time division. I do not want at this point to get into the debates which Delphy and others are engaged in about who benefits from women's household work, but whether it is men alone or capitalism alone or both, there is no doubt that women themselves benefit little and that the necessity to do household work quite dramatically affects women's free time and their leisure.

The task, time and complicated relationships implicated in household work increases still further when a household contains dependent children[26] or sick or disabled adult dependants.[27] As Berk and Berk[28] show, although male partners do get involved in child-care, this is often the more pleasant tasks such as playing, rather than nappy changing or feeding or washing. Where men are significantly involved in the more mundane aspects of childcare, it is often because they are unemployed or are middle class fathers with professional jobs, flexible hours and a political commitment to gender equality in the household.[29] But for women, child-care is double edged anyway – it both prevents them from having leisure or much leisure, and is a source of enjoyment in itself, both in terms of children's play and company.[30] Also, as one woman in the Dixey and

Talbot[31] study said, 'Children help you discover all sorts of things. You wouldn't dream of going out and putting a pair of ice-skates on but when you've got children with you you don't think twice about it.' Adult dependants such as ageing relatives or a sick or handicapped husband however are much more likely to destroy leisure than to provide it, especially since such 'caring' work is seen to be properly the task of women. As Ungerson[32] demonstrates, the nature of caring for the sick, mentally-ill and disabled and the time this takes are extremely demanding and usually undertaken by females alone. Where it is a handicapped child that requires care, Ungerson's material suggests fathers may help with tasks like lifting, but not with washing, feeding or nappy-changing.

Time, tasks and the nature of the relationships underlying caring and housework then can be seen to be significant constraints on the leisure of many women, although there are of course life cycle variations in this.

Household routines and leisure

One of the arguments that used to be used by sociologists of leisure about housewives was that as they were largely responsible for organizing their own day's work, they therefore had more freedom than others (i.e. those in paid employment) for organizing their work and leisure.[33] This argument has also surfaced again more recently.[34] Such arguments ignore the extent to which housework and child-care are actually organized around and made necessary by sets of power relationships, principally those between men and women. As Delphy[35] points out, there is a big difference between the work which an individual does to sustain themselves in their household and the work which is necessary to sustain others. The former is not really housework or familial work but the latter is, and is made more difficult by the fact that it then has to satisfy others' demands and ideas about how it should be done. Thus while a young single woman living alone can decide for herself whether to dust or hoover the carpet, a woman with a male partner and children, especially if she is financially dependent on the man, has also to take into consideration the effects on those other household members and on herself if she does not carry out certain tasks.

Dixey and Talbot[36] argue that whilst women are aware that there is some degree 'in practice' of autonomy involved in housework, in fact they rarely make use of this (that is, the power relationships and ideologies surrounding it are influential). In addition to setting their own standards (the Leeds study found women who preferred to wash by hand even though they had washing machines because they felt hand washing got clothes cleaner), 'housewives are reminded each day of the standards they are expected to reach. If not from husbands and children, from the television, magazines, hoardings and from other women; housewives are bombarded with images of standards which they cannot reach'.[37] These standards often involve setting up weekly and monthly lists of tasks and organizing some aspects of housework round a routine which though it may frequently be broken by children or by husbands' unexpected arrivals, departures or demands, is rarely broken for reasons to do with women's personal leisure. Not only this, but the nature of housework is that much of it is repetitive and once done soon needs redoing. [. . .]

> sometimes I will get finished early, before the kids get home, and I'll sit down in the front room with a magazine – but then I'd often start looking at the nets or the carpet and think – maybe I should have washed the nets or hoovered round again – more often than not having thought of it I put down my book and go and do it (woman with three children, Milton Keynes study B, no paid employment).

In the Milton Keynes research I found that women with no paid employment and who claimed not to be currently seeking a job (a category I am aware is problematic) [. . .] were the most likely to have organized their housework into a routine, which both structured their day and possibly allowed them a small amount of space for themselves. Women with jobs had less need for a routine in the house because they already had a more immutable structure provided by the times during which they were at their jobs, and housework as well as leisure had to be fitted into what was left over. The Sheffield study found that almost half the women interviewed in the NOP survey had no free time during the day at all (weekends excepted) and that the likelihood of this was greatest (not least) amongst those *in employment*. Those who did have free time said they took it when they could, rather than trying to plan it in advance. But having free time and feeling able to use it *as you wish* are not the same, and even those women who do have time available to them in the day may only use it for certain kinds of activities, involving either their own homes or the homes of friends and relatives, rather than out-of-home leisure.

Women do not, as I have already indicated, act as free agents in determining their own routines when they live in households with men and/or children. Even where they live alone, the ideologies of marriage and female roles are still influential. Men's jobs and leisure interests were a significant determinant of what women were able to do in their nonwork time in the Milton Keynes study, influencing when and whether leisure was possible on a regular and predictable basis. As Finch[38] shows, some male jobs (including self-employment) are so all-encompassing both of their encumbent and his wife that very little in the way of leisure may be planned by the women concerned. Certain kinds of jobs, for instance those of the clergy, armed forces and police may even determine who women may make friends with and who not. Shift work or work which involves long periods of time away from home (oilrig workers, those with jobs abroad, merchant seamen, etc.) can also seriously disrupt women's free time and cause radical rearrangements of the time spent and what is involved in doing housework. Children's school hours and out-of-school activities may also have the same effect. But it is not only the appearance or absence of others in the household at particular times which affects women; it is also their presence. Studies of unemployed men suggest that one source of strain is that women used to being at home all day on their own find it hard to get used to having men around too[39] because this destroys not only their routine but also even the illusion of autonomy. Murcott[40] has also drawn attention to the ways in which men's expectations about meals and women's own ideas about 'a proper meal' in South Wales (i.e. 'meat and veg', not beans on toast or fish and chips) may also influence what women expect to do in the way of cooking and how long this will take them. Employed working class men in manual jobs are expected to require, and indeed expect themselves, a substantial meal at least once a day. Delphy[41] notes this tendency in French peasant families where men also have to have the best cut of meat or the largest portion and significant attention is paid to preparing their meal. Cooking 'proper' meals takes time and usually has to be set into a routine which takes into account a man's working hours (which may be variable or unsocial) and shopping as well as preparation.

Ideologies about female gender roles and marriage, as well as the power relations of households and the structures of family life, are very influential on women's at-home leisure. Household routines and their structuring around other household members, are also a significant factor shaping what leisure time a woman has available to her, when and the quality of that time. Although much housework is predictable and repetitive, in households of several people there are always likely to be contingencies which upset or alter any routine which has been established. It is this unpredictability and fragmentation which women (especially those without paid employment of their own which can form time boundaries around which they are not available for housework) may find difficult to manage in terms of setting aside time where they are able to choose what to do or whether to do anything at all, quite apart from the extent to which women's leisure is seen by the rest of the household as at all legitimate.[42]

[. . .]

Homes as places for leisure

[. . .] There are many reasons why women are likely to have at-home leisure. It is usually cheaper, easier and requires no travel or transport; at-home activities or interests can be more easily adjusted than out-of-home ones to fit the requirements of domestic obligations, child-care commitments and the needs of other dependants, and there are likely to be fewer objections from male partners, especially if that leisure takes place when they are out. But as Glyptis and Chambers[43] pointed out when embarking on their ESRC/Sports Council sponsored 'Leisure in the Home' project, the home

> must accommodate individual and communal activity, and perhaps several activities simultaneously for different members of the household . . . Few people have the luxury of designing or fitting a home principally with leisure needs in mind . . . But the leisure opportunities and constraints posed by the physical characteristics of the home and its immediate surroundings must critically affect the quality of leisure of its occupants.

They suggest that there are a number of attributes of homes which affect leisure, including size, division of space into indoor and outdoor, design (layout and access to rooms, as well as competing uses of space), flexibility, and the way space is managed by the household. For most women the only space (in other than single households) which is likely to be given over to them is the kitchen, which at busy times of the day is likely to offer anything but a peaceful haven and whose design is often oriented to servicing a household rather than towards providing privacy and a basis for leisure.

My Milton Keynes in-depth interview data [. . .] suggested that even where house-holds were living in small houses (in Milton Keynes these are mostly privately built rather than rental houses which despite some other disadvantages, have tended to be spacious) men and children often had some space they could call their own – a bedroom, shed, allotment, corner of the garden or garage, or in middle class house-holds even a study, but that women rarely had such a space. Kitchens, as I have already suggested, whilst often occupied by women, do not provide privacy or solitude quite apart from the other disadvantages associated with being in a place designed for and used as a work-base. Cookery and listening to the radio apart, there are few solitary, leisure activities which are happily located in a kitchen unless it is exceptionally large. Partly this is because the kitchen is an ever-present reminder of undone chores. Although women who are at home during the day in a household where other members are out at work or school theoretically have access to the whole of their home during that time, during winter or cold weather this may be of little use if the rooms thus avail-able are cold and unheated. Several women in the course of my interviews said that although their house had central heating, reasons of economy (sometimes imposed by male partners safely out of freezing cold homes during the day and so unaware of the consequences) dictated turning off the heating during the day. Gardens are an important leisure space for some women and may provide at certain times of the day or week a private place, but this is seasonal and also subject to invasion by others at certain times (weekends, school holidays etc.). Gardens may also accommodate work (e.g. washing) or represent work for those women who hate gardening.

The home also stores and contains as Glyptis and Chambers note, various forms of leisure equipment (the nature of which is mainly dictated by commercial concerns) for members of the household, but the leisure equipment most women use certainly appears from the Milton Keynes, Sheffield and Leeds studies to be fairly limited in extent, is acquired primarily for its work related usefulness – sewing machines, baking tins, knitting machines – or is something all the household has access to (television, radio, hi-fi). In the case of the latter there are often bitter disputes over who should use it and what should be viewed or listened to. Homes as leisure bases for women thus tend to have severe disadvantages relating to their dual work/leisure use, the presence of other household members and lack of privacy.

This chapter has tried to explore both the kinds of leisure activities (or non-activities) which women pursue in the home, and those processes and constraints which are based on the household and affect all leisure, not just that which is home-based. The fact that much of women's leisure at particular stages in the life cycle (especially mothers of dependent children and women over sixty) takes place in the home cannot auto-matically be assumed to mean that women are quite satisfied with that state of affairs, although some of them clearly are. Nor is the home necessarily the kind of peaceful haven for women that it is often presumed to provide for other family members. Not only is the home a workplace for most women, whether in employment or not, but it is also the site of conflictual power relationships between men, women and children. Women's role in the home is also shaped by powerful ideologies about marriage and gender. Women whose leisure takes place in the home are not at risk from sexual assault or harassment whilst travelling to leisure activities, but are still at risk from sexual assault, rape and other forms of violence from men whilst they are at home.[44] Money (and struggles over it) is less important for home-based activities than it is for leisure outside the home, but it is still a relevant consideration and influences how much status, confidence and power women have. [. . .] The leisure of others in the household also takes place in the home or is fought out in the household, and the leisure of males and children can and often does, take precedence over the leisure of women. Women's leisure does not seem to command the same degree of legitimacy as men's leisure, either in the home or out of it and whether we are talking about time, space, money or resources. Leisure in the home is affected by many factors external to the home, including employment, working hours, school hours and terms, social structure and cultural ideological beliefs about what is acceptable. Capitalism dictates how houses are designed and what leisure equipment is available. For women from certain ethnic minority groups cultural factors may result in them being even more confined to home-based leisure than other women (for example Asian small-shop owners); it is significant that ethnicity is something missing from most of the existing research on women's leisure and is partly related to the invisibility of women from some ethnic minority groups. But there are also many other things which we do not know about women's leisure in the home and which are not easily accessible to us, either through interviews or diary-based budget studies. The trend towards privatization of family life originally noted by sociologists in the 1960s and 1970s does not seem to have decreased, but many of the implications and processes of that privatization are actually hidden from view. Almost no studies of female leisure for instance, mention sexual activity. But it is not apparent whether this is because women don't want to talk about their sex lives (some researchers looking at more general family life have not found this problem[45]) or because women don't think of sexual activity as leisure. Whilst it is possible to pick out certain categories of women whose at-home leisure seems more varied or more facilitated than others (those without young children, single women, women with co-operative partners and children, women with high incomes and large houses) it is not yet possible to say, other than on the basis of region-specific studies, which combinations of social and economic factors are most or least likely to provide women with leisure. It may be that the patterning is more random than we might suppose, or that it is possible to do something about improving the home-based leisure of many women only in conjunction with very far reaching and radical changes in the organization of our society; certainly what we know so far suggests the latter.

Notes

1. There were two main stages in the research. The first stage (known hereafter as Study A) took place in 1980–81. The second phase of the study (hereafter referred to as Study B) occurred in 1981 and 1982. A combination of questionnaires and interviews was used. Overall, the project involved 497 women.

2. S. Parker, *The Future of Work and Leisure*, London: MacGibbon and Kee, 1971; S. Parker, *The Sociology of Leisure*, London: Allen and Unwin, 1976.
3. *Social Trends 1985*, London: HMSO, 1985.
4. Ibid.
5. E. Green, S. Hebron and D. Woodward, 'Leisure and gender: Women's opportunities, perceptions and constraints', Unpublished report to ESRC/Sports Council Steering Group, 1985.
6. Ibid.
7. R. Dixey and M. Talbot, 'Women, leisure and bingo', Trinity and All Saints College, Leeds, 1982, p. 61.
8. E. Wimbush, 'Conceptualising and researching the work–leisure complex', Presentation to Women, Well-Being and Leisure Workshop, Dunfermline College of Physical Education, 1985.
9. R. Dixey and M. Talbot, op. cit.
10. P. Hunt, *Gender and Class Consciousness*, Basingstoke: Macmillan, 1980.
11. Ibid., pp. 49–50.
12. C. Delphy, *Close To Home: A materialist analysis of women's oppression*, London: Hutchinson, 1984. For an extract, see Reading 1.1, this volume.
13. J. Thompson, *Learning Liberation*, London: Croom Helm, 1983.
14. R. Finnegan, 'Working outside formal employment', in R. Deem and G. Salaman, eds, *Work, Culture and Society*, Milton Keynes: Open University Press, 1985; R. Pahl, *Divisions of Labour*, Oxford: Blackwell, 1985.
15. R. Pahl, op. cit., p. 213.
16. Ibid., pp. 270–2.
17. P. Hunt, op. cit.
18. E. Green, S. Hebron and D. Woodward, op. cit.
19. R. Pahl, op. cit.
20. S. Wyatt, 'Science Policy Research Unit: Time budget studies', Presentation to Women, Well-Being and Leisure Workshop, Dunfermline College of Physical Education, 1985.
21. R. Pahl, op. cit., p. 111.
22. M. Maynard, 'Houseworkers and their work', in R. Deem and G. Salaman, op. cit., p. 81.
23. J. Finch, *Married To the Job*, London: Allen and Unwin, 1983.
24. Ibid., pp. 56–7.
25. C. Delphy, op. cit., p. 90.
26. M. Maynard, op. cit.
27. J. Finch and D. Groves, *A Labour of Love*, London: Routledge and Kegan Paul, 1983.
28. R. Berk and S. Berk, *Labour and Leisure at Home*, London: Sage, 1979.
29. M. O'Brien, 'The working father', in N. Beail and J. McGuire, eds, *Fathers: Psychological perspectives*, London: Junction Books, 1982; G. Russell, *The Changing Role of Fathers*, Milton Keynes: Open University Press, 1983; P. Hunt, op. cit.
30. E. Green, S. Hebron and D. Woodward, op. cit.; Milton Keynes Study B.
31. R. Dixey and M. Talbot, op. cit., p. 60.
32. C. Ungerson, 'Women and caring: Skills, tasks and taboos', in E. Gamarnikow, D. Morgan, J. Purvis and D. Taylorson, eds, *The Public and the Private*, London: Heinemann, 1983.
33. S. Parker, 1971, op. cit.
34. S. Gregory, 'Women among others: Another view', *Leisure Studies*, 1: 47–52, 1982.
35. C. Delphy, op. cit.
36. R. Dixey and M. Talbot, op. cit.
37. Ibid., p. 23.
38. J. Finch, op. cit.
39. J. Burgoyne, 'Unemployment and married life', *Unemployment Unit Bulletin*, 18: 7–10, 1985; L. Fagin and M. Little, *The Forsaken Families*, Harmondsworth: Penguin, 1984.
40. A. Murcott, See Reading 2.1, this volume.

41. C. Delphy, op. cit.
42. In Deem's original chapter, there follows a section on money and household budgeting which has been omitted from this version for reasons of space.
43. S. Glyptis and D. Chambers, 'No place like home', *Leisure Studies*, 1: 247–62, 1982, pp. 247–8.
44. J. Pahl, 'Household budgeting', Presentation to Women, Well-being and Leisure Workshop, Dunfermline College of Physical Education, 1985; S. Brownmiller, *Against Our Will: Men, women and rape*, New York: Simon and Schuster, 1975; J. Hanmer and M. Maynard, *Women, Violence and Social Control*, Basingstoke: Macmillan, 1986.
45. L. Holly, 'Feminist methods in the study of middle class wives and mothers', Unpublished paper to Feminist Methods Workshop, Open University, 1985.

3.2 □ *Dorothy Hobson*

Here, Dorothy Hobson presents an early ethnographic account of domestic media consumption based on her observations and discussions with young working-class housewives. Focusing on their routine viewing and listening practices, she considers the everyday social uses of television and radio, and argues that there are distinctive masculine and feminine genres of media output.

Housewives and the mass media

Mass communication, in the form of radio and television, has emerged as an important aspect of the day-to-day experience of the women in the study.[1] Television and radio are never mentioned as spare-time or leisure activities but are located by the women as integral parts of their day. (The exception to this is the television viewing which is done after the children are in bed, but even then the period is not completely free for the woman because she still has to provide drinks or food if her husband wants them.) There is a separation between the consumption of radio and television, but both provide crucial elements in the experience and management of their lives.

Radio

You've got a friend, the happy sound of Radio 1. (Radio 1 jingle)

[. . .]

The radio, for the most part, is listened to during the day while they are engaged in domestic labour, housework and child care. As Anne said, 'It's on in the background all the time'. In some cases switching on the radio is part of the routine of beginning the day; it is, in fact, the first *boundary* in the working day. In terms of the 'structurelessness' of the experience of housework, the time boundaries provided by radio are important in the women's own division of their time.

> *Lorna* We do have the radio on all day. You know, from the time we get up till the time the tele comes back on. I usually put it on at 4 o'clock for the kids' tele. . . .
> *Linda* I listen to the radio. I put it on as soon as I get up.

Anne Six o'clock I get up (laughs), er, put on the radio full blast so that me husband'll
   get up . . .

The constant reference to time during the programmes on Radio 1 also helps to structure the time sequences of the work which women perform while they listen to the
radio. Programmes are self-definitional, as *The Breakfast Show, Mid-morning
Programme*, which includes *Coffee Break* at 11 a.m. At the time of the study Tony Blackburn was running the morning show (9 a.m.–12 noon), in which he had the 'Tiny Tots'
spot at 11 a.m., during which a record was played for children and Blackburn attempted
to teach a nursery rhyme to the children listening while the 'mums' had a coffee break.
During David Hamilton's afternoon programme (2 p.m.–5 p.m.) the 'Tea at Three' spot
is included, when once more women are encouraged to 'put their feet up'. The disc
jockeys (DJs) use points of reference within the expected daily routines of their listeners,
and some of these references are responded to by the women in the study. The
programmes which are listened to are Radio 1 and BRMB local radio, the former being
the more popular. Responses to questions about radio are always given in terms of the
disc jockey who introduces the programme, with the records referred to in a secondary
capacity.

Pat
P. I like Radio 1. Tony Blackburn. I think he's corny but I think he's good. Dave Lee Travis
   I like and Noel Edmunds. Noel Edmunds, I think he's absolutely fantastic. . . .
D. So do you prefer the radio?
P. During the day, yes.
D. Would you have the radio on while you were doing housework?
P. Oh yes, yes.
D. Why do you like the people you like?
P. rm . . . their personality – it comes over on the radio. Noel Edmunds, I think he's really
   fantastic, you know, the blunders he makes, you know [. . .] I think he is really lovely
   (laughs).
D. And do you do your housework at the same time?
P. Oh yes.

Anne
A. I listen to BRMB, you know, that's quite a good programme. I like listening to the
   people that phone in, erm. . . . I like the conversations.
D. Why do you think that is?
A. Er. . . . I suppose it's 'cos I'm on me own.
D. Is it the music as well that you like or . . . ?
A. Yes, 'cos I find that nearly all my records are a bit old-fashioned and I like to hear a
   bit of the modern music. I don't want to get way behind the times, you know.

The predominance of presenters or DJs in the respondents' reactions to radio
programmes can be seen from various aspects. First, it is necessary for the personality
of the disc jockey to be a prominent feature in the programme, since all the records
which are played throughout the day on Radio 1 are the same; the only variation which
exists is in the chatter between records which the disc jockeys provide. Inevitably, then,
it is their ability to form a relationship with their audience which gives the disc jockeys

their appeal. The disc jockeys have become personalities in their own right, as have the presenters of television current affairs programmes, and the increasing professionalism and development of the necessary features and components of the successful disc jockey could be seen as analogous with the professionalization of other television presenters [. . .] The disc jockeys are prominent as a structural feature of the production process of these programmes, and it is they who direct the discourse of the radio programmes towards their known audience – in this case the housewives. Secondly, the women respond to that notion of themselves as 'feminine domestic subjects' of radio discourse which is presented by the disc jockeys. [. . .]

Within the overall picture of isolation which has emerged in the lives of the women in this study, the disc jockey can be seen as having the function of providing the missing 'company' of another person in the lives of the women. As well as helping to combat isolation, it is not too far fetched to see the DJ as also playing the role of a sexual fantasy-figure in the lives of the women who listen. Pat's comments about Noel Edmunds (above) are certainly not limited to his role as someone who breaks the isolation in her life; it includes references to his attractiveness and physical appearance, although she does not make this explicit. Nevertheless, my *reading* of the role of the DJs is that they play the role of a safe, though definitely sexually attractive man, in the lives of the women. The responses to other DJs confirm this assumption. Tony Blackburn is talked about more in terms of the content of his programme and his manner of presentation than in terms of endearment or enthusiasm. However, Blackburn himself obviously realizes the potential for fantasy relationships with his audience. When he was suffering from a throat infection, which made his voice sound rather husky, he said: 'I hope I am not turning you ladies on too much. I know your husbands have left for work, it's you and I together, kids' (Recorded from Radio 1, autumn 1977).

Blackburn is a disc jockey whom it is impossible to ignore. Rather like *Crossroads*, the women either like him or hate him, but rarely do they remain indifferent to him. Blackburn himself provides interesting comments on his own views on radio and pop music, describing his show as 'a pleasant bit of entertainment in the background if you like – inane chatter. I think there's room for a station that comes on and is full of a lot of people talking a load of nonsense' (*Guardian*, 9 January 1976).

Fortunately for him, he does not have to listen to his own programme for, as he says, 'It would drive me mad if I had to physically sit down and listen to David Hamilton's show, or mine, for that matter' (ibid). And fortunately for the women in this study, they do not have to sit and listen either; they can treat the programme as background chatter. But if by chance they happen to listen to what Tony Blackburn has to say, they will be subjected to an onslaught of chatter which definitely reinforces the ideology of the sexual division of labour and places women firmly in their 'correct' place – in the home. It is in the direct comments which he makes about the records and current topics of interest that Blackburn reveals the depth of his conservatism. The 'working man', strikers, punk rockers, women involved in divorce actions (in the wake of his own recent divorce) all warrant criticism from him. Women who are playing their traditional role as housewives and mothers constantly earn praise from him. In one programme in which he was promoting a record by Nancy Wilson (which was supposedly sung by a woman who had enjoyed a 'liberated' life, yet still yearned for the love and security of a husband and family and wanted to tell her 'sisters' of the truth of her misspent life), Blackburn fervently 'plugged' the record and consistently reminded his listeners of the 'truth' of the theme, saying, 'If you understand this, ladies, you understand everything'. In case his listeners did not fully get the message of the song, he took the trouble to explain it, using his own interpretation: 'I hope you understood these lyrics. Nothing is more important, no matter what the press and the media tell you, there is nothing more wonderful than bringing up a child, nothing more difficult either' (recorded from Radio 1, autumn 1977).

Perhaps Tony Blackburn does represent an extreme form of the reinforcement of the ideology of domesticity of the housebound listeners of Radio 1, but far from providing background chatter which can be ignored, he obviously intends his comments to be heard by his audience – and he knows who his audience is. The reinforcement of the dominant ideology of domesticity is definitely a function of the encoded media messages emanating from Radio 1.

The disc jockey, as well as providing relief from isolation, links the isolated individual woman with the knowledge that there are others in the same position.[2] Similarly, this can be seen as a functional effect of 'phone-in' programmes. One of the women says: 'I like listening to the people that phone in. I like the conversations. . . . I suppose it's 'cos I'm on me own'. These programmes not only provide contact with the 'outside' world; they also reinforce the privatized isolation by reaffirming the consensual position – there are thousands of other women in the same situation, in a sort of 'collective isolation'.

Radio can be seen, then, as providing women with a musical reminder of their leisure activities before they married.[3] It also, as they say, keeps them up to date with new records. Since they do not have any spare money to buy records, this is an important way in which they can listen to music. Since listening to music and dancing are the leisure activities which they would most like to pursue, radio is also a substitute for the real world of music and discos which they have lost. Also, it provides a crucial relief from their isolation. The chatter of the disc jockey may appear inane and trivial, but the popularity of radio, both in national and local terms and in the responses of the women in this study, would appear to suggest that it fulfils certain functions in providing music to keep them 'happy and on the move'. Radio creates its own audience through its constant reference to forthcoming programmes and items within programmes. As the jingle at the beginning of this section suggests, the women in this study do appear to regard Radio 1 as a friend, and they certainly view the disc jockeys as important means of negotiating or managing the tensions caused by the isolation in their lives.

Television – 'two worlds'

Linda No, I never watch the news, never!

The ideology of a masculine and a feminine world of activities and interests and the separation of those gender-specific interests is never more explicitly expressed than in the women's reactions and responses to television programmes. Here both class- and gender-specific differences are of vital importance, in terms of both which programmes the women choose to watch or reject and their definition and selection of what are appropriately masculine and feminine programmes and topics. Also, they select television programmes much more consciously than radio programmes. This must partly be a consequence of the fact that they have more freedom during the evenings, and they can make active choices because they are no longer subject to constant inter- ruptions caused by their responsibility for domestic labour and child care. This is in contrast to their listening to the radio during the day, when radio programmes are selected primarily as 'easy listening', a background while they do their housework or look after the children.

There is an *active* choice of programmes which are understood to constitute the 'woman's world', coupled with a complete *rejection* of programmes which are presenting the 'man's world'. However, there is also an acceptance that the 'real' or 'man's world' is important, and the 'right' of their husbands to watch these programmes is respected: but it is not a world with which the women in this study wanted to concern themselves. In fact, the 'world', in terms of what is constructed as of 'news' value, is seen as both alien and hostile to the values of the women. For them television programmes appear to fall into two distinct categories. The programmes which they watch and enjoy are: comedy series (*Selwyn Froggitt, Are You Being Served?*); soap operas (*Emmerdale Farm, The Cedar Tree, Rooms, Crown Court* and, predominantly, *Crossroads* and *Coronation Street*); American television films (*MacMillan and Wife, Dr Welby, Colombo*); light entertainment and quiz shows (*Whose Baby?, Mr and Mrs*); and films. All these programmes could be broadly termed as 'entertaining' rather than 'educational and informative'. The programmes which are actively rejected deal with what the women designate the 'real world' or 'man's world', and these predominantly cluster around the news, current affairs programmes (*Panorama, This Week*), scientific programmes (*Tomorrow's World*), the subject-matter of politics or war, including films about war, and, to a lesser extent, documentary programmes. Selected documentaries will be viewed as long as the *subject-matter* is identified as of feminine interest. The following are extracts from responses to questions about television, and it can be seen from these that there is a clear distinction between what men and women watch and what is seen to be the *right* of the husband to watch (news and current affairs programmes).

Anne

D. What programmes do you watch on television?

A. Er . . . *Crown Court, Rooms, Cedar Tree, Emmerdale Farm, Mr and Mrs.* What else is there? *Dr Welby.* Then there's a film on of a Friday.

D. This is all on ITV, isn't it?

A. (Long pause while she thinks of other programmes) Yes, er . . . yes, that's another programme. *Whose Baby?*

D. There's a film on on Mondays as well, isn't there?

A. No, no . . . oh, yes, there is. It's *Mystery Movie.* I don't like, I'm not very interested in them, you know. I sort of half-watch them.

D. So it's more the short series. [. . .] What do you like about the programmes that you watch?
A. Something to look forward to the next day 'cos most of them are serials.
D. Do you like them to . . . . Which do you like the best, which type?
A. Er, I like *The Cedar Tree* more than *Emmerdale Farm*. I'm not really keen on that. I only watch it through habit. Er, more romantic, I think, you know, there's sort of, er, family life, that is, more than *Emmerdale Farm*. I don't know, I . . . something about that isn't so good.
D. That only really takes you up to tea time, so do you watch the television at night?
A. Yes, in between half-five and eight, that's me busiest time, feed him, change him, sometimes bath him. I don't bath him very often, erm, get Richard's dinner and I always clean up straight away, the washing up, and then I get everything settled and that takes me up to about 8 o'clock, 'cos I stop at half-past six to watch *Crossroads* (laughs). And then from 8 onwards I just sit and watch the box (laughs).
D. Why do you like *Crossroads*?
A. Just that you like to know what's going to happen next, you know. I mean they're terrible actors, I know that, and I just see through that, you know. I just, now and then I think, 'Oh my God, that's silly', you know, but it's not the acting I'm interested in, it's what's going on. l suppose I'm nosy . . . .
D. The time then between that – do you watch the news?
A. I watch a little bit of it, erm (pause). I don't really like the news much because it's all politics; generally and British Leyland out on strike again, and this and that. I like to hear the news things if, er, – if there's been a murder, I know that sounds terrible, but I like to hear – 'Oh what's happening next, what have they found out?' That sort of news I like, you know – gossip.
D. Do you ever watch documentaries?
A. Now and then I find an interesting one. I watched one the other night about people who'd got diseases.

Lorna
L. We have the radio on all day, you know, from the time we get up till the time the tele comes back on. I usually put it on at 4 o'clock for the kids' tele and they watch all the children's programmes, and it might come back off at 6 and it might not go back on again till half-past seven.
D. So you don't watch the news?
L. No, I never watch the news, never.
D. Why don't you watch it?
L. I don't like it, I don't like to hear about people dying and things like that. I think about it afterwards and I can't sleep at all. Like when I watched that thing, *World at War*, and I watched it once and all I could see were people all over the place, you know, heads and no arms and that and at night I could not sleep. I can't ask him to turn it over 'cos he likes it, so I go in the kitchen till it's finished.

It is clear that the news, current affairs, political programmes and scientific programmes, together with portrayals of war (real or in the guise of war films) are actively rejected by the women. They will leave the room rather than sit there while the news is on. The world as revealed through the news is seen to be (a) depressing, (b) boring, but (c) important. The 'news values', as realized in agendas, are 'accepted', but they have *alternative* values which the women recognize but do not suggest should form an alternative coverage. In fact, the importance of accepted 'news values' is recognized, and although their own world is seen as more interesting and relevant to them. it is also seen as secondary in rank to the 'real' or 'masculine' world. In terms of what the news is seen to present, they only select items which they *do not wish to see*. Comments or judgements are made in terms not only of what the items are but also of the effect which they have on the individual. Thus the items are not judged solely for their 'news value' but also for the way they affect the individual. There would appear to be a model for the programmes which are discussed and then rejected.

The news

Content	Conceptualization of value of content	Effects on individual
Politics	Boring	Depressing
War	Male orientated	Causing nightmares
Industrial troubles		and sleeplessness

The women [. . .] may mis-identify the foci of some news reports, but this perhaps reinforces their claim not to watch these programmes. For instance, when Lorraine says 'It's all Vietnam, on the news', she is not necessarily identifying specific examples. In fact, Northern Ireland is much more likely to have been the exact focus of the news at the time. The general point is clear enough: 'Vietnam' has become a generic term for war.

The grouping together of the news and current affairs programmes by the women is a response to the circularity of these programmes, which is determined by the interrelation between the news and current events programmes and the prior selection of news items for their news value. A news 'story' becomes a 'current events topic', and the selection of news items according to the hierarchy of 'news value' puts political and military concerns, industrial relations and economic affairs at the head of topics for inclusion.[4] The editorial selection of these items is premised on their 'news value', and this also reflects a masculine bias in terms of the ideology of the subjects of the items included. The women find little of interest for them in the news except for any 'human interest' items, which are necessarily low in news value and rarely occur. When domestic affairs do reach the news it is often in terms of deviation or murder, and this in turn reinforces the accepted absence of these items from 'normal' news bulletins. This is illustrated when Anne says that she likes to hear news about murders (see above). It is not the fact that someone has been murdered which she finds interesting in the news but the fact that *there are elements within the situation to which she can relate*.

The ideology of femininity and feminine values over-determines the structures of what interests women. It is topics which can be regarded as of 'domestic' interest which they see as important or interesting, and it is also significant that 'domestic affairs', constructed in terms of 'news values' to include the economy and industrial relations, are not defined as 'domestic' in the categories which the women construct for themselves. 'Domestic' clearly relates to their own interests and not to the definition which is constructed through the hierarchy of 'news values'. It can be said that the majority of items which are included in news, current affairs and documentary programmes have a content which has little or no intrinsic interest for these women, and the way that they are presented means that they exclude these women from 'participation' at the point of identification with the items included. At the same time, the women accept that these are *important*, and this reinforces the split between the masculine values, which are interpreted as being important, and the interests which they see as representing their own feminine values.

The feminine 'world' of television

[. . .]

First, in conjunction with the programmes which women reject, there are programmes which they choose to watch and to which they obviously relate. These can be defined as those which are related to their own lives, the programmes which can loosely be termed 'realistic' – *Coronation Street, Crossroads, Emmerdale Farm, The Cedar Tree*. Secondly, the programmes which can be described as having 'fantasy content' (horror movies, or American movies or television movies), although not seen as representing 'real life' in the women's own terms, are seen as an alternative to the reality of their own lives. Finally, there are the programmes which can be categorized as light entertainment (quizzes, or competitions which often have an 'everyday' or 'domestic' theme, either because the contestants are seen as ordinary people or because of the subject-matter). In *Whose Baby?*, for example, the children of celebrity guests appear and the panel has to guess who is the famous father or mother – a direct link of parenthood between the 'famous' and the 'ordinary' viewer (in this case, the woman).

[. . .] Within the programmes which are seen as 'realistic' there are common elements of identification. Many of the characters in the series *Coronation Street* and *Crossroads* are women who themselves have to confront the 'problems' in their 'everyday' lives, and the resolution or negotiation of these problems within the drama provides points of recognition and identification for the women viewers. It is in the 'living out' of problem areas that much of the appeal of the series is located. However, the resolution of areas of conflict, contradiction or confusion within a dramatic situation is double-edged. The woman can be confronted with the problems and also informed of the different elements which have to be considered in any 'living out' or resolution of problems. It is in the forms that the resolutions are made within programmes that the ideological basis of consensual femininity is *reproduced* and *reinforced* for women. As with the problems that are discussed in phone-in programmes and in the chatter of DJs, the very fact of recognition and *seeming* discussion or consideration by some 'outside' or 'independent' authority gives an impression that the problems have been aired. The outcome remains the same. The resolutions within either the soap opera series or the telephone conversations or talks are not revolutionary; what emerges is the reinforcement of the fatality or inevitability of the situation, without the need to change it.

It is impossible to attempt a detailed analysis of the decoding of the programmes which is made by the women because at this stage this would be only supposition.[5] What is clear, however, is that the programmes which the women watch are differentiated specifically in terms of both class and gender. Overall the programmes fall into the categories of popular drama and light entertainment, and although it is obvious that the women reject news and the political content of current affairs programmes, it would be wrong to contend that they do not have access or exposure to news or politics. Within comedy programmes, news and current affairs topics are presented in a mediated form – and often in a more easily accessible or even 'joking' or parodying manner. The news on Radio 1, which is transmitted every hour, is relatively accessible; it is also introduced by music which is recognizable, bright and repetitive and demanding of attention. The women in this study are exposed to news in this form, but they do not mention finding that unacceptable. Clearly, what is important is the definition of specifically feminine interests which women select from media output and the rejection of items which they see as specifically of masculine interest. They combat their own isolation through their interest in radio programmes during the day, and they see television programmes as a form of 'leisure' or relaxation. Radio is integral to their working day, but early-evening television is secondary to the domestic labour which they perform. The programmes which the women watch and listen to, together with the programmes which they reject, reinforce the sexual division of spheres of interest, which is determined both by their location in the home and by the structures of femininity that ensure that feminine values are secondary (or less 'real') than those of the masculine world of work and politics, which the women regard as *alien*, yet *important*.

Notes

1. This extract is part of a longer study which looks at the culture of young working-class housewives at home with young children. The research was conducted by tape recorded interviews and observation in their homes, and it covered many aspects of their personal experience both before they were married and in their present situation. For a fuller discussion, see D. Hobson, 'Housewives: Isolation as oppression', in Women's Studies Group CCCS, eds, *Women Take Issue: Aspects of women's subordination*, London: Hutchinson, 1978a; D. Hobson, 'A study of working class women at home: Femininity, domesticity and maternity', Unpublished MA Thesis, University of Birmingham, 1978b.
2. The essential finding of the research from which this extract is taken was that it was the isolation of their lives which the women found most oppressive, coupled with their inability to escape from the home either to paid work or leisure activities.
3. For a fuller discussion of the absence of leisure activities, see Hobson, 1978b, op. cit.
4. I. Connell, L. Curti and S. Hall, 'The "unity" of current affairs television', in CCCS, *Working Papers in Cultural Studies 9*, University of Birmingham, 1976.
5. Herzog looked at the structure of audiences and their responses to programmes of a similar kind: daytime radio serials. She was predominantly concerned with the psychological responses of the audience to features within the text and relied on the 'uses and gratifications' theory. Also, Arnheim looked at the content of daytime radio serials in an attempt to identify features to which the audience responded. Both these works are important starting points for future research into the possible identification which women may make

to radio and television programmes, since many of the features of the programmes analyzed in Arnheim are common to the present television series watched by the women in my study. My own work in this study starts at a point where the audience selects from a given range of available programmes. I have not been concerned, in this article, so much with how they decode those programmes as with the structures which have mediated in their choice of programmes. See H. Herzog, 'What do we really know about daytime serial listeners?', in P. Lazersfeld and F. Stanton, eds, *Radio Research 1942–43*, New York: Duell, Sloan and Pearce, 1944; R. Arnheim, 'The world of the daytime serial', in P. Lazersfeld and F. Stanton, eds, ibid.

3.3 □ *Janice Radway*

Like Hobson, American researcher Janice Radway is interested in how media reception is woven into the fabric of daily household life, although she chooses to look in detail at women's uses and interpretations of romantic fiction. The following extract illustrates her proposition that this reading activity must be understood as a social event in a familial context. Radway begins by reflecting on her first encounters with Dot, bookshop worker and avid romance reader, and with a group of the shop's regular customers.

The act of reading the romance

By the end of my first full day with Dorothy Evans and her customers, I had come to realize that although the Smithton women are not accustomed to thinking about what it is in the romance that gives them so much pleasure, they know perfectly well why they like to read. I understood this only when their remarkably consistent comments forced me to relinquish my inadvertent but continuing preoccupation with the text. Because the women always responded to my query about their reasons for reading with comments about the pleasures of the act itself rather than about their liking for the particulars of the romantic plot, I soon realized I would have to give up my obsession with textual features and narrative details if I wanted to understand their view of romance reading. Once I recognized this it became clear that romance reading was important to the Smithton women first because the simple event of picking up a book enabled them to deal with the particular pressures and tensions encountered in their daily round of activities. Although I learned later that certain aspects of the romance's story do help to make this event especially meaningful, the early interviews were interesting because they focused so resolutely on the significance of the *act of romance reading* rather than on the meaning of the romance.

The extent of the connection between romance reading and my informants' understanding of their roles as wives and mothers was impressed upon me first by Dot herself during our first two-hour interview which took place before I had seen her customers' responses to the pilot questionnaire.[1] In posing the question, 'What do romances do better than other novels today?,' I expected her to concern herself in her answer with the characteristics of the plot and the manner in which the story evolved. To my surprise, Dot took my query about 'doing' as a transitive question about the *effects* of romances on the people who read them. She responded to my question with a long and puzzling answer that I found difficult to interpret at this early stage of our discussions. It seems wise to let Dot speak for herself here because her response introduced a number of themes that appeared again and again in my subsequent talks with other readers. My question prompted the following careful meditation:

> It's an innocuous thing. If it had to be . . . pills or drinks, this is harmful. They're very aware of this. Most of the women are mothers. And they're aware of that kind of thing. And reading is something they would like to generate in their children also. Seeing the parents reading is . . . just something that I feel they think the children should see them doing. . . . I've got a woman with teenage boys here who says 'you've got books like . . . you've just got oodles of da . . . da . . da . . . [counting an imaginary stack of books].' She says, 'Now when you ask Mother to buy you something, you don't stop and think how many things you have. So this is Mother's and it is my money.' Very, almost defensive. But I think they get that from their fathers. I think they heard their fathers sometime or other saying, 'Hey, you're spending an awful lot of money on books aren't you?' You know for a long time, my ladies hid' em. They would hide their books; literally hide their books. And they'd say, 'Oh, if my husband [we have distinctive blue sacks], if my husband sees this blue sack coming in the house . . . .' And you know, I'd say, 'Well really, you're a big girl. Do you really feel like you have to be very defensive?' A while ago, I would not have thought that way. I would have thought, 'Oh, Dan is going to hit the ceiling.' For a while Dan was not thrilled that I was reading a lot. Because I think men do feel threatened. They want their wife to be in the room with them. And I think my body is in the room but the rest of me is not (when I am reading).[2]

Only when Dot arrived at her last observation about reading and its ability to transport her out of her living room did I begin to understand that the real answer to my question, which she never mentioned and which was the link between reading, pills, and drinks, was actually the single word, 'escape,' a word that would later appear on so many of the questionnaires. She subsequently explained that romance novels provide escape just as Darvon and alcohol do for other women. Whereas the latter are harmful to both women and their families, Dot believes romance reading is 'an innocuous thing.' As she commented to me in another interview, romance reading is a habit that is not very different from 'an addiction'.

Although some of the other Smithton women expressed uneasiness about the suitability of the addiction analogy, as did Dot in another interview, nearly all of the original sixteen who participated in lengthy conversations agreed that one of their principal goals in reading was their desire to do something *different* from their daily routine. That claim was borne out by their answers to the open-ended question about the functions of romance reading. At this point, it seems worth quoting a few of those fourteen replies that expressly volunteered the ideas of escape and release. The Smithton readers explained the power of the romance in the following way:

> They are light reading – escape literature – I can put down and pick up effortlessly.

> Everyone is always under so much pressure. They like books that let them escape.

> Escapism.

I guess I feel there is enough 'reality' in the world and reading is a means of escape for me.

Because it is an Escape [*sic*], and we can dream and pretend that it is our life.

I'm able to escape the harsh world for a few hours a day.

They always seem an escape and they usually turn out the way you wish life really was.

The response of the Smithton women is apparently not an unusual one. Indeed, the advertising campaigns of three of the houses that have conducted extensive market-research studies all emphasize the themes of relaxation and escape. Potential readers of Coventry Romances, for example, have been told in coupon ads that 'month after month Coventry Romances offer you a beautiful new escape route into historical times when love and honor ruled the heart and mind.'[3] Similarly, the Silhouette television advertisements featuring Ricardo Montalban asserted that 'the beautiful ending makes you feel so good' and that romances 'soothe away the tensions of the day.' Montalban also touted the value of 'escaping' into faraway places and exotic locales. Harlequin once mounted a travel sweepstakes campaign offering as prizes 'escape vacations' to romantic places. In addition, they included within the books themselves an advertising page that described Harlequins as 'the books that let you escape into the wonderful world of romance! Trips to exotic places . . . interesting places . . . meeting memorable people . . . the excitement of love. . . . These are integral parts of Harlequin Romances – the heartwarming novels read by women everywhere.'[4] Fawcett, too, seems to have discovered the escape function of romance fiction, for Daisy Maryles has reported that the company found in in-depth interviewing that 'romances were read for relaxation and to enable [women] to better cope with the routine aspects of life'.[5]

[. . .] It is [. . .] essential to add, however, that although the women will use the word 'escape' to explain their reading behavior, if given another comparable choice that does not carry the connotations of disparagement, they will choose the more favorable sounding explanation. To understand why, it will be helpful to follow Dot's comments more closely.

In returning to her definition of the appeal of romance fiction – a definition that is a highly condensed version of a commonly experienced process of explanation, doubt, and defensive justification – it becomes clear that romance novels perform this compensatory function for women because they use them to diversify the pace and character of their habitual existence. Dot makes it clear, however, that the women are also troubled about the propriety of indulging in such an obviously pleasurable activity. Their doubts are often cultivated into a full-grown feeling of guilt by husbands and children who object to this activity because it draws the women's attention away from the immediate family circle. As Dot later noted, although some women can explain to their families that a desire for a new toy or gadget is no different from a desire to read a new romantic novel, a far greater number of them have found it necessary to hide the evidence of their self-indulgence. In an effort to combat both the resentment of others and their own feelings of shame about their 'hedonist' behavior, the women have worked out a complex rationalization for romance reading that not only asserts their equal right to pleasure but also legitimates the books by linking them with values more widely approved within American culture.[6] [. . .]

Both the escape response and the relaxation response on the second questionnaire immediately raise other questions. Relaxation implies a reduction in the state of tension produced by prior conditions, whereas escape obviously suggests flight from one state of being to another more desirable one.[7] To understand the sense of the romance experience, then, as it is enjoyed by those who consider it a welcome change in their day-to-day existence, it becomes necessary to situate it within a larger temporal context and to specify precisely how the act of reading manages to create that feeling of change and differentiation so highly valued by these readers.

In attending to the women's comments about the worth of romance reading, I was particularly struck by the fact that they tended to use the word escape in two distinct ways. On the one hand, they used the term literally to describe the act of denying the present, which they believe they accomplish each time they begin to read a book and are drawn into its story. On the other hand, they used the word in a more figurative fashion to give substance to the somewhat vague but nonetheless intense sense of relief they experience by identifying with a heroine whose life does not resemble their own in certain crucial aspects. I think it important to reproduce this subtle distinction as accurately as possible because it indicates that romance reading releases women from their present pressing concerns in two different but related ways.

Dot, for example, went on to elaborate more fully in the conversation quoted above about why so many husbands seem to feel threatened by their wives' reading activities. After declaring with delight that when she reads her body is in the room but she herself is not, she said, 'I think this is the case with the other women.' She continued, 'I think men cannot do that unless they themselves are readers. I don't think men are *ever* a part of anything even if it's television.' 'They are never really out of their body either,' she added. 'I don't care if it's a football game; I think they are always consciously aware of where they are.' Her triumphant conclusion, 'but I think a woman in a book isn't,' indicates that Dot is aware that reading not only demands a high level of attention but also draws the individual *into* the book because it requires her participation. Although she is not sure what it is about the book that prompts this absorption, she is quite sure that television viewing and film watching are different. In adding immediately that 'for some reason, a lot of men feel threatened by this, very, very much threatened,' Dot suggested that the men's resentment has little to do with the kinds of books their wives are reading and more to do with the simple fact of the activity itself and its capacity to absorb the participants' entire attention.

These tentative observations were later corroborated in the conversations I had with other readers. Ellen, for instance, a former airline stewardess, now married and taking care of her home, indicated that she also reads for 'entertainment and escape.' However, she added, her husband sometimes objects to her reading because he wants her to watch the same television show he has selected. She 'hates' this, she said, because she does not like the kinds of programs on television today. She is delighted when he gets a business call in the evening because her husband's preoccupation with his caller permits her to go back to her book.

Penny, another housewife in her middle thirties, also indicated that her husband 'resents it' if she reads too much. 'He feels shut out,' she explained, 'but there is nothing on TV I enjoy.' Like Ellen's husband, Penny's spouse also wants her to watch television with him. Susan, a woman in her fifties, also 'read[s] to escape' and related with almost no bitterness that her husband will not permit her to continue reading when he is ready to go to sleep. She seems to regret rather than resent this only because it limits the amount of time she can spend in an activity she finds enjoyable. Indeed, she went on in our conversation to explain that she occasionally gives herself 'a very special treat' when she is 'tired of housework.' 'I take the whole day off,' she said, 'to read.'

This theme of romance reading as a special gift a woman gives herself dominated most of the interviews. The Smithton women stressed the privacy of the act and the fact that it enables them to focus their attention on a single object that can provide pleasure for themselves alone. Interestingly enough, Robert Escarpit has noted in related fashion that reading is at once 'social and asocial' because 'it temporarily suppresses the individual's relations with his [*sic*] universe to construct new ones with the universe of the work.'[8] Unlike television viewing, which is a very social activity undertaken in the presence of others and which permits simultaneous conversation and personal interaction, silent reading requires the reader to block out the surrounding world and to give consideration to other people and to another time. It might be said, then, that the characters and events of romance fiction populate the woman's consciousness even as she withdraws from the familiar social scene of her daily ministrations.

I use the word ministrations deliberately here because the Smithton women explained to me that they are not trying to escape their husbands and children 'per se' when they read. Rather, what reading takes them away from, they believe, is the psychologically demanding and emotionally draining task of attending to the physical and affective needs of their families, a task that is solely and peculiarly theirs. In other words, these women, who have been educated to believe that females are especially and naturally attuned to the emotional requirements of others and who are very proud of their abilities to communicate with and to serve the members of their families, value reading precisely because it is an intensely private act. Not only is the activity private, however, but it also enables them to suspend temporarily those familial relationships and to throw up a screen between themselves and the arena where they are required to do most of their relating to others.

It was Dot who first advised me about this phenomenon. Her lengthy commentary, transcribed below, enabled me to listen carefully to the other readers' discussions of escape and to hear the distinction nearly all of them made between escape from their families, which they believe they do *not* do, and escape from the heavy responsibilities and duties of the roles of wife and mother, which they admit they do out of emotional need and necessity. Dot explained their activity, for instance, by paraphrasing the thought process she believes goes on in her customers' minds. 'Hey,' they say, 'this is what I want to do and I'm gonna do it. This is for me. I'm doin' for you all the time. Now leave me, just leave me alone. Let me have my time, my space. Let me do what I want to do. This isn't hurting you. I'm not poaching on you in any way.' She then went on to elaborate about her own duties as a mother and wife:

As a mother, I have run 'em to the orthodontist. I have run 'em to the swimming pool. I have run 'em to baton twirling lessons. I have run up to school because they forgot their lunch. You know, I mean, really! And you do it. And it isn't that you begrudge it. That isn't it. Then my husband would walk in the door and he'd say, 'Well, what did you do today?' You know, it was like, 'Well, tell me how you spent the last eight hours, because I've been out working.' And I finally got to the point where I would say, 'Well, I read four books, and I did all the wash and got the meal on the table and the beds are all made, and the house is tidy.' And I would get defensive like, 'So what do you call all this? Why should I have to tell you because I certainly don't ask you what you did for eight hours, step by step.' But their husbands do do that. We've compared notes. They hit the house and it's like 'Well all right, I've been out earning a living. Now what have you been doin' with your time?' And you begin to be feeling, 'Now really, why is he questioning me?'

Romance reading, it would seem, at least for Dot and many of her customers, is a strategy with a double purpose. As an activity, it so engages their attention that it enables them to deny their physical presence in an environment associated with responsibilities that are acutely felt and occasionally experienced as too onerous to bear. Reading, in this sense, connotes a free space where they feel liberated from the need to perform duties that they otherwise willingly accept as their own. At the same time, by carefully choosing stories that make them feel particularly happy, they escape figuratively into a fairy tale where a heroine's similar needs are adequately met. As a result, they vicariously attend to their own requirements as independent individuals who require emotional sustenance and solicitude.

Angie's account of her favorite reading time graphically represents the significance of romance reading as a tool to help insure a woman's sense of emotional well-being. 'I like it,' she says, 'when my husband – he's an insurance salesman – goes out in the evening on house calls. Because then I have two hours just to totally relax.' She continued, 'I love to settle in a hot bath with a good book. That's really great.' We might conclude, then, that reading a romance is a regressive experience for these women in the sense that for the duration of the time devoted to it they feel gratified and content. This feeling of pleasure seems to derive from their identification with a heroine whom they believe is deeply appreciated and tenderly cared for by another. Somewhat paradoxically, however, they also seem to value the sense of self-sufficiency they experience as a consequence of the knowledge that they are capable of making themselves feel good.

Nancy Chodorow's observations about the social structure of the American family in the twentieth century help to illuminate the context that creates both the feminine need for emotional support and validation and the varied strategies that have evolved to meet it. As Chodorow points out, most recent studies of the family agree that women traditionally reproduce people, as she says, 'physically in their housework and child care, psychologically in their emotional support of husbands and their maternal relation to sons and daughters.'[9] This state of affairs occurs, these studies maintain, because women alone are held responsible for home maintenance and early child care. Ann Oakley's 1971 study of forty London housewives, for instance, led her to the following conclusion: 'In the housekeeping role the servicing function is far more central than the productive or creative one. In the roles of wife and mother, also, the image of women as servicers of men's and children's needs is prominent: women "service" the labour force by catering to the physical needs of men (workers) and by raising children (the next generation of workers) so that the men are free *from* child-socialization and free *to* work outside the home.'[10] This social fact, documented also by Mirra Komarovsky, Helena Lopata, and others, is reinforced ideologically by the widespread belief that females are *naturally* nurturant and generous, more selfless than men, and, therefore, cheerfully self-abnegating. A good wife and mother, it is assumed, will have no difficulty meeting the challenge of providing all of the labor necessary to maintain a family's physical existence including the cleaning of its quarters, the acquisition and preparation of its food, and the purchase, repair, and upkeep of its clothes, even while she masterfully discerns and supplies individual members' psychological needs.[11] A woman's interests, this version of 'the female mystique' maintains, are exactly congruent with those of her husband and children. In serving them, she also serves herself.[12]

As Chodorow notes, not only are the women expected to perform this extraordinarily demanding task, but they are also supposed to be capable of executing it without being formally 'reproduced' and supported themselves. 'What is . . . often hidden, in generalizations about the family as an emotional refuge,' she cautions, 'is that in the family as it is currently constituted no one supports and reconstitutes women affectively and emotionally – either women working in the home or women working in the paid labor force.'[13] Although she admits, of course, that the accident of individual marriage occasionally provides a woman with an unusually nurturant and 'domestic' husband, her principal argument is that as a social institution the contemporary family contains no role whose principal task is the reproduction and emotional support of the wife and mother. 'There is a fundamental asymmetry in daily reproduction,' Chodorow concludes, 'men are socially and psychologically reproduced by women, but women are reproduced (or not) largely by themselves.'[14]

That this lack of emotional nurturance combined with the high costs of lavishing constant attention on others is the primary motivation behind the desire to lose the self in a book was made especially clear to me in a group conversation that occurred late in my stay in Smithton. The discussion involved Dot, one of her customers, Ann, who is married and in her thirties, and Dot's unmarried, twenty-three-year-old daughter, Kit. In response to my question, 'Can you tell me what you escape from?,' Dot and Ann together explained that reading keeps them from being overwhelmed by expectations and limitations. It seems advisable to include their entire conversation here, for it specifies rather precisely the source of those felt demands:

Dot: All right, there are pressures. Meeting your bills, meeting whatever standards or requirements your husband has for you or whatever your children have for you.
Ann: Or that you feel you should have. Like doing the housework just so.
Dot: And they do come to you with problems. Maybe they don't want you to – let's see – maybe they don't want you to solve it, but they certainly want to unload on you. You know. Or they say, 'Hey, I've got this problem.'
Ann: Those pressures build up.
Dot: Yeah, it's pressures.

Ann: You should be able to go to one of those good old – like the MGM musicals and just . . .

Dot: True.

Ann: Or one of those romantic stories and cry a little bit and relieve the pressure and – a legitimate excuse to cry and relieve some of the pressure build-up and not be laughed at.

Dot: That's true.

Ann: And you don't find that much anymore. I've had to go to books for it.

Dot: This is better than psychiatry.

Ann: Because I cry over books. I get wrapped up in them.

Dot: I do too. I sob in books! Oh yes. I think that's escape. Now I'm not gonna say I've got to escape my husband by reading. No.

Ann: No.

Dot: Or that I'm gonna escape my kids by getting my nose in a book. It isn't any one of those things. It's just – it's pressures that evolve from being what you are.

Kit: In this society.

Dot: And people do pressure you. Inadvertently, maybe.

Ann: Yes, it's being more and more restrictive. You can't do this and you can't do that.[15]

This conversation revealed that these women believe romance reading enables them to relieve tensions, to diffuse resentment, and to indulge in a fantasy that provides them with good feelings that seem to endure after they return to their roles as wives and mothers. Romance fiction, as they experience it, is, therefore, *compensatory literature*. It supplies them with an important emotional release that is proscribed in daily life because the social role with which they identify themselves leaves little room for guiltless, self-interested pursuit of individual pleasure. Indeed, the search for emotional gratification was the one theme common to all of the women's observations about the function of romance reading. Maureen, for instance, a young mother of two intellectually gifted children, volunteered, 'I especially like to read when I'm depressed.' When asked what usually caused her depression, she commented that it could be all kinds of things. Later she added that romances were comforting after her children had been especially demanding and she felt she needed time to herself.

In further discussing the lack of institutionalized emotional support suffered by contemporary American women, Chodorow has observed that in many preindustrial societies women formed their own social networks through which they supported and reconstituted one another.[16] Many of these networks found secondary institutional support in the local church while others simply operated as informal neighborhood societies. In either case, the networks provided individual women with the opportunity to abandon temporarily their stance as the family's self-sufficient emotional provider. They could then adopt a more passive role through which they received the attention, sympathy, and encouragement of other women. With the increasing suburbanization of women, however, and the concomitant secularization of the culture at large, these communities became exceedingly difficult to maintain. The principal effect was the even more resolute isolation of women within their domestic environment. Indeed, both Oakley in Great Britain and Lopata in the United States have discovered that one of the features housewives dislike most about their role is its isolation and resulting loneliness.[17]

I introduce Chodorow's observations here in order to suggest that through romance reading the Smithton women are providing themselves with another kind of female community capable of rendering the so desperately needed affective support. This community seems not to operate on an immediate local level although there are signs, both in Smithton and nationally, that romance readers are learning the pleasures of regular discussions of books with other women.[18] Nonetheless, during the early group discussions with Dot and her readers I was surprised to discover that very few of her customers knew each other. In fact, most of them had never been formally introduced although they recognized one another as customers of Dot. I soon learned that the women rarely, if ever, discussed romances with more than one or two individuals. Although many commented that they talked about the books with a sister, neighbor, or with their mothers, very few did so on a regular or extended basis. Indeed, the most striking feature of the interview sessions was the delight with which they discovered common experiences, preferences, and distastes. As one woman exclaimed in the middle of a discussion, 'We were never stimulated before into thinking why we like [the novels]. Your asking makes us think why we do this. I had no idea other people had the same ideas I do.'

The romance community, then, is not an actual group functioning at the local level. Rather, it is a huge, ill-defined network composed of readers on the one hand and authors on the other. Although it performs some of the same functions carried out by older neighborhood groups, this female community is mediated by the distances of modern mass publishing. Despite the distance, the Smithton women feel personally connected to their favorite authors because they are convinced that these writers know how to make them happy. Many volunteered information about favorite authors even before they would discuss specific books or heroines. All expressed admiration for their favorite writers and indicated that they were especially curious about their private lives. Three-fourths of the group of sixteen had made special trips to autographing sessions to see and express their gratitude to the women who had given them so much pleasure. The authors reciprocate this feeling of gratitude and seem genuinely interested in pleasing their readers. [. . .] Many are themselves romance readers and, as a consequence, they, too, often have definite opinions about the particular writers who know how to make the reading experience truly enjoyable.[19]

It seems highly probable that in repetitively reading and writing romances, these women are participating in a collectively elaborated female fantasy that unfailingly ends at the precise moment when the heroine is gathered into the arms of the hero who declares his intention to protect her forever because of his desperate love and need for her. These women are telling themselves a story whose central vision is one of total surrender where all danger has been expunged, thus permitting the heroine to relinquish self-control. Passivity *is* at the heart of the romance experience in the sense that the final goal of each narrative is the creation of that perfect union where the ideal male, who is masculine and strong yet nurturant too, finally recognizes the intrinsic worth of the heroine. Thereafter, she is required to do nothing more than *exist* as the center of this paragon's attention. Romantic escape is, therefore, a temporary but literal denial of the demands women recognize as an integral part of their roles as nurturing wives and mothers. It is also a figurative journey to a utopian state of total receptiveness where the reader, as a result of her identification with the heroine, feels herself the *object* of someone else's attention and solicitude. Ultimately, the romance permits its reader the experience of feeling cared for and the sense of having been reconstituted affectively, even if both are lived only vicariously.

[. . .]

Dot's daughter, Kit, observed that an unhappy ending is the most depressing thing that can happen in a romance. She believes, in fact, as does nearly everyone else, that an unhappy ending excludes a novel that is otherwise a romantic love story from the romance category. Kit is only one of the many who insist on reading the endings of the stories *before* they buy them to insure that they will not be saddened by emotionally investing in the tale of a heroine only to discover that events do not resolve themselves as they should. [. . .] It is indicative of a tendency among Dot's customers to avoid any kind of reading matter that does not conform to their rigid requirements for 'optimism' and escapist stories. Romances are valuable to them in proportion to their lack of resemblance to the real world. They choose their romances carefully in an attempt to assure themselves of a reading experience that will make them feel happy and hold out the promise of utopian bliss, a state they willingly acknowledge to be rare in the real world but one, nevertheless, that they do not want to relinquish as a conceptual possibility.

In discussing the therapeutic function of true fairy stories and folk tales, Bruno Bettelheim has argued that they perform the fundamental service for children of creating and maintaining *hope*.[20] [. . .] Bettelheim believes that children are actually encouraged by their experience of identification with a character whose remarkably similar problems are happily resolved. 'We know,' he writes, 'that the more deeply unhappy and despairing we are, the more we need to be able to engage in optimistic fantasies.'[21] He continues that 'while the fantasy is *unreal*, the good feelings it gives us about ourselves and our future *are real*, and these good feelings are what we need to sustain us.'

I want to argue similarly that by participating in a fantasy that they are willing to admit is unrealistic in some ways, the Smithton women are permitting themselves the luxury of self-indulgence while simultaneously providing themselves with the opportunity to experience the kind of care and attention they commonly give to others. Although this experience *is* vicarious, the pleasure it induces is nonetheless real. It seems to sustain them, at least temporarily, for they believe reading helps to make them happier people and endows them with renewed hope and greater energy to fulfill their duty to others.

[. . .]

In summary, romances can be termed compensatory fiction because the act of reading them fulfills certain basic psychological needs for women that have been induced by the culture and its social structures but that often remain unmet in day-to-day existence as the result of concomitant restrictions on female activity. From the Smithton readers' experiences, in particular, it can be concluded that romance reading compensates women in two distinct ways. Most important, it provides vicarious emotional nurturance by prompting identification between the reader and a fictional heroine whose identity as a woman is always confirmed by the romantic and sexual attentions of an ideal male. When she successfully imagines herself in the heroine's position, the typical romance reader can relax momentarily and permit herself to wallow in the rapture of being the center of a powerful and important individual's attention. This attention not only provides her with the sensations evoked by emotional nurturance and physical satisfaction, but, equally significantly, reinforces her sense of self because in offering his care and attention to the woman with whom she identifies, the hero implicitly regards that woman and, by implication, the reader, as worthy of his concern. This fictional character thus teaches both his narrative counterpart and the reader to recognize the value they doubted they possessed.

Romance fiction is compensatory in a second sense because it fills a woman's mental world with the varied details of simulated travel and permits her to converse imaginatively with adults from a broad spectrum of social space.

[. . .]

Notes

1. Radway's methods included questionnaire surveys as well as lengthy conversational interviews with groups of the Smithton women. For fuller details, see J. Radway, *Reading Their Romance: Women, patriarchy and popular literature*, London: Verso: 1987, pp. 47–8.
2. All spoken quotations have been taken directly from taped interviews. . . . Pauses in a speaker's commentary have been marked with dashes.
3. These coupon ads appeared sporadically in national newspapers throughout the spring and summer of 1980.
4. B. Neels, *Cruise to a Wedding*, Toronto: Harlequin Books, 1980, p. 190.
5. D. Maryles, 'Fawcett launches romance imprint with brand marketing techniques', in *Publishers Weekly*, 3 September 1979, p. 70.
6. That is, values of education and instruction. The latter part of Radway's chapter – left out here for reasons of space – deals with women's justification of their reading in terms of its instructional potential. Radway sees this as a response to the guilt they experience as romance readers.
7. As Escarpit has observed, 'there are a thousand ways to escape and it is essential to know from what and towards what we are escaping'. See R. Escarpit, *The Sociology of Literature*, Painesville, OH: Lake Erie College Press, 1965, p. 91.
8. Ibid., p. 88. Although Dot's observations are not couched in academic language, they are really no different from Escarpit's similar observation that 'reading is the supreme solitary occupation'.
9. N. Chodorow, *The Reproduction of Mothering: Psychoanalysis and the sociology of gender*, Berkeley: University of California Press, 1978, p. 36.
10 A. Oakley, *The Sociology of Housework*, New York: Pantheon Books, 1974, p. 179. See also A. Oakley, *Woman's Work: The housewife, past and present*, New York: Vintage Books, 1976,

pp. 60–155; R. McDonough and R. Harrison, 'Patriarchy and relations of production', in A. Kuhn and A. Wolpe, eds, *Feminism and Materialism: Women and modes of production*, London: Routledge and Kegan Paul, 1978; A. Kuhn, 'Structures of patriarchy and capitalism in the family', in A. Kuhn and A. Wolpe, eds, ibid.; K. Sacks, 'Engels revisited: Women, the organization of production and private property', in M. Rosaldo and L. Lamphere, eds, *Women, Culture and Society*, Stanford: Stanford University Press, 1974; H. Lopata, *Occupation: Housewife*, New York: Oxford University Press, 1971.

11. In addition to Lopata, see M. Komarovsky, *Blue Collar Marriage*, New York: Random House, 1964; A. Myrdal and V. Klein, *Woman's Two Roles: Home and work*, London: Routledge and Kegan Paul, 1968; B. Friedan, *The Feminine Mystique*, New York: Norton, 1963; J. Mitchell, *Woman's Estate*, New York: Pantheon Books, 1971; A. Steinmann, 'A study of the concept of the feminine role of 51 middle class American families', *Genetic Psychology Monographs*, 67: 275–352, 1963.

12. With respect to this view of woman as a natural wife and mother, Dorothy Dinnerstein has observed that women are treated as 'natural resources to be mined, reaped, used up without concern for their future fate': see D. Dinnerstein, *The Mermaid and the Minotaur: Sexual arrangements and human malaise*, New York: Harper and Row, 1976, p. 101.

13. N. Chodorow, op. cit., p. 36.

14. Ibid.

15. It is worth remarking here that the feeling that housework ought to be done according to some abstract standard is apparently common to many women who work in the home. For a discussion of these standards, and the guilt they produce in the women who invariably feel they seldom 'measure up', see A. Oakley, 1974, op. cit., pp. 100–12.

16. N. Chodorow, op. cit, p. 36. For studies of contemporary working-class versions of these networks, see C. Stack, *All Our Kin: Strategies for survival in a black community*, New York: Harper and Row, 1974; M. Young and P. Willmott, *Family and Kinship in East London*, Harmondsworth: Penguin, 1966; L. Lamphere, 'Strategies, co-operation and conflict among women in domestic groups', in M. Rosaldo and L. Lamphere, eds, op. cit.

17. A. Oakley, 1974, op. cit., pp. 52–4, 75, 88–92; A. Oakley, 1976, op. cit., pp. 101–2; H. Lopata, op. cit., pp. 36, 244–5.

18. A few months before I arrived in Smithton, several of Dot's customers expressed an interest in getting together with other romance readers. Accordingly, Dot arranged an informal gathering in her home at which 5 to 10 women socialized and discussed romances. Although the women claimed they enjoyed themselves, they have not yet met again.

19. There is ample evidence to indicate that writers' and readers' perceptions of romances are remarkably similar. This holds true not only for the subject of the story itself but also for conceptions of the romance's function. For comments very similar to Dot's, see H. Van Slyke, '"Old fashioned" and "up to the minute"', *Writer*, 88: 14–16, 1975.

20. B. Bettelheim, *The Uses of Enchantment: The meaning and importance of fairy tales*, New York: Alfred Knopf, 1976, pp. 121–3.

21. Ibid., p. 126.

3.4 □ *David Morley*

Referring to his lengthy conversational interviews with members of 18 South London families, David Morley discusses the practices and power relations of domestic TV viewing, and builds on the insights of previous pieces in this section. He sees television consumption as a social event situated within broader patterns of household leisure and labour, and explores issues such as genre preference and control over programme choice.

The gendered framework of family viewing

[...]

Too often the fact that television is pre-eminently a domestic medium, and that viewing is largely done in the family, is either ignored, or is registered only to be assumed away (as a pre-given backdrop to other activity) rather than being directly investigated itself. Television viewing may be a privatized activity – by comparison with going to the movies, for example – but it is still largely conducted within, rather than outside, social relations (except in the case of those who live in single-person households).

In this research, I took the premise that one should consider the basic unit of consumption of television to be the family/household rather than the individual viewer. This was done to raise questions about how the television set is handled in the home, how decisions are made – by which family members, at what times, what is watched – and how responses to different kinds of materials are discussed within the family, and so on. In short, this represents an attempt to analyse individual viewing activity within the household/familial relations in which it commonly operates.

Audience research that ignores this context cannot comprehend a number of key determinations relating to both viewing 'choices' and responses – those involving questions of differential power, responsibility, and control within the family at different times of the day and night.

[...]

Methodology

The methodology adopted was a qualitative one, whereby each family was interviewed in depth in order to elucidate their various accounts of how they understand the role of television in their overall leisure activities. The aim was to gain insight by this means into the terms within which respondents themselves defined their viewing activities.

[. . .]

The families were interviewed in their own homes during the spring of 1985. Initially the two parents were interviewed, then later in each interview their children were invited to take part in the discussion along with their parents. The interviews lasted between one and two hours and were audiotape-recorded and later transcribed in full for analysis.

Moreover, the interviewing method – unstructured discussion for a period of between one and two hours – was designed to allow a fair degree of probing. Thus, on points of significance I returned the discussion to the same theme at different stages in the interview from different angles. This means anyone 'putting me on' (consciously or unconsciously) by representing themselves through an artificial/stereotyped persona which has no bearing on their 'real' activities would have to be able to sustain their adopted persona through what could be seen as a quite complex form of interrogation. One powerful safeguard was provided by the presence of other members of the family, who often chipped in with their own queries or sarcastic comments when their husbands or wives seemed to them to be misrepresenting their activities.

Sample design

The sample consisted of eighteen families. All were drawn from one area of south London. All possessed a video recorder. All consisted of households of two adults living together with two or more dependent children up to the age of 18. All were white.

Because of the nature of the area where respondents were recruited, my sample contains a high proportion of working-class/lower-middle-class families – not necessarily in terms of income (my sample includes quite a wide range of income) but in terms of all the other aspects of class (cultural capital, education, etc.). Another limitation is indexed by the fact that the population of the area is very stable. Many of the families in my sample have lived there all their lives (and often their parents before them), and are a particularly stable group geographically, with strong roots in their local community – hence their strong and favourable responses to programmes set in the working-class areas of London with which they identify. Conversely, geographically mobile families are absent from my sample. Doubtless my findings would be very different with a sample recruited from the professional, geographically mobile 'non-nuclear' viewers of a more up-market area.

All of this has an obvious bearing on the strength of gender differentiation within the families in my sample. I am not arguing that all families in the UK repeat this pattern. Indeed, I would be amazed if it were repeated among more highly educated professional families. However, I am claiming that gender differentiation and traditional sex-role stereotyping are very strong among working-class/lower-middle-class families in stable inner-city areas, and that this has consequences to which I refer later in terms of viewing patterns.

Television and gender: the framework of analysis

The following major themes were identified in the interviews. They recur frequently enough with the different families to point to a reasonable degree of consistency of response. Clearly, one structural principle working across all the families interviewed is that of gender. These interviews raise important questions about the effects of gender in terms of:

1 power and control over programme choice;
2 styles of viewing;
3 planned and unplanned viewing;
4 television-related talk;
5 technology: use of video;
6 solo viewing and guilty pleasures;
7 programme-type preferences;
8 national versus local news programming.

Before describing the findings under these particular headings, I would first like to make some general points about the significance of the empirical differences which my research revealed between the viewing habits of the men and women in the sample. As will be seen, men and women offer clearly contrasting accounts of their viewing habits in terms of their differential power to choose what they view, how much they view, their viewing styles, and their choice of particular viewing material. However, I am not suggesting that these empirical differences are attributes of their [. . .] biological characteristics as men and women. Rather, I am trying to argue that these differences are the effects of the particular social roles that these men and women occupy within the home. Moreover, I am not suggesting that the particular pattern of gender relations within the home found here (with all the consequences which that pattern has for viewing behaviour) would necessarily be replicated either in nuclear families from a different class or ethnic background or in households of different types with the same class and ethnic backgrounds. Rather, it is always a case of how gender relations interact with, and are formed differently within, these different contexts.

Aside from these qualifications, there is one fundamental point which needs to be made concerning the basically different positioning of men and of women within the domestic sphere. The dominant model of gender relations within this society (and certainly within that sub-section of it represented in my sample) is one in which the home is primarily defined for men as a site of leisure – in distinction from the 'industrial time' of their employment outside the home – while the home is primarily defined for women as a sphere of work, whether or not they also work outside the home. This simply means that, in investigating television viewing in the home, one is by definition investigating something which men are better placed to do wholeheartedly, and which women seem only to be able to do distractedly and guiltily, because of their continuing sense of domestic responsibility. Moreover, this differential positioning is given a greater significance as the home becomes increasingly defined as the prime sphere of leisure.

When considering the empirical findings that follow, care must be taken to hold in view this structuring of the domestic environment by gender relations, as the backdrop against which these particular patterns of viewing behaviour have developed. Otherwise, we risk seeing this pattern as somehow the direct result of 'essential' or biological characteristics of men and women *per se*.

As Brunsdon has put it, commentating on research in this area, we could:

> mistakenly . . . differentiate a male – fixed, controlling, uninterruptable – gaze, and a female – distracted, obscured, already busy – manner of watching television. There is some empirical truth in these characterisations, but to take this empirical truth for explanation leads to a theoretical short-circuit. . . . Television is a domestic medium – and indeed the male/female differentiation above is very close to the way in which cinema and television have . . . been differentiated. Cinema, the audio-visual medium of the public sphere [demands] . . . the masculine gaze, while the domestic, 'feminine' medium is much less demanding, needing only an intermittent glance. This, given the empirical evidence . . . offers us an image of male viewers trying to 'masculinise' the domestic sphere. This way of watching television, however, seems not so much a masculine mode, but a mode of power. Current arrangements between men and women make it likely that it is men who will occupy this position in the home.[1]

Ang extends the argument

> Women's viewing patterns can only be understood in relation to men's patterns: the two are in a sense constitutive of each other. What we call 'viewing habits' are thus not a more or less static set of characteristics inhabited by an individual or group of individuals; rather they are the temporary result of a . . . dynamic . . . process . . . male/female relationships are always informed by power, contradiction, and struggle.[2]

So, as Ang argues, male and female modes of watching television are not two separate, discrete types of experience, clearly defined and static 'objects' of study, or expressions of essential natures. Rather than taking differences between male and female relations to television as an empirical given, one must look to how the structure of domestic power relations works to constitute these differences.

Power and control over programme choice

Masculine power is evident in a number of the families as the ultimate determinant on occasions of conflict over viewing choices. ('We discuss what we all want to watch and the biggest wins. That's me, I'm the biggest'.) It is even more apparent in the case of those families who have a remote-control device. None of the women in any of the families uses the remote-control device regularly. A number of them complain that their husbands use the device obsessively, channel-flicking across programmes when their wives are trying to watch something else. Characteristically, the remote-control device is the symbolic possession of the father (or of the son, in the father's absence), which sits 'on the arm of Daddy's chair' and is used almost exclusively by him. It is a highly visible symbol of condensed power relations:

Daughter: Dad keeps both of the automatic controls – one on each side of his chair.
Woman: Well, I don't get much chance, because he sits there with the automatic control beside him and that's it . . . I get annoyed because I can be watching a programme and he's flicking channels to see if a programme on the other side is finished so he can record something. So the television's flickering all the time, while he's flicking the timer. I just say, 'For goodness sake, leave it alone'. I don't get the chance to use the control. I don't get near it.
Woman: I don't get the chance to use the automatic control. I leave that down to him. It is aggravating, because I can be watching something and all of a sudden he turns it over to get the football result.
Daughter: The control's always next to Dad's chair. It doesn't come away when Dad's here. It stays right there.

Interestingly, the main exceptions to this overall pattern are those families in which the man is unemployed while his wife is working. In these cases it is slightly more common for the man to be expected to let other family members watch what they want to when it is broadcast while he videotapes what he would like to see in order to watch that later at night or the following day, because his timetable of commitments is more flexible than those of the working members of the family. Here we begin to see the way in which the position of power held by most of the men in the sample (and which their wives concede) is based not simply on the biological fact of being men but rather on a social definition of a masculinity of which employment (that is, the 'breadwinner' role) is a necessary and constituent part. When that condition is not met, the pattern of power relations within the home can change noticeably.

One further point needs to be made in this connection. It has to be remembered that this research is based on people's accounts of their behaviour, not on any form of direct observation of behaviour outside the interview itself. It is noteworthy that a number of the men show some anxiety to demonstrate that they are 'the boss of the household', and their very anxiety around this issue perhaps betokens a sense that their domestic power is ultimately a fragile and somewhat insecure thing, rather than a fixed and permanent 'possession' which they hold with confidence. Hence, perhaps physical possession of the channel-control device has symbolic importance to them.

Styles of viewing

One major finding is the consistency of the distinction made between the characteristic ways in which men and women describe their viewing activity. Essentially, men state a clear preference for viewing attentively, in silence, without interruption, 'in order not to miss anything'. Moreover, they display puzzlement at the way their wives and daughters watch television. The women describe viewing as a fundamentally social activity, involving ongoing conversation, and usually the performance of at least one other domestic activity (ironing, etc.) at the same time. Indeed, many women feel that just to watch television without doing anything else at the same time would be an indefensible waste of time, given their sense of their domestic obligations. To watch in this way is something they rarely do, except occasionally, alone or with other women friends, when they have managed to construct a situation in which to watch their favourite programme or video. The women note that their husbands are always 'on at them' to shut up, and the men can't really understand how their wives can follow the programmes if they are doing something else at the same time:

Man: We don't talk. They talk a bit.

Woman: You keep saying 'sshh'.

Man: I can't concentrate if there's anyone talking while I'm watching. But they can, they can watch and just talk at the same time. We just watch it, take it all in. If you talk, you've missed the bit that's really worth watching. We listen to every bit of it. If you talk you miss something that's important. My attitude is sort of 'go in the other room if you want to talk'.

Man: It really amazes me that this lot [his wife and daughters] can talk and do things and still pick up what's going on. To my mind it's not very good if you can do that.

Woman: Because we have it on all the time it's like second nature. We watch, and chat at the same time.

Woman: I knit because I think I am wasting my time just watching. I know what's going on, so I only have to glance up. I always knit when I watch.

Woman: I can't think of anything I'll totally watch. I don't just sit and watch. I'll probably sew, maybe knit. I very rarely just sit – that's just not me.

Woman: There is always something else, like ironing. I can watch anything while I'm doing the ironing. I've always done the ironing and knitting and that . . . you've got things to do, you know, and you can't keep watching television. You think, 'Oh my God, I should have done this or that'.

Brunsdon[3] offers a useful way of understanding the behaviour reported here. As she argues, it is not that women have no desire to watch television attentively, but rather that their domestic position makes it almost impossible for them to do so unless all other members of the household are 'out of the way'

[. . .]

Again, we see that these distinctive viewing styles are not simply characteristics of men and women as such but, rather, characteristics of the domestic roles of masculinity and femininity.

Planned and unplanned viewing

It is men, on the whole, who speak of checking through the paper (or the teletext) to plan their evening's viewing. Very few women seem to do this at all, except in terms of already knowing which evenings and times their favourite series are on and thus not needing to check the schedule. This is also an indication of a different attitude to viewing as a whole. Many of the women have a much more take-it-or-leave-it attitude, not caring much if they miss things (except for their favourite serials):

> *Man*:   Normally I look through the paper because you [his wife] tend to just put on ITV, but sometimes there is something good on the other channels, so I make a note – things like films and sport.
>
> *Woman*:   I don't read newspapers. If I know what's going to be on, I'll watch it. He tends to look in the paper. I don't actually look in the paper to see what's on.

One extreme example of the greater tendency for the men to plan their viewing in advance in this way is provided by one man, who at points sounds almost like a classic utilitarian aiming to maximize his pleasure quotient, in terms of both viewing choices and calculations of programme time in relation to video-tape availability, and so on:

> *Man*:   I've got it [the video – D. M.] on tonight on BBC, because it's *Dallas* tonight and I do like *Dallas*, so we started to watch *EastEnders* . . . and then they put on *Emmerdale Farm* because I like that, and we record *EastEnders* so we don't have to miss out. I normally see it on a Sunday anyway . . . I got it all worked out to tape. I don't mark it in the paper, but I register what's in there. Like tonight it's *Dallas* then at 9 o'clock it's *Widows*, and then we've got *Brubaker* on till the news. So the tape's ready to play straight through . . . what's on at 7.30? Oh, *This Is Your Life* and *Coronation Street*. I think BBC is better to record because it doesn't have the adverts. *This Is Your Life* we'll record because it's only on for half an hour, whereas *Dallas* is on for an hour, so you only use half an hour of tape . . . Yeah, Tuesday if you're watching the other programme it means you're going to have to cut it off halfway through. I don't bother, so I watch the news at 9 o'clock . . . yes, there's a film at 9 o'clock on a Tuesday, so what do I do? I record the film so I can watch *Miami Vice*, so I can watch the film later.

Or, as he puts it elsewhere, 'Evening times, I go through the paper, and I've got all my programmes sorted out'.

Television-related talk

Women show much less reluctance to 'admit' that they talk about television with their friends and workmates. Very few men (see below for the exceptions) say they do this. It is as if they feel that to admit that they watch too much television (especially with the degree of involvement that would be implied by finding it important enough to talk about) would be to put their very masculinity in question (see the section on programme-type preferences below). The only standard exception is where the men say that they talk about sports on television. Some part of this has simply to do with the fact that femininity is a more expressive cultural mode than is masculinity. Thus, even if women watch less, with less intent viewing styles, they are none the less inclined to talk about television more than men, despite the fact that men watch it more attentively:

Woman: Actually my Mum and my sister don't watch *Dynasty* and I often tell them bits about it. If my sister watches it, she likes it. And I say to her, 'Did you watch it?' and she says no. But if there's something especially good on one night, you know, you might see your friends and say 'Did you see so and so last night?' I occasionally miss *Dynasty*. I said to a friend, 'What happened?', and she's caught me up, but I tend to see most of the series. Marion used to keep me going, didn't she? Tell me what was happening and that.

Man: I might mention something on the telly occasionally, but I really don't talk about it to anyone.

Woman: At work we constantly talk about *Dallas* and *Dynasty*. We run them down, pick out who we like and who we don't like, what we think should happen next. General chit-chat. I work with quite a few girls, so we have a good old chat . . . we do have some really interesting discussions about television [at work]. We haven't got much else in common, so we talk a lot about television.

Woman: I go round my mate's and she'll say, 'Did you watch *Coronation Street* last night? What about so and so?' And we'll sit there discussing it. I think most women and most young girls do. We always sit down and it's 'Do you think she's right last night, what she's done?', or 'I wouldn't have done that', or 'Wasn't she a cow to him? Do you reckon he'll get . . . wonder what he's going to do?' Then we sort of fantasize between us, then when I see her the next day she'll say, 'You were right', or 'See, I told you so'.

Woman: Mums at school will say, 'Have you seen any good videos?' And when *Jewel in the Crown* was on, yes, we'd talk about that. When I'm watching the big epics, the big serials, I would talk about those.

Man: I won't talk about television at work unless there's been something like boxing on. I wouldn't talk about *Coronation Street* or a joke on *Benny Hill*.

There is one exception in the sample to this general pattern. In this case, it is not so much that the woman is any less willing than most of the others in the sample to talk about television as that her programme tastes are at odds with those of most of the women on the estate where she lives. However, in describing her own dilemma, and the way in which this disjunction of programme tastes functions to isolate her socially, she provides a very clear account of why most of the mothers on her estate do spend so much time talking about television:

Woman: Ninety-nine per cent of the women I know stay at home to look after their kids, so the only other thing you have to talk about is your housework, or the telly – because you don't go anywhere, you don't do anything. They are talking about what the child did the night before or they are talking about the telly – simply because they don't do anything else.

It could be argued that the claims many of the male respondents (see below) make about only watching 'factual' television are a misrepresentation of their actual behaviour, based on their anxiety about admitting to watching fictional programmes. However, even if this were the case, it would remain a social fact of some interest that the male respondents felt the compulsion to misrepresent their actual behaviour in this particular way. Moreover, this very reluctance to talk about some of the programmes they may watch has important consequences. Even if it were the case that men and women in fact watch the same range of programmes (contrary to the accounts they gave me), the fact that men are reluctant to talk about watching anything other than factual programmes or sports means that their viewing experience is profoundly different from that of the women in the sample. Given that meanings are made not simply in the moment of individual viewing, but also in the subsequent social processes of discussion and 'digestion' of material viewed, the men's much greater reluctance to talk about (part of) their viewing will mean that their consumption of television materials is of a quite different kind from that of their wives.

Technology: use of video

None of the women I interviewed operate the video-recorder themselves to any great extent, relying on their husbands or children to work it for them. Videos, like remote-control devices, are largely the possessions of fathers and sons:

Woman: There's been things I've wanted to watch and I didn't understand the video enough. She [the daughter] used to understand it more than us.

Woman: I'm happy with what I see, so I don't use the video much. I mean lots of the films he records I don't even watch. He watches them after we've gone to bed.

Man: I use it most – me and the boys more than anything – mostly to tape racing and pool, programmes we can't watch when they [the women] are watching.

Woman: I can't use the video. I tried to tape *Widows* for him and I done it wrong. He went barmy. I don't know what went wrong . . . I always ask him to do it for me because I can't. I always do it wrong. I've never bothered with it.

It is worth noting that these findings have also received provisional confirmation in the research that Gray[4] has conducted. Given the primary fact of women's tangential relation to the video machine, a number of consequences seem to follow. For instance, it is common for the woman to make little contribution to (and have little power over) decisions about hiring video tapes; it is rare for the woman actually to go into a video-tape shop to hire tapes; when various members of the family all have their 'own' blank tape on which to tape time-shifted material, it is common for the woman to be the one to let the others tape over something on her tape when theirs are full, and so on.

Given that many women routinely operate sophisticated pieces of domestic technology, it is clearly these gender expectations – operating alongside and framing any particular difficulties the woman may experience with the specific technology of video – that have to be understood as accounting for the alienation which most of the women in the sample express towards the video recorder.

Clearly there are other dimensions to the problem – from the possibility that the expressions of incompetence in relation to the video fall within the classic mode of dependent femininity which therefore 'needs' masculine help, to the recognition, as Gray points out, that some women may have developed what she calls a 'calculated ignorance' in relation to video, so that operating the video does not become yet another domestic task expected of them.

Solo viewing and guilty pleasures

A number of the women in the sample explain that their greatest pleasure is to be able to watch 'a nice weepie' or their favourite serial when the rest of the family isn't there. Only then do they feel free enough of their domestic responsibilities to indulge themselves in the kind of attentive viewing in which their husbands routinely engage. [. . .] The point is expressed most clearly by the woman who explains that she particularly enjoys watching early-morning television at the weekends, because these are the only occasions when her husband and sons 'sleep in' providing her with a rare chance to watch television attentively, without keeping half an eye on the needs of others.

Several of these women will arrange to view a video with other women friends during the afternoon. It is the classically feminine way of dealing with conflict – in this case over programme choice – by avoiding it, and 'rescheduling' the programme (often with someone's help in relation to the video) to a point where it can be watched more pleasurably:

> *Woman*:   That's one thing we don't have on when he's here, we don't have the game programmes on because he hates them. If we women are here on our own, I love it. I think they're lovely . . . if I'm here alone, I try to get something a bit mushy and then I sit here and have a cry, if I'm here on my own. It's not often, but I enjoy that.
>
> *Woman*:   If I get a good film on now, I'll tape it and keep it, especially if it's a weepie. I'll sit there and keep it for ages – especially in the afternoon – if there's no one here at all. If I'm tired, I'll put that on – especially in the winter – and it's nice then, 'cause you sit there and there's no one around.
>
> *Woman*:   If he's taped something for me, I either watch it early in the morning about 6 o'clock . . . I'm always up early, so I come down and watch it very early about 6.00 or 6.30 Sunday morning. Now I've sat for an hour this afternoon and watched *Widows*. I like to catch up when no one's here – so I can catch up on what I've lost . . . I love Saturday morning breakfast television. I'm on my own, because no one gets up till late. I come down and really enjoy that programme.
>
> *Woman*:   I get one of those love stories if he's not in.
>
> *Man*:   Yes, I don't want to sit through all that.
>
> *Woman*:   Yes, it's on his nights out. It doesn't happen very often.

What is at issue here is the guilt that most of these women feel about their own pleasures. They are, on the whole, prepared to concede that the drama and soap opera they like is 'silly' or 'badly acted' or inconsequential. They accept the terms of a masculine hegemony which defines their preferences as having low status. Having accepted these terms, they then find it hard to argue for their preferences in a conflict because, by definition, what their husbands want to watch is more prestigious. They then deal with this by watching their programmes, when possible, on their own, or only with their women friends, and will fit such arrangements into the crevices of their domestic timetables:

> *Woman*:   What I really like is typical American trash, I suppose, but I love it . . . all the American rubbish, really. And I love those Australian films. I think they're really good, those.

Woman: When the children go to bed he has the ultimate choice. I feel guilty if I push for what I want to see because he and the boys want to see the same thing, rather than what a mere woman would want to watch . . . if there was a love film on, I'd be happy to see it and they wouldn't. It's like when you go to pick up a video, instead of getting a nice sloppy love story, I think I can't get that because of the others. I'd feel guilty watching it because I think I'm getting my pleasure while the others aren't getting any pleasure, because they're not interested.

Programme-type preferences

My respondents displayed a notable consistency in this area, whereby masculinity was primarily identified with a strong preference for 'factual' programmes (news, current affairs, documentaries) and femininity identified with a preference for fictional programmes. The observation may be banal, but the strength of the consistency displayed here was remarkable whenever respondents were asked about programme preferences, and especially when asked which programmes they would make a point of watching and of doing so attentively:

Man: I like all documentaries . . . I like watching stuff like that . . . I can watch fiction but I am not a great lover of it.
Woman: He don't like a lot of serials.
Man: It's not my type of stuff. I do like the news, current affairs, all that type of stuff.
Woman: Me and the girls love our serials.
Man: I watch the news all the time, I like the news, current affairs and all that.
Woman: I don't like to so much.
Man: I watch the news every time, 5.40 pm, 6.00 pm, 9.00 pm, 10.00 pm, I try to watch.
Woman: I just watch the main news, so I know what's going on. Once is enough. Then I'm not interested in it.

There is a refrain among the men that to watch fiction, in the way that their wives do, is an improper and almost 'irresponsible' activity, an indulgence in fantasy of which they disapprove (compare nineteenth-century views of novel-reading as a 'feminizing' activity). This is perhaps best expressed in the words of the couples below, where in both cases the husbands clearly disapprove of their wives' enjoyment of 'fantasy' programmes:

Woman: That's what's nice about it [*Dynasty*]. It's a dream world isn't it?
Man: It's a fantasy world that everybody wants to live in, but that – no, I can't get on with that.

The husband quoted below takes the view that watching television in this way is an abrogation of civil responsibility:

Man: People get lost in TV. They fantasize in TV. It's taken over their lives . . . people today are coming into their front rooms, they shut their front door, and that's it. They identify with that little world on the box.
Woman: To me, I think telly's real life.
Man: That's what I'm saying. Telly's taken over your life.
Woman: Well, I don't mind it taking over my life. It keeps me happy.

The depth of this man's feelings on this point is confirmed later in the interview when he discusses his general leisure pursuits. He explains that he now regularly goes to the library in the afternoons and comments that he didn't realize the library was so good – 'I thought it was all just fiction'. Clearly, for him 'good' and 'fiction' are simply incompatible categories.

Second, men's programme-genre preference for factual material is also framed by a sense of guilt about the fact that watching television is 'second-best' to 'real' leisure activity, a feeling not shared by most of the women:

> Man: I'm not usually here. I watch it if there's nothing else to do, but I'd rather not ... In the summer I'd rather go out. I can't bear to watch TV if it's still light.
> Man: I like fishing, I don't care what's on if I'm going fishing. I'm not worried what's on the telly then.
> Man: If it's good weather, we're out in the garden or visiting people ... I've got a book and a crossword lined up for when she goes out, rather than just watch television.

Moreover, when the interviews move to a discussion of the fictional programmes that the men do watch, consistency is maintained by their preference for a 'realistic' situation comedy (a realism of social life) and a rejection of all forms of romance. These responses seem to fit fairly readily into a crude kind of syllogism of masculine/feminine relationships to television:

MASCULINE	FEMININE
Activity	Watching television
Factual programmes	Fictional programmes
Realist fiction	Romance

It could be claimed that my findings in this respect exaggerate the 'real' differences between men's and women's viewing and underestimate the extent of 'overlap' viewing as between men and women. Certainly my respondents offer a more sharply differentiated picture of men's and women's viewing than is ordinarily reported in survey work, which shows substantial numbers of men watching fictional programmes and equally substantial numbers of women watching factual programmes. However, this apparent contradiction largely rests on the conflation of 'viewing' with 'viewing attentively and with enjoyment'. Moreover, even if it could be demonstrated that my respondents had systematically misrepresented their behaviour to me (offering classic masculine and feminine stereotypes which belie the complexity of their actual behaviour), it would remain as a social fact of considerable interest that these were the particular forms of misrepresentation that respondents felt constrained to offer of themselves. Further, these tendencies – for the men to be unable to admit to watching fiction – themselves have real effects in their social lives.

National versus local news programming

As has been noted, it is men and not women that tend to claim an interest in news programming. Interestingly, this pattern varies when we consider local news programming, which a number of women claim to like. In several cases they give very cogent reasons for this. For instance, they say that they do not understand what international economic news is about and, as it has no experiential bearing on their lives, they are not interested in it. However, if there has been a crime in their local area, they feel they need to know about it, both for their own sake and for their children's sakes. This connects directly to their expressed interest in programmes like *Police Five*, or programmes warning of domestic dangers. In both these kinds of case the programme material has a practical value to them in terms of their domestic responsibilities, and thus they will make a point of watching it. Conversely, they frequently see themselves as having no practical relation to the area of national and international politics presented in the main news, and therefore do not watch it.

Conclusion

We need to broaden the framework of our analyses to focus on the contexts in which processes of communication occur, including especially those instances where class and gender considerations are articulated.

[. . .]

We need [. . .] to understand the phenomenology of domestic television viewing – that is, the significance of various modes of physical and social organization of the domestic environment as the context in which television viewing is conducted. There is more to watching television than what is on the screen – and that 'more' is, centrally, the domestic context in which viewing is conducted.

Notes

1. C. Brunsdon, 'Women watching television', Paper to Women and the Electronic Mass Media Conference, Copenhagen, 1986.
2. I. Ang, 'Wanted: Audiences. On the politics of empirical audience studies', in E. Seiter, H. Borchers, G. Kreutzner and E. Warth, eds, *Remote Control: Television, audiences and cultural power*, London: Routledge, 1989, p. 109.
3. C. Brunsdon, op. cit.
4. A. Gray, 'Behind closed doors: Video recorders in the home', in H. Baehr and G. Dyer, eds, *Boxed In: Women and television*, London: Pandora, 1987.

3.5 □ *Marie Gillespie*

Whereas Morley's sample of households was made up entirely of white nuclear families, Marie Gillespie's essay turns our attention towards very different viewing contexts. She writes about the responses of immigrant families to popular Hindi movies watched on video at home. Gillespie maps out the specific generational meanings which these films have for their domestic consumers.

Technology and tradition: audio-visual culture among South Asian families in West London

Introduction

This ethnographic account is based on research among South Asian families in Southall, Middlesex. Southall is a 'town', formerly an autonomous London borough, with a population of some 65,000. Its demographic majority is of South Asian origin, predominantly of Sikh religion, but divided along cross-cutting cleavages of national, regional, religious, and caste heritage.

The study evolved over seven years of teaching in two Southall high schools where the popularity of 'Indian' films was evident; and yet various manifestations of resistance to its pleasures seemed to signify a great deal more than mere expressions of taste or preference.

The extensive use of the VCR at home to view 'Indian'[1] films represents a powerful means for grandparents and parents to maintain links with their country of origin. Second-generation children, however, born and educated in Britain, position themselves and are positioned rather differently in relation to notions of 'Asian' and 'British' culture. [. . .]

[. . .] This paper therefore is an attempt to re-present 'their voices', concentrating on their interpretations of popular Indian films and the themes and issues arising from their viewing experiences and which they find salient.

The ethnographic data are based on interviews carried out with young people predominantly of Punjabi origin and aged 15–18. A set of basic questions was used to spark off each interview. When do you watch? What do you watch? With whom do you watch? Who chooses what you watch in which situations? [. . .] This account will be structured around four main concerns:

First, it will contextualize the study by briefly outlining the history of Indian cinema in Southall, and the shift from public exhibition to private viewing in the home. Secondly, it will examine the implications of this shift by focusing on the family-viewing context. It will explore questions of choice and preference alongside issues of family power and control. The third part will examine the responses of young people to Indian films and the factors mediating their various interpretations. Finally, it will bring together the diverse strands of the study in order to highlight the different ways in which viewing experiences are used.

Indian cinema in Southall: from public pleasure to private leisure

The first 'Indian' films were shown in Southall in 1953 in hired halls and then in three local cinemas. During the 1960s and 1970s the cinema provided the principal weekend leisure activity in Southall and represented an occasion for families and friends to get together; the social event of the week.

In 1978, when VCRs came on the market, many families were quick to seize the opportunity to extend their choice and control over viewing in the home. Many Asian communities obtained them as early as 1978/9 before most other households in Britain. It is now estimated that between 40 and 50 per cent of households in Britain now own or rent a VCR but in Southall the figure is held to be 80 per cent.[2]

Most shops rent popular Hindi (also known as 'Bombay') films and although films in Punjabi and Urdu are also obtainable from shops they lack the broad-based appeal of the popular Hindi movie. In fact the Bombay film has gained something of a cultural hegemony in South Asia and among many 'Asian' settlers across the world. To understand this one has to look to the specific evolution of the popular Hindi genre which, in order to appeal to a mass audience, had to produce films which would cross the linguistic, religious, and regional differences that exist within India, as indeed within Southall.

Many of the films combine a catholicity or universality of appeal with a careful handling of regional and religious differences. A distinctive form of Bombay Hindi, characterized by a certain 'linguistic openness' has evolved which makes most films accessible also to speakers of other South Asian languages. The distinctive visual style, often foregrounded over dialogue, combines with successive modes of spectacle, action and emotion which facilitates cross-cultural understanding.[3] In the light of this we can understand the huge uptake of Hindi films on cassette among the diverse linguistic groups in Southall.

With the arrival of video, the adventure, romance, and drama of the Bombay film was to be enjoyed in domestic privacy. A small piece of home technology brought the cinema hall into the home, or so it appeared. A lot was gained but much was lost. The weekly outing became a thing of the past as the cinemas closed and the big screen image shrunk into the TV box and entered the flow of everyday life in the living room.

[. . .]

But the consequences of a decade of video use are perceived in contradictory ways by the youth of Southall. Many young people feel that the VCR has served further to isolate the community from mainstream British society. It is also seen to have specific effects on the lives of women: 'The video has isolated the community even more. They might as well be in India, especially the women'. Others see it as a liberating pleasure, especially for females: 'Some girls can't get out of the house that much so they can get a film and keep themselves occupied within the four walls of the house. It's an advantage for them'.

Such contradictory evaluations need to be seen in the contexts in which they originate.

Domestic viewing contexts

[. . .] For the purpose of this account I shall concentrate on weekend family viewing because this situation was so frequently and consistently discussed by all interviewees, and due to the importance given to it within this cultural context.[4]

The VCR is used predominantly at the weekend in most families. Viewing 'Indian' films on video is the principal, regular family leisure activity. Weekend family gatherings around the TV set is a social ritual repeated in many families. The VCR and TV screen become the focus and locus of interaction. Notions of togetherness and communality are stressed: 'It's probably the only time in the week that we are all together so when we're watching a film at least we're all together.'

This togetherness is by no means that of passive viewers: 'No one is silent, we're all talking through the film about what's happening here and there and generally having a chat . . . it sort of brings you closer together'.

The weaving of conversation through the narrative is facilitated by an impressive familiarity with films brought about by repeated viewings. The episodic structure of films which moves the spectator through the different modes of spectacle, song and dance, drama, action, and affect also provides natural breaks for talk, emotion and reflection.

With such large family gatherings the question of power and control over viewing becomes important. The interviews highlight the way in which parents actively set and maintain viewing rules which govern viewing patterns and modes of parent–child interaction.

While the father is usually seen to determine when children are allowed access to the screen by his absence or presence in the home, the mother is perceived as exercising a greater degree of power and control over the choice of what is watched. This was a significant pattern across the interviews, emphasizing the important role mothers play in socializing their children in the domestic context. It also makes clear that the relationship between family power structures and family viewing patterns is not one of simple correspondence.

There are also clear differences in the attentiveness and in the degree of salience of Indian films to various family members, which are obscured by the simple observation that the family all watched the same programme.[5] Many young people say they sit with parents and view parts of the films just to please them or that their parents encourage or even 'force' them to watch.

As gender differences are important to understand parental control over viewing they are also a significant factor in understanding young people's viewing preferences and behaviour. Boys tend to experience greater freedom in deciding how they use their leisure time and spend more time engaged in activities outside the home. In contrast, girls are usually socialized to remain within the domestic realm and often participate in strong and supportive female cultures in the home where the viewing of Indian films on video frequently plays an important role. This explains to some extent the generally greater engagement with popular Hindi videos on the part of most girls interviewed. In one interview two boys rather begrudgingly claim: 'It doesn't hurt to watch an Indian film with the parents.' 'No, it kills you.'

In spite of this repeatedly expressed reluctance the way in which the screen can serve social interaction in the family tends to override individual preferences and return young people to the family situation. One boy commented to the general agreement of the group: 'Well we don't usually stay in another room while they're watching, if you've got something to yourself, you isolate yourself don't you?' It is clear that what might be seen on the one hand as 'enforced' or 'reluctant' viewing can take on pleasurable connotations where the emphasis is on 'being together'. Parents do not have much time for leisure due to long working hours and shift work, so the time when the family is together around the TV set is often much appreciated by all concerned.

Conversely, the family audience is frequently fragmented by English and American films: 'When it's Indian films it's all of us together but when it's English films it's just me and my brother.' This fragmentation is partly due to the texts of English and American films themselves. Given parental reservations about the language, sensuality, and references to sexuality, young people may often prefer to view them on their own to escape parental censure or vigilance.

You may now have the impression that the avid consumption of VCR films falls into two neat categories. While Hindi films tend to be viewed in large family gatherings and to be celebrated by intense social interaction, British and American films tend to be consumed on their own in a more or less assertive circumvention of parental control and preferences. While viewing patterns tend indeed to correspond to this dichotomy, young people's viewing of Hindi films raises further ethnographic questions about perceptions of 'Indianness' and Britain or India and 'Britishness'.

Representations of India

For young people in Southall who have little or no direct experience outside the UK, perceptions of India will be founded on a complex combination of factors. But invariably they will also be influenced by 'Indian' films. Even for those who have lived or spent long periods in India the films provide a counterpoint to their own personal experiences.

Throughout the interviews a series of related binary oppositions frame and structure accounts of how India is perceived through the films:

Village	City
Poverty	Wealth
Communality	Individualism
Tradition	Modernity
Morality	Vice

The interviewees' accounts are in some measure reconstructions of and responses to patterned social and moral discourses prevalent in popular Hindi films, where a pristine and moral rural India is often constructed by opposing it to an exotic and decadent 'other' – usually signified by symbols of the west and city life.

Thus, across the interviews, village life is frequently contrasted with city life. The village community is seen as one of extended kin where co-operation and communality prevail, notions of individualism are absent. Village life is seen as 'pure' because 'people are so honest there, they never look with the "evil eye", they help each other even though they're poor, they never "skank" [betray] one another'.

Such interpretations contrast with those of city life which, through the films, is perceived as decadent, immoral, and polluted – a place 'where prostitutes hang out and where even pundits [priests] try to rape girls'.

There was considerable criticism of the 'unrealistic' portrayal of village life and an often acute awareness is shown of the selective and ideological nature of representations: 'There's not so much about the landless labourers and the position of women, you know, who spend hours and hours looking for water and fuel . . . in the scorching heat.'

[. . .]

Striking gender differences emerge in the framing of accounts. Girls often express their perceptions of India through an exploration of the social and moral values inherent in the films via a 'retelling' of the narratives. In contrast boys seem to be much more concerned with representational issues, particularly 'negative images' and, in many cases, reject Hindi films *per se* on that basis.

Several male respondents see Indian films as offensive in their emphasis on poverty and corruption: 'They should not portray India as if it's really poor and backward even though they're Indians themselves, it's degrading; that's a lot of the reason I don't like Indian films.'

Others ridicule the 'backward image' of 'Indians' in the films because of the different norms associated with fashion and style but they also remark upon the selective nature of images: 'they follow up too late in India, they still wear flares, though I must admit they're not backward in everything they're very advanced in technology but they don't show you those aspects of India.' One boy vehemently rejected the films and wished to dissociate himself from both films and India but not without some irony: 'I didn't learn anything from the films apart from the fact that India is one of the most corrupt countries in the world', and later, 'that country has nothing to do with me any more'.

Such discussions often provoke comments on representations of India in British media more generally which is seen on the whole to reinforce an 'uncivilized', poverty-stricken image of India: 'Documentaries shown in this country degrade India badly as well.' Strong resentment is expressed at the way India is 'degraded' in the west by the circulation of images of poverty, underdevelopment, death, and disease. Such images are linked to the 'degradation' of Indians in Britain where they 'get racist harassment'.

In identifying 'salient' themes and making selective interpretations, a range of 'meanings' are projected onto the films which undoubtedly derive from experiences of racism in Britain. Such experiences underpin and sensitize responses to constructions of Indian society in Hindi films and in the media generally. Boys, in particular, show an understanding of how Indian films may be rebuked and ridiculed as 'backward', 'foreign' and 'ludicrous' by 'outsiders' (for example their white peers) but they also, clearly, feel somewhat estranged from the sense of 'Indianness' and from the 'India' represented in the films. At the same time, there is a tacit acknowledgement that the films may be used to confirm what constitute dominant discourses on India in British society, and an underlying awareness of how they function as racist discourses. As a result the boys would appear to occupy shifting and often contradictory positions from which they view and interpret the films – positions which vary according to context.

It would appear that experiences of racism as well as the reading of films are gender specific. A similar connection may be detected between gender and genre.

Genre

For nearly a century Hindi films have been either rebuked or ignored in the west by critics, academics, and film enthusiasts alike. Such institutionalized disdain and ignorance is not only a symptom of racism but feeds directly into it. The fierce rejection of the popular Hindi film, seen as a genre in itself, especially among the boys interviewed, echoes western critical discourses about the genre. Films are consistently criticized for being 'all the same', based on 'ideas got from Westerns . . . just a mixture of everything . . . commercial . . . full of songs and running round trees and rose gardens'.

An 18-year-old male interviewee in a rather eloquent condemnation of Indian films claims: 'With the standards of media appreciation in the west it's hard to understand the sort of psyche that would appreciate these kinds of film again and again and again. . . . If you've been exposed to a film culture based on plots and detailed cinematography then you'd expect the same from the other culture and if it doesn't match up to that standard you don't want to see it anymore . . . it's like driving a Morris Minor after you've driven a Porsche.'

The widespread condemnation of popular Indian films and the coincidence of views held by both film critics and many of the boys interviewed does not confirm a 'truth' about Hindi cinema but, rather, exposes a common frame of reference which is based on dominant Hollywood and western film-making practices. Clearly, a cultural experience dominated by western film genres will initially militate against an engagement with popular Hindi films, which are likely to disorientate the spectator by subverting generic conventions, even where language presents no barrier.

The focus of this study on South Asian families should not exclude consideration of the context of power relations in which this community lives and between western and 'Third World' countries and cultures. It should, rather, lead us further to consider the nature of white norms and white cultural practices, especially when they entail the abrogation of measures for culturally distinct genres which are clearly incommensurate. Otherwise such a study becomes merely a descriptive exercise, devoid of political responsibility, intent, or analysis.

What becomes clear from the interviews is that for those who do find pleasure in popular Hindi films, the skilful blending of certain generic ingredients is crucial: the screenplay, the music and songs, the emotional appeal, spectacle, production values, and, of course, the stars. But it is above all when narrative is discussed in the interviews that one becomes aware of a deeper engagement with the films. The pleasures involved become apparent but we can also begin to unravel some further causes of resistance to films.

Narrative

According to many writers, the popular Hindi film has evolved from village traditions of epic narration, and the dramas and characters, as well as the structure of the mythological epics, are regularly and openly drawn upon. Film-makers and theorists claim that there are only two stories or 'metatexts', the *Mahabharata* and the *Ramayana*, and that every film can be traced back to these stories.

[. . .]

What seems to distinguish the Hindi film most from its western counterparts is the form and movement of the narrative. The balance between narrative development, spectacle, and emotion is rather different from that in western films. Spectacle alone risks losing an audience. Skilled narration involves the swift transition between well-balanced modes of spectacle and an emotional involvement invited by the reassuring familiarity of many narratives, structured by discourses, deeply rooted in Indian social, moral, and psychic life.[6]

One of the most common assertions across the interviews is that the films all have the same type of stories. Usually this means that the films are 'totally predictable' and therefore not worth watching: 'who wants to sit and watch a film where you can work out the whole plot in the first five minutes?'

Three basic narrative themes of Hindi cinema particularly popular in the late 1970s and 1980s are repeatedly identified and referred to by interviewees: (1) 'Dostana', where the bond of male friendship overcomes the desire for a woman; (2) 'lost and found' parents and children are separated and reunited years later following the revelation of mistaken identities; and (3) revenge, villains get their just deserts at the hands of the heroes they wronged.

Interviewees frame their accounts with references to the discourses which commonly structure these narratives, which are those of kinship duty, social obligation, solidarity, respect or 'izzat', and trust. A sense of social 'order' and 'ideal social relations' is related to living in harmony with fate and respecting social obligations and ties of friendship and family.

Hindi film aesthetics, it is argued, are based not on cognition, as in the west, but in re-cognition. Like Hindu epics whose familiar stories form part of the fundamental myths of Indian society, the Hindi film is said to have evolved a broad framework of its own. Anil Saari[7] claims: 'thus one film is like another, each film confirms once again the world as it is and has been and is likely to remain. The very hopelessness created by poverty and social immobility demands that the world and distractions from it remain as they are. That is indeed how the world is for the average Indian who is not a member of the ruling elite.'

Many interviewees analyse the narrative closure of contemporary Hindi films and compare them with the older, black and white, social-realist films prevalent in the 1950s and 1960s, in which there is an upsurge of renewed interest among young and old alike: 'They all have happy endings by the way . . . unlike the older films, tragedies are being solved by lucky, fortunate events that turn everything upside down, if a heroine's about to die these days she's saved by a handsome doctor at the last moment . . . everything turns out all right and people have nothing to think about, nothing to cry about, unlike the older films.'

Certain fundamental differences in the narrative structures of 'Hindi' and 'western' films are highlighted in the interviews. English films are seen as 'continuous all the way . . . they just continue, no songs, no dances . . . that's why I find them boring'. Pleasure is taken in the non-linear narratives. The intricate and convoluted nature of story-telling becomes apparent through attempts at narrative reconstructions. Hindi films are not tightly linear but build in more or less circular fashion through a number of climaxes which are counterposed with scenes of humour, spectacle, and 'pure' emotional import. It is not so much a question of *what* will happen next that drives the narrative but of *how* it will be framed, not so much an enigma to be solved as a moral disordering to be resolved.

Affective involvement is a crucial component of films and is ensured not only by cinematic techniques which encourage identification and involvement, e.g. the use of close-ups, subjective point of view shots, shot reverse shots, but also through the songs: 'The songs back up everything . . . they have real feeling in them and it's not just any old songs, they relate to the actual situations of the films, they get you emotionally involved and influence you'. As in melodrama, undischarged emotion which cannot be accommodated within the action is expressed in song and music: 'Whenever that song comes on I cry, I can't control myself . . . it's the father of a girl singing to her before she leaves the family to get married, he sings about how you are leaving us now and saying how when you were young I used to hold you in my arms, how I used to play with you. . . . I can't listen to that song without tears pouring out . . . and I think of my sister when she will be leaving us.'

This passage highlights the way in which the Hindi film tends to address and move its spectator by way of affect. This positioning depends for its full effect on certain kinds of cultural competence, most notably a knowledge of the 'ideal moral universe' of the Hindi film. Such cultural knowledge is acquired by young people to very varying degrees and while clearly lending enormous spectator power to some, disallows others from any deep engagement with the films. Conventions of verisimilitude also affect the relationship between text and viewer.

Fantasy and realism

'When I watch an Indian film after that I'm in heaven but I don't relate to the real world like I did . . . they're in rose gardens and the music just springs up from nowhere . . . that's why people like watching them to get away from their own lives, what do drugs do? They take you to another world . . . so do Indian films but they are a safer way out of your problems.'

For those who enjoy Hindi films fantasy is a chief source of pleasure. The songs and dances as well as their settings often provide discrete dream-like sequences and 'a moment of escape from reality' for the spectator. In comparing drug-induced euphoria with the sensations provoked by the fantasy sequences in films this young girl gives us some insight into the desire provoked by the fantasy films: 'I wouldn't mind sitting around in rose gardens or deserts being loved and things like that.'

Such anti-realism is seen by some as escapist: 'They're fantasies for the poor they show them what they cannot afford . . . they're satisfied with the songs . . . they create the dream sequences for them.' They are also seen as exploitative and politically reactionary: 'Most of them are just sheer escapism. . . . I think that has quite a negative effect because it allows people to ignore the reality of their situation, the political realities of India, the exploitation and oppression of the masses.' Several interviewees compared Hindi films of the 1970s and 1980s to the 'social realist' films of the 1950s: 'I think people could identify their immediate lives with them, they were true to life, if they showed a farmer losing his crops after years of hard labour that was a reflection of life and that used to happen to people and they would sit in the cinema and say "well that's true!" There was nothing magical about it as it is now. After this period, people didn't want tragedies, they wanted fantasies, they wanted a means of escape, they wanted to break out of reality and that's when the "masala" films started coming out.'

However, in spite of such criticisms, many of the interviewees do not ignore the cathartic and therapeutic aspects of films. Indeed they are seen to enable a temporary release from the tensions of everyday life and to help discharge distressful emotions: 'I must admit I'm scared of my parents (finding out I have a boyfriend) but after I've watched a film, and listened to a few songs and calmed myself down, I'm not scared of my parents anymore so they give you courage in a way.'

Selective but contradictory judgements about conventions of realism in films are frequent across the interviews as with this girl who on the one hand claims: 'Indian films don't really relate to reality, they're really sheltered . . . it's just fantasy they make it out so perfect.' And yet, later the film's realistic portrayal of love is endorsed: 'Sometimes we'll just sit there and wonder if there's a thing called love . . . whereas in an Indian film you're so convinced that love is real . . . that it's true, that it's really there.'

It is clear that an exposure to western conventions of realism influence responses considerably. Attention is paid to *mise-en-scène* and anachronism is not easily tolerated. A determined fidelity to details of period representation and dress is adhered to by young male respondents: 'They'll show a man fighting for Independence and you'll see a man on a motorbike with sunglasses and jeans they should at least have the clothes of the period.'

'They'll be showing a scene in the eighteenth century with horse-drawn carriage and at the back you'll see 1980s taxis, scooters, and high-rise buildings. It spoils everything. If only they [the directors] thought more about what they were doing, it looks as though they haven't planned it.' Western conventions of realism also provide expectations about the way characters should behave, dress, and act. The reality status of stunt sequences is rebuked where production values are low: 'It's stupid motorbikes crossing lakes when you know it's a cartoon.'

There is in Hindi films an acceptable realism and logic beyond the material which is unbelievable. In fact the criteria of verisimilitude in Hindi cinema appears to refer primarily to the skill demonstrated in manipulating the rules of the film's moral universe. Among regular viewers one is more likely to hear accusations of unbelievability if the codes of ideal kinship are flouted than if the hero performs some outrageously unrealistic feat as is the case with disaffected viewers. [. . .]

Social and cultural uses of viewing experiences

The final part of this account concerns the social and cultural uses of viewing experiences, broadening the scope beyond that of contemporary popular Hindi films to include the full range of films viewed.

For the older members of the community, nostalgia is a key element in the pleasure experienced through film. In one particularly moving account by a man in his 70s, tears welled in his eyes as he recounted: 'When we see black-and-white films it reminds us of our childhood, our school days, our school mates, of what we were thinking, of what we did do, of our heroes . . . and I tell you this gives us great pleasure.' The films would appear to act as a form of collective popular memory and some parents are able to convey a sense of their past in India to their children.

With the emergence of second-generation children, parents and grandparents have found new uses for films. These uses are primarily defined in terms of linguistic, religious, and socio-cultural learning. In viewing Indian films together many families are enabled to come together on a 'shared' linguistic basis. Both parents and children see this as a major advantage of watching films: 'They help children get a hold of the language.'

For many children the films provide one of the rare opportunities, outside communication in the family and community, to hear that language used and legitimated: 'They can hear and see how the language is used and should be used.' One boy put it more directly: 'They teach not only the language but how "to be" in an Indian environment.' The notion of language as transmitter of culture is prevalent among parents: 'If the children don't speak the language they lose their culture.' Language is a potent symbol of collective identity and often the site of fierce loyalities and emotional power. In the context of a society which constructs linguistic difference as a problem rather than as a tool, the desire to defend and maintain one's linguistic heritage becomes strong.

In a community faced with religious distinctiveness and at times division, it is not surprising that cultural identity is often construed as being based not only on linguistic but also on religious continuity. 'Religious' or mythological films are also watched for devotional purposes, particularly by Hindu families, and often integrated with daily acts of worship: 'When we start fasting we always watch these films, sometimes five times a day . . . you kind of pray to God at the same time you know.'

The films are also used as a form of religious education: 'They help parents teach their children about the Holy Books like the *Ramayana*, the *Mahabharata*, and the *Bhaghavat Gita*. It's the tradition in families to tell the young children the stories but some families don't have the time and so there are children who don't know who is Rama.' In some families viewing devotional films has come to replace reading the holy books. Certainly, the video is seen as a great advantage in familiarizing children with parables and religious stories, largely due to the widespread illiteracy of second- and third-generation children in their mother tongue. Not only are the religious and moral values inherent in the films an important aspect of viewing but the visual representation of the deity plays an extremely important symbolic role in the devotional and ritual acts of worship. This relates to the importance of popular forms of religious iconography in Indian society.

Parents use the films to talk about religious festivals: 'Here we can never really celebrate festivals like Holi which involves the whole village and people smearing each other's faces with colour. No one does that here but when you watch you can really appreciate what it's like in India. Here the kids just know about the fireworks but they don't know the real basic thing about why, they don't know about the religious aspects of the festivals.'

Young people and their parents use the films to negotiate, argue, and agree about a wider range of customs, traditions, values, and beliefs. Together, they often enjoy films which encourage discussion: 'films which bring out the contradictions in families, the arranged marriage system, the caste or class system'. The films function as tools for eliciting attitudes and views on salient themes; family affairs and problems, romance, courtship, and marriage were often discussed. There is a recurrent recognition of the 'influence' and value of the films in the lives of girls in particular. There are frequent references to the 'meanings, the really deep meanings, which reflect the way we think, it's just so . . . so . . . so I don't know, so influential'.

It would appear that Hindi films can serve to legitimate a particular view of the world

and at the same time to open up contradictions within it. So while young people sometimes use films to deconstruct 'traditional culture' many parents use them to foster certain
'traditional' attitudes, values and beliefs in their children. Films are expected to have
both an entertainment and a didactic function and are seen by parents as useful agents
of cultural continuity and as contributing to the (re)-formation of cultural identity.

Various degrees of scepticism are registered among the boys about parents' attempts
to 'artifically maintain a culture' through film: 'Parents want their children to maintain certain religious values, beliefs and customs but that doesn't mean that Indian films
are necessarily going to educate them in that way. They may well do the opposite
. . . I think the moral standards in most recent films is pretty appalling.' But clear distinctions are made between religion and a sense of cultural identity and whilst firmly
upholding the Sikh faith one boy claims: 'Parents use the films to represent their culture
to their children but that will not work because those are not my roots, that place [India]
has nothing to do with me anymore.'

Many parents lament what they see as a process of progressive 'cultural loss' in each
generation of children. Looking to the past they attempt to re-create 'traditional
culture'. Meanwhile young people, with eyes to the future, are busy re-creating something 'new'. The striving after cultural continuity and the negotiation of cultural identity are thus inescapably dialectical processes and they must, moreover, be seen in the
widest possible context. The notion of viewing as a social activity which takes place
in families needs to be extended to include more detailed explorations of the wider
social, cultural, and ideological contexts and uses of the VCR.

What is clear is that for the young people interviewed a sense of ethnic, national,
and cultural identity does not displace or dominate the equally lived and formed identities based on age, gender, peer group, and neighbourhood. Static notions of culture
are extremely disabling as are absolutist views of black-and-white cultures as fixed,
mutually impermeable expressions of 'racial' or national identity. Notions of national
culture with unique customs and practices understood as 'pure' homogeneous nation-
ality need to be challenged.

One is reminded in this context of the arguments put forward by Benedict Anderson[8]
about the use of cultural artefacts in constructing 'imagined communities' based on
notions of nation and nationness. The 'imagined communities', constructed and created
through the viewing of films on VCR may link Asian communities across the world.
However, these communities, with their origins in history and experience, are not fixed
but change, develop and combine, and are in turn redispersed in historic processes.

If cultural practices are detached from their origins they can be used to found and
extend new patterns of communication which can give rise to new common identities. Perhaps most of all this study provides a contemporary example of how 'traditional' ties are created and recreated out of present rather than past conditions.[9]

Notes

1. The term 'Indian' film is used most commonly by interviewees, but distinctions between
   films are also drawn according to language (i.e. Hindi, Punjabi and Urdu) as well as genre.
2. This estimated figure is based on surveys carried out in three Southall schools.

3. A. Lutze, 'From Bharata to Bombay: Change and continuity in Hindi film aesthetics', in B. Pfleiderer, ed., *The Hindi Film*: *Agent and re-agent of cultural change*, Manohar, 1985.
4. Other contexts documented in the research included siblings viewing together in the home, viewing with friends/peers, women/girls-only groups, women solo viewing and male-only viewing.
5. For further accounts of family contexts of viewing see, for example, D. Morley, *Family Television*: *Cultural power and domestic leisure*, London: Comedia, 1986; P. Simpson, ed., *Parents Talking Television*: *Television in the home*, London: Comedia, 1987.
6. R. Thomas, 'Indian cinema pleasures and popularity', *Screen*, 26: 123–35, 1985.
7. A. Saari, Contribution to B. Pfleiderer, ed., op. cit.
8. B. Anderson, *Imagined Communities*: *Reflections on the origin and spread of nationalism*, London: Verso, 1983.
9. From 1988 to 1991, Marie Gillespie conducted further fieldwork in Southall. For details of this later work, see M. Gillespie, 'Soap viewing, gossip and rumour amongst Punjabi youth in Southall', in P. Drummond, R. Paterson and J. Willis, eds, *National Identity and Europe*: *The television revolution*, London: British Film Institute, 1993; M. Gillespie, 'The Mahabharata: From Sanskrit to sacred soap. A case study of the reception of two contemporary televisual versions', in D. Buckingham, ed., *Reading Audiences*: *Young people and the media*, Manchester: Manchester University Press, 1993; M. Gillespie, *Television, Ethnicity and Cultural Change*, London: Routledge, 1995.

3.6 □ *Derek Wynne*

Derek Wynne offers a fascinating ethnographic description of taste wars on a middle-class housing estate – examining the divergence of residents' consumer preferences and lifestyle choices. His piece is particularly useful in reminding us that domestic contexts are set within wider neighbourhood cultures, and the emphasis he places on social class and class fractions also helps to balance a focus on gender in many of the other readings we have selected.

Leisure, lifestyle and the construction of social position

Using Bourdieu's[1] conceptualization of economic and cultural capital this paper provides an ethnographic analysis of the leisure practices of residents living on a private housing estate in the north-west of England.

Their socio-economic location is examined and it is suggested that their leisure practices can be understood as one of the ways in which social position is constructed.

[. . .]

Setting

The estate, which I will refer to as 'The Heath', is located [. . .] between two major conurbations and close to motorway and rail networks connecting both. It is situated on a 100 acre site between two small villages, and is bounded by two country lanes and agricultural land. There are approximately 400 houses on the estate, together with a common green area in the centre. Built alongside the common green area is a leisure club for the use of residents. It contains a lounge bar and poolroom, a dance floor/meeting hall, indoor swimming pool, sauna and two squash courts with a viewing gallery. Adjacent to this complex are two floodlit tennis courts; in addition, the construction company's former sales offices have been extended and are currently being used as a youth club for residents' children. It is interesting to note that this 'youth club' is in fact known by some residents as the young persons' club. Conversations with such residents indicate that they feel that such a title is more appropriate than 'youth club' as it allows for some social distance from the image of the 'youth club' and conno-tations of working class 'folk devils'. Each household pays an annual sum, currently £130, for the use and maintenance of the facilities described above. A manager, gardener and cleaners are employed by residents, whose elected committee has overall responsibility for the estate and its facilities.

With respect to the residents' use of the facilities, analysis reveals considerable differ-ences according to their possession of cultural and economic capital. For the purposes of this analysis I wish to distinguish between those whose socio-economic mobility has been attained primarily by entry into the economic field, achieving middle and senior management positions without the experience of full-time higher education, and those who have attained similar socio-economic positions following their experience of full-time higher education and the obtaining of professional qualifications. Employing Bour-dieu's terminology, the first of these groups could be said to have invested primarily in economic capital, and the second primarily in cultural capital. The resultant analysis reveals considerable differences in the leisure lifestyles of these socially mobile groups. However, in spite of these differences, each can be seen as constructing social posi-tion through the leisure activities in which they engage.

Both groups can be described as 'new middle class': new, in the sense that both came from family backgrounds in which their fathers were employed in manual labour; middle class, in the sense that they are in the highest income-earning groupings, have occupations in middle and senior management, and/or are professionally/technically qualified, and own homes valued at at least two, in some cases three, times the average for this area of the country. The home owning history of both groups exhibits a series of moves within the housing market and a considerable degree of geographical mobility. [. . .] Nevertheless, as [. . .] the ethnography proceeded it became clear that there were at least two different fractions of the new middle class on this estate, identified not just by me but by the residents themselves. Both are highly visible in terms of their use of the leisure facilities available, but these different groups use the facilities in very different ways.

Employing the categories produced by residents themselves, the first group I have called 'the drinkers', and the second 'the sporters'. As stated above, although members of both groups share similar socio-economic origins, they can be distinguished with respect to their educational backgrounds and current occupations. The major differ-ences with respect to these two features are as follows:

Their educational backgrounds. Formal, full time education for 'the drinkers' is most likely to have finished at the age of 16, and any further qualifications will have been attained while in full time employment. By contrast 'the sporters' are more likely to have continued with full time higher education, entering employment as graduates.

Their employment activities. 'The drinkers' are employed in middle and senior manage-ment positions in industry, manufacturing and distributing, whereas 'the sporters' are more likely to be employed as professionals in either the public or private sector. Occu-pational 'advancement' for 'the drinkers' has been accomplished primarily through work rather than education, although some have obtained vocational or technical skills through 'night school' or in-service training. In contrast, most 'sporters' entered employment at graduate level with professional qualifications. Although there are self-employed members of both groups, those categorized as 'drinkers' tend towards the more traditional positions, whereas those in the other group tend towards the new services. For example, among 'the drinkers' are a self-employed electrical contractor, a distributor to the retail trade whose business has developed from a market stall-holding and a supplier of bathroom fittings. In 'the sporters' category are a self-employed accountant, a partner in a computer software house, the owner of a franchized estate agency and a land surveyor specializing in legal contract work for building firms. All of the latter developed their own businesses after having worked as professional employees of larger companies.

Leisure practices

The case study material looks at some of the more general features associated with leisure lifestyles and examines the use of the recreational facilities on the estate by the two groups identified above.

Observation notes and case study material on the leisure lifestyles of 'drinkers' indicates a series of preferences which Bourdieu finds amongst the French petit bourgeois. This group exhibits a preference for the hotel based family holiday in the Mediterranean or North America at the height of summer, weekends away at country hotels, horse racing, football matches and a minority interest in golf, although this is played by occasional visits to a variety of clubs rather than by specific club membership. Eating out is a favoured weekend activity, although choice of restaurants is primarily the steak-house.

In the home, emphasis is placed on comfort and tidiness, rather than design, and their homes are furnished with the 'solid' furniture of the established company: heavily upholstered and cushioned, fitted carpeting and 'heavy' curtains. Visits to the theatre or cinema are rare (the video is more popular), but, when taken, such visits are usually to see the spectacular film or star vehicle, and theatre visits are to see shows and musicals at venues such as the Palace in Manchester, a favourite venue for promoters of 'West End' productions. With respect to such visits, it is not uncommon for this group to organize themselves into a 'coach party' to attend the latest musical revival, or other 'off the Heath' entertainments. On one occasion I was invited to accompany them on a trip to a Liverpool brewery that had been arranged by someone who worked for a company that had supplied the brewery with electrical fittings. I was under the impression that the visit would consist of a tour of the brewery but when we arrived I discovered that the evening consisted of being entertained, free drinks, food and live music, in one of the brewery company's executive suites.

In comparison with some of the leisure activities engaged in by other residents, membership of voluntary associations is very small and none of those I spoke to had ever been invited or expressed a desire to join any of the groups created by other residents, such as the gardening club, or those associated with the sports facilities. In spite of the fact that this grouping's children make up many of the members of the young residents club, only two adults were members of the 'help rota' created for the club's supervision.

By contrast, 'sporters' exhibit what Featherstone[2] has termed 'a learning mode to life . . . consciously educating [themselves] in the field of taste, style [and] lifestyle.'

Their homes are more likely to exhibit style as opposed to comfort. The leather chesterfield or sofa grouping, rather than the three piece suite; the feature coffee table and magazine rack, even the magazines themselves; parquet or tiled flooring, rather than the fitted carpet; component 'hi fi' rather than the 'one piece enclosed system', associated record collections are likely to be of a particular style of music rather than compilations of popular music or established classics. Taste in holidays is for the *à la carte*, a *'gite'* or campsite in France, rather than the tour company construction.

Rather than the 'star vehicle' or 'musical', they are more likely to attend the established or *avant garde* theatre, associated in Manchester with the Royal Exchange or Cornerhouse. The adoption of a learning mode to their leisure activities can be seen in their attendance at evening centres to take courses such as those offered in foreign languages, musical or artistic appreciation and games such as Bridge. Other indicators relate to their membership of the voluntary associations that they have been primarily responsible for creating, such as the clubs associated with the sports facilities, the care of children, the swimming and aerobics clubs.

In examining the use of the lounge bar in the recreational complex, observation work indicates that it is 'the drinkers' who are predominant in the production of this social space. The group is comprised of both sexes, but is primarily constructed by the practice of 'males only drinking' on returning 'home' from work. Shortly after opening at 5.30 pm on weekday evenings a small but regular number of males enter the lounge bar. Their drinking is done at the bar itself, rather than at one of the tables. This practice allows for the development of sociability amongst those who drink at this time. Joining a group standing at the bar is more easily accomplished than taking one's drink over to a table. When any of the tables are in fact occupied this is usually taken as a sign that those at such tables are engaged in conversational projects unsuited to the development of casual group drinking. The tables then, for those involved in these drinking practices, confer the status of privacy for those using them. Conversation at the bar for 'the drinkers' might relate to the nature of the workday experience, a review or preview of a national sporting event, or conversation around an aspect of recent news. Such conversations, however, tend not to be discursive, in the sense that varying points of view will be expressed. Rather, such conversational work will encourage the expression of commonly held beliefs with respect to either working practices or opinions on news items. This group tends to develop in size until about 7.00 pm, after which the men tend to leave for dinner in order to return later in the evening with their spouses and partners. By 10.00 pm many have returned and can be seen occupying similar positions at the bar to those they had vacated some two or three hours earlier. Sitting at tables close by are their spouses and partners. This gender segregation appears related to beliefs pertaining to what is deemed proper conversation, and proper drinking practices for the sexes. Drinks are bought for all in turn, but it is invariably the males who are responsible for their purchase. [. . .]

For the most part, members of this group do not avail themselves of the other recreational facilities of the complex. Most have not played a sport since leaving school and do not make regular use of the sports facilities available, apart from games of pool in a small room annexed from the bar. Indeed, this room is almost the sole preserve of males belonging to this group.

I would suggest that members of this group are a petit bourgeois created from the ranks of the traditional working class whose advancement has occurred without the development of what Bourdieu[3] terms cultural capital. Their position has developed primarily from the economic field, and their leisure practices can be understood as an amplified version of those traditionally associated with the urban working class. Attendance at football matches is still important for some males, although they are more likely to be sitting in season-ticket stands or the executive boxes owned by companies rather than the terraces that they stood on as children. Other sporting events likely to be visited include golf matches, horse racing, snooker and motor sports events, but such visits are likely to be made via company 'complimentary tickets' rather than as enthusiasts for the particular sport. With respect to such visits to these sporting occasions, being at such an event is perhaps more important for the status it confers rather than any intrinsic enjoyment of the sport itself.

The guarded animosity which exists between 'drinkers' and 'sporters' is illustrated in the conduct of the annual raffle for Wimbledon tickets run by the 'tennis section'. Affiliation to the Lawn Tennis Association provides the 'tennis section' with a number of tickets for the Wimbledon Championships, and one way of raising funds to pay for 'match balls' and league affiliation fees is to hold a raffle for these tickets. However, in order to raise as large a sum as possible the purchase of such tickets is open to any member of the community. I have been present at two of the annual occasions when the 'draw' for these tickets has taken place and on both occasions have witnessed scenes of dismay and disgust amongst 'sporters' when the 'finals day' tickets have been won by 'drinkers'. Muffled comments such as, 'God, would you believe it!' and, 'They don't deserve them' are drowned by shouts of glee as members of the 'drinking' group realise that the 'sporters' have failed to obtain one of the major rewards for their organizational efforts.

However, the leisure practice most visible to other residents is their drinking. [. . .] Their preference for standing at the bar, ordering large rounds of drinks at 'last orders', and the sexual segregation practices associated with their drinking, are evidenced by others as indicative of their social origins and the kind of people they are seen to be. Such 'drinking practices' ensure a high visibility for this group of regular drinkers. They represent for less frequent and non-users 'what the bar is like', in that their domination of both the physical and social space of the lounge bar helps determine how the rest of the population use this facility. Some of the less frequent users have commented that the atmosphere in the bar reminds them of, 'a posh working men's club'. Others have said that obtaining a drink at the bar is so difficult, because its whole length is always full with the same people: 'why can't they sit at one of the tables and make it easier for everyone'.

Sitting at one of the tables, however, would present 'the drinkers' with a number of problems. As we have seen this group develops during the course of the evening, beginning when the bar opens at 5.30 pm with male-only drinking. At this time men will mainly enter the bar alone, waiting the arrival of other male drinking partners. Standing at the bar not only facilitates the serving of drinks by the steward but also allows for the development of the group via a series of 'recognition practices'. Later in the evening when mixed sex company is the norm, males and females may be separated by the practice of the latter sitting at the nearest table to the bar. It is their utilization of the bar frontage in this way that allows for, and is part of, their drinking practices.

In response to the views held of them, members of this group claim an authenticity for their actions which they deny to others. Those who do not engage in regular drinking are defined variously as being 'under the thumb', understood as wanting to but not being allowed by family commitments; 'living in hock', a reference usually to the size of a mortgage, financial commitments not allowing some to 'enjoy themselves'; or 'miseries', those who do not use the facilities yet complain about the behaviour of those who do. Such complaints are usually concerned with late drinking, but also with the style of drinking referred to above. 'The drinkers' do not understand why anyone would buy a house on this estate and not avail themselves of this facility. Those who use the sports facilities but not the bar are seen as not being able to afford the drink that 'everyone needs after playing tennis or squash!' 'The drinkers' evaluate most 'sporters' as poseurs, recognizing a similarity in their working class origins and a realization of the 'learning mode' in which 'sporters' are engaged, as expressed in such comments as, 'They're just trying to be something they're not'.

For this group then, social position is understood primarily in economic terms. It is constructed through an indulgence in activities associated with having more of the same rather than a reconstruction of lifestyle. The 'signs of arrival' associated with this group are the ability to pay cash rather than live on credit, to 'stand a round' without concerning oneself with the cost, to holiday abroad in a hotel rather than a tent, even if it is pitched for you, and generally not to have to worry about financial matters.

Such expressions are perhaps more embedded in certain aspects of respectable working class, rather than middle class culture. Their achievement has been a respectability by the standards of a working class that is fragmenting, rather than a move into what one might term the new middle class. They look back with satisfaction to their social origins and regularly bring parents to the bar so that they too can be shown the successes of their children. A belief in hard work, and being in the right place at the right time, serve for them as an explanation of their material success.

By contrast, the most frequent users of the sports facilities could, in Bourdieu's terms, be said to relate more to the 'new bourgeois'. One of the 'signs of arrival' associated with this group are related to how and what one plays, and it is in this sense that I would argue that leisure is becoming increasingly important in the construction of social position. The high visibility produced by the practices of the regular drinkers is replicated in the practices of the most frequent tennis and squash players. To understand the importance of these sporting practices it is necessary to examine their associated meanings, which as Bourdieu points out, requires an examination of a variety of variables such as

> how long ago, and how, the sport was learnt, how often it is played, the socially qualified conditions (place, time, facilities, equipment) and how it is played (position in a team, style etc).[4]

Three areas of investigation help provide an understanding of the sporting practices associated with the playing of tennis and squash. These are team selection, clothing and equipment, and court management.

The Heath has four tennis teams which play in local tennis leagues. Three of these compete in the summer, two for men and one for women, and a winter team primarily comprised of men, but which co-opts women on the relatively few occasions when not enough men are available to play. There are three squash teams, two for men and one for women. Although these numerical differences are understood by residents to reflect the demands they themselves make for competitive play, it is interesting to note that while [. . . the . . .] data might support this belief with respect to squash, it does not do so for tennis, where in fact slightly more women than men play on a regular basis. Recent discussions with female tennis players are interesting in that they express a desire for more competitive play, but feel that any demands that they might make would be unacceptable because of its effects on the reduction of 'open court' time that would be available for the majority of residents who do not wish to engage in competitive tennis. [. . .]

An indication of the importance of team selection and its role in sociability can be gained from the following conversation that took place in the lounge bar of the recreational facility. I approached three squash players who were standing at the side of the bar opposite to that usually occupied by the 'regular drinkers'. Jon, Ray and Martin were talking about a forthcoming squash match in which Martin was unable to play. When asked why, he replied, 'I've got to be in a dinner jacket by eight-thirty.' This turned out to be a reference to a business evening in Liverpool that he needed to attend on the same night as the squash match, from which Ray and Jon developed the conversation in terms of business meals they had had in various restaurants in the North-West, each seemingly vying with the other to recount a story of more exclusivity and greater cost.

The conversation then returned to the forthcoming squash match and in what follows we can gain some insight as to the importance attached to social position and sports ability. Jon, the team captain, informed Ray that he was considering playing him at number three rather than two, his usual position. In effect this was demotion for Ray who appeared 'put out' by this possibility. Jon informed him that Harry was currently playing well enough to beat him at the moment. Shortly after this Harry and his opponent came into the bar, and the following conversation ensued:

Jon: 'We'll see how Harry got on against Alan.'
Ray: 'If he beat him 3–0 then I'll worry.'
Jon (to both players):   'What was the score?'
Alan (Harry's opponent):   'We're not talking about the score.' (This was correctly taken to be an indication that he had not lost the match.)

Ray: 'Three–love?'
(Harry nodded his head in confirmation.)
Ray: – 'Hmmmm.'
Jon (looking at Ray):   'I told you so.'

Although moving down in the squash team ranking would not pose an immediate threat to Ray's membership of the team and the social scene afforded by such membership, should he find himself left out of matches for a period of time it would undoubtedly affect the quality of his wider social life with respect to the opponents he would then be playing against, and therefore the social group with which he might find himself associated. It is certainly the case that the two former team tennis players have, through serious injury, not only been unable to play in team matches but have also forfeited attendance at some of the social events associated with the 'tennis clique'.

With respect to the importance of clothing and equipment to the understanding of a sporting practice, in tennis one of the easiest distinctions is made with respect to the racket itself. For this 'new bourgeois' tennis is a recently discovered sport, and evident in the newcomers' approach is an acute awareness of the distinctions associated with the equipment. On 'The Heath', a tennis racket carries with it a symbolic meaning. The old wooden Dunlop Maxply has been almost completely replaced by a variety of midheads and largeheads in an exotic collection of materials, ranging from magnesium alloy through fibreglass to carbon graphite. Such rackets carry not only a financial price tag but also a symbolic one. They allow for a categorisation of the newcomer, even prior to stepping onto the tennis court, allowing distinctions to be made between someone who does not really play tennis (the old and cheap, or dug-out-of-the-cupboard wooden racket), the beginner (the metal or alloy Prince style largehead), and the serious player (the carbon fibre graphite, indicating a financial investment of around £100, and therefore a likely measure of serious intent and ability in the sport itself).

The tennis courts themselves, in addition to providing the physical space in which the game is played, act as stages on which reputations may be won or lost. Their importance as a symbolic arena can be gauged by one incident involving a 'handicap' tournament for women. Feeling confident of the outcome, two first team players agreed with their 'non-team playing opponents' to play their match off a revised handicap in order to quicken the outcome of the game. This resulted in a slight increase of the handicap, and the non-team players duly won the match. The implications of defeat for the first team players was of such enormity that after the game confusion reigned as to who had agreed to the revised handicap and following frantic conversation with the tournament referee, also a first team player, the match was begun again and did not finish until 11.45 pm, by which time the first teamers had secured their victory, establishing not only a win, but also what many saw as a 'correctness' in the result! Only those not immersed in the 'tennis playing practices' felt that the eventual winners had cheated.

The estate management, in order to facilitate court use and the maintenance of equipment associated with them, such as tennis nets, measuring sticks, floodlights and backstop netting, leave the everyday control of facilities to what are identified as 'user groups'. As such, a number of 'user group committees' have been created, for tennis, squash, 'mother and toddler', 'ladies circle', etc. Therefore effective control over how activities 'get done' resides in large measure with these committees, especially when such committees comprise the most prolific users, which is certainly the case in the playing of tennis and squash. To the extent that the 'tennis committee' has created a set of practices for how the game should be played, this has had the effect of helping to limit participation to those who play the game in this way. Consequently, although on occasion one does see 'rabbits' on court, the condescending phrase of 'those who play properly' used to describe those who do not, it is rare to see them playing at the same time that 'serious' players are on the adjacent court. When this does happen it is likely that the 'rabbits' will terminate their game, with explanatory comments such as, 'We'd spoil their game with our mishit balls crossing their court all the time'. Dressed in casual clothing rather than the designer wear of the 'serious' player, such 'casual' players appear intimidated by the arrival of the 'serious' player.

The system used to 'obtain' a tennis court also possesses consequences, particularly for children's use of the facilities. One of the most often voiced criticisms of the estate's children relates to their relatively limited use of the facilities.

> I don't understand why the kids don't play more, they have everything they need here, but instead they just hang around saying they're bored.

However, this is not so surprising when one realises that in order to play a game of tennis, or squash, one needs to write one's name in an appropriate 'time slot' on the 'booking sheets' located in the recreation centre. During the most popular seasons for these sports, spring and summer for tennis, autumn and winter for squash, this usually means booking at least one week in advance in order to obtain the most popular, early evening, playing times. However, for children, and the casual player, tennis or squash is not the organized activity that it is for the 'serious' player. As such, when children do appear on the courts at these times, it is invariably because a court has suddenly become available. On certain occasions when this has happened, 'serious' players have entered the recreational centre, crossed out the name of the person who had booked the court but failed to play, and then returned to the court and dismissed the playing children for failing to comply with the rules for booking courts! When younger children do manage successfully to book courts at these times then the impatient 'serious' player will, on occasion, challenge those who they see as not playing the game 'properly'. Not wearing 'correct' clothes or footwear, not keeping score in the prescribed manner, or failing to change ends at the correct times, are reasons which 'serious' players give for challenging children to 'either play properly or get off the court'.

An understanding of such behaviour would be only a partial understanding if it were to be simply seen as selfish. Attempts have been made by both 'serious' tennis and squash players to introduce children to their respective sports and for a very few children these have been successful in that they have taken up the sport in the manner deemed 'proper' by the 'serious' players. However, I would suggest that it is the control of the facility, and the practices which maintain that control, which underlie the distinctions observed with respect to the frequency of the facilities' use. Conversations with occasional players, and with some of those who do not play at all, indicate the 'seriousness' with which the sports are played as one of the main obstacles which limit their involvement in the activity: 'the courts are always booked by the team players . . . I'd like to occasionally but it's difficult to get a court . . . It might be fun but I'd feel such a fool, I can't play properly' are some of the comments that I have encountered in these conversations.

Conclusion

In conclusion, I have attempted to describe the ways in which leisure is used by two different groups of residents found on this estate. The two groups, 'drinkers' and 'sporters', have been shown to engage in quite distinct leisure practices. Although both share similar socio-economic backgrounds with respect to father's occupation, both their educational experiences and current occupational positions can be differentiated. By employing Bourdieu's [. . .] differentiation between economic and cultural capital, [. . .] I have attempted to examine the distinctions in the leisure practices of these two fractions of the new middle class, and have argued that such practices can be understood as one of the principal ways in which social position is constructed.

Both groups owe their existence to industrial and economic change in the post-war period, and/or to the increase in higher education provision in the 1960s, although such provision has been relatively more important for 'the sporters'. In moving through the social space both groups have had to be geographically mobile, but such geographical mobility is welcomed for the accompanying social mobility they see as having been attained. Indeed, as Bell[5] comments, such geographical mobility is perhaps a necessary condition of social mobility.

Both, in Featherstone's terms, could be said to be the perfect consumers, although their consumption patterns are very different. 'The drinkers' could be understood as constructing social position based very much on the promise of material success held out to working class youth in the late 1950s and early 1960s, commented upon by Cohen,[6] albeit in different circumstances, in his analysis of Mod youth culture in the early 1960s. They are the working class grammar school kids who 'made it'. Their sense of social position is constructed through a 'looking back' to their social origins. From where they are now, a detached house in the countryside, a company car and a suit for work, and their leisure practices, become part of a statement which affirms change. However, as an affirmation of change such practices, to be recognized in the parent culture, need to stay the same.

'The sporters' engage in very different leisure practices, and construct social position through the promotion of a particular style of life related to the acquisition of cultural, rather than economic, capital. This group, largely college educated, could be said to be searching more for the cultural requirements of middle classness such as those associated with an appreciation of culture used in this term's 'high or sacred sense'. As such, their construction of social position concerns itself more with what is perceived as the 'correct' form of consumption, rather than its amount. Their disposition towards certain leisure activities, rather than others, and more so the practice of such dispositions, lends support to Bourdieu's contention that this class fraction can be seen to promote itself through the acquisition of cultural capital. Rather than a 'looking back', theirs is a 'looking forward'; a search to acquire the cultural hallmarks which they associate with a class they see themselves as entering. As such, their leisure practices, particularly their involvement with the 'learning mode', are essentially attempts at 'becoming'.

The struggle in the social space between these two fractions is evidenced by the way in which the leisure practices of each subverts the use of the facilities by others. 'The drinkers' have constructed the lounge bar in a way which best accommodates their use, while 'the sporters', through their creation of various competitions and rules associated with the use of the facilities, provide themselves with a series of opportunities to construct what they take to be a 'middle classness'. Both have succeeded in eliminating others from effective participation – effective in the sense that these activities are done on the terms of the group which controls the practices of use by which the facilities are used.

What the above points towards is the need for an examination of leisure practices, not as appendages to an existent lifestyle, but as part of the construction and affirmation of social position. To observe that people drink and play tennis, or badminton, golf or rugby for that matter, is not enough. Neither is it enough simply to quantify the frequency with which these things are done. A sociology of leisure must locate such leisure practices within a wider social order if it is to explain the nature of the choices made. The leisure practices outlined above are practices by which these class fractions announce and establish their position, and they reflect the position of these class fractions in the changing economy.

[. . .]

Notes

1. See P. Bourdieu, *Distinction: A social critique of the judgement of taste*, London: Routledge and Kegan Paul, 1984.
2. M. Featherstone, 'Lifestyle and consumer culture', *Theory, Culture and Society*, 4: 55–70, 1987, p. 65.
3. P. Bourdieu, op. cit.
4. Ibid., p. 211.
5. C. Bell, *Middle Class Families*, London: Routledge and Kegan Paul, 1968.
6. P. Cohen, 'Subcultural conflict and working class community', in CCCS, *Working Papers in Cultural Studies* 2, University of Birmingham, 1972.

4 □ *The Uses and Interpretations of Household Technologies*

4.1 □ *Cynthia Cockburn*

This brief piece is extracted from a much wider study of gender and technological change, in the course of which Cynthia Cockburn interviewed 113 men and 83 women from 11 workplaces. She discusses their responses here to questions about technology in the home and its relationship to domestic divisions of labour.

Black & Decker versus Moulinex

[. . .] If a woman's work is non-technological, the closest she may come to having to deal with the demands of the physical environment and of machinery and equipment is in the home. I therefore asked both men and women to spell out with some precision the actual practical tasks each carried out at home.

Before I had got beyond the introductory phrase, 'I'm interested to know how responsibilities are divided in the home', it often happened that whoever I was talking with, woman or man, would break in with 'Oh, we share everything.' It seemed something that confirmed a loving relationship, to believe that all work is shared. My first question then was, 'In general, do you feel that you divide things up between you, or do you each do the *same* things?' And again, very often the answer was 'We do the same things.' However, once the individual tasks were mentioned a different story began to emerge. It appeared that both women and men wanted to think that equality and similarity prevailed between partners, but in actual fact a sharp distinction in the tasks done by the sexes in practice defeated this object.

Here are some such sequences. First, a woman's account. Barbara Sheldrick is a keyboard operator on a computer terminal in a warehouse. 'We just share everything,' she started. *Who does the cooking*? I asked. 'I do, because I get in first.' *Who shops for food*? 'I do. Because I go past Tesco's on my way home. But if I needed something when he comes in at night, he'll go out for it. And he washes the pots after we've had our tea. So I do all the cooking and he does the washing up.' *What about the jobs that mean using tools, like hammers and screwdrivers, that kind of thing*? 'He'd have to do it. I'm not – I don't know nothing about those things.'

Secondly, here is a man: [. . .] Tom Delaware, warehousing consultant. 'Not a sharp division. No. I tend to do as much cooking, if not more, than my wife.' *What about repairs, electrical things say*? 'She wouldn't do any of those things, no.' *Decorating*?

213

'Painting yes. I have a preference for papering. She doesn't have any skill in papering but she likes to have a paintbrush in her hand.' *Sewing curtains*? 'She would do all those. Up to a point, and then she might decide to get a woman she knows down the road who might do them for her.' *What about the garden*? 'Combined.' *Tell me in detail*. 'I tend to do the hedges, eight hours on Saturday, with a machine. Whereas she would do the flowerbeds. She would tend to do the weeding. Not the heavy vegetable patch, which I would maintain. And she has a total knowledge of flowers. I have a zero knowledge of flowers. It is her background as a farmer's daughter.' *Does she ever use the hedge cutter*? 'No. I've trained her in the lawn mower, but not to a great extent. No, no.' And then he added what might appear to be a *non sequitur*. 'It's quite a nice comfortable life, I suppose.'

Donald Ramsey demonstrates that, though men may do some conventionally feminine tasks and even *vice versa*, a division of labour of some kind, quite humorous in the detail in which it is known and understood, continues to exist. That is the important thing. 'I always cook the meal, during the week. Monday to Friday, because she has other things to do. She has her washing and ironing and cleaning and hoovering. I never do that. Ever. If we are having people round for a meal, I do the cooking [ie., even at weekends]. Or rather my wife does the starter, I do the main course and she does the sweet. Because I can't bake. She is good at some things, I'm good at others.' *She does your washing, your clothes*? 'Yes. She does all the washing, hoovering, ironing and cleaning and I never help on that side because she is a perfectionist. The only thing I clean is the kitchen, after I have cooked. Then after the meal we do the dishes together. I wash, she dries. And then if we are going out we go out. If we are staying in, she will do whatever she wants to do and I'll read, or go and play chess with the neighbour.'

Barny Short, ex-field engineer, I pursued through a detailed and specific sexual division of labour in cooking, cleaning, shopping and finally through to decorating ('she paints, but I don't like her hanging wallpaper, that's a man's job') and gardening ('I do the digging, she does the rest') until we arrived finally at a hobby they shared: upholstery. Ah, I thought. Something that *both* of them do? 'I repair the wooden frames, she puts on the fabric.'

Where the reality is a division of labour systematically denied, it is refreshing to encounter someone who says frankly, as Alice Morrison does:

> No (firmly), we don't share things equally. I do practically everything. I do cooking, cleaning, shopping. But if I were ill then he completely takes over. He is very capable of doing everything. He's a better cook than what I am and he knows how to wash, clean and sew and everything. But because I'm there he thinks I should do it. On the odd occasion he has given me a hand. He'll say, 'Is there anything you want doing?' Like, for instance, this weekend, because we wanted the weekend free, being nice, he said, 'Is there anything you want doing?' and I said, 'Yes, will you just do the front door step' and he says (putting on a peevish tone), 'I don't like doing that'.

Alice explained that he disliked being observable by neighbours when contributing to housework.

It is beginning to be clear that technology is just as significant a factor in the division of labour at home as it is at work. Very few women were saying they did any DIY in the house, beyond painting and decorating. Few used hammer or screwdriver for more than hanging the occasional picture or 'mending' the proverbial plug. Fewer still would use an electric drill, even a lawn mower. Men were proprietorial about these tools and the role that goes with them: 'I've fitted our central heating system, I've re-wired the house. I built a shower, knocked up a bit of a bedroom,' an engineer said to me. 'Oh, it's beautiful.' I asked, *What is your wife's role in this?* 'I keep making the point,' he said, 'if you can keep the kids out of the tool kit, out of the paint, that's making a contribution. That's helping as much. Do a bit of painting, wallpapering, of course. Not a job *I* like much. I like hammering up the stud wall, doing a bit of wiring, things like that.'

And another: 'If I'm working on the car, she'll do little bits. Hand me tools and that.' And another: 'She's not averse to picking up a screwdriver but no, generally . . . She wouldn't do anything electrical . . . She wouldn't do things needing a lot of strength.' *Where do you keep your tools?* 'In the garage.' *Does your wife ever use them?* 'Never, ever.'

Of course, as several women pointed out, if men are not doing the cooking, cleaning, shopping, washing and child care, the least they can be expected to contribute is the physical repairs. Jen Gouldner, a packer at Delta, says of DIY, 'I think to myself, "I could have a bash at that." So I do. That's me personally. But a lot of my friends, well, yes some of them do think I'm a bit daft because "That's his job, you should let him do it."'

Nonetheless, it is still surprising and sad that a woman like Maureen Casey, who at work uses pliers, screwdrivers, Allen keys, soldering iron and other tools, sees herself as technologically illiterate at home. *Do you feel a different person when you are at home, to when you are at work?* 'Oh, yes. I think I *am* a different person.' *Would you take a socket set like that to your car for instance?* 'No, I don't know anything about cars. I wouldn't know how to.' *You don't have a set of tools of your own at home?* 'No.' *You don't want to, you're not interested?* 'If I had to I would. But because I have someone there that will do it, well, I suppose I've always had someone there who will do it, so I don't . . . I don't think I could do it efficiently enough, good enough. I think my job is to clean the house.'

Just occasionally, especially but not exclusively in middle-class professional couples, you find a woman reporting that she is the practical one, the husband the intellectual, the dreamer, the incompetent one. In these situations the woman may use tools about the house. But it is noteworthy that this is predicated on the 'freak man' who is inadequate with technology: 'He's one of those, you want it done, you end up doing it yourself.' Such men are in the main gaining their gender identity through intellectual work and achievement.

Being close to a man who is technically competent seems to stop women gaining know-how. An electrician's wife, it was understood, knew *less*, not more, about electrical repairs than other women. A marriage, like Jen Gouldner's, in which the two of them stripped down and rebuilt a car together, knocked down a chimney, cleaned off the bricks and rebuilt it together, is very rare. Where women do do these things they feel better: 'It gives you more self-respect. It does, yes. Especially if you can say, "Look, I've done this." It's great. It's good. Yeah.'

Normally, women use utensils and implements – the dishwasher, vacuum cleaner, car. They don't use tools. The utensils and implements are, in their way, tools, of course, and they are used by women with skills (making food, sewing clothes) certainly equal to the male skills of their husbands. But women cannot fix these utensils and implements when they go wrong. It is men on the whole who are in control of women's domestic machinery and domestic environment. Women depend on men, husbands or tradesmen, for the completion of many necessary physical tasks.

Men gain social status in the community by the skills they learn at work. The mechanic and engineer are known among their friends as 'the one who can fix things.' What boys are taught early at home also helps them gain their status at work. Women are cut out of this process. The women apprentices studied by Ina Wagner realized the asset they would gain from breaking their way in:

> They are aware that technological competence acquired through work extends to their role outside the workplace, by giving them a symbolically visible share in what is commonly considered men's domain: participation in discussions on technical issues and in socially highly valued leisure activities. The young women themselves highly value these more general benefits they draw from technological competence. They perceive themselves as more well-rounded personalities who are able to take an active part in what they themselves consider a privileged world.[1]

The secret world from which women are excluded, the world of the man and boy, is symbolized in 'the shed at the bottom of the garden': 'My grandfather was a maker of things. He had a workshop at the bottom of the garden and he was always making things. And going to my grandparents, I can remember it being an Aladdin's cave, all these lovely things. Boats and trains and cars and toys. And I used to have endless fun standing and watching my grandfather make things.' This engineer himself had had a room which he had made into the equivalent of this remembered Aladdin's cave. It had been his own place. And he felt it hard that 'once the children had come along, I lost it and was banished to a shed . . . But all the same it is a place that is mine and I don't get lumber slung in it. It is my work shop.' *Does your son come down and join you there?* I asked. 'Yes. He'll come down there and suck a chisel and play with the electric saw (happy laugh). Yes. I can remember my grandfather being quite an influence in that way.' He was talking energetically, enthusiastically. Three generations of men here, the passing down of knowledge and proprietorial rights over technology. The shutting out of one generation of women after another from Aladdin's cave.

Note

1. I. Wagner, 'New work experiences for women: The case of women apprentices in Austria's metal and construction industries.' Draft Report, University of Vienna, 1983.

4.2 □ *Judy Wajcman*

Like Cockburn, Judy Wajcman locates domestic technology within divisions of labour in the home. Her contribution is a critical review of the existing literature in this area. She draws our attention to a variety of extra-domestic determinants of technological development – underlining the need to connect what goes on inside households with far broader social processes.

Domestic technology: labour-saving or enslaving?

Since the 1970s housework has finally become the object of serious academic study by historians, sociologists and even a few economists. This was part of a general concern with the relationship between the changing structures of industrial capitalism and the shaping of everyday life within the household. *The Sociology of Housework* by Ann Oakley[1] published in 1974 marked an important break in treating housework as work within the framework of industrial sociology. In the same year, Joann Vanek's[2] article on 'Time Spent on Housework' compared the findings of the US time use studies of housework from the 1920s to the late 1960s. She argued that the aggregate time spent on housework by full-time housewives had remained remarkably constant throughout the period, although there had been some redistribution of time between individual tasks. Her surprising conclusion, that the introduction of domestic technology had practically no effect on the aggregate time spent on housework, soon became the orthodoxy amongst feminists working in the area.

In recent years feminist scholars in North America, Britain and Australia have produced excellent material on the history of housework and domestic technology.[3] Considerable attention has been devoted to countering the myth that housework is the creation of discontented housewives in that it 'expands to fill the time available'. Feminists (commonly quoting Vanek's data) have emphasized that women's household tasks have not decreased with so-called 'labour-saving' appliances. Much of this literature has pointed to the contradictions inherent in attempts to mechanize the home and standardize domestic production. Such attempts have foundered on the nature of housework – privatized, decentralized and labour-intensive. Thus, in the words of one writer on the subject, 'substantial changes in household technology left the sex, hours, efficiency, and status of the household worker essentially unaltered'.[4]

[. . .]

Industrialization of the home and creation of the housewife

What was the relationship between the technological developments in the economy and those in the home? To what extent did new technologies 'industrialize' the home and transform domestic labour? Why, despite massive technological changes in the home, such as running water, gas and electric cookers, central heating, washing machines, refrigerators, do studies show that household work in the industrialized countries still accounts for approximately half of the total working time?[5]

The conventional wisdom is that the forces of technological change and the growth of the market economy have progressively absorbed much of the household's role in production. [. . .] Modern technology is seen as having either eliminated or made less arduous almost all women's former household work, thus freeing women to enter the labour force. To most commentators, the history of housework is the story of its elimination.

Although it is true that industrialization transformed households, the major changes in the pattern of household work during this period were not those that the traditional model predicts. Ruth Schwartz Cowan,[6] in her celebrated American study of the development of household technology between 1860 and 1960, argued exactly that.[7] For her, the view that the household has passed from being a unit of production to a unit of consumption, with the attendant assumption that women have nothing left to do at home, is grossly misleading. Rather, the processes by which the American home became industrialized were much more complex and heterogeneous than this.

Cowan provides the following explanations for the failure of the 'industrial revolution in the home' to ease or eliminate household tasks. Mechanization gave rise to a whole range of new tasks which, although not as physically demanding, were as time consuming as the jobs they had replaced. The loss of servants meant that even middle-class housewives had to do all the housework themselves. Further, although domestic technology did raise the productivity of housework, it was accompanied by rising expectations of the housewife's role which generated more domestic work for women. Finally, mechanization has only had a limited effect on housework because it has taken place within the context of the privatized, single-family household.

It is important to distinguish between different phases of industrialization that involved different technologies. Cowan characterizes twentieth-century technology as consisting of eight interlocking systems: food, clothing, health care, transportation, water, gas, electricity, and petroleum products. While some technological systems do fit the model of a shift from production to consumption, others do not.

Food, clothing, and health-care systems do fit the 'production to consumption' model. By the beginning of the twentieth century, the purchasing of processed foods and ready-made clothes instead of home production was becoming common. Somewhat later, the health-care system moved out of the household and into centralized institutions. These trends continued with increasing momentum during the first half of this century.

The transportation system and its relation to changing consumption patterns, however, exemplifies the shift in the other direction. During the nineteenth century, household goods were often delivered, mail-order catalogues were widespread and most people did not spend much time buying goods. With the advent of the motor car after the First World War, all this began to change. By 1930 the automobile had become the prime mode of transportation in the United States. Delivery services of all kinds began to disappear and the burden of providing transportation shifted from the seller to the buyer.[8] Meanwhile women gradually replaced men as the drivers of transport, more and more business converted to the 'self-service' concept, and households became increasingly dependent upon housewives to provide the service. The time spent on shopping tasks expanded until today the average time spent is eight hours per week, the equivalent of an entire working day.

In this way, households moved from the net consumption to the net production of transportation services, and housewives became the transporters of purchased goods rather than the receivers of them. The purchasing of goods provides a classic example of a task that is generally either ignored altogether or considered as 'not work', in spite of the time, energy and skill required, and its essential role in the national economy.

In charting the historical development of the last four household systems, water, gas, electricity, and petroleum, Cowan reveals further deficiencies in the 'production to consumption' model. These technological changes totally reorganized housework yet their impact was ambiguous. On the one hand they radically increased the productivity of housewives: 'modern technology enabled the American housewife of 1950 to produce singlehandedly what her counterpart of 1850 needed a staff of three or four to produce; a middle-class standard of health and cleanliness.'[9] On the other hand, while eliminating much drudgery, modern labour-saving devices did not reduce the necessity for time-consuming labour. Thus there is no simple cause and effect relation between the mechanization of homes and changes in the volume and nature of household work.

Indeed the disappearance of paid and unpaid servants [. . .] and the imposition of the entire job on the housewife herself, was arguably the most significant change. The proportion of servants to households in America dropped from 1 servant to every 15 households in 1900, down to 1 to 42 in 1950.[10] Most of this shrinkage took place during the 1920s. The disappearance of domestic servants stimulated the mechanization of homes, which in turn may have hastened the disappearance of servants.

This change in the structure of the household labour force was accompanied by a remodelled ideology of housewifery. The development in the early years of this century of the domestic science movement, the germ theory of disease and the idea of 'scientific motherhood', led to new exacting standards of housework and childcare.[11] As standards of personal and household cleanliness rose during the twentieth century women were expected to produce clean toilets, bathtubs and sinks. With the introduction of washing machines, laundering increased because of higher expectations of cleanliness. There was a major change in the importance attached to child rearing and mother's role. The average housewife had fewer children, but modern 'child-centred' approaches to parenting involved her in spending much more time and effort. These trends were exploited and further promoted by advertisers in their drive to expand the market for domestic appliances.

Housework began to be represented as an expression of the housewife's affection for her family. The split between public and private meant that the home was expected to provide a haven from the alienated, stressful technological order of the workplace and was expected to provide entertainment, emotional support, and sexual gratification. The burden of satisfying these needs fell on the housewife.

With home and housework acquiring heightened emotional significance, it became impossible to rationalize household production along the lines of industrial production.[12] Domestic technology has thus been designed for use in single-family households by a lone and loving housewife. Far from liberating women from the home it has further ensnared them. This is not an inevitable, immutable situation, but one whose transformation depends on the transformation of gender relations.

The relationship between domestic technology and household labour thus provides a good illustration of the general problem of technological determinism, where technology is said to have resulted in social changes. The greatest influences on time spent on housework have in fact come from non-technological changes: the demise of domestic servants, changing standards of hygiene and childcare, as well as the ideology of the housewife and the symbolic importance of the home.[13]

[. . .]

Technological innovation and housework time

Attempts by 'post-industrial utopians' to conceive of the likely shape of the household in the future suffer from many of the intellectual defects that have misled analysts of domestic technology in the past. Much of the work of these theorists is speculative. The British economist and sociologist, Jonathan Gershuny[14] has made the most sustained attempt to give empirical weight to post-industrial predictions about the household.

Gershuny's starting point has little in common with that of the feminist commentators. His work is directed at theories of post-industrial society which see the economy as being based increasingly on services rather than on manufacturing production. By contrast, Gershuny's main thesis is that the economy is moving toward the provision of services within the household, that is, to being a self-service economy.

[. . .]

Gershuny describes a shift from the purchase of final services (going to the cinema, travelling by train, sending washing to a commercial laundry) to the purchase of domestic technologies (buying a television, buying a car, buying a washing machine). A degree of unpaid domestic work is necessary in order to use such commodities to provide services. This model is used to explain the economic expansion of the developed economies in the 1950s and 1960s, which was based on the creation of new mass markets in consumer durables, electronics and motor vehicles. In this way domestic technology is of enormous economic significance, affecting the pattern of household expenditure, the industrial distribution of employment and the division of labour between paid and unpaid work.

Like Cowan, Gershuny argues that people make rational decisions in this area. However, whereas her emphasis is on moral values and the social nature of human desires and preferences, his emphasis is on prices. The household will choose between alternative technical means of provision on the basis of the household wage rate, the relative prices of final services and goods, and the amount of unpaid time necessary to use the goods to provide the service functions. However, Gershuny assumes that people have unchanging desires and respond to market signals, making narrowly economic decisions primarily in terms of prices but also in terms of domestic labour time per item. But human beings do change and the introduction of machines alters people's preferences and values. The main weakness in Gershuny's analysis is that he ignores the social and cultural dimensions of human desires.

Implicit in this analysis is the assumption that the household can be treated as a unity of interests, in which household members subordinate their individual goals to the pursuit of common household goals. Gershuny shies away from any attempt to explain decisions as to whether men or women should do domestic labour, instead simply referring to 'the traditional segregation of domestic tasks' and 'people's perception of their roles'. What this approach overlooks is that there are conflicts of interest between family members over the differential distribution of tasks and money, and this may well influence how decisions actually come about.

Let us see how this theory explains the widespread purchase and use of washing machines, as opposed to commercial laundries. Gershuny's account differs quite sharply from Cowan[15] who explicitly considers and rejects an economic-rationality argument on laundry. He argues that as the time needed to use a washing machine has fallen, and the price of washing machines relative to the price of laundry has fallen so their popularity has increased. These developments are not linear however. A central feature of Gershuny's model is that it predicts first a rise, then a plateau, and then a decline in the time spent on domestic labour.

The first phase constitutes the shift from the service to the goods – for example from commercial laundries to domestic washing machines. According to the model this is a rational decision because it is cheaper, even counting the housewife's labour. But clearly, the domestic time spent on laundry goes up at this point. And precisely because it is a cheaper form of washing clothes, it becomes rational to wash more clothes more often, to satisfy (high) marginal desires for clean laundry.

In the second phase, where washing machines are fairly widely diffused, competition between manufacturers at least partly takes the form of offering more efficient machines, replacing the twin tub with the automatic. At the same time, the desire for clean laundry will begin to stabilize – slowing the rate of growth in clothes to be washed. Hence, eventually, time spent in laundry will start to fall. Thus, Gershuny argues, an effect of this move to a self-service economy, is that the amount of time spent on house-work has declined since 1960.[16]

Gershuny is so convinced that new technologies increase the productivity of domestic labour that, in a recent paper with Robinson,[17] he takes issue with the feminist 'constancy of housework' thesis. Whilst conceding that prior to the 1960s the time spent by women on domestic work did remain remarkably constant, he insists that a shift occurred at that point. Drawing on evidence from time–budget surveys in the USA and UK, as well as Canada, Holland, Denmark and Norway, he concludes that domestic work time for women has been declining since the 1960s, and even that men do a little more than previously. It is central to his argument that this is so, even after taking into account the effects of such socio-demographic changes as more women having paid jobs, more men being unemployed, and the decreasing size of families. Therefore the diffusion of domestic equipment into households must have had some effect in reducing domestic work time.

In fact on closer inspection, these findings are more in line with feminist theories about constancy of domestic work than the authors would lead us to believe. Although the central argument is that domestic work time has been declining for women between the 1960s and the 1980s, this is only the case with respect to 'routine' domestic work. Unpaid work is subdivided into three categories: routine domestic chores (cooking, cleaning, other regular housework), shopping and related travel, and childcare (caring for and playing with children).[18] While routine domestic work has declined, the time spent in childcare and shopping have substantially increased.

This finding, however, is entirely consistent with the feminist emphasis on the added time now devoted to shopping and childcare. [. . .] To argue that domestic labour time has reduced is only meaningful if it means that leisure or discretionary free time has increased. If however mechanization results in less physical work but more 'personal services' work in the sense of increased time and quality of childcare, then surely this does not mean a real decrease in work. [. . .]

It seems that the preoccupation with increases in productivity due to technological innovation blinds many analysts to more fundamental social factors. For example, the presence or absence of children, their age and their number all have significantly greater effects on time spent in housework than any combination of technological develop-ments. Similarly, the presence of men in a household increases women's domestic work time by at least a third. In contrast, for men, living with women means that they do less domestic work.[19] Furthermore, it has repeatedly been found that the amount of time women spend on housework is reduced in proportion to the amount of time they spend in paid employment.[20]

A major problem with most time–budget research is that it does not recognize that the essence of housework is to combine many things, usually concurrently. This has a profound bearing on the interpretation of time spent in childcare and the apparent growth of leisure time. For example, watching television or listening to the radio can be combined with childcare, cooking, ironing and washing laundry. [. . .] Time budgets do not analyse whether activities are undertaken exclusively or in combination with another activity. Perhaps, as Michael Bittman[21] suggests, the private and gendered character of the household promotes the kinds of technological innovations that maximize the number of tasks that can be performed simultaneously. To resolve such issues we would need more detailed information about the extent of use of consumer durables, the material output of services performed in the home and the social significance that these activities have for people. Gershuny's focus on technological innovations and tasks *per se* seems indicative, once again, of a technicist orientation which sees the organization of the household as largely determined by machines.

A technicist orientation is also evident in much of the futuristic literature on 'home informatics'. [. . .] There is much speculation about the fully automated home of the future known as a 'smart house' or 'interactive home system', where appliances will be able to communicate with each other and to the house within an integrated system. Ian Miles predicts that home informatics will bring substantial changes to people's ways of life, one of which will be to improve the quality of domestic work both in terms of the convenience and effort required. However, Miles[22] gives no reasons whatsoever for his hope that this will result in 'the sexual redivision of labour between men and women in families'.

The sociological literature on the electronic, self-servicing home of the future remains remarkably insensitive to gender issues. In particular, it ignores the way in which the home means very different things for men and women. Many of the new information and communication technologies are being developed for the increasing trend towards home-centred leisure and entertainment. But leisure is deeply divided along the gender lines. Many of these technologies, such as the home computer, demand that the user spend considerable time and concentration mastering it. But women have a lot less time for play in the home than men and boys. Programming the electronic system for the 'smart house' may enhance men's domestic power. Furthermore, the possibilities of home-based commercial operations, from 'telebanking' and shopping to 'teleworking', are likely to involve more housework for women in catering for other home-based family members. [. . .]

Alternatives to individualized housework

Even the most forward looking of the futurists have us living in households which, in social rather than technological terms, resemble the households of today. A more radical approach would be to transform the social context in which domestic technology applies. [. . .]

During the first few decades of this century there were a range of alternative approaches to housework being considered and experimented with. These included the development of commercial services, the establishment of alternative communities and co-operatives and the invention of different types of machinery. Perhaps the best known exponent of the socialization of domestic work was the nineteenth-century American feminist Charlotte Perkins Gilman. Rather than men and women sharing the housework, as some early feminists and utopian socialists advocated, she envisaged a completely professionalized system of housekeeping which would free women from the ties of cooking, cleaning and childcare.

The call for the socialization of domestic work was not unique to the early feminist movements. Revolutionary socialists such as Engels, Bebel and Kollontai also saw the socialization and collectivization of housework as a precondition for the emancipation of women. And they embraced the new forces of technology as making this possible. [. . .]

The modern socialist states of Eastern Europe took up some of these ideas, establishing collective laundry systems in apartment blocks and communal eating facilities. Whilst these initiatives certainly represented a different use of technology, they did not challenge the sexual division of labour insofar as women remained responsible for the housework, albeit collectivised. [. . .]

History thus provides us with many examples of alternatives to the single-family residence and the private ownership of household tools. Why then, in the USA in particular, has the individualized household triumphed? In particular, why should women apparently be so complicit in a process that was so damaging to them?

> Shall we believe that millions upon millions of women, for five or six generations, have passively accepted a social system that was totally out of their control and totally contrary to their interest? Surely there must have been at least one or two good reasons that all those women actively chose, when choices were available to them, to reside in single-family dwellings, own their own household tools, and do their own housework.[23]

To argue that women just welcomed the new domestic technologies because they became available is to come perilously close to technological determination. On the other hand, how can women have consciously and freely chosen to embrace the new methods when they have been so discredited as a liberating force? It is tempting in these circumstances to see women as duped, as passive respondents to industrialization, and as victims of advertisers.[24]

Cowan argues that women embraced these new technologies because they made possible an increased material standard of living for substantially unchanged expenditure of the housewife's time. To this extent women were acting rationally in their own and their families' interests.

However, as the following passage illustrates, Cowan seems to find the most convincing explanation of the paths chosen in a set of values to which women subscribed – the 'privacy' and 'autonomy' of the family.

> . . . when decisions have to be made about spending limited funds, most people will still opt for privacy and autonomy over technical efficiency and community interest . . . Americans have decided to live in apartment houses rather than apartment hotels because they believe that something critical to family life is lost when all meals are eaten in restaurants or all food is prepared by strangers; they have decided to buy washing machines rather than patronize commercial laundries because they prefer to wash their dirty linen at home . . . When given choices, in short, most Americans act so as to preserve family life and family autonomy. The single-family home and the private ownership of tools are social institutions that act to preserve and to enhance the privacy and autonomy of families.[25]

Cowan does here depict women as active agents of their own destiny rather than passive recipients of the process. However, an approach that gives such primacy to values and to the symbolic importance of the home inevitably plays down the material context of women's experience.

[. . .]

It is important to recognize the extent to which individual choice is constrained by powerful structured forces. The available alternatives to single-family houses were extremely limited, especially for the working class. In fact, state policy in the area of housing and town planning played a key role in promoting privatism. Without the extensive provision of different options, it is not clear to what extent people freely chose private domestic arrangements.

It is even less clear to what extent women, as opposed to men, exercised the degree of choice available. Oddly Cowan separates this American preference for domestic autonomy from the sexual division of domestic labour. No role is granted to men in choosing this single-family home even though Cowan's own historical findings point to men being well served by the private domestic sphere.

The common feminist stress on the negative effects of domestic technology has contributed to the view that women have been duped. [. . .] Once we recognize that the mechanization of the home did bring substantial improvements to women's domestic working conditions, even while it also introduced new pressures, women seem less irrational. 'When manufacturers then, in their own interests, marketed washing machines in terms of "make your automatic your clothes basket and wash every day", they were tapping into women's experience of the problems of organizing laundry and the physical drudgery it entailed. They were also opening up greater flexibility in managing some domestic tasks.'[26]

Against this there is no doubt that people can be taken in by false promises, especially where advanced technology is involved. Wanting to save time and improve the quality of their housework and in turn the quality of their home life, housewives are susceptible to well-targeted advertising about the capacity of new appliances to meet their needs. The irony is that women have commonly blamed themselves for the failure of technology to deliver them from domestic toil, rather than realizing that the defects lie in the design of technologies and the social relations within which they operate.

Men's designs on technology

Most domestic technology is designed by men in their capacity as scientists and engineers, people remote from the domestic tasks involved, for use by women in their capacity as houseworkers. And, as we have seen, modern household equipment is designed and marketed to reinforce rather than challenge the existing household-family pattern.

It is not only gender relations that influence the structure of domestic technology. Like other technologies, domestic technology is big business. Particular technologies are produced not in relation to specific and objectively defined needs of individuals, but largely because they serve the interests of those who produce them. The design and manufacture of household appliances is carried out with a view to profit on the market. And the economic interests involved are not simply those of the manufacturers, but also those of the suppliers of the energy needed by these appliances.

[. . .] There is nothing the owner of an electricity supply system, for example, likes better than the widespread diffusion of an electricity-using household appliance that will be on at times of the day when the big industrial consumers are not using electricity. Residential appliances (including heating and cooling equipment) use about a third of the electricity generated in the US today; the refrigerator alone uses about seven per cent. Unlike most other household appliances, the refrigerator operates twenty-four hours a day throughout its life. In fact, many American kitchens now contain between 12 and 20 electric motors. Indeed the drive to motorize all household tasks – including brushing teeth, squeezing lemons and carving meat – is less a response to need than a reflection of the economic and technical capacity for making motors.[27]

[. . .]

An important dimension glossed over in the literature on the development of domestic equipment is the culture of engineering. After all, engineers do not simply follow the manufacturers' directives; they make decisions about design and the use of new technologies, playing an active role in defining what is technically possible. [. . .] The masculinity of the engineering world has a profound effect on the artefacts generated. This must be particularly true for the design of domestic technologies, most of which are so clearly designed with female users in mind.

When women have designed technological alternatives to time-consuming housework, little is heard of them. One such example is Gabe's innovative self-cleaning house.[28] Frances Gabe, an artist and inventor from Oregon spent 27 years building and perfecting the self-cleaning house. In effect, a warm water mist does the basic cleaning and the floors (with rugs removed) serve as the drains. Every detail has been considered. 'Clothes-freshener cupboards' and 'dish-washer cupboards' which wash and dry, relieve the tedium of stacking, hanging, folding, ironing and putting away. But the costs of the building (electricity and plumbing included) are no more than average since her system is not designed as a luxury item. Gabe was ridiculed for even attempting the impossible, but architects and builders now admit that her house is functional and attractive. One cannot help speculating that the development of an effective self-cleaning house has not been high on the agenda of male engineers.

Domestic technology: a commercial afterthought

The fact is that much domestic technology has anyway not been specifically designed for household use but has its origins in very different spheres. Consumer products can very often be viewed as 'technology transfers' from the production processes in the formal economy to those in the domestic informal economy.

Typically, new products are at first too expensive for application to household activities; they are employed on a large scale by industry only, until continued innovation and economies of scale allow substantial reduction in costs or adaptation of technologies to household circumstances. Many domestic technologies were initially developed for commercial, industrial and even defence purposes and only later, as manufacturers sought to expand their markets, were they adapted for home use. Gas and electricity were available for industrial purposes and municipal lighting long before they were adapted for domestic use. The automatic washing machine, the vacuum cleaner and the refrigerator had wide commercial application before being scaled down for use in the home. Electric ranges were used in naval and commercial ships before being introduced to the domestic market. Microwave ovens are a direct descendant of military radar technology and were developed for food preparation in submarines by the US Navy.[29] They were first introduced to airlines, institutions and commercial premises before manufacturers turned their eyes to the domestic market.

Despite the lucrative market that it represents, the household is not usually the first area of application that is considered when new technologies are being developed. For this reason new domestic appliances are not always appropriate to the household work that they are supposed to perform nor are they necessarily the implements that would have been developed if the housewife had been considered first or indeed if she had had control of the processes of innovation.

It is no accident that most domestic technology originates from the commercial sector, nor that much of the equipment which ends up in the home is somewhat ineffectual. As an industrial designer I interviewed put it, why invest heavily in the design of domestic technology when there is no measure of productivity for housework as there is for industrial work? Commercial kitchens, for example, are simple and functional in design, much less cluttered with complicated gadgets and elaborate fittings than most home kitchens. Reliability is at a premium for commercial purchasers who are concerned to minimize their running costs both in terms of breakdowns and labour-time. By contrast, given that women's labour in the home is unpaid, the same economic considerations do not operate. Therefore, when producing for the homes market, manufacturers concentrated on cutting the costs of manufacturing techniques to enable them to sell reasonably cheap products. Much of the design effort is put into making appliances look attractive or impressively high-tech in the showroom – for example giving them an unnecessary array of buttons and flashing lights. In the case of dishwashers and washing machines, a multitude of cycles is provided although only one or two are generally used. [. . .]

In tracing the history of various domestic appliances, Forty[30] shows how manufacturers have designed their products to represent prevailing ideologies of hygiene and housework. Thus, in the 1930s and 1940s manufacturers styled appliances in forms reminiscent of factory or industrial equipment to emphasize the labour-saving efficiency which they claimed for their products. At that time, domestic equipment was still intended principally for use by servants. However such designs made housework look disturbingly like real work and in the 1950s, when many of the people who bought these appliances were actually working in factories, the physical appearance of appliances changed. A new kind of aesthetic for domestic appliances emerged which was discreet, smooth, and with the untidy, mechanical workings of the machine covered from view in grey or white boxes.[31] The now standard domestic style of domestic appliances '. . . suited the deceits and contradictions of housework well, for their appearance raised no comparisons with machine tools or office equipment and preserved the illusion that housework was an elevated and noble activity', of housework not being work.[32]

[. . .]

Conclusion: more work for social scientists?

[. . .]

An adequate analysis of the social shaping of domestic technology cannot be conducted only at the level of the design of individual technologies. The significance of domestic technology lies in its location at the interface of public and private worlds. The fact that men in the public sphere of industry, invention and commerce design and produce technology for use by women in the private domestic sphere, reflects and embodies a complex web of patriarchal and capitalist relations. [. . .] By refusing to take technologies for granted we help to make visible the relations of structural inequality that give rise to them.

This portrait of domestic technology is certainly incomplete. [. . .] I have concentrated on domestic technology as a set of physical objects or artefacts and argued that gendered meanings are encoded in the design process. This process involves not only specifying the user but also the appropriate location of technologies within the house. For example, domestic appliances 'belong' in the kitchen, along with women, and communications technology such as the television are found in the 'family room'. This signals the way in which the physical form and spatial arrangement of housing itself expresses assumptions about the nature of domestic life.

Notes

1. A. Oakley, *The Sociology of Housework*, Oxford: Martin Robertson, 1974.
2. J. Vanek, 'Time spent on housework', *Scientific American*, 231: 116–20, 1974.
3. One of the earliest articles enquiring into the historical impact of domestic technology on housework is A. Ravetz, 'Modern technology and an ancient occupation: Housework in present-day society', *Technology and Culture*, 6: 256–60, 1965. For detailed references see the bibliographic essays at the back of R. Schwartz Cowan, *More Work for Mother: The ironies of household technology from the open hearth to the microwave*, New York: Basic Books, 1983; M. McNeil, ed., *Gender and Expertise*, London: Free Association Books, 1987,

pp. 229–30. For a comprehensive review of the contemporary research see C. Bose, P. Bereano and M. Molloy, 'Household technology and the social construction of housework', *Technology and Culture*, 25: 53–82, 1974. As they point out, this research is limited by its focus on the 'ideal' white middle-class family, and contains virtually no evidence on variations across class and ethnic groups; neither does it encompass single-parent households or people living alone. The data is also limited by its failure to reflect different stages of the life-cycle. A similar problem exists with much of the historical literature, as McGaw notes. See J. McGaw, 'Women and the history of American technology', *Signs: Journal of women in culture and society*, 7: 798–828, 1982, p. 813. This has led many authors to exaggerate the rate of diffusion of domestic devices.

4. J. McGaw, op. cit., p. 814.
5. I. Sirageldin, *Non-Market Components on National Income*, Ann Arbor: University of Michigan Survey Research Centre, 1969.
6. R. Schwartz Cowan, 1983, op. cit.
7. See also R. Schwartz Cowan, 'The "industrial revolution" in the home: household technology and social change in the twentieth century', *Technology and Culture*, 17: 1–23. 1976; R. Schwartz Cowan, 'From Virginia Dare to Virginia Slims: Women and technology in American life', *Technology and Culture*, 20: 51–63, 1979.
8. S. Strasser, *Never Done: A history of American housework*, New York: Pantheon, 1982.
9. R. Schwartz Cowan, 1983, op. cit., p. 100.
10. Ibid., p. 99.
11. There is now quite an extensive feminist literature on the domestic science movement and its attempt to elevate the status of housekeeping. On America, see B. Ehrenreich and D. English, 'The manufacture of housework', *Socialist Revolution*, 26: 5–40, 1975; B. Ehrenreich and D. English, *For Her Own Good: 150 years of experts' advice to women*, London: Pluto Press, 1979; M. Margolis, *Mothers and Such: Views of American women and why they changed*, Berkeley: University of California Press, 1985. For Britain, see L. Davidoff, 'The rationalization of housework', in D. Barker and S. Allen, eds, *Dependence and Exploitation in Work and Marriage*, London: Longman, 1976; E. Arnold and L. Burr, 'Housework and the appliance of science', in W. Faulkner and E. Arnold, eds, *Smothered By Invention: Technology in women's lives*, London: Pluto Press, 1985. For Australia, see K. Reiger, *The Disenchantment of the Home: Modernising the Australian family, 1880–1940*, Melbourne: Oxford University Press, 1986. Reiger's book is the most interesting sociologically as she attempts to combine a feminist analysis of the role of the professional and technical experts of the period with a critique of instrumental reason. The infant welfare and domestic science movements are seen as part of a general extension of 'technical rationality' in the modern world.
12. A. Ravetz, op. cit.
13. I am only referring to domestic technology here, as clearly medical technology is central to demographic changes in life expectancy and to birth control.
14. J. Gershuny, *After Industrial Society: The emerging self-service economy*, London: Macmillan, 1978; J. Gershuny, *Social Innovation and the Division of Labour*, Oxford: Oxford University Press, 1983; J. Gershuny, 'Economic development and change in the mode of production of services', in N. Redclift and E. Minigione, eds, *Beyond Employment: Household, gender and subsistence*, Oxford: Basil Blackwell, 1985; J. Gershuny and J. Robinson, 'Historical changes in the household division of labour', Unpublished Manuscript, 1988.
15. R. Schwartz Cowan, 1983, op. cit., p. 110.
16. J. Gershuny, 1983, op. cit., p. 151.
17. J. Gershuny and J. Robinson, op. cit.
18. A fourth residual category, odd jobs, is not considered in this article.
19. S. Wyatt, G. Thomas and I. Miles, 'Preliminary analysis of the ESRC 1983/4 time budget data', Science Policy Research Unit, University of Sussex, 1985, p. 39.

20. This might lead one to expect that women in the paid labour force might use their income to substitute consumer durables for domestic labour. Surprisingly however women in employment have slightly less domestic equipment than full-time housewives. From an analysis of the Northampton household survey data as part of the British ESRC 'Social change in economic life' initiative, Sara Horrell found that there were no significant differences in the ownership of consumer durables between working women and non-working women.

21. M. Bittman, 'Service provision, women and the future of the household', Unpublished Paper, 1988.

22. I. Miles, *Home Informatics: Information technology and the transformation of everyday life*, London: Pinter, 1988.

23. R. Schwartz Cowan; 1983, op. cit., p. 148.

24. In her 1976 essay Cowan has a tendency to adopt the latter position, seeing the corporate advertisers – 'the ideologues of the 1920s' – as the agents which encouraged American housewives literally to buy the mechanization of the home. The interest of appliance manufacturers in mass markets coincided exactly with the ideological preoccupations of the domestic science advertisers, some of whom even entered into employment with appliance companies. According to W. and D. Andrews, nineteenth-century American women, anxious to elevate their status, believed that technology was a powerful ally. See W. Andrews and D. Andrews, 'Technology and the housewife in nineteenth-century America', *Women's Studies*, 2: 309–28, 1974.

25. R. Schwartz Cowan, 1983, op. cit., p. 150.

26. K. Reiger, op. cit., pp. 115–16.

27. The Australian Consumer Association magazine, *Choice*, recently found that many appliances were useless and that a lot of jobs were better done manually. For example, they found that a simple manual citrus squeezer was overall better than many of the electric gadgets.

28. J. Zimmerman, *The Technological Woman: Interfacing with tomorrow*, New York: Praeger, 1983.

29. This point is made by M. Hicks, 'Microwave ovens', MSc Dissertation, University of New South Wales, 1987.

30. A Forty, *Objects of Desire: Design and society, 1750–1980*, London: Thames and Hudson, 1986.

31. One can only speculate whether covering up the mechanical workings of appliances assisted in alienating women from understanding these machines and how to mend them.

32. A. Forty, op. cit., p. 219.

4.3 □ *Ann Gray*

Taken from her book on video cassette recorders in the home, this extract by Ann Gray considers the gendered meanings of household technologies – pursuing Cockburn's earlier arguments about the distribution of technical competences in domestic culture. Gray's interviewees speak at length here about their feelings towards a new household leisure gadget, and she reveals some quite complex negotiations of power and resistance being played out around the VCR.

Technology in the domestic environment

[. . .]

It was obvious from the interview material that these women[1] had an incomplete knowledge of the workings of the video recorder. The similarity of the women's reported experience in relation to technology was striking and I have therefore chosen to discuss this aspect of the VCR generally across the sample, aiming to provide an account of the range of attitudes and approaches they have in relation to entertainment technology. It is important to point out that technologies such as the VCR have a life even before they enter the household, for example, in discussions about the appropriateness, or otherwise, of its purchase,[2] and also that technologies have a developing biography within households after they have been acquired. The contours of the biography are determined by, amongst other things, different and changing patterns of use and their relation to other forms of technology. [. . .] I will begin by exploring the processes whereby the women actually gained the knowledge and skill required to use the recorders. Very few of the women learnt how to operate the video recorders on their own; this generally means that whatever knowledge they have has been mediated mainly through their male partners. This in many cases relates back to decisions about the purchase or rental of the VCR.

> We got an instruction book but he had a rough idea anyway; he was probably more familiar with it anyway because until we'd started looking he'd been the one who was up on them, as it were. (Lynne)

[. . .] It is important to note here that the five women who were most at ease with the operation of the video recorder were either instigators of the acquisition or, in one case, already familiar with the machine before the current domestic arrangement began.

When new pieces of domestic technology are acquired there are, under current consumer supply practices, two main channels through which user information is gained. The first is that the person who delivers the machine will set up the VCR, tune it to the existing television set and, perhaps, run through the operating procedure. The second is the manual or instruction booklet provided with all machines. The former is usually a quick 'run down' given at speed and not sufficient in itself for the user to become totally competent. The latter, of course, is a permanent source which can be referred to when necessary, as the user develops her or his competence.

The majority of women interviewed said that their partners had initially studied the instruction manual and learnt how to operate the video recorder.

> Well when we got it my husband read the instructions and, you know, he told me. (Janet)

> Michael used to work it at first, he got the knack of it great, he knows how to do it. (Cathy)

> He learnt, then showed me . . . I mean because he bought it. (Beth)

This in turn led to the men operating the recorder more often and on a regular basis, thereby becoming familiar with the various modes of operation and gradually reducing the necessity for consulting the manual. The women, on the other hand, did not use the machine regularly enough to become familiar with it and had to consult the manual if they were to use the recorder, particularly for setting the timer switch for pre-recording.

> I can programme the video – I need the handbook because I don't do it very often. (Beth)

> I can put the tape in, switch it on and find the bit without having to consult the manual, but it is the pre-programming to make it come on at certain times, on which channel and so forth, I don't have the facility to do that, I haven't done it frequently enough to know how to do it without consulting the manual. (Caroline)

> Jim can set the timer, but I have to look it up in the book . . . and whereas I can do it I always have to check back in the book . . . so I suppose most of the time he does that. When he's away I cope with it perfectly well. (Jenny)

Many of the women felt inadequate because of their lack of knowledge and some explained this in terms of not being technically minded.

> I don't even know how to work the thing properly . . . I mean I'll try if I'm desperate, I'll press every button and I'll eventually get on what I want, but I'm certainly not . . . I'm not machine minded really. (Kay)

> I do feel it's passed me by, this technological revolution. (Shirley)

> He does the recording for me. The first video we had I could do it myself, it was just very basic, but as we progressed it got very complicated and I still to this day can't work out the timer, it's just a joke; I'm not very good at that sort of thing. (Susan)

Some insisted in a self-deprecating way that it was their own fault through sheer laziness, or not having bothered to learn.

Well I still have to think about the video. Mainly my own fault because I haven't bothered to do it often enough and bothered to look in the instruction book . . . the timing bit I haven't bothered with, because, then again I don't say that I couldn't do it because there aren't many things I can't do if I put my mind to it . . . I just haven't bothered, you know, there's always somebody here to do it and, then again, it's just pure laziness and apathy because, you know there'll come a time when I probably may want to use it then I'll have to learn how to do it. (Sheila)

I operate it to record when I'm there. I'm not very good at programming it, in fact I tend not to. But it's never really arisen much. I suppose it's laziness, I ought to learn how to programme it but I never need to do it; I suppose if I did I'd sit down and learn to do it, but I've never actually needed to. (Hilary)

It must be noted that a stated lack of enthusiasm for television and video in many cases accounted for a disinclination to become more familiar with the technicalities of the machine. Those women who were keen television viewers made it their business to get to know how to operate the machine, even though the knowledge was mediated by their male partners.

He was the one who read the book and found out how it worked. (Rene)

But Rene soon familiarized herself with the operation of all aspects, including the timer, so that she could record programmes of interest when her husband was away.

For one woman there was more at stake. Her male partner assumed not just knowledge, but control over the video so that her son (not his child) had to ask him to record things on his behalf. She and her son took steps to alter this situation.

I've just learnt. Me and Mark [son] did it last week together, we got the book out, but right from us having it we've never sat down and done it. We fathomed it out between us. Because sometimes Mark feels he wants to record something and Brian'll [partner] say you can't do it . . . and he wants to tape things for himself. (Alison)

Other reasons given for not having gained the knowledge were more complex and were much more to do with the division of labour in the home and appropriate 'territories' mapped out across gender. Two of the older women had been quite calculating in their maintenance of ignorance, a tactic based on years of practical experience.

What about setting the timer?

Oh no, I haven't got a clue, no. If there's anything I want recording I ask one of the boys to do it for me. This is sheer laziness I must admit because I don't read the instructions. When I'm reading the instructions it will not go through, it's like a knitting pattern or a sewing pattern, I just cannot get it through into my thick skull, but the minute I start and work with it, then I carry on quite happily just looking at the directions as I go on . . . but to sit and read it, you know, you've to do this and do that, and hold this button when you're pressing that [shaking head].

So you're not . . .

No, I'm not going to try. No. Once I learned how to put a plug on, now there's nobody else puts a plug on in this house but me . . . so [laugh] there's method in my madness, oh yes. (Edna)

The second woman, in her fifties, living with her husband and grown-up son, could use the video to put a tape in, play it back and rewind it. But, when it came to the timer switch:

> I have been explained to very quickly, and I've looked at the instructions [giggle]. I am what I am, I'm termed as being a bit thick . . . it took me a long time to learn to drive [laugh] and it takes a long time for things to sink in. But on top of that I really don't want to be taught how to do it, really deep down, I know that, because if so it will be my job to deal with it . . . that's the truth. (Audrey)

Some of the younger women also had their reasons for not operating certain parts of the video and one, referring to it as her husband's 'preserve', said,

> Roger uses it more than I do, in fact I'd probably be hard pressed to actually work it myself, I've always left it I must admit to him.
>
> *Have you ever set the timer?*
>
> No, I don't think I have, no.
>
> *Has there not been an occasion when you've needed it?*
>
> No, because I would say to him, I'm going to be out tomorrow night, could you set it up . . . a weak and feeble woman [laugh] . . . I have put it on for the children sometimes, not the timer, but I can put a disc [*sic*] in and turn it on.
>
> *Did you make a conscious decision not to learn?*
>
> I don't know, really, I mean I'm sure I could if I read it up and did it but, erm . . . I suppose I have consciously decided in effect.
>
> *You said earlier that it was Roger's preserve, is that why you don't . . .*
>
> Erm . . . no, I didn't mean, you know, that he would be cross or anything if I did, I just meant, you know, traditionally it has been his affair, the technicalities of it. (Shirley)

Tradition, custom and practice, already established as family routines before the arrival of the video recorder, obviously play an important part in the division of labour, especially where there are children in the household.

> *Who decides normally whether you're going to record something?*
>
> I would say Craig because he's usually the one that gets around to doing the actual setting it up, if it's going to be a setting the timer up job and what have you. Although I must admit that I often say tape that, tape this, so I suppose really, it seems that he does it more because he actually gets the job of doing the setting up.
>
> *Is that because you can't do it?*
>
> No, I can do it, but I usually find that it's one of those jobs that he's capable of doing and he can be getting on with that whilst I'm doing something else that he's not capable of doing . . . usually if we're going out I'm usually brushing hair and putting bobbles in and saying 'Set that up' and we're sort of rushing out and I say, 'Oh, I want to watch that, set that up' and, erm . . . (Lynne)

It would seem that there are decisions made by the women, either consciously or subconsciously, to remain in ignorance of the workings of the VCR, so that it is their husband or partner's job to set up the timer. This, of course, has the function of a 'service' for the household unit, that of timing an off-air recording for joint watching; the more calculatedly ignorant women had perhaps recognized this latent servicing element and resisted it in view of their already heavily committed domestic servicing roles. One woman had learnt her lesson with the plug (as we have seen) but the other, interestingly, had learnt hers through knowing how to erect the screen for the showing of home movies, which was her job every Christmas and some Sundays.

> All this time and I'm just learning. I had to set it all up, I had to put the screen up [laugh] we'd say on a Sunday night 'we haven't seen any films for a long time' and he'd say 'get it all set up' [laugh] you see my reluctance [pointing to the video]. (Audrey)

For those women who have not made a conscious decision to remain in ignorance, but for whom it simply 'just happened' or 'there's always someone there to do it for me', this has negative repercussions. It means that they never get to use the recorder, or not often enough to become familiar with it, relying on their partners or their children to set it for them. The same effect is produced by both strategies: the women remain ignorant. What is important, though, is that they feel stupid because of their lack of knowledge in this area. That can be accounted for in terms of material restriction – having particular domestic duties to perform rather than being able to sit down and study an instruction manual and its application – is then turned back on the women, often in their own consciousness, as a presumed basic inability to understand technical things. For three of the women I talked to, the same was true of the home computer.

> When we first got the computer and we were all learning to play with it and fiddling, I had much less time and everybody got computer literate, they were all much more adept at it much more quickly than me and I got really left behind and I felt really pissed off with it. They had all this time and they can now play the games and Jim's got into the first stages of programming. They left me way behind so that I couldn't really appreciate it and enjoy it and I was very much aware at the time that I resented that and that it was purely a time thing. (Jenny)

She has recognized that whilst her family were free to devote themselves to playing with the computer, she had other calls on her time which placed her on the margins of the learning process. She goes on:

> I keep thinking I'll set it up again now I've got some more time when this work finishes, but I probably won't because the initial impetus has gone . . . the novelty has worn off for everybody else . . . it would be a very deliberate thing for me to settle down to do it and anyway nobody else would be interested now [laugh] so I'd just be doing it for myself . . . And I think that happens perhaps in other areas because I feel I've got less time or I'm doing something else or I've got other responsibilities . . . I'll get left behind, or I'll simply 'agree' rather than 'suggest' sort of thing. (Jenny)

It is also interesting to note her prediction about her future use of the computer when she may have more time. The likelihood is that she will not learn how to use it because it would, in her words, be 'doing it for myself'. This relates to [. . .] reluctance to indulge in activities which are motivated by self-interest. Another woman was very keen to learn how to operate the computer; her husband used it a lot 'as a computer, not just for games'. I asked her if she had tried to learn.

> When we first got it and that yes . . . but I find that if things don't go in straight away I lose interest, there seems to be such a lot to take in, like I sat reading some of the books, he has a lot of books on it, some very basic ones, but I think . . . I'm all right so far, then you get . . . mind you, you've always got other things on your mind, what we're going to have for tea and things like that . . . you've got to be able to concentrate . . . (Janet)

These two men were 'hobbyists' and were envied by their wives for their ability to switch off from the daily routine and concentrate on their chosen pastime. Although the first speaker is quite aware that it is lack of time which prevents her from engaging fully with the computer, the latter fails to make the connection between the many and frequent demands made upon her time and her inability to concentrate, simply believing that her husband is much cleverer than she is. What is important to note in both cases is the significance given to those particular activities chosen by their male partners. This is not a simple matter of available time, but of the right to time which is claimed by the men, as if what they are doing is significant by virtue of the fact that they are doing it. This [. . .] obviously has far-reaching implications for the organization of domestic life, but here we can see that this claim to time and how it is spent gives the male of the household the opportunity to become techno-literate much more quickly and effectively than his female partner.

The third woman in a home-computer-owning household had managed to familiarize herself with the computer. She did not have children; the computer was used in her husband's work, and they had decided to learn together about it; but in order to do so she had to overcome certain barriers.

> Well I hated it at first, I didn't even want to turn it on. I thought, no, this is far too advanced for me, I don't know what it does and I don't want it to do anything. I was frightened of the computer because everybody was saying women can't pick up computers as easily as men and children. (Susan)

She had overcome these prejudices and found that she 'had a brain' after all, although her husband had enabled her to 'find' it.

> He's a very clever person and he educates me in silly little things. I mean, I left school at 15 and I didn't have a full education because my parents weren't interested in me having one, they wanted me to get married and that was it. But John's educated me, and I have got a brain . . . it sounds terrible doesn't it? People say, oh, women haven't got brains, well they have, they're just not allowed to put them to use properly, and I have got one. (Susan)

This 'mastering' of the computer had given her confidence to find out how to work the video, but again she blames her lack of knowledge on 'laziness'.

> It was just laziness, like the computer, you know, there were too many knobs and too many . . . it's one of these complicated ones and I couldn't be bothered learning how to do it,

I was depending on him to do it, like at first I was depending on him to play with the computer. That's his. But now I can do it . . . so if I can do a computer I can certainly do a video, my God. (Susan)

This woman performs complex ideological work in order to explain her relationship to technology. She recognizes the social constraints which agencies like the family and education place on women, but ultimately the blame rests upon her own personal 'laziness'. Her husband, although he had a very similar education to her, is seen by her as naturally more intelligent and inhabiting a world of knowledge which he is able to offer her through an educative process. Janet had a very similar attitude towards her own background and her male partner, although he did not perform the same educative role.

I left school and went to work in Boots . . . and I was only young when I met my husband . . . and I just wanted to get married and have children, that was my only aim in life . . . I mean it didn't seem important if I did anything. But then when you've got them you think oh, I wish I could do something . . . just to say, I've done that. Like, I keep telling my husband that I'm going to write a book, so buy me a typewriter. He says, just get a word processor and goodness knows what, and a printer . . . but whether or not I will do . . . I might do.

And what about the computer, would you think about learning how to use that?

I would like to really I think, just to say, well yes I can do it . . . I don't mean just for playing games . . . I mean as a computer . . . yes because there again I can say well, I can do that . . . I think I get riled at it because I can't . . . I think ooh I wish I could and then I could speak more on a level with my husband . . . you know I could, you know, converse with him and be on his level type of thing . . . mind you, I suppose I haven't sat and read like he has, he reads hours, you know, about goodness knows what. (Janet)

This woman, a self-defined full-time housewife, implicitly suggests the ways in which women are ideologically placed by the notion of the 'feminine career', and its limitations; her ambitions to write a children's book were not to seek external recognition necessarily, but to show her family that she could do something too. Her aspirations in this respect have been deflected on to the necessity for her to learn how to operate a word processor, but furthermore, to break into the masculine world of the computer and the 'knowledge' which she sees her husband as possessing. This woman goes into the library with her children and sees children's books and thinks to herself, 'I could write something better than that', but at home the possibility of her writing a book is, paradoxically, undermined by her ignorance of computer technology. This particular kind of technology therefore is used in these two homes as a symbol of technological and intellectual ability, of indisputably male territory to which a woman can only gain entry via her husband.

One of the 'calculated ignorance' strategists, referring to the more mundane example of changing a plug, claimed that this kind of technical knowledge 'makes the men feel superior' and she, for one, was willing to be complicit in this state of affairs. Although less explicit, neither Susan nor Janet in any way seriously challenged that male superiority.

Although [. . .] the majority of the women did not operate the timer functions on the video, the reasons they gave for this and their implications are complex and far-reaching. I have discussed the right to time, but it is also clear that the 'cleverness' or 'superior knowledge' which the males are able to accrue enables them to maintain their position of authority and superiority in the eyes of many of the women.

Most VCRs and many television receivers are supplied with a remote control unit which facilitates the changing of channels and the operation of record and playback of the VCR from 'the comfort of your own armchair' (Sony VCR manual). Indeed, compact disc players and other video or sound systems are now also supplied with this facility. The remote control unit itself assumes a single viewer or controller, but very often, of course, several members of the household will be watching television or video at the same time. The majority of the women reported that, if they were in the television room, then the male members of the household, either father or son, would invariably hold the remote control.

[. . .]

This male domination of the remote control unit has also been noted by Dave Morley[3] in his study of families in London [. . .] and observed by Peter Collett when he videotaped households watching televisions.[4] This obviously has ramifications for the question of control over the material to be viewed. [. . .]

What of the women who did regularly operate the video recorder? One of these, a young woman teacher married to an often out-of-work actor, had already owned a video recorder when living alone. She therefore was quite at ease with all functions of the recorder, and often used VCRs in connection with her work. However, even her case is not straightforward.

Who sets the pre-recorder?

Well, whoever's in. [*If you're both in?*] I'd probably let Tony do it. I mean if he was upstairs, I'd do it, but if he was in the same room as me I'd probably say 'do that'. I can do it, but I'd rather sit and watch him do it, in the same way that I would always sit in the passenger seat of the car, because I'd much rather be driven, and I would sit in a chair and say, 'Would you get me a drink'. I like to have things done for me. (Michelle)

This partnership was unusual in the sample in that she was the main regular earner. Michelle and her husband 'shared' most household tasks – shopping, cooking and washing – but in fact, because of his irregular employment he did most of the domestic work. However, she shows her desire to maintain some distinction, or to return to more traditional male and female roles, where he does things for her. But this could well be the effects of a rather complicated 'barter' system within which she was usually in credit because her full-time work enabled him to pursue his rather uncertain career.

Of the four other video-competent women, two were unmarried women living with their parents – Christine and Sandra [. . .] and here age is an important factor.

My Dad won't touch it at all, he gets me to set the timer for him . . . I think he's scared of blowing himself up, he goes mad if I ask him to touch it. (Sandra)

Another was a divorcée living with her grown-up daughters and occasionally her boyfriend. She did, however, admit to not using the timer switch very often, although she did know how to operate it.

> I'm good at fiddling, I didn't look at the book, I just worked it out as it came, I'm quite good at fiddling like that. (Barbara)

The young full-time mother, Julie, was totally in command of the video recorder. In fact, before beginning our discussions she set the timer to record a programme she would be missing because I was there. Her husband never used the video.

> Occasionally he'll say 'will you record something?' if he knows it's on, but that is sort of my department [pointing to the video], is the television and the video.

How did you learn how to do it?

> Well the man who brought it showed me, but it didn't really sink in I don't suppose, and then I learnt from the book. Andrew still can't operate the timer and everything, but it's just because he hasn't sat down and worked it out, he just leaves it to me, it's easy. (Julie)

Here we have a male partner who makes no claims to technical knowledge of the VCR and his partner experienced no difficulty in studying and applying the manual to the operating procedures.

Very few women experienced any kind of 'block' with, say, the hi-fi or cassette players, and many of them used these machines quite often. Those women who used them very regularly expressed a keen enjoyment in listening to music, some taping off the radio, others playing records or tapes during the day or if they were on their own in the house in the evening. The pleasure that these women gained from listening to music seems to have been a motivating factor in learning how to operate the equipment, but in general they considered hi-fis and cassette players to be much easier to use than the VCR.

> Well we've always had one [cassette player] at home . . . it's just the video. (Cathy)

> I make up a tape for myself with the songs that I like. Usually on a Sunday when the Top Twenty's on, I record the songs that I like. (Kay)

We have already noted that Kay does not work the video and is 'not that interested really' in recording off television, but will regularly record music on to a sound tape. She often sits in the same room as the family whilst they are watching television.

> No, I never sit anywhere else. I always sit where the television is . . . I can read, or I put a record or tape on and sit with the headphones on and totally ignore the lot of them [laugh]. I sit and listen to music. (Kay)

However, some of the women experienced difficulties with the more technologically advanced pieces of entertainment equipment in their houses, often referring to these as 'gadgets'.

> We've got so many gadgets in this house you see . . . so many radios, computer radios where you punch a thing in and it goes to the station, but I live with it and, well, I feel

as if it's nothing to do with me. Not that I'm frightened of it, I think being in an all-male household it's rubbed off. I carry a screwdriver, I can fix plugs and if anything's broken I can do it. But I don't know whether it's easier not to do things yourself, or whether I see men doing it so much, messing about with the electrical things, soldering irons and that. And I think I could do it just as good as they can . . . I think I could work all these radios and things, and do the timer on the video. (Jean)

This woman is a teacher in a large inner-city middle school where she regularly operates a VCR and tape cassettes as part of her job. At home, living with her two grown-up sons and husband she feels as if 'it's nothing to do with me' and, indeed, doesn't work the timer on the video recorder. She realizes, of course, that she can, or could do it, but within the household there seems to be an assumption about what men do which is carried over into practice. This is confirmed by Cynthia Cockburn's research, in which she notes that some women who work with technology or 'tools' in paid work outside the home relinquish this expertise to their male partners in the home.[5]

Many of the households had more than one television set. The main colour television and VCR were mostly in the sitting-room, with portables in either the kitchen or bedroom. Some of these second televisions were complicated and also presented problems in their operation.

The TV in our bedroom is one of these really complicated things which is TV, radio, cassette player and an alarm thing in it . . . I don't know how to switch the TV on, it's got so many knobs and things on it, and it's also got a peculiar switch whereby it'll switch off after an hour and I'm forever in the middle of watching something and it goes off . . . you've to get out of bed and work out how to switch it back on again . . . it's probably because I've never bothered to say, look just show me how to do this . . . erm . . . Then on the occasions that you have to do it, I'll fiddle around and not remember what I've done the next time . . . I'm the same with the alarm clock, setting it or changing the setting . . . you see I haven't done it that number of times that I can remember . . . I think it is the number of times you do it. (Jenny)

It appears that older pieces of equipment and perhaps those with which the women were familiar before their current domestic circumstances, present no problem in terms of operation. Added to this are motivational factors, such as, wanting to record music, or, in some specific circumstances, wanting to record television programmes off air, which will be sufficient reason for the women to become familiar with the machines, and to use them regularly enough to achieve ease of operation. On the other hand, the newer and, almost by definition, more 'complicated' or technologically advanced pieces of entertainment equipment tend to be off-putting for women and they are largely the preserve of the adult male or children of the household. In some of the households there is a reproduction of 'appropriate' tasks with the children.

What about your children, how do they use the video recorder?

Erm . . . my son, erm . . . well if his dad is out on business and can't get back for a certain programme, I mean, he knows it all, he's been primed . . . so when father's not there my son takes over.

What about the girls?

My youngest daughter definitely not, but my eldest daughter, yes, she knows how to work it, yes, but there again if she wants anything recording she'll ask her brother, you know, she won't be bothered. If he's not here she'll do it, but she'll say to him, 'Will you record so and so?' if he's in. (Kay)

These women, of course, routinely operate quite sophisticated pieces of technology in the course of their domestic work: washing machines, cookers, microwave ovens, food mixers, sewing machines, etc. Almost all the women were perfectly at ease with these machines and most registered surprise when they were referred to as technology. The one exception to this was Caroline who had adopted a 'Luddite' attitude towards technology in general and resisted what she saw as the pressure to technologize the home. She believed this to be 'technology for its own sake' and that rather than simplifying household tasks it had the effect of making them much more complicated. However, the rest of the women did not appear to share this view and when new kitchen equipment had been purchased they had read through manuals and instruction books and had quickly become familiar users. In the majority of cases, their male partners had not staked their claim to this knowledge, leaving the women to work things out for themselves. This is important for two main reasons. First, it is an indication of assumptions about appropriate 'female' technology and second, when knowledge or expertise is not rendered 'masculine' then the women appear to have a less problematic relationship with technology.

We noted that the video recorder timer switch seemed to present the biggest difficulties for the women, although many of their cookers also had a time-setting function. The women used this facility without difficulty, but very few of the men could operate the cooker timer; for example:

Does your husband operate the cooker timer?

Only the minute timer, not the pre-set timer . . . he uses it so he doesn't forget something that's on, but if we were going out and I was putting something in the oven to cook for when we got back, that would be my job. (Shirley)

He can't set the timer on the cooker [laugh]; it's disgusting. (Jenny)

When I went away we discovered that my husband didn't know how to operate the timer on the oven. (Hilary)

These are glaring examples of the gendered division of labour which have nothing to do with technological competence but everything to do with social use. However, it goes further than this in that the fact that the men cannot work the cooker timer is not seen by the women as evidence of masculine technological incompetence, in the way that their own inability to operate the video timer might demonstrate – in their own eyes – such inadequacy in themselves. It seems that women's technical competences are rendered invisible, along with the invisibility of their domestic work. Hilary, for example, argues that it is her husband's lack of time which leads to his lack of expertise in the kitchen, whereas she felt that her own lack of expertise with the video recorder was due to her laziness, or 'natural' lack of technical competence.

[. . .]

Summary

[. . .] Gender is the key determinant in the use of and expertise in specific pieces of domestic equipment. This in turn can be seen to relate to the gendered division of labour within the home and its associated technology. Recent research into the acquisition of radio and television has identified very similar patterns of use [. . .].[6] In the light of the women's attitudes to older forms of entertainment technology such as radio and cassette recorders, we can perhaps see their resistance to video technology as a passing phase. This would certainly find support in Sherry Turkle's arguments[7] in relation to 'computerphobia', which she argues is transitional. However, we can see from this study that there is more at stake for many of the women. One point to make is that it seems that the women will always be 'lagging behind' in mastery of entertainment and information technology. However, the crucial point to be drawn from this analysis is that the domestic context and the social relations within it have quite powerful consequences in relation to women and new technology.

Notes

1. Gray provides brief biographical details of all 30 women featured in her study, using fictitious names listed alphabetically. Here are those to whom she refers in this extract:

   Alison

   Full-time housewife. Aged 35. Living with a sheet metal worker, with his 12-week-old baby, and her three children from a previous marriage aged 15, 13 and 10. They own their detached modern house. She left school at 15, worked in Marks and Spencer doing office work until she had her first child.

   Audrey

   Part-time doctor's receptionist. Aged 51. Married to a self-employed haulage contractor, with one son who is 27 and unemployed. They own a 1930s semi-detached house. She left school at 15 and worked as a telephonist until her child was born. Has held her present job for 10 years.

   Barbara

   Casual worker for her boyfriend who is a jobbing builder. Aged 38. Divorced, and lives with her two daughters aged 19 and 17 in a rented council house. She left school at 15 and worked in offices until she left to have her children.

   Beth

   University lecturer and practising architect. Aged 37. Married to a lecturer: they run their own joint practice. Three children aged 11, 8 and 6. They own a large old semi-detached house. She has a degree in architecture and has had a continuous career.

Caroline

Full-time research fellow. Aged 43. Lives with an architect, with her daughter aged 12 and their son aged 5 in a large Edwardian terrace house. She read English at university and after a postgraduate certificate of education year, taught in school, but took a break to have her first child.

Cathy

Evening packer at the biscuit factory. Aged 21. Married to a maintenance engineer. One son aged 2. They own a modern terrace house. She left school at 15 and worked in the retail industry until she had her child.

Christine

Full-time supermarket assistant. Aged 21. Unmarried, living with her parents in their rented council terrace house. Left school at 16, since when she has worked in the same supermarket.

Edna

Newsagent. Aged 52. Recently widowed, but lives with her four children, two sets of twins aged 25 and 17. Left school at 16 and worked as a telephonist until having her children. She now runs her shop with some assistance.

Hilary

Part-time ESL supply teacher. Aged 44. Married to a university professor. They have two children, 16 and 13. Own their large Victorian terrace house. She has a degree in English and had been a secondary school teacher before having her children.

Janet

Full-time housewife. Aged 34. Married to an electrical engineer who often works abroad. Three children aged 12, 10 and 7. Owners of modern semi. She left school at 15 and worked behind the counter at Boots the Chemist.

Jean

Full-time teacher in a middle school. Aged 44. Married to a fireman. Three sons, 24, 23 and 19. The 23-year-old lives at home. They own their own semi. She left school at 17 and worked in the civil service until she had her first child. Qualified as a teacher as a mature student.

Jenny

Part-time research administrator. Aged 36. Married to a process worker. Two children aged 10 and 8. Rented council house. Read German at university and did a postgraduate certificate of education. Taught in middle school, but left the area. Had a break to have her children and is now employed in clerical administration on short-term contracts.

Julie

Full-time housewife. Aged 27. Married to a fitter-engineer, shift-worker. One daughter aged 2. They own a small terrace house. She left school at 16 and trained as a nursery nurse. She left this job to have her child.

Kay

Part-time nursery assistant. Aged 39. Married to a pensions consultant. Three children aged 17, 15 and 10. They own a modern detached house. She left school at 15 and worked as an insurance clerk before having her children.

Lynne

Part-time plant displayer. Aged 29. Married to a self-employed plumber. Two children aged 7 and 4. They own their semi-detached house. She left school at 15 and worked for a mail order company before leaving to have her first child.

Michelle

Full-time primary school teacher. Aged 33. Married to an actor. They do not have children. They own their own Victorian terrace house. She trained as a teacher and has been employed since leaving college.

Rene

Part-time assistant in wine bar. Aged 50. Married to a leisure executive. No children at home. Owners of a modern detached house. She left school at 14 and worked as a comptometer operator, before having children by her first marriage.

Sandra

Unemployed. Aged 19. Single, living with her parents in their rented council house. Has worked on YTS and at the biscuit factory.

Sheila

Part-time clerical assistant. Aged 48. Married to a car sales executive. Two children, 20 and 18, living at home. Owners of large detached house. Left school at 15, trained as a secretary and worked for the Post Office until having the first of her children.

Shirley

Voluntary tutor in English as a Second Language. Aged 36. Married to a solicitor. Two children, aged 5 and 2. Owners of modern detached house. Read French at university and worked as a bilingual secretary until she had her first child.

Susan

Part-time hairdresser's receptionist. Aged 29. Married to a self-employed motor accessories distributor and expecting their first child. They own their modern flat. Left school at 15, worked mainly in retail fashion and hairdressing since then. Intends to leave her job to bring up her child.

2. A section from Gray's book, on decisions to have a VCR, has been left out here for reasons of space.
3. D. Morley, *Family Television*: *Cultural power and domestic leisure*, London: Comedia, 1986.
4. P. Collett, 'Watching the TV audience', Paper to Second International Television Studies Conference, London, 1986.
5. C. Cockburn, *Machinery of Dominance*: *Women, men and technical know-how*, London: Pluto, 1985, p. 219; and see Reading 4.1, this volume.
6. S. Moores, '"The box on the dresser": Memories of early radio and everyday life', *Media, Culture and Society*, 10: 23–40, 1988; T. O'Sullivan, 'Television memories and cultures of viewing, 1950–65', in J. Corner, ed., *Popular Television in Britain*: *Studies in cultural history*, London: British Film Institute, 1991.
7. S. Turkle, *The Second Self*: *Computers and the human spirit*, New York: Simon and Schuster, 1984.

4.4 □ *Graham Murdock, Paul Hartmann and Peggy Gray*

Following extensive research on the consumption of home computers and other domestic media – carried out in the English Midlands during the mid-1980s – Graham Murdock, Paul Hartmann and Peggy Gray chart the shifting career of this technology across time. They show how computing can have a contested significance in the private sphere, and they insist that work of this sort pays careful attention to the different material and cultural resources available to families.

Contextualizing home computing: resources and practices

Along with the video cassette recorder, the Walkman and the compact disc player, home computers were one of the most conspicuous consumer products of the 1980s. From their first appearance at the beginning of the decade, they attracted an increasing amount of research aimed at finding out who was entering the domestic micro market and who wasn't, identifying barriers to adoption and how they might be overcome, and exploring what people were actually doing with their machines. This work, which began in the United States but spread rapidly to other advanced economies, employed a variety of methods, ranging from nationwide surveys[1] to studies of early adopters and computer enthusiasts[2] and ethnographies of computer households.[3] But beneath the differences of approach, virtually all these studies were united in viewing home computing activity in a radically decontextualized way. They [...] focused on the practical activities of [...] users but took little account of the way these activities were structured by the resources that consumers could draw upon, or were excluded from.

These resources are material, social and symbolic. Home computers are not just commodities that are traded for a price in the market. They are also the site of a continual cultural struggle over the meaning of the machine and its appropriate uses. In Britain, this has taken the form of a contest between official discourses stressing

245

home computing's educational and instrumental potentials, and commercial discourses promoting its entertaining, playful and expressive uses. Each discourse offers particular user identities, which intersect with the material resources and social relations inside and outside the household to produce specific patterns of use or disuse.

[We] set out to explore the relations between practices and resources, drawing on material gathered in the course of a longitudinal study of domestic communication technologies based on samples of just over one thousand households, drawn from four contrasted locations in the English Midlands.[4] All respondents were interviewed at three points in time about their use of media and new technology, including home computers. These indexical data were supplemented by focused interviews with computer users, drawn from the main samples. [. . .]

The period covered by the research, 1983 to 1987, coincided with the British home computer market's takeoff to growth. At the end of 1981 (when the first cheap, easy-to-use machines were launched) less than a quarter of a million households had a micro. By the spring of 1986, this figure had climbed to 3.06 million.[5] Because the Midlands interviews were conducted over this crucial period, they provided clues to the complex interplay between the user careers of individuals and households and the general development of the home computer industry as a whole.

Most research on home computing has either ignored the diachronic dimension, and settled for a snapshot at a particular moment, or approached it from the point of view of the computer industry's interest in devising more effective marketing strategies.[6] Work on the diffusion of innovations is a partial exception, however. This is centrally concerned with the social dynamics of adoption and use over time but until recently has paid little attention to material constraints, and no attention at all to the role of public discourse in organizing use.

Material resources: from diffusion to differential access

Writers in the 'diffusion of innovations' tradition are concerned with the processes whereby a novel object or practice comes to be adopted by the members of a society or social group and incorporated into everyday routines and practices.[7] Diffusion models were originally developed in relation to studies of agricultural innovations in rural America in the 1940s, in an attempt to explain why some farmers were more willing to adopt new techniques. After World War II they became one of the major theoretical linchpins of US-sponsored 'modernization' strategies in the Third World.

In the early 1980s, one of the key figures in developing the diffusion perspective, Everett Rogers, began to apply it to the spread of home computers in the United States. As a resident of southern California, living close to Silicon Valley, one of the major sites of commercial activity concerned with microcomputing, he was particularly well placed to observe its development as both an industry[8] and a market.[9] In seeking to explain patterns of adoption and use, Rogers and his co-workers originally focused on the interplay between the capacities and characteristics of the available machines

– what they could do and how easy they were to use – and the personal needs and dispositions of users and potential users – what they wanted a machine for, whether they had any relevant skills or experience, and whether their attitude towards technology in general was positive or hostile. They paid comparatively little attention to the role of material resources in regulating market entry.

This was largely because their model took it for granted that everybody was a potential computer owner and that the diffusion curve would follow other major innovations in consumer electronics, such as the television set, with adoption trickling steadily down the income scale. This ignored the widening income gap and rising levels of unemployment produced by Reaganomics. As the decade wore on, however, research showed quite clearly that, despite a massive promotional effort, home computer ownership remained concentrated within the professional and managerial strata. The diffusionists accordingly modified their position, and accepted that 'differential access seems to be primarily based on income differentials across socio-economic status groups'.[10] This pattern was repeated in other advanced capitalist societies.[11] It was particularly marked in Britain, where the Family Expenditure Surveys revealed a clear linear relation between income and computer ownership. In 1986, for example, only 7.6 per cent of households with a weekly income of under £125 had a home computer, compared to 26.6 per cent of households in the income band £325–75.[12]

The Midlands study confirms and extends this point. Economic capacity not only played a central role in determining whether or not a household entered the home computer market, it also shaped subsequent patterns of use in significant ways. A number of applications, such as word processing, are either made much more difficult or ruled out altogether if the machine owned is one of the cheaper models without a dedicated monitor or a printer. The last wave of the panel study, conducted in 1987, revealed that, despite the rapid growth of the Amstrad PCW range and the proliferation of relatively cheap IBM PC 'clones', the majority of computer households in the study still only had the machine they had first bought, more than half of which were basic Sinclair or Commodore models. Only one in four had traded up and acquired a more sophisticated model.

Behind these figures lay experiences of disillusion, particularly among those who had bought into 'the home computer revolution' in its first phase. The limits of these early cheap machines were not obvious at first. On the contrary, as one teenager recounted, in 1983 when sales first boomed, they seemed exciting and full of possibility.

> 'I don't know really why, because it suddenly started didn't it, computers everywhere. The first one I ever saw was the [Sinclair] ZX81, which I thought was really good when I first saw it. It's nothing really is it? Because it can only print the name on the screen'.

This restriction was a source of considerable disappointment to users who bought one thinking it could do more than it could.

> 'I wanted it as a word processor, but of course it's no good for that at all. I didn't appreciate it at the time. You can't get enough words on the screen, unless you get one that's about four or five times the price. . . . With this one you can only read four or five words

across and you've had it. I just went round a bit and I thought, well this was the best for the price you know. I wanted it for a word processor and they said, "Oh yes they can do this" and "Oh yes they do that", you know. And of course it does, but not satisfactorily for proper use.'

Programming also proved to be a problem, with naïve users often finding that it took far longer than they anticipated to master the skills they needed to pursue their own projects. As one young teacher explained: 'I quite enjoyed the programming side of it, but found that it was a lot of work to achieve very, very simple results. Although it was quite a challenge.'

Often initial enthusiasm dwindled rapidly, as in this account by a woman who had seen her husband and son lose interest:

'I think they thought they were going to do great things with it, and make programs and use it in all sorts of ways. But then they realized what a long time it was going to be to learn to do this, and a long time putting the program in. They haven't had the time.'

The problems of using the basic models to produce self-generated material were often compounded by two other material limitations.

One of the attractions of the early Sinclair and Commodore machines, besides their relatively low price, was the fact that they did not need a disc drive or dedicated monitor. They could be operated using a standard black-and-white television set as a display screen and a portable audio cassette recorder to load and store software. But both these selling points imposed important limitations on use. Whilst tape technology was cheap and convenient, it was not particularly robust in use and took a considerable time both to load programs into the machine and retrieve stored material. Even in 1987, however, when the third wave of the Midlands survey was conducted, three-quarters of computer households still relied entirely on tape technology. An even higher proportion, 80 per cent, had computers without their own screens, and were still using a domestic television set for visual display facilities.

This was less of a problem where the machine was connected to a set reserved for the purpose and placed in a permanent location. As the survey results showed, however, this was a luxury that poorer households could not always afford. Because they were less likely to own a second or third television set, the home computer became a literal extension of the main set, competing with broadcast programming and video cassette recorder use for access to the screen. This meant that computing activity was restricted both spatially and temporally, with the keyboard and television set having to be connected and disconnected each time the machine was used. Not having an integral computer screen will become even more of a disadvantage if and when Britain's fifth terrestrial television channel comes on stream. This will employ the same frequency as home computers currently using a television set as a monitor and, though these machines could be re-tuned, the industry consensus is that most owners will not bother.

To sum up: the available evidence reveals a consistent relationship between patterns of home computer ownership and use and a household's income and class position. The more affluent the household the more likely it is to own a home computer and the more likely that this will be one of the more expensive and versatile machines with a built-in screen, a disc drive and a printer, capable of supporting a wide range of uses and applications.

The material resources at a household's disposal – in the form of discretionary income, domestic space and related technologies – can be said to be determinant in 'the first instance', in the sense that they establish the basic conditions of access to and exclusion from the various configurations of computing equipment.[13] To explain why this equipment is used in particular ways, however, or why it falls into disuse, we need to go on to explore the social resources at the user's disposal.

Social resources: networks and disconnections

One of the strengths of the 'diffusion of innovations' perspective is its emphasis on the role of social networks in fostering and sustaining new practices. According to this argument, the maintenance of particular forms of computer use will depend in large part on access to other users who can offer advice, encouragement and practical support. Conversely, users who are isolated from or marginal to such networks may find it difficult to acquire competences and sustain interest over time. The centrality of networks emerged strongly from the Midlands data. As the following interview account makes clear, contacts can play an important role in providing back-up support at key moments.

> 'My friend down round the estate, who's got the same machine, which is useful because he has a lot of system software that I don't have. He's into computers as a job. It's useful. The other day when I was using the word processor, I was trying to save it. I had spent all morning keying it in. It's only an extract from a magazine. Started at 8 o'clock and finished about lunch. You make one mistake and it's rubbish. Terrifies you. Oh it's a swine to type in, and I wanted to make sure I'd save it. So, I saved a load of tape without turning the machine off. I then carried my tape recorder round to his machine to see if it would load on his machine. If it would then I was alright. So I was lucky, because if I'd turned it off I'd have wasted eight hours of work.'

Contacts also help to legitimate particular patterns of use through the swopping of information and anecdotes and exchanging software. Almost 60 per cent of the computer users interviewed in the Midlands study said that they often talked about computing to friends and acquaintances, and around half claimed to borrow and exchange software on a regular basis. Significantly, those with little or no contact with other users were more likely to have stopped using their machines once the initial novelty had worn off. They tended to live in households where no one had a job that involved using computers or gave them access to relevant expertise and contacts, and in neighbourhoods with relatively few other users. These patterns of social and spatial segregation interacted with the differential distribution of material resources described earlier to reinforce the disadvantaged position of users and would-be users in low-income households.

At the same time, we must be careful not to overstate the importance of class location. Computer use is also very strongly inflected by generation and gender. Among the Midlands sample, domestic micros were overwhelmingly concentrated in households with children and adolescents. By 1985, when the second wave of interviews was conducted, over a third (35 per cent) of 'nuclear families' had acquired one, as against 5 per cent of couples without children and 6 per cent of people living alone. When households with computers were asked to say who the main user was, only one in seven nominated a female. In fact, apart from a small number of adults in professional and managerial jobs, who mainly used their machines for work-related tasks, and a scattering of hobbyists, home computing was the province of children and teenagers and of boys rather than girls, a pattern confirmed by Jane Wheelock's recent research[14] on Wearside. To explain these age and gender biases we need to go beyond the differential distribution of material and social resources, and explore the way the promotional discourses around home computing have drawn on activities and identities associated with youth and masculinity.

Discursive resources: the multiple meanings of the home mirco

From its first entry into the British market, the home computer has been enmeshed in a web of competing definitions of uses and users, as the promotional discourses of the hardware and software industries[15] jostled for public attention with governmental discourses about information technology and education. By defining the micro's potentialities and pleasures in different ways, these discourses played an important role in structuring the ways it was used.

The push to market a micro for home use came initially from firms selling kits that purchasers assembled themselves. These began to appear in the late 1970s and were aimed firmly at committed hobbyists who wanted to explore the possibilities of the technology and had the competence to cope with the machines' far from 'user-friendly' characteristics, including the complete lack of pre-written software. They were, in Leslie Haddon's useful phrase, 'self-referring', in the sense that the pleasures they offered derived not from particular applications but from the possession of the technology itself and from solving the problems involved in getting it to perform.

This notion of the 'self-referring' machine was generalized by the British entrepreneur, Clive Sinclair, whose consumer electronics company had grown out of his own interest in inventing and brainstorming. He launched his first model, the ZX 80, in 1980, as a machine for learning to program on. Since there was no supporting software, this was more of a necessity than an invitation. Not surprisingly, it found its main market among enthusiasts with computer skills. They were also among the first to buy his second and more powerful model, the ZX 81, launched the following year. This extract from an interview captures the computer hobbyist's pleasure in possession particularly well.

'I caught the bug over ten years ago at college on the mainframe there. I was so keen that one summer holiday period I conned this company that I was just a little guy with a couple of "O" levels and I wanted to be an operator, and they trained me up. It was 8K. So, an expanded ZX 81 is more powerful. And this was a mainframe. This took up a whole room. I always thought one day I would have my own, you know. I just can't believe it now, I still haven't got over the shock.'

At the same time, the ZX 81 began to pick up sales in the general consumer market among households with little or no previous computer experience. Within twelve months of its launch, 400,000 had been sold, establishing it as the brand leader in the British home computer market. Its nearest rival was the VIC 20, produced by the American company, Commodore, which, like the Sinclair, used an ordinary domestic television as a display screen and a portable audio cassette recorder in place of a disc drive.

1981 also saw the launch of the government's scheme to put a microcomputer into every secondary school as part of its plan to help 'prepare children for life in a society in which devices and systems based on microelectronics are commonplace and pervasive'.[16] In line with the diffuse 'Buy British' policy in information technology, schools were directed to the machines manufactured by two domestic companies, Acorn and Research Machines. Acorn had a distinct advantage in this competition since the BBC's well-publicized computer literacy course, launched at the beginning of 1982, was built around their model. In October 1982, the Micros in Schools scheme was extended to primary schools, and once again Acorn was on the list of approved suppliers. This double seal of official approval, from the government and the BBC, gave a considerable fillip to Acorn's push into the general consumer market, and by the end of 1983 their machines had achieved sales of around 250,000.

Their marketing strategy resonated strongly with official discourse about the coming 'information age', and played on parents' hopes and fears about their children's future employment prospects. The advertisement for the second generation of Acorn machines is a good example. Headed 'Think of it as a downpayment on your child's future uniform', it featured a girl in her graduation robes, bathed in sunlight, standing in the cloisters of one of the country's ancient universities. The accompanying copy was addressed directly to parental worries.

> Your child's degree ceremony might seem a long way off. But the BBC Master Compact is equipment to help at every step of the way. Our new micro can provide your child with constant support throughout education, eventually graduating into business and professional use. Put it on your Christmas list. It should help to put a few letters after your child's name.

A contemporaneous advertisement, for the colour monitors approved for use with BBC micros in schools, underlined this message, arguing that:

> This year, no less than 20,000 schools rely on the high resolution of Cub monitors to make computer-related education more clearly understood. . . . Now Microvite have made this same range available for home use. . . . It has never been more vital to ensure that your child has the benefit of the finest teaching aids. . . . The Microvite Cub is the colour monitor which your child will expect and is unlikely to out-grow.

These promotional appeals presented home computing as a form of rational recreation, in which domestic space becomes an extension of the classroom and the office, and the user practises 'useful' skills, gradually moving on to more complex tasks and becoming a fully functioning member of the computerized society.

This vision of the micro as an essential aid to educational and career advancement played a key role in encouraging parents to invest in one. Altogether, three-quarters of all the households in the Midlands survey that had a computer claimed to have purchased a machine with children and teenagers in mind. Many had gone out and bought one in much the same spirit as they might earlier have bought a set of encyclopaedias. Its acquisition often coincided with the development of computer studies in school. Sometimes the push came from the children, as in this teenager's account of using his BBC micro:

> 'It was the time when everybody was getting a computer really, and I wanted one for school. So I thought I'd get one like the stuff I used at school, so I used it to get through my "O" level. . . . We did a project in the Fifth Form, which was handy, 'cause I could do it at home you see.'

He also experimented with uses linked to his interests: 'what I used to like writing was sound programs. Doing, you know, making? 'cause I used to have a music book and I used to type in. That's what I used to do a lot of.'

This form of micro use as rational recreation was the exception rather than the rule, however. With the prices of basic models starting at around £300, comparatively few families in the Midlands sample could afford an Acorn/BBC machine, and most therefore settled for one of the cheaper machines, in the belief that simply having one in the house would be beneficial. The following account is typical.

> *Son (14):*   We didn't have anything to do with it. It was him over there [indicating the father]. We got in from school one day and he said, 'Right we're going to go and get a computer'.
> *Father:*   We'd obviously got a bit of spare cash like. I'd got some money coming at the end of the summer, and I said we'd go out and buy it at the beginning of the summer, didn't I?
> *Son:*   Yes.
> *Father:*   They were just about to start learning it at school when we got it, and I thought it wouldn't be fair if they got left behind. . . . I thought I could try it anyway, and then I found that I couldn't drive it at all [laughs].

In common with many parents with little or no knowledge of computers, this father hadn't realized that the cheaper machines were not well suited to educational applications. Their primary uses were being constructed by a quite different discourse.

The initial wave of parental decisions to buy a basic Sinclair or Commodore coincided with the point in time when the cheap micro was beginning to emerge as a games-playing machine. The major push in this direction came from the software companies rather than the hardware producers, several of whom feared that too close an identification with games would undermine the micro's status as a general-purpose machine. As the executive who handled Commodore's advertising campaign in the early 1980s put it: 'We wanted always to see our product as a proper piece of technology: but fun technology. We didn't want to see it as a toy.'[17] By 1983, however, this precarious balance between 'proper' and playful uses had been tipped in favour of games-playing by the promotional activities of the entertainment entrepreneurs who were entering the software market. They saw home computer games as a logical extension of two other screen-based entertainment systems: the video games console that plugged into a domestic television set, and the coin-operated video games machines installed in amusement arcades.

In the United States, higher levels of disposable income combined with tax breaks encouraged households to invest in relatively powerful domestic computers, leaving a definable market niche for dedicated games consoles. Sales took off in 1975, when Atari launched its tennis game, 'Pong' and grew substantially after 1976, when reprogrammable cartridges were introduced. In contrast, the British console market started a little later and was undercut by cheap computers before it had a chance to establish itself. As a result, only 2 per cent of households had acquired a video games console by the end of 1982, compared to 15 per cent in the United States. Price was again a significant factor. In 1983, reprogrammable video consoles cost between £70 and £140, with games cartridges selling for between £20 and £30. By that time, consumers could purchase a basic Sinclair machine for less than £70, and select games from a rapidly expanding catalogue of titles for around £5 each. Moreover, the ubiquity of cassette recorders meant that games borrowed from other users could be copied for the price of a blank tape, despite the software manufacturers' best efforts to protect their sales with anti-piracy devices. Breaking these security systems became a popular pastime among computer hobbyists. For some, the main pleasure was in beating the system. Actually playing the game was secondary. As one teenager recounted: 'I must admit, I do have great fun trying to crack protection systems. But that's more to do with the fun of it, rather than anything to do with the program once you've got it on tape'.

Other hobbyists, like this 21-year-old unemployed male, experimented with altering standard software and writing their own games. As he explained in interview:

> 'Games are nice to play, but I always have a go. I say, "I wonder if I could make that game", and then I try it myself. Sometimes people come and say "That's a nice program. Did you buy it?" and I say "No, I made it." My talent seems to lie in making it look better. . . . For a start, I look for a different presentation, the title screen, etcetera, adding all little items like that. . . . One of me greatest achievements was writing me own adventure programs, where I could slot in any adventure I wanted.'

Most users, however, were content to buy commercially produced games tapes. These drew on a range of sources, including the genres that had proved popular in the arcades.

Video games began to replace pinball machines in the arcades in the late 1970s. Their iconography was overwhelmingly masculine. Most were either simulations of glamorized male activities, such as flying a fighter aircraft or driving a Grand Prix racing car, or variants on the scenario where the player defended territory against enemy attack. The most famous of these games, 'Space Invaders', was introduced in 1979, to be followed by hosts of others. According to one American study, by the mid-1980s, women appeared in only 8 per cent of arcade games, and then mostly in passive roles.[18] The more polymorphous games such as 'Pac-Man', were less obviously gendered, but overall, the imaginary world of arcade games was overwhelmingly masculine. This bias was reinforced by the social organization of the arcades themselves and the fact that they had mostly been commandeered by adolescent male peer groups as arenas for competitive display.

This masculine orientation carried over into the home computer market when the most popular arcade games were adapted for domestic use. It was also evident in the other major games genres: sports and adventure games. Although some adventures drew on sources popular with girls as well as boys, such as J.R.R. Tolkien's fantasy, *The Hobbit*, many relied on predominantly masculine genres such as horror and science fiction.[19] A recent survey of Midlands teenagers, conducted in 1989, confirms the continuing gender bias of games-playing, with boys being twice as likely as girls to play once or twice a week and six times as likely to play three or more times a week.[20] Arcade games were still far and away the most popular genre, followed some way behind by simulations, sports and adventure games. There was also a strong age pattern, with games-playing falling away sharply by the age of 15, when activities outside the home become more central in peer group life. Nevertheless, it remains easily the most common use of micros by young people.

Despite its centrality, games-playing has never quite shaken off the connotations of addiction that surrounded the early arcade games. In 1981, the Labour MP George Foulkes narrowly failed to push through his 'Control of Space Invaders (and Other Electronic Games) Bill' in the House of Commons. Concern continued through the decade, but in 1988 a Home Office study concluded that there was no need for further legislation, and placed the responsibility for controlling adolescent use of arcades firmly on the shoulders of parents and managers.[21] Early worries about harmful 'effects' had already carried over into the domestic market, however, and home computer games were included in the terms of the 1985 Video Recording Act, which was introduced to regulate pre-recorded video tapes and eradicate the so-called 'video nasties'. Beneath these debates lay the familiar Victorian concern with the 'proper' use of leisure, and the continual clashes between contrasted definitions of rational recreation, trivial pursuits and dangerous pleasures.

By mid-decade, then, there were at least four major discourses around home computing, offering competing definitions of its potentialities and pleasures: the discourse of self-referring practice in which the machines appeared as a space for creative activity and problem-solving; the discourse of 'serious' applications related to the schoolroom and workplace; the discourse of games-playing and fun which presented the micro as another screen-based entertainment facility; and the discourse of righteous concern for the welfare of the young. These discourses provided the symbolic context within which the parents and children in the Midlands study negotiated and struggled over the uses of their machines.

Micros and moral economies

The outcomes depended on the way households were organized as economic and cultural units, their moral economies[22] and, in particular, on the structure of authority and the distribution of computing expertise among family members.

Parents familiar with computers sometimes made a determined effort to encourage 'serious' use, as in this mother's account of activities with her 10-year-old son and 12-year-old daughter:

> 'The first computer came when we had the children, even though my husband used to be a computer engineer and I use a computer at school with the children I work with. It is for educational purposes. We have always encouraged them. It is not just for playing games. Even when we had the Spectrum, before this Atari, we had a word processing package. They would write little stories, and we had a comprehension package, and a maths package, even when they were little. We all use the Atari. . . . We play games together. We have chess and so on.'

Other parents, even those used to working with computers, had given up an unequal struggle and accepted that the machine would be mainly used for games, though some rationed computer use in an effort to encourage their children to spend more time on 'improving' activities. As one mother (who taught computing in a secondary school) explained:

> 'On the whole they use it mainly for games, and therefore I do restrict how long they use it, because a lot of games I consider as not very worth while, and, like television, I believe in restricting what they do in some way.'

Other families resorted to more stringent measures, such as packing the computer away. As another mother related:

> 'We don't like to get it out too often because it's a temptation to them to give up their swotting. 'Cause once they start playing games, it's difficult to stop, we found that. . . . They are quite good and disciplined about it. They know that they've got work to do at the moment. So I say, "Right, we'll put it away".'

In all three of these cases, the parents attempted to exercise control over use, either positively or negatively. But, as the Midlands interviews revealed, this was much more difficult with older teenagers, particularly where the parents had little or no computer competence themselves. In these situations children could use their time on the micro to win space and privacy within the household and assert their separation and independence from their parents. This was particularly important in the case of fathers and sons, as in this account by an unemployed man in his early twenties living at home. His father, a skilled tradesman, had never attempted to master the computer but valued practical expertise.

> 'It's a program that's very simple to make. It just keeps jiggling through all the numbers. It's a system a lot have used to crack telephone numbers. 'Cause this place is ex-directory, and me dad said "You can't do it in a week", and I said, "Yes, I can". And using the number plan and the telephone book and a bit of guesswork as well, I located the number. And he says, "I backed you twenty pound that you can't do it in a week", he says. And I got my sister involved in as well, and we ended up taking forty pounds off him. Served him right.'

Conclusion

These tales from the field afford fleeting glimpses of complex processes, deeply embedded in the sedimented structures of families' interior lives. To tell these tales in the detail they deserve, we will certainly need better and deeper ethnographies of everyday consumption. But, as we have also argued, if we are interested in explanation as well as description, we will [. . .] need to look for better ways of linking these micro processes to the wider economic, social and symbolic formations that surround and shape them. We need more sensitive explorations of the continual traffic between public and private, interiors and exteriors, and of connections between user careers and the general trajectory of the computer industry, between biographies and history.

As we have argued, the British home computer market was divided, almost from the outset, into a 'serious' sector based around relatively powerful machines of the type being introduced into schools and offices, and a games-playing sector in which cheap computers became another extension of screen-based entertainment, often literally, since many families used a television set as a monitor. There is every sign that this bifurcation will continue. The recent *rapprochement* between the two leading personal computer companies, Apple and IBM, looks likely to consolidate their control over the market for 'serious' machines, whilst the Japanese companies, Nintendo and Sega, have revivified the market for dedicated games consoles, selling half a million units by the middle of 1991.

The Midlands data suggest that this industrial segmentation will be mapped onto social divisions, and that self-determined computing will remain concentrated in the relatively affluent and well-educated households of the professional and managerial strata, whilst the rest of the population are largely confined to participating in professionally crafted fantasies. They will have interactivity without power. The consequences of this situation for democratic participation, in a society increasingly organized around screen-based systems, deserves more extended discussion than it has so far received.

Notes

1. For example, W. Danko and J. MacLachlan, 'Research to accelerate the diffusion of a new invention: The case of personal computers', *Journal of Advertising Research*, 23: 39–43, 1983.
2. For example, M. Dickerson and J. Gentry, 'Characteristics of adopters and non-adopters of home computers', *Journal of Consumer Research*, 10: 225–34, 1983; P. Hall, J. Nightingale and T. MacAulay, 'A survey of micro-computer ownership and usage', *Prometheus*, 3: 156–73, 1985.
3. For example, C. Tinnell, 'An ethnographic look at personal computers in the family setting', *Marriage and Family Review*, 8: 59–69, 1985.
4. The research was made possible by grants from Central Independent Television, the Economic and Social Research Council and the Research Board of Leicester University.
5. 'Mediabank: Videographics', in *Marketing Week*, 17 October 1986.
6. For example, A. Venkatesh and N. Vitalari, 'Computing technology for the home', *Journal of Product Innovation and Management*, 3: 171–86, 1986.
7. E. Rogers, *Diffusion of Innovations*, New York: Free Press, 1983.

8. See E. Rogers and J. Larsen, *Silicon Valley Fever: Growth of high-technology culture*, New York: Basic Books, 1984.

9. For example, W. Dutton, E. Rogers and S. Jun, 'The diffusion and impacts of information technology in households', *Oxford Surveys in Information Technology*, 4: 133–93, 1987.

10. W. Dutton, P. Sweet and E. Rogers, 'Socio-economic status and the diffusion of personal computing in the United States', Paper to Conference of International Association for Mass Communication Research, Barcelona, 1988, p. 14.

11. For example, J. Jouet, 'Social uses of micro-computers in France', Paper to Conference of International Association for Mass Communication Research, Barcelona, 1988.

12. See G. Murdock and P. Golding, 'Information, poverty and political inequality: Citizenship in the age of privatised communications', *Journal of Communication*, 39: 180–95, 1989.

13. G. Murdock, 'Critical inquiry and audience activity', in B. Dervin, L. Grossberg, B. O'Keefe and E. Wartella, eds, *Rethinking Communication, Volume 2: Paradigm Exemplars*, London: Sage, 1989.

14. J. Wheelock, 'Personal computers, gender and an institutional model of the household', in R. Silverstone and E. Hirsch, eds, *Consuming Technologies: Media and information in domestic spaces*, London: Routledge, 1992.

15. See L. Haddon, 'The home computer: The making of a consumer electronic', *Science as Culture*, 2: 7–51, 1988.

16. Department of Education and Science, *Microelectronics Education Programme: The strategy*, London: DES, 1981, p.1.

17. Quoted in L. Haddon, 'Electronic and computer games: The history of an interactive medium', *Screen*, 29: 52–73, 1988, p. 71.

18. T. Toles, 'Video games and American military ideology', in V. Mosco and J. Wasko, eds, *The Critical Communications Review, Volume 3: Popular culture and media events*, Norwood, NJ: Ablex, 1985.

19. G. Skirrow, 'Hellivision: An analysis of video games', in C. MacCabe, ed., *High Theory/Low Culture: Analysing popular television and film*, Manchester: Manchester University Press, 1986.

20. This study, based on a survey of 460 11 to 15-year-olds in six schools in a Midlands town, was conducted by Robert Cromwell in 1989 as part of the research for his doctoral thesis at the University of Loughborough.

21. J. Graham, *Amusement Machines: Dependency and delinquency*, Home Office Research Study 101, London: HMSO, 1988.

22. R. Silverstone, 'From audiences to consumers: The household and the consumption of communication and information technologies', *European Journal of Communication*, 6: 135–54, 1991; R. Silverstone. E. Hirsch and D. Morley, 'Information and communication technologies and the moral economy of the household', in R. Silverstone and E. Hirsch, eds, op. cit.

4.5 □ *Ann Moyal*

Ann Moyal investigates a medium which she believes is of crucial importance in the lives of many women. Her work on the feminine culture of the telephone involved interviews with 200 Australian women from various social backgrounds – and was designed to uncover their routine uses of the technology. Moyal concludes that there is a feminine information flow which holds together family and friendship networks over sometimes vast spatial distances.

The gendered use of the telephone: an Australian case study

Introduction

The telephone is not a 'new' technology, yet its diverse role in society, its evolution as both a business and a household instrument since its inception in 1876, and the vital part it continues to play in our changing societies and in the rapid extension of the Information Age, focus it as a technology of central relevance to studies of gender, interactive media and information technologies.

The point is the more crucial in the light of the long neglect that the telephone has experienced in communication and information scholarship. While a steady stream of monographs and journal articles has examined television, broadcasting, video, cable and satellite communication, and the organization and politicization of telecommunication, the ubiquitous, pervasive, invisible but culturally significant connector – the telephone – has been taken for granted and ignored.

[. . .]

Such studies of telephone use that are available, conducted primarily by telecommunication carriers, have focused on traffic flows.[1] [. . .] Some differences in gender use have been observed, notably in studies by French and German researchers in Lyons[2] and Berlin.[3] It fell, however, to Lana Rakow to open up the study of women's specific telephone use in a qualitative study of forty-three women from the rural American town of Prospect, Illinois.[4]

The Australian study marks the first national survey of women's telephone use to be conducted in any country.

[. . .]

Research strategy

Since the aim of the research was to collect the views, attitudes and voices of women across Australia, in all states, the research sample embraced 200 women aged from 16 to 87; women at home and in the workforce; single, married, divorced and widowed women; single parents, teenagers, women from migrant backgrounds; urban, rural and remote region women, some Aborigines, and a group of women without access to a domestic telephone – the 'telephone poor'. With this object, a qualitative, ethnographic methodology was selected which assumed the nature of 'a dialogic approach . . . contiguous with female-gendered communications patterns'.[5] [. . .] Fifteen women research assistants were engaged, scattered across Australia, recruited from different backgrounds, professional and personal experience, and with access to different aspects of Australian life. Each assistant was equipped with the research protocol and a forty-question questionnaire, and required to provide seven to ten respondents of different ages from their network of contacts, to record, tape and transcribe interviews and present written reports. Interviews were seen as flexible and open-ended offering the opportunity to retrieve direct, candid and reflective material.

Questions covered demographic data, occupation, living situation, telephone use (including local, long distance and international calls), call timing and duration, the last call, the respondent's network of contacts, access to transport, volunteer work, hobbies and interests, attitudes to the telephone (positive and negative), historical conditioning and, where relevant, responses to public call box use. A distinction was drawn between 'instrumental' and 'intrinsic' calls, the first being calls of a functional nature made in connection with shopping, making appointments or business arrangements, seeking information and dealing with emergencies or household crises; and the latter covering personal communication with relatives and friends, volunteer work, counselling and all intimate discussion and exchange.[6] Respondents were issued with time sheets and asked to monitor a week's incoming and outgoing calls. [. . .]

A further series of interviews, with additional questions to cover aspects of acculturation were conducted by multilingual women interviewers to bring in a sample of Greek, Italian, Vietnamese, Lebanese, Polish and Spanish women, while, as chief investigator, I oversaw the research and conducted interviews through direct contact and by telephone with rural, remote region and some Aboriginal women, to ensure geographical balance and diversity. In this, significantly, the telephone itself served as a key instrument of research both in maintaining contact with dispersed researchers and in gathering direct and detailed information from isolated country women. Its use, moreover, confirmed a key finding of the study that women can establish close, reflective and warm communication in telephone talk with women whom they have never met.

No methodology is free from problems. Some researchers drew richer material; some tended, for efficiency, to compress and stereotype some attitudinal responses. More important, half of the sample respondents failed to complete the weekly time sheet on the grounds of the 'atypicality' of the check week, and opted to furnish a less precise 'observed average' of their weekly pattern of calls.[7] The sample, of course, does not claim to cover 'everywoman'. With a female population of just over eight million in Australia, such an expectation would be unrealistic, and no attempt was made lo look for occupational or social categories. It is, nonetheless, indicative of the validity of the methodology that it closely reflected the Australian demographic profile. Ten women were aged 15–19; seventy aged 20–39; fifty-two aged from 40–54; thirty-two from 55–64; twenty-four were aged 65–74, and twelve were over 75.[8] As one in every five Australians is a migrant, forty-four migrants (22 per cent) featured in the survey. Moreover, despite sample size, respondent inputs on attitudes and telephone usage reached a degree of repetition well before data collection was complete.

Women interviewed ran the gamut from straightforward, practical countrywomen, migrants of complex and restricted experience, home-based mothers of wide diversity, women working in 'electronic cottage' situations, through urban teenagers, sporty and intellectual women, the aged living at home, through primary, secondary, tertiary and postgraduate educated women, and on to high profile women in the workforce. Their frank participation, reflective viewpoints, and sense that their evidence was of relevance and interest, yielded data that a statistically larger quantitative methodology could not retrieve.

Survey findings

Women's telephone use

The survey illuminated distinctive feminine patterns of telephone use. One major finding related to the distinction made between kinds of telephone calls. Consistent with evidence from overseas, the great proportion of use involved local calls (such calls in Australia being 'flat rate' or 'untimed' at a fixed charge per call). Women surveyed in all states made, on average, 2–6 local 'instrumental' calls a week, with the exception of women who worked at home, home-based women temporarily involved in a family health crisis or renovation, and telephone-dependent, physically disadvantaged women whose instrumental calls reached 10–12 per week.

Instrumental calls were made throughout the day (only emergency calls tending to be made at night) and occupied 1–3 minutes, a uniform 2 minutes being most frequently cited except when the call involved Commonwealth or state government departments and utilities when the broadly established 'queueing mechanism' for handling calls pushed the telephone call up to 10–20 minutes and elicited widespread criticism from respondents. Evidence on women's personal 'instrumental' use of the telephone in Australia thus suggested that users conducted these calls with despatch; that, in this context, the telephone was a valued substitute for personal contact, many using the telephone 'to let their fingers do the walking', but that the concept of teleshopping had not taken root among the sample, young, middle-aged and even older women[9] preferring to go out to do their shopping. In short, the domestic telephone was used as a constructive aid for the efficient and time-saving control and handling of their weekly tasks. Migrant women tended to contribute to the top range of instrumental calls (often using language-skilled kin to make the transaction) in order to obtain information from government departments, ethnic agencies and organizations to help in their process of acculturation.

Respondent patterns, however, were very different for 'intrinsic' calls. Here women in the sample made 14–40 personal calls a week, averaging 20–28 in metropolitan centres and 14–25 in rural domains. While again the majority were local calls, a rising trend in intrinsic trunk line calling marked an increasing mobility and distribution of Australian families across the states. While a group of young mothers living close to parents (who preferred daily or weekly contact face to face), British women migrants and a small number of women over 75, contributed to the low end of the user curve, the highest number of calls, from 25 to 48 each week, attached to women who worked at home, some older women aged 65–75, and women from different ethnic groups.

Significantly, only 39 per cent of the sample attested that their intrinsic calls occupied less than 5 minutes; 20 per cent averaged these calls at 10–15 minutes, and the remaining 61 per cent affirmed that their intrinsic calls commonly centred around 15–20 minutes, not infrequently 30–45 minutes and, on occasion, an hour. Survey evidence on 'intrinsic' calling thus clearly confirmed that the duration of Australian women's telephone calls rarely fell within the 3-minute time span characterized by telecommunications carriers as an 'average' local call,[10] and that the call's duration, and the sense of unpressured communication it contained, was perceived as a key component of the purpose and gratification of the call.

Women's telephone networks

In his broad and critical overview 'The Sociology of the Telephone', American sociologist Sidney Aronson observes that 'that which we take for granted usually needs to be most closely examined', and the questions concerning telephone use yet to be answered are 'who talks to whom, for how long, and for what reasons and with what results?'[11]

What then did the telephone networks and messages of Australian women reveal? 'Kinkeeping' floods the lines. Survey evidence suggested that Australians are a deeply familial people and enjoy a society in which ongoing telephone communication between female family members constitutes an important part of their support structure and contributes significantly to their sense of well-being, security and self-esteem. No less than 184 of the 200 respondents confirmed that the prime importance of the telephone in their daily lives related to 'sustaining family relationships', and to their contact with children, parents and, less regularly, with siblings, grandchildren and the extended family. A significant proportion of these calls was devoted to communication between mothers and daughters who established telephone contact daily, or regularly throughout the week, and maintained an intimate and caring telephone relationship across their lives. The communication link appeared at its most concentrated when the daughters had moved away from home, were in their childbearing/childrearing period, worked in the same town or city, and lived within an area of local call. Costs clearly governed the shorter duration of calls between more geographically distant mothers and daughters and their regret at this constraint emerged in their replies. But the importance of this telephone connection – regular, caring and detailed in its content – appeared undiminished by geography.

Women's voices

Women's voices from the survey illustrate the gratification derived from telephone use and the individual character of the response. From these voices, a distinctly gendered communication process can be discerned, a process that frequently takes responsibility for men's as well as women's family contact tasks; is widely conditioned by the challenge of distance; reflects at times problems of access, patriarchal conflict and guilt but, in a country where telephone penetration reached 94 per cent in 1991, emerges as an entrenched social support system that has vital consequences for the nation.

Fundamentally, the voices reflect a family theme. A retired resident of a country town records: 'Each night my daughter and I talk for half an hour by 'phone. We discuss the routine of the day, things we want to do when we meet. It helps my life entirely. It helps my daughter too.' An older city woman reported ringing her daughters and sisters regularly, and they in turn kept in frequent touch with her. 'Family contact is very important with one's children scattered and hard at work,' she confirmed. 'I need the 'phone for ongoing contact. My brother has a terminal illness and needs constant reassurance, as does my sister-in-law. Some days, with illness, I seem never to be off the 'phone.' Another older mother noted, 'You offer a forum on the telephone for listening to your children's problems.' A mother in the workforce reported that she began each day for a four-month period with a 'phone call to her son who, devastated by marital breakdown, needed her call to 'get him going'. 'It was the support he needed', she said, 'just to speak to someone.' Conversely, young mothers raising new babies and young children made daily telephone calls to mothers and, at times, to sisters to report on their child's progress, and to gain confirmation and reassurance from the exchange. Two suburban sisters interviewed, both young mothers, found that talking by telephone to each other each day 'certainly helped with our babies, we establish greater intimacy on the telephone', while a town-based mother recalled that her daughter, who had moved to a city where other young wives were out at work, would telephone her with the desperate cry, 'Mum, I've put the egg-timer on, talk to me for 3 minutes!'. Even when family members cohabited, one ethnic respondent revealed how a 10-minute telephone call could break the isolation and bleakness experienced by an elderly, frail mother at home. 'My daughter rings daily from work for 10 minutes and sometimes more', said an 83-year-old Greek interviewee. 'Just the contact with my daughter's voice is a comfort to me and I look forward to her call as my loneliness grows.'

Transgenerational telephone relationships between grandmother and grandchild were also highlighted in the data. Several older women recalled how grandchildren could command lengthy telephone calls, taking over from a call to a parent with 'Grandma I want to tell you something' and recounting a story that continued for 45 minutes. Another emphasized the value of this kind of communication in a society where distance prevented frequent face-to-face contact with grandchildren and where a grandchild could enjoy ongoing and uninterrupted converse with the grandmother. Another suburban grandmother noted, 'A great deal of my contact with my grandchildren is by 'phone. It is extremely important that they feel free to 'phone me often and hold these detailed conversations when they don't have to compete for my attention as they do when other family members are present face-to-face'. The telephone, as one grandmother pointed out, 'becomes a cultural resource early and is an element in the lives of very small children'.

Clearly, the filial connection and its impetus to the process of discourse between women in the nuclear family feeds a major strand of telephone traffic in Australia. Contact breeds more contact, frequency gives continuity to the talk, and the very detail of the communication – a point stressed independently by many women – gives particular value to the calls. There were some negative images – the demanding mother who, when feeling lonely, 'would not let her daughter off the 'phone', or the interfering mother who telephoned to 'overadvise' on child care. But, in the total sample, the negatives were small. Significantly, the last call made registered by many women was 'to my daughter' or 'to Mum'.

Friends

Beyond the inner family, the second most important site of telephone networking was between close women friends, an area of communication which, in both range and kind, has extended significantly in the past two decades. Not only do more women live alone, undergo marital break-up or separation, and assume responsibilities as single parents, but, in a period of rising feminist influence and ideas, they find increasing support and emotional and intellectual stimulus from women friends. In this, evidence from the sample appeared undifferentiated by education, social environment or age. The sociological importance of confidantes, girlfriends and women's enduring friendships is well understood. What emerged conspicuously from this study was the high importance of the telephone in maintaining and enhancing these key feminine links. Most women interviewed gave their close friendship calls a high priority, 'top' for women without parents or children, and very important for married women of all ages, widows, the retired, the elderly, those distant from relatives overseas, and those 'in relationships' with men. The exceptions in terms of volume of use were students or single women living in communal situations, a small cluster of married or partnered women in exclusively close relationships, and women with access only to a public telephone.

'Talking by 'phone to a close friend', said one young, home-bound mother, 'is a life-saver. When you're feeling lonely, these calls can transform your view.' 'My calls to close friends are the longest calls I make,' a young city mother summed up for many women, 'It's difficult to get to see them and I need frequent contact to exchange ideas about our children and what we're all doing. After my last child's birth I was depressed and these 'phone calls helped me to get back to normal.' Another suburban mother, married to a busy professional, maintained,

> The telephone is very important to me because suburban home life is lonely and the 'phone is a link with colour and variety and with people one loves. There's a need to communicate feeling and caring: the telephone is more personal than letters. What I want to know is how my friends 'feel' and I can hear this on the telephone.

The survey's reiterated finding, indeed, was that women talk more freely and intimately on the telephone with close friends than they do face-to-face, that the telephone highlights warmth and sympathy in the voice, that (as one respondent put it) 'you can convey "I know you're worried" even if you don't say it', and that women can reach 'greater depth in conversation on the telephone'. A postgraduate student, studying to re-enter the workforce, pinpointed a salient trend in society when she said,

> When I was younger and in the workforce and sharing accommodation I was much more gregarious, and there was no great need to use the telephone as a lifeline. Now the telephone is the 'frontline' when it comes to giving or receiving news, good and bad. With friends, it's grabbed instantly in all sorts of situations – in response to mail, about something I'm reading or have heard on the radio, to air a grievance, share a success, seek support for an injustice or unlucky break, share news about health or holidays. It contributes to my sense of direction and participation, and is vital when I need to discuss professional ideas I'm turning over.

Another tertiary student confirmed,

> With the 'phone it's instant gratification. If you are lucky, and if there is something preying on your mind, you can solve it speedily. The 'phone creates this psychological neighbourhood for women. We are not doing all the same thing now, not all staying at home in the family, we're moving about and talking to people. Professional women working at home may not have anything in common with their immediate neighbours, but they've created a close-knit 'phone neighbourhood. It alleviates loneliness which is very important. My 'phone calls now are a lot deeper. I need people and I'm more attentive to the needs of my women friends. Feminism has made us not feel ashamed of being close to women; we encourage and support each other.

Women with secondary education brought other perspectives to this view. Older women with children scattered interstate, sometimes widowed, some retired, carried on regular telephone networking with their circle of close friends, at times making daily contacts in late afternoon or evening to enquire how each fared. Such networking was essential to women who had moved through their share of life crises and, through telephone contact, they found and gave important mutual support and care. Many respondents testified to long call durations from '30 to 45 to 60 minutes or more' with friends who, for example, had been widowed and who found telephone discussion often the only accessible communication for their grief. Women of all ages readily engaged in 'reflective listening' with friends in stress or personal need. Even women who avoided personal telephone initiatives appeared responsive in this listening art,[12] accepting long calls, often disruptive to their own programmes, from distressed or traumatically involved friends. A 41-year-old single parent identified the trend:

> Friends telephone me with their troubles. My 'last call' was from a friend who was very depressed; it lasted 2 hours which is normal for such calls. People seem to be feeling more stress these days and need to talk to others without getting their children out of bed to go and visit. The telephone relieves a lot of tension.

'Telephoning is a form of care-giving', Rakow concluded in her study of women and the telephone in Prospect, USA. 'It is "gendered work" and "gender work" in that it is work that women do to hold together the fabric of the community, build and maintain relationships, and accomplish important care-giving and receiving functions'.[13] The point is amply illustrated in Australia. Women in country towns, cities and suburbs engaged widely in the process of maintaining telephone contact with elderly relatives, mothers-in-law, extended family members, a father living alone, and with frail older friends and members of the community who lived alone or in nursing homes, and were isolated or without family. Volunteer work also ranked high. In a 'nation of joiners', 23 per cent of women contributed to diverse volunteer activities. 'The purpose of volunteer work', one woman summed up, 'is to get the best out of our lives.' But it was recognized that it also conferred a substantial contribution of time, saved costs and personal effort on the nation. For volunteer workers in every kind of activity, 'the telephone', said one, 'is the tool'. While many friendships, recognizably, grew from volunteer involvement, this part of women's telephone care remained a hidden and taken-for-granted activity, and one that could be highly vulnerable to pricing change.[14]

Across the broad community, patterns of telephone contact reflected altered, more turbulent and clearly more socially alienating conditions in Australia. For example, children of divorced families frequently took the initiative in sustaining a close telephone relationship with a non-custodial parent. A single mother, typically, reported that her three children made regular calls to their 'non-supporting' father in an effort to arrange outings or 'merely to talk', and quite young children felt it their right to have telephone access to key adults. The single mothers' evidence added potent testimony on the telephone's parenting and supportive role. Single mothers were heavy telephone users, dependent on extended local calls with family and friends, commonly constrained by cost factors in trunk use, and keen adapters of this communication form for difficult instrumental or other dealings with a former husband. One working single mother summed up the value of the telephone for this growing and vulnerable group in graphic terms:

> Without this form of parenting check, to ring my daughter when she comes home from school, I would be unable to work. The telephone allows me to earn an income and sustain some social contact. As a single parent, there's little margin for the optional 'extras' of social life. It's an unrelenting lifestyle and seldom of one's choice. What sustains me are

lengthy late evening phone calls to a small nucleus of friends (often in the same boat). Without this lifeline I would very likely be a candidate for suicide or hospitalisation.

The aged

There is no group in the Australian community to whom the telephone offers more effective functional communication or a sense of personal participation and well-being than the aged. For the purposes of this survey, the classification 'aged' is applied to women over 75. The Australian Bureau of Statistics demarks its 'aged' category at 65. There was, however, too great a commonality in the life and telephone patterns of the 24 members of the sample aged 65–74 and the 32 aged 55–64, to group women aged from 65 to 90 as a cohesive division in terms of telephone use, or to identify a cohort of predominantly active, part-work/part-volunteer involved women in the analysis of a long-living, but frailer, senior group. Accordingly, 12 respondents over 75 were allocated to the 'aged' subset drawn from women living in cities and country towns, living alone, with family members, or in retirement villages, but not living in nursing homes or hostel accommodation.

The interest and significance of the experience of this small subset lies in the fact that women outlive their male contemporaries to a noted degree and that, to date, there is a dearth of literature that examines the importance of 'telephone relationships' in the daily lives, and care of the aged. Conspicuously, this particular set of interviewees emerged as an articulate and positive group of women who enjoyed autonomy, independence and fellowship in their lives. In their very selection for survey, they represented a distinctive and outgoing set. Many elderly women would be less fortunate, and less able to express their attitudes in such striking terms. Yet their needs are likely to correspond, and the majority would find the sustaining telephone behavourial habits described directly threatened by pricing change and the introduction of timed local calls.

All the women interviewed in this group gave first priority to the sense of security the telephone conferred and to its importance in providing instant connection for their well-being and health. Most kept their telephone beside the bed. For those who lived alone (9 out of 12), their evidence indicated that instrumental calls were essential for their continuing maintenance and autonomy, bringing them support care systems, home deliveries and linking them with shopping, banking, taxis and important pharmaceutical and medical needs. The lone dwellers conformed with the national sample in setting the greatest store by the contact the telephone gave them with immediate family members, frequently a daughter who kept in daily touch to monitor their needs and health and to furnish the companionship of a 'chat'. For this subset, the telephone emerged as an 'indispensable' human connector, a 'vital link' that brought encouragement, a sense of participation, and feelings of adequacy and worth.

To an 87-year-old respondent who shared a home with her daughter in Sydney, the telephone had, she informed us, assumed great importance over the past five years when she was often unwell, could not use public transport easily, and did not wish to obtrude on her daughter's plans. As her intimate circle of friends shrank through death, she depended greatly on incoming calls to bring her a connection with a wider world. 'The telephone', she said, 'is very important to me to maintain contact. I ring less often as so many old friends have gone, but my life is invigorated by the people who 'phone in.' Similarly a 75-year-old woman acknowledged that she had been greatly comforted by telephone communication in her recent widowhood. 'People have helped me in my bereavement', she said, 'talking to me. It has been wonderful and made easier through the privacy of the telephone.' For her, the changed nature of personal telephone behaviour was clearly apparent in the last two decades. While women, she reflected, used the telephone formerly for family purposes and friends, 'these calls were not the relaxed and long type of calls we enjoy today'.

In the country, where widowed, elderly women stayed alone on their farms, inter-view data suggested that they used the telephone among confidantes in their peer group to 'recollect their lives'. While several women indicated that they would prefer contact face-to-face, the problems of mobility, public transport and ill health proved limiting. Widowhood and other life events led to change of residence into smaller units or retire-ment villages, and the value of the telephone for retaining friends in former places rose. Stimulus, connection to the community and a lessening of feelings of 'depression' and 'invisibility' flowed along the lines. Older women enjoyed communication with younger women, often the friends of daughters, and proved receptive listeners in periods of stress. A representative of the elderly blind, using a telephone with twenty pre-set numbers, found her personal life 'empowered' by this 'upgrading technology' and looked to a time when there would be teleconferencing and telecounselling for the rising numbers of elderly blind women to assist them with the grief of loss of sight.

While the size of the aged sample was small, it yielded fertile insights. In an ageing community, with women at its forward edge, any resource that can increase the number of non-institutionalized elderly, and reduce their occupation of nursing homes, hospital and special accommodation offers positive social gain. Clearly, this aged set's intrinsic telephone calling patterns demonstrated the value to their well-being and independence of telephone links with confidantes and friends. The 'invisible' telephone, in its gendered role, may thus furnish a crucial, if widely neglected, clue to women's signif-icant staying and survival power.[15] In 1977, Martin Mayer suggested for the USA that 'we do not know how the telephone functions in the delivery of social services or in the lives of those who need them'.[16] In Australia, in 1991, the telephone appears to stand as a major option for innovative public and private sector aged care.

Migrant women

Little (if any) substantial research has yet been conducted on the telephone needs of migrant women and, beyond my own exploratory investigation, the subject has attracted no attention in Australia, a nation of immigrants where one in five residents was born overseas and no less than 40 per cent of the population has parents born in countries elsewhere. Yet women migrants, housebound and restricted in their social contact and exchange, have proved especially vulnerable to adaptation and have, in some ethnic groups, remained hidden members of their new environment, under-privileged and depressed. In these circumstances, it is useful to enquire whether the telephone has played a timely part in the acculturation process of this sample of 44 women, whether it has kept their links with their homeland firm, and whether it has, in the privacy of their own language, offered them a sense of 'ethnic place'.

Survey results, in fact, showed a striking commitment by women of different ethnic communities to telephone use and its impact upon old patterns of communication. They revealed how women with little or no telephone experience in their own countries became significant telephone users and how, in multicultural Australia, there is a daily concourse of many languages across the telecommunication lines. At first, women arriving with no or very limited telephone experience, made little use of the telephone: costs of installation were high, they found the technology 'alien' and few could afford to telephone kin 'at home'. When, after several years, they installed a telephone, they 'used the telephone a good deal'. The experience was common to all ethnic groups. 'The 'phone' said one Greek woman who had lived in Australia for 40 years, 'has become very important to me though I used it only occasionally for many years.' This Sydney woman made some 40 calls a week, received 5 calls daily, and called members of her extended family trunk line in Melbourne 4 or 5 times a week. She used the telephone in lieu of going out, calls often lasting for half an hour. They relieved her, she affirmed, from a 'sense of imprisonment'.

For women from migrant backgrounds instrumental calls loomed large. Here, conspicuously they used the telephone for information-seeking from government departments and agencies to ascertain their rights, while the telephone served as a key access route to jobs, community services and medical care. Older women from all ethnic groups with poor language skills called on relatives and their increasingly skilled English-speaking children to conduct this exchange. The ongoing role of the younger family member as the household telephone interpreter emerged as a recurring theme and for some testators was a source of tension and strain. 'I always had to make calls for my parents', a 30-year-old Polish woman recalled. 'It really "freaked" me because the responsibility was so great and I was too young to deal with bureaucracy.'

On the intrinsic front, however, the telephone developed as a welcome connector in the migrants' own language, communicating with immediate and extended family, cultivating friendships within their ethnic community, and reducing their sense of alienation and 'loss'. For some, participation in the workforce overcame their resistance to unfamiliar telephone use, and migrant women in general testified that using the telephone in their own language encouraged their confidence in moving into the community and attempting to communicate with Australians. Among the home-based, there was evidence of marked 'telephone apprehension' about incoming calls, and these language-handicapped women shrank from answering the telephone's ring. Yet, as one elderly Italian summed up, 'Having the security of knowing that I can call my family and friends in my native tongue, has given me confidence to try to communicate face-to-face with my Australian neighbours.' The one outstanding difference in the migrant sample attached to British women whose telephone use, predominantly instrumental and brief, derived, it is suggested, from calling habits established in the United Kingdom where high daytime timed charging for each call (as well as a preference for measured friendship contact face-to-face) induced hesitation and some guilt in the making of non-business or lengthy intrinsic calls.

But in sum, for the migrant sample, the gendered use of the telephone and the support it conferred, marked a positive contribution to the process of acculturation in Australia. And it signalled some significant cultural changes. Notably in the male-dominated Greek, Italian and Lebanese cultures, telephone technology offered an accepted opportunity for building a feminine network of family solidarity, communication and control. Male members, like their Australian brothers, frequently deputed the task of family and extended family contact to the wife. Thus the traditional function of preserving cohesion, particularly in the large Lebanese kinship groups, was passing, via telephone usage, from the senior male figure to the senior wife.

Working women and the 'electronic cottage'

It was revealing that in respect of attitudes to telephone use, women in the workforce (40 in the sample), found telephone friendship and kin contact as vital in their personal lives as women anchored at home. Those married or in relationships found that they made long intrinsic calls either in the early morning or late at night when, away from their partner, they were free to discuss their own relationship, joys and problems with a friend. Most attested that telephone calls had replaced letters, the telephone was a major transport replacement and for some their only means of maintaining important feminine networking. Those with the smallest number of intrinsic calls were women who used the telephone extensively in their jobs, but even for those who had access to personal calls at work,[17] they sought fellowship and the giving and receiving care of the 'telephone neighbourhood' in the evening with close family and friends.

The sample contained a number of self-employed professional 'home-workers' drawn from such traditional fields as editing, writing, consulting and counselling, who occupy an expanding place in the work structure of society. Their 'compensatory patterns' of high intrinsic telephone calling at intervals across the day for the purpose of sustaining a sense of personal stimulus and participation, marks an aspect of gendered telephone communication whose importance will continue to grow. Evidence, however, from a group of young women solicitors, who worked from home connected telephonically to a central office so that they could rear young children while retaining their expertise, suggested that such alternatives would prove temporary. Here the 'electronic cottage' experiment appeared, at best, 'a timely solution for a few but a calamity for others, and simply difficult for most'.[18] It seems evident that despite innovative approaches to harnessing women for decentralized work at home, any future 'wired city' must depend not only on the technical proficiency of new communication forms, but on the human and caring function of the voice telephone.

The sociology of the telephone in Australia

Much of the evidence from this survey indicated a very positive attitude from Australian women to telephone use, a finding reaffirmed and strengthened by ongoing feedback from women and women's organizations since the study's publication in 1989. There were, however, negative attitudes, qualifications and tensions arising from telephone use. A number of young urban women living in close radius of mother or siblings used the telephone for very brief calls to make arrangements for meetings or baby-sitting and preferred contact face-to-face. Others kept telephone communication short and resented mothers or friends who kept them 'hanging on the 'phone'. Weekly calls to a mother-in-law conducted for a husband were perceived as a 'telephone chore' although in more than one case it became a route to real communication and exchange. A small cohort of older women were pragmatic about telephone use. A widow, 70, tertiary educated, did not find the telephone 'a place for exchanging ideas'. Nor did it provide her with 'vital contact' but was simply an easy means of communication. She believed that people could 'condense their calls to three minutes if necessary'. Another found telephone conversations 'time-consuming with many tasks staring you in the face'. She rationed talk and felt guilty if she spent time enjoying conversations on the telephone. Feelings of guilt were also harboured by several who loved the comfort of telephone talk. Some women felt guilty about 'tying up the line'; for others the guilt appeared to flow from a deep psychological reservoir fed by the puritan ethic or by culturally imposed concepts of women's 'silly talk' or 'gossiping' on the telephone.

A number of respondents expressed marked ambivalence about the telephone. The telephone could be Janus-faced. Hence, while there was widespread evidence of 'telephone obedience' – 'a telephone *must* be answered', and most women went to extreme, even at times dangerous, lengths to get to a ringing telephone ('You miss it, you make a cup of coffee and wait for the caller to try again: they don't'), there were criticisms of its intrusiveness, the caller's lack of respect for the time, convenience or occupation of the receptor, and the lack of contemporary 'telephone etiquette'. There was also stringent criticism from many on the spread of telephone marketing and charity fund-raising calls, both of which were seen as 'an unacceptable invasion of privacy'. As one respondent summarized: 'The 'phone is private and for my use, and that's what I tell them.' Attempts to circumvent such invasions of privacy through technology, however, did not have wide appeal and there was considerable opposition among those interviewed to answering machines, an 'answered' call, for many, representing a 'wasted call'.

While exposing the telephone as 'a critical index of social relationships' in its communicative practices,[19] survey data also disclosed a measure of tension, conflict and power play arising from some women's telephone use. A major source of tension attached to a husband's attitude to his wife's calls. Men arriving home from work, it was reported by women in young and middle age groups, objected to finding their wife talking on the telephone. Several women, with children dispersed about the country, testified that their husbands were resistant to their calling trunk line. Sometimes cost lay at the core; at other times a husband objected to his wife's overcommitment to distant young. 'My husband', one woman summed up, 'did not worry about the cost: he was jealous about my time spent away from him.' Husbands in retirement were prone to contribute to tension of this kind. Many men teased their wives or joked about time spent on the telephone and the time wastage it implied. Tension could run high. Women in close relationships with a partner therefore tended to reduce their intrinsic calls with women friends or to arrange times for calling in the partner's absence 'to communicate without male jealousy'. Young mothers were also familiar with patterns of obstreperous child behaviour that made telephone conversations with friends challenging, while one respondent recounted: 'When the telephone rings, my answering it and talking for any time certainly annoys the cats!'

While the majority of the evidence revealed the extensive and important networks developed between women on the telephone, men's presence and voices came through. Some respondents maintained intimate relations with a distant lover through contact long distance by telephone; some women shared strong bonds with brothers through sharing long intrinsic calls; other women maintained a caring role towards a widowed father through constant 'keeping in touch' telephone calls. Some men appeared to use the telephone as women do and a comparative study needs to be made. While most respondents concurred that telephone communication could never be 'total' in terms of affective communication, many found it superior to face-to-face contact for 'performing sensitive tasks'. It was easier to handle emotional contact by telephone. It was an excellent venue for 'straightening out a situation that is getting out of hand'; it could be 'an easy valve for anger aggression not available face-to-face'; or, with considerable diversity, it could be a vehicle for 'tact', 'diplomacy' or 'power'.

Conclusions

The telephone neighbourhood has thus become a key environment for women in Australia. Essentially the study [. . .] has revealed a pervasive, deeply rooted, dynamic feminine culture of the telephone in which kinkeeping, caring, mutual support, friendship, volunteer and community activity play a central part and which, through its ongoing and widening functioning, contributes substantially to women's sense of autonomy, security, participation and well-being. As Rakow identified in the USA, women's telephone talk 'fits into the appropriate spheres of activity and interests designated for women . . . taking responsibility for the emotional and material needs of husbands and children, the elderly, the handicapped, the sick and unhappy'.[20]

[. . .] Women's telephone communication constitutes a major private sphere activity the role and importance of which has been overlooked. The message content of telephone talk disclosed by the Australian evidence exhibited a striking breadth that reached from family matters, child rearing, aged care, health, emergency decisions, grief, bereavement, trauma, household maintenance, crafts, hobbies, community and religious needs and interests; through sporting, environmental and diverse cultural activities, counselling and volunteer care, to wide-ranging political, economic and intellectual exchange. As such, the feminine 'information flow' may be seen to represent a critical social support system that underlies family, community and national development, and to be, arguably, as important to national well-being and progress as the more politically visible and highly rated masculine business information flow.

[. . .]

In our changing information society, there is a clear need for cultural studies of the telephone that will shed light on our social relationships, behavioural patterns, the sociology of communities, the response to advancing technology, and on individual, gender and household use. There is a concomitant need for such studies to inform the policy process.

[. . .]

Notes

1. B. Brandon, ed., *The Effect of Demographies of Individual Households on Their Telephone Usage*, Cambridge, MA: Ballinger, 1981; W. Infosino, 'Relationship between demand for local telephone calls and household characteristics', *Bell Telephone Technical Journal*, 59: 31–53, 1980.
2. G. Claisse and F. Rowe, 'The telephone in questions on communication', *Computer Networks and ISDN Systems*, 24: 209–19, 1987.
3. U. Lange, 'The Berlin telephone study: An overview', in A. Moyal, ed., *Research on the Domestic Telephone*, Melbourne: CIRCIT, 1991.
4. L. Rakow, 'Gender, communication and technology: A case study of women and the telephone', Unpublished PhD Thesis, University of Illinois, 1987a.
5. H. Roberts, ed., *Doing Feminist Research*, London: Routledge and Kegan Paul, 1981.
6. See S. Keller, 'The telephone in new (and old) communities', in I. De Sola Pool, ed., *The Social Impact of the Telephone*, Cambridge, MA: MIT Press, 1977.
7. Telecommunication carriers suggest that survey respondents relying on memory overestimate the average number and duration of local calls. This is confirmed by M. Mayer. 'The telephone and the uses of time', in I. De Sola Pool, ed., op. cit. In the Australian survey, there were indications that respondents tended to underestimate the number and duration of their local calls.
8. In comparison with population figures produced by the Australian Bureau of Statistics, there is a slightly higher percentage representation in each of these age categories – but this arises from the absence of any respondents in the survey sample aged 0–14.
9. As also appears in Japan, see T. Morris-Suzuki, '"The communications revolution" and the household: Some thoughts from the Japanese experience', *Prometheus*, 6: 237–48, 1988.
10. The concept of 3 minutes as the basic unit of telephone 'conversation time' is internationally accepted. Yet the calculation is based on recorded call time measured in telephone exchanges at the busiest time of day, and encompasses an average over all types of business and residential voice calls, and unanswered (unsuccessful) calls.
11. S. Aronson, 'The sociology of the telephone', *International Journal of Comparative Sociology*, 12, 1971 – reprinted in C. Gumpert and R. Cathcart, eds, *Inter/media*, 3rd edition, New York: Oxford University Press, 1986.
12. As Dale Spender has pointed out, little research has yet been done on listening, a form of interactional work particularly associated with women and 'as complex and important as talk', L. Rakow, op. cit., p. 175.
13. L. Rakow, 'Looking to the future: Five questions for gender research', *Women's Studies In*

Communication, 10: 10–86, 1987b; L. Rakow, 'Women and the telephone: The gendering of a communications technology', in C. Kramerae, ed., *Technology and Women's Voices*, New York: Routledge and Kegan Paul, 1988.

14. H. Leonard, 'Creating community: The use of telephones as sources of information and support', in A. Moyal, 1991, op. cit.
15. See A. Day, 'Family caregiving and the elderly: Myths, realities and environmental implications', Seminar in Human Sciences, Canberra: Australian National University, 1988.
16. M. Mayer, 'The telephone and the uses of time', in I. De Sola Pool, ed., op. cit.
17. The uses of the office telephone, widespread in most industrial countries, awaits research. See H. Dordick, 'The social uses of the telephone: A US perspective', in U. Lange, K. Beck and A. Zerdick, eds, *Telefon und Gesellschaft*, Berlin: Volker Speiss, 1989.
18. A. Moyal, *Women and the Telephone in Australia*, Melbourne: Telecom Australia, 1989, pp. 33–4.
19. C. Marvin, 'When the telephone was new', in U. Lange, K. Beck and A. Zerdick, eds, op. cit.
20. L. Rakow, 1987a, op. cit.; L. Rakow, 1987b, op. cit.

5 □ The Cultural Construction of Home

5.1 □ Leonore Davidoff and Catherine Hall

The work of Leonore Davidoff and Catherine Hall considers how a new ideal of home was constructed in middle-class family life during the late eighteenth and early nineteenth centuries. They demonstrate that much of what we now take for granted was then innovatory: the residential suburbs, a separation of home and workplace, the specialized division of interior space and notions of domestic privacy.

'My own fireside': the creation of the middle-class home

On a rainy afternoon in August 1832, a 12-year-old vicar's daughter recorded in her diary that, while walking near the rural parsonage, she had seen 'a poor miserable woman in a tent by the roadside . . . she has a bad drunken husband who has quite starved her; and now that they cannot pay their rent they have been turned out of their house. To add to her miseries, she is very ill, having just given birth to a child. Mama has been once or twice to see her and given her broth'. A few weeks later, she saw a figure lying by the roadside who she assumed was sleeping but later discovered was dead from cholera.[1]

The recording of such incidents by a young, delicately raised girl brings home the concrete threats which surrounded many middle-class families. Along with continuing political unrest, the exigencies of poverty, brutality, pressing sexuality, disease and death were all too familiar. Against these, people struggled to control their destiny through religious grace and the bulwark of family property and resources. These shields took practical as well as symbolic form in middle-class homes and gardens.

[. . .]

The search for segregated living patterns and housing was in two stages. Productive work first had to be banished from the domestic area. Within this space, cooking, eating, washing, sleeping and other 'back stage' functions then began to be separated from polite social intercourse and eventually to have special places for each function.

In the 1793 renovations of the Taylor's house in Lavenham, the parlour had a sliding panel 'for convenient communication with the kitchen'.[2] This informal proximity was soon phased out of middle-class homes and not reintroduced until the 1930s.

The second separation was epitomized by the suburban villa: physically, financially and socially removed from the enterprise. [. . .] While the aristocracy and gentry had segregated some functions and spaces since the seventeenth century, their leisured lifestyle incorporated both estate management and honorific legal and political duties in the design of country seats.[3] At the other extreme, wage labourers, whether in factories or on the land, daily experienced a disjunction between the small space where they slept and ate and the employers' premises where their work-filled days were spent, with streets, open spaces and taverns serving their brief leisure. It was the middle ranks who erected the strictest boundaries between private and public space, a novelty which struck many early nineteenth-century travellers in England.

[. . .]

A [. . .] desire for privacy marked property boundaries with gates, drives, hedges and walls around house and garden. Humphrey Repton strikingly demonstrated the effect in his paper model of the space in front of his Essex 'cottage' where the view of shops, road and passing public was cut off by fencing, shrubbery and trees; a strong contrast to the communal squares and terraces of Georgian styles.[4] The novel device of the semi-detached house, combining the privacy and economy of a smaller house with the appearance of one twice the size, was peculiar to suburban development.[5] The inherent anti-urbanism of middle-class culture was reflected in the quintessential image of early nineteenth-century desirable housing, the *white cottage* with thatched roof and porch embowered with honeysuckle and roses. 'The White Cottage' in the commonplace book of an Essex farmer's daughter is the place where 'the world's cares and sorrows might cease, for all was humility, comfort and peace'.[6] But middle-class housing had to provide more than just a haven for family withdrawal for the home was also a stage for social ritual and outward manifestation of status in the community.

Undoubtedly, some details in housing and furnishing came from gentry emulation. For example, there are hints that visiting professional men, the local attorney calling to draw up a document and stopping for a glass of wine or the doctor attending a prestigious patient, noted and imitated the accoutrements of upper-class style. The homes of local gentry were regularly opened to a select public, providing a glimpse of taste to be followed even if it was electroplate rather than solid silver which graced middle-class sideboards. But the middle classes used and transformed gentry settings for their own purposes. Their type of housing, its distribution in towns and villages, its gardens and surroundings were part of the bid for independence from traditional aristocratic dictates. Neither was this pattern in direct line with the eighteenth-century mansions of merchants built next to counting houses and packing sheds or of professionals inhabiting eighteenth-century terraces and squares.

Part of the need for more segregated living space came from new activities made possible through time and labour freed from subsistence needs: reading, writing, music, fancy needlework, pursuit of scientific hobbies and the entertainment of friends. The capacity to create and beautify this type of home was becoming an expectation of natural feminine identity. A farmer prayed that God would permit his family 'the great gift of a new or restored, more commodious dwelling' that 'my Lizzie will have more scope for her tasteful devices. She understands the adornment of a home'. This contrasted with his childhood, for he found a great change towards a 'loftier and more refined civilization hallowing our dwellings', which he identified with women's influence.[7]

The demand for middle-class housing had built up over the latter half of the eighteenth century and blossomed in the boom of the first two decades of the nineteenth.[8] All levels, from the residences of gentlemen to the refitting of modest shops, were affected by the new ideals.

[. . .]

The separation of home from work

The expansion of middle-class housing, whether through the conversion of existing buildings or the building of new structures, provided a source of lucrative investment and made fortunes for local families. These homes were designed to enhance privacy and respectability even when next to or part of the enterprise. At first there was some ambivalence about the desirability of separation. Families moved between premises near the works at the town centre and villas on the outskirts as the prosperity of the business waxed and waned. It is significant that in a moral tale by a Suffolk clergyman, 'A Merchant's Wife', the young husband's desire to move away from rooms over the counting house is portrayed as striving for status and due to 'false shame'. His more modest Christian wife does not mind 'living above'. She argues: 'you have no fatiguing walk, now, after a wearisome day; and while the counting house is so near me, I have more of your society.' Proximity and interest in the business allows her to save them from bankruptcy by her opportune intervention.[9] Yet such proximity ran counter to valued privacy and protection from public gaze. In 1819, two young ladies visiting Birmingham's Galton and James Bank complained: 'Called . . . on Mr and Mrs James, the only unpleasant part of which was, the being ushered as usual through the Bank.'[10]

Since for merchants goods were processed in workers' cottages, the business had only contained the counting house and space for storing raw materials and packing finished goods. For generations, spaces for these activities had been part of residential premises. In Birmingham and Colchester sumptuous houses were adjoined by such offices and could, for example, include 'tenting grounds' for cloth, although hedges, walls and shrubbery might be used to screen productive activities from the living quarters.[11]

Manufacture such as brewing, where success depended on the entrepreneur's supervision, kept brew houses sited next door to the works, not a great inconvenience since brewing had to ensure ingredients free from smoke and smuts. But even where a process was noisy and dirty, the family might still live beside or near even such noisome works as a tannery. [. . .]

Into the nineteenth century, banking operations were usually carried on in the front room of the bank house partly as a security measure when specie was kept in cash boxes or chests.[12] In one such bank house even the privileged youngest daughter was banned from entering the sanctum of the 'Bank Parlour'.[13] Similarly, accommodation for schoolmasters usually adjoined the school if not below or above the single school room. Birmingham's King Edward VIth School, built in the 1830s, was typical, with a centre and two wings on three sides of a small quadrangle with a dwelling-house for the head-master, three school rooms and a library and behind it a smaller house for the second master.[14]

Professional men had little practical motivation to separate family life from those business premises which were neither dirty, nor noisy and which did not involve the social threat of a large workforce. In market towns, most doctors and attorneys remained in the centre, although they were beginning to cluster in more genteel streets. The Pattissons, whose legal practice and land holdings made them one of Witham's wealthiest families, lived in a large, double-fronted brick house in a central position on the main street. It was connected to the building used for law offices by a gangway between the first floors.[15] Doctors saw patients and mixed drugs in their front rooms and boarded their apprentice assistants in the house. In the main street of an Essex village, an early nineteenth-century surgeon occupied a handsome house with 'three parlours, three elegant bedrooms and a coach house'.[16] Even when Birmingham's prominent physician, Withering, a member of the Lunar Society, made the decision to rent Edgbaston Hall, he was assured that such a residence 'near Birmingham would be equally well adapted for his professional employment'.[17]

The separation of functions in shops took the form of removing preparation processes from rooms used for eating and sleeping. An eighteenth-century Ipswich butcher kept his chopping block and 'cliver' in the backroom/kitchen, the front room being used for living and sleeping and, significantly, still housing a spinning wheel. By the early nineteenth century, the hall as a place for living and sleeping had dwindled to an entry while the two main rooms became dining room and parlour. The shop was now a separate room holding stock and/or tools.[18]

[. . .]

In a manufacturing town the size of Birmingham, demand for specialized middle-class enclaves grew, as large tracts of working-class housing jostled commercial development in the town centre. The Rev. William Marsh, when in Colchester, lived in the vicarage on the High Street around the corner from his church of St Peter's and next door to the Corn Market. In 1829 when he was called to the town centre church of St Thomas's, Birmingham, the family chose to live in the recently developed suburb of Edgbaston over a mile away.[19]

Edgbaston represented the largest, most exclusive suburb in the town:

See Edgbaston, the bed of prosperous trade,
Where they recline who have their fortunes made;
Strong in their wealth, no matter how possessed,
There fashion calls, and there at ease they rest,

The beauteous suburb swells with lofty pride;
The vulgar poor are there forbid to hide.
With longing eye, the favoured of the day
Towards the loved purlieu make their eager way;
And as their broughams by our dwellings wheel,
We think how nice it is to be genteel.[20]

Clergy and professionals were some of Edgbaston's most enthusiastic residents as befitting their espousal of domestic ideals. By the 1850s, twenty-one clergymen (including John Angell James) lived in the suburb although there were only three local churches.[21] Such as area also appealed to those on independent incomes or retired, for although totally separated from the town's overcrowded courts, it was within 10 minutes' carriage drive or a brisk half hour's walk from the centre. According to a contemporary, the soil, the air and elevation overlooking the open country, the 'exclusion of manufactories and small houses render Edgbaston a favourite place of domestic retreat'.[22] Yet the still active businessman could feel comfortably free from the social exclusion he might experience in villages dominated by gentry.

Unlike earlier developments, Edgbaston maintained its momentum through increased demand and the dominance of the landowner, Lord Calthorpe, with his far-sighted agent. Calthorpe was an Evangelical and for such Christians who favoured the provision of aids to morality, improved housing was a moral duty as well as an attractive long-term investment. Through careful control of leases and aid for amenities such as the Botanical and Horticultural Society, he ensured that the suburb remained residentially segregated despite the variety of its housing.[23] Edgbaston prided itself on its rural ambience; the old church and Edgbaston Hall helped maintain the aura of village life. The roads were bordered with trees and hedges securing privacy from the public gaze so that 'few points in England exhibit such an assemblage of architectural beauty amidst a landscape of so strictly a rural character', according to the local guide.[24]

[. . .]

Despite the control exercised by Calthorpe, house design in Edgbaston was typical of the middle-class villa style, allowing for much individual taste and moving away from Georgian uniformity.[25] The final effect was variation within a basic pattern, as with the Rev. Swann's 'family residence' in 1830s Edgbaston: 'an elegant veranda standing at an agreeable distance from the road, shielded by neat shrubbery with a garden entrance for servants and tradesmen and a large well cultivated garden', while inside were two parlours, five bedrooms plus kitchen and all the now expected offices.[26]

[. . .]

The lay-out of the home

In turning living quarters into a home, the first change was in the lay-out of the buildings. When James Oakes renovated his house and made the bank parlour, he also pulled down the back to make way for a new wash house, brew house, scullery and 'offices'.[27]

When possible, rooms were being set aside for children, to be called 'nurseries' as Loudon instructed his readers in 1838.[28] These arrangements were promoted by the rationalization of domestic tasks, the more manual being increasingly taken over by servants who were doing less work connected to the enterprise. As more servants became available, family members were released for more cultural and social activities, now carried on in rooms kept for that purpose.[29]

[. . .]

By the 1830s, a range of modifications and additions had unquestionably added both comfort and gentility. The early nineteenth-century taste which favoured lightness and space was giving way to the heavy upholstered cluttered effect of the mid and late Victorians. Cowper's sparse domesticity, the sofa, shutters and tea urn, had now burgeoned with carpets, curtains, redesigned grates, mahogany furniture, wallpaper, chintz covers and bedsteads.

Where possible, eating now took place in a separate dining room with linen table-cloths, napkins, pottery and china and, at least, silver plate. Everyday goods were separated from best, which were used to mark the Sabbath and family rituals like Christmas or, more rarely, for formal entertaining. Arthur Biddell, the bluff Suffolk farmer who prided himself on his simplicity despite a substantial income, maintained: 'Gay Plates require Silver Spoons, Glasses instead of Black and White Mugs – a clean cloth and nice knives and forks and all this necessitates food and wine to match the plates; real China Tea things, a silver Cream Jug and Plated Pot.'[30] There was the apparatus of a more literate culture: books and bookcases, desks, music stands and instruments, a proliferation of cabinets and tables for sewing and embroidery, games and scientific collections.

These changes came slowly. Household needs and resources varied and many had to make do with older-styled premises. Families inherited furniture and household goods or bought from sales and auctions for few could afford to start housekeeping with completely new stock.

The aristocracy and gentry had begun adding halls and corridors in the seventeenth century to give more privacy and mark the family from the public domain, and by the 1770s, servants had been banished to back premises to be summoned by bell pulls.[31] But in smaller houses, the most important late eighteenth-century innovation was setting aside one room specifically for social intercourse: the middle-class equivalent to the (with) drawing room was the parlour (parler, to speak). In the 1790s, a Suffolk village family who ran a bakery-cum-haberdashery spent their time in the brick-floored kitchen with the master's wooden chair in the warm chimney corner and doors opening to the shop and garden. Only at Christmas was the parlour with its spinnet used for family gatherings.[32] Birmingham in the same period was no different. A family who operated a profitable print works lived in the kitchen, the liveliness of that room being 'a great point . . . for there they received their company and there were we entertained with chocolate and coffee'.[33]

By the 1830s, the parlour was coming into more regular use. An Ipswich town house, functioning as a genteel residence for a shopkeeper's family in 1827, included a vestibule, dining room and parlour with separate kitchen, backhouse and laundry.[34] Experts like Loudon made it a cardinal principle that the parlour or drawing room should have better fittings and furniture with a superior appearance. In everyday life, the dining room with more homely furnishings and large central table, fire and lamps was more often used, doubling as library, study, sewing room and general gathering place.

The use of rooms partly depended on the formality of social circles but more obviously on the size and composition of the household. [. . .] When John Cadbury and his family moved to Edgbaston from living over the shop in Birmingham town centre, their home had an 'almost cottage like appearance' and needed extensive alterations. The kitchen was turned into a children's room first for play and later a school room and two new kitchens were built. As the children grew up this room, with large windows overlooking the newly laid out garden, became 'our prettiest sitting room'. Later three more bedrooms and back staircase were added as servant numbers increased.[35]

Given the large numbers of children, it was usual to share beds as well as rooms. Even substantial residences might have only three bedrooms to house parents, children, relatives, visitors and servants. The privilege of an individual bedroom was unusual. A vicar's eldest daughter gained her own 'dear little room' when in her teens, a 'true delight . . . which was quite my property, and I feel completely independent'. She glowingly described its large proportion, two white curtained windows, four posted bed, handsome carved chimney piece, bookshelves, wash stand, bonnet press, dressing table, mahogany chest of drawers and writing table.[36]

Perhaps the most striking example of changes wrought by the separation of functions and the desire for privacy was on the farm, where the house remained part of the working complex. During the phasing out of farm service, labourers were segregated at their own table in the living kitchen, or fed a midday meal in the back kitchen or 'bakhus' (Suffolk), while the family ate separately and sat in a parlour.[37] A door to the parlour avoided entrance through the kitchen, keeping family and hands apart. In a small Essex farmhouse the best parlour remained a 'houseplace' where 'the men were admitted to regale themselves – master and man together after their daily labour unless there was company', a pattern already considered old-fashioned by the 1800s.[38] Maids and daughters no longer shared bedrooms reached through the parents' room. Parents and children now had separate premises opening off an upstairs hall.[39]

[. . .]

Local sources reveal a clear rise in the standard of furnishings for all occupational groups. Inventories taken after the destruction of homes of prominent Birmingham nonconformist families in the Priestley Riots of 1791 show living rooms without carpets and only a few pieces of mahogany furniture. Priestley himself had a mahogany sofa covered with material to match his curtains, impressively affluent for that period.[40] In 1806, a small Essex farmer proudly listed two tables and six chairs made locally for £4 'out of my own tree in my yard'.[41] By the 1830s and 1840s, inventories for William Marsh in Edgbaston, a Birmingham lawyer, and Bernard Barton, a bank clerk, all reveal a collection of Brussels and Axminster carpets, a variety of sofas, settees, stools, tables cabinets, sideboards (the furniture mostly of mahogany), together with smaller pieces for special functions: sewing boxes, a medicine case and umbrella stand.[42]

Living rooms blossomed with decorative additions: 'Rich china ornaments' on the new mantlepieces, and paintings, both amateur and professional. [. . .]

Running the home

Within the middle-class rubric, maintaining privacy and the hallmark of respectability presented logistical problems when households were large, especially with numerous young children. In the census sample, children under 16 (whether or not related to the household head) made up 27 per cent of the household population, 15 per cent being children under 10. Shared beds as well as sleeping quarters were the rule; space for eating, washing, or just sitting was cramped by later standards. Regimented proce-dures for the minutiae of behaviour were the only way of keeping order under such conditions and entailed a strict distribution of both objects and activities. 'A place for everything and everything in its place' was, for good reason, an often quoted maxim.

Yet within this general framework, visual images could be more important than the functional use of labour and materials. Polished surfaces and mirrors reflected candle (later oil) light; warm colours and textures gave a domestic cosiness and rich feeling, physical warmth was provided by open coal fires, shutters, heavy curtains, carpets and upholstered furniture.[43] [. . .]

Technical changes in lighting made a longer day for leisure or business, for time spent with the family together after dark. The poor might struggle on with rush lights and inferior tallow candles; a benefit of higher income was wax tapers and, by the 1830s, oil for lamps.[44] The gleam of silver (or plate) on polished wood gave the impression of good housekeeping, evoking the time and energy spent rubbing with beeswax. In fact, carpets, curtains, canopied beds and soft chairs could harbour more dirt and dust than sanded stone flags and sparse wooden furniture. Large towns presented special problems in keeping a house really clean; housewives had to battle with coal smoke, smuts and waste products like wet rubbish which in the country had been recycled on the land.[45] Concern with dirt and disorder drew new boundaries between what was valuable and what was waste and in the process, moral or social criteria were often used rather than the hygienic standards of the twentieth century based on a germ theory of disease.

Cleanliness was also associated with individual behaviour. Arthur Young, travelling in late eighteenth-century France, was impressed with the refined table manners, that each person kept his own glass at the dinner table and had clean napkins and linen.[46] Changes in hygienic practice partly took this personal form because water supplies suffi-cient for standards of modern household cleanliness depended not on moral oversight, but communal action and large-scale capital investment which neither households nor local organizations were willing to undertake until after mid century. Many villages remained dependent on brooks and fetid ponds. Even in small towns pumps were only slowly erected, and often depended on philanthropy or were run for profit, while middle-class homes had to ensure their supplies with wells which often ran dry.[47] In larger towns, even when piped water had been brought into the back premises of wealthier homes, supplies were intermittent and cheap servant labour delayed efforts for raising water above ground level. In any case, personal cleanliness was directed to washing hands and faces rather than overall bathing, so that wash stands with ewer and basin (another lucrative item for pottery manufacturers) were becoming standard bedroom furniture. Women now had to carry up water and empty slops, either themselves or overseeing servants.

If the provision of water supplies suffered from the vagaries of local politics and desire for profit, waste disposal lagged even further behind and most houses made do with ash pits and outdoor earth closets. Well into the late nineteenth century outdoor privies for men and servants reserved the one indoor facility for the modesty of ladies.[48] Keeping up even an appearance of cleanliness in town centres must have been daunting. In 1819, two young Quaker women visiting Birmingham were impressed with the neat appearance of their co-religionists' houses, given the grime and smoke of the town. Clean steps, doors, and window ledges, gleaming brass knockers, and starched white curtains dramatically demonstrated the break between private rectitude and public squalor.[49]

Moving to the leafy purlieus of Edgbaston did not necessarily solve the problem. A report to the Public Health Authorities covering Hagley Road (with villas renting from £60 to £180 per annum and the home of Rev. John Angell James) stated that, even in the 1840s, there was no drainage and that open ditches on each side of the road were 'full of green and fetid matter' where water closets were discharged. Many premises had cess pools which overflowed into local wells. R. T. Cadbury complained in his evidence that ditches surrounding his Edgbaston home were 'in a most putrid state, reeking with the content of water closets in the finest neighbourhood of Birmingham'.[50] Without the means for proper washing, bugs, nits and other insect pests remained a plague, on which mistress and maid waged constant time and energy consuming attacks. Yet even then, moral and social concern often superseded physical health. Mid century Ipswich was particularly backward in water supply and drainage. A local commentator – and political radical – denounced the fact that one 'out office' (euphemism for privy) had to serve for several houses: 'Are not these circumstances sufficient to destroy all modesty, to blight the beauty of the female character and to banish all feelings of self-respect from the human mind?'[51]

It was often the offensive smell, signifying both health and moral hazards which concerned middle-class people. According to scientific ideas of the time, diseases were spread by 'myasmic contagion' signified by smell.[52] For example, at a time when the middle ranks were using soap for laundry, many labourer's families still used urine. Given their resources, the gap in personal hygiene between the habits of poor and moderately well off was widening. The importance of odour in maintaining social hierarchy remained until the mid twentieth century. [. . .]

Ideas about the nature of cleanliness and order directly affected the lay-out of middle-class housing. Segregating the mess and smell of food preparation from the social ritual of eating became an important hallmark of respectability and meant that the kitchen became ideally as remote as possible from the living rooms, no matter the cost in servants, or wife's time and labour. The English obsession with fresh air also stems from this period. Light and air let in from the enlarged sash windows allowed that 'ventilation and mitigation of smell' which it was claimed 'helped to make a population moral and happy'.[53] Maintaining and running such homes required greater investments of time and energy as well as money. For example, closed ranges had to be cleaned with blacking and brushed liberally with 'elbow grease'. Oil lamps needed careful cleaning and trimming if the wicks were to burn brightly, fires had to be lit laboriously from a tinder box until the invention of matches in the 1830s.

[. . .]

Cooking was now banished to the kitchen except for a tiny hob where the lady of the house might make tea, or in less elevated households, pancakes or drop scones over the parlour fire. A good portion of the enhanced middle-class income was being spent on more elaborate food. Eighteenth-century innovations of tea, sugar and chocolate were augmented by more 'made up dishes', coffee and wines. [. . .]

Overseeing the buying in of provisions was an important part of a mistress's role. At this period, most still did their own marketing but the stigma of being seen in public carrying parcels was growing. Fiction picked up these sensitive areas. In the early 1800s, Jane Austen ridiculed Mrs Bennett's preening herself that her daughters had nothing to do with the kitchen.[54] By the 1830s, Harriet Martineau has one of her pretentious characters urge the heroine not to let down her family's social position by carrying a basket through the town with the small end of a carrot peeping from under the lid.[55] Town grocers began to solve the dilemma by delivering for those who could not send servants, although undoubtedly many women and children continued to shop for themselves, particularly in the countryside, and the breadwinners of Edgbaston were not above stopping at the butcher's or grocer's on their way home from town.

Another major task for women was laundry work. This had grown since the eighteenth century when more frequent changes of the recently introduced cotton clothing became desirable. Sheets, towels, the linen napkins admired by Arthur Young, not only had to be purchased and hemmed, but laundered, along with white linen around the neck and wrists for men, aprons, kerchiefs and nightwear for women and a variety of children's clothing. New habits of hygiene and also signs of morality were displayed by such fashions. For example, the spotless starched headgear of Quaker women was remarked upon favourably in local records. By the 1840s, we find an array of tea cloths, tray napkins, cheese tray cloths, oyster cloths and dusters besides the ordinary linen, all to be laundered in a merchant's Essex household.[56] The early eighteenth-century orgies of washing once or twice a year were no longer sufficient for the higher standards of cleanliness and amount or variety of linen – local records indicate washing days at about monthly intervals.

The monthly wash day now meant routine upheaval for the household. All lent a hand; women of the family, servants and extra washerwomen. In a bank manager's menage, coloured clothes, whites and muslins were soaked separately for several days and simmered on the stove, put out to bleach, then washed and, in bad weather, dried on stretchers before the fire (whites had first to be blued).[57] [. . .]

The finishing processes of starching and ironing made linen look clean for longer and strengthened the image of order and purity, but they were heavy consumers of female energy, using weighty ember-filled irons constantly in danger of scorching or marking the linen with soot. Women's caps and children's clothes had ruffles and frills necessitating special goffering irons and elaborate starching and steaming.[58] [. . .]

Women were responsible for overseeing the appearance of all household members. In addition to laundering, they bought, made and mended all clothing. Although written evidence is scarce, one of the great silences about women's lives was undoubtedly filled with needlework. From the long flat-fell seaming of sheets to the embroidered chair cushions, from making up boys' suits to exquisitely worked velvet slippers for papa at Christmas, middle-class women were constantly sewing, and their daughters were taught to do so from the age when they could grasp a needle. The 'work' boxes and sewing chests listed in local inventories, and the samplers, quilts and other surviving artefacts speak forcefully for what is seldom said in words.

However, men also took an active part in setting up the home. [. . .] Men were responsible for buying certain items: wine, books, pictures, musical instruments and wheeled vehicles. They accompanied their wives to buy furniture and carpets, while both men and women painted and papered rooms. In the 1820s, a civil engineer in a West Midlands ironworks made drawings for alterations to the house, shopped with his wife for furnishings in Birmingham and carpets in Kidderminster and papered the rooms.[59] A commercial traveller in the same decade also shopped for a carpet while in Kidderminster, and he constantly wrote details about servants and household affairs to his wife while away from home.[60]

Who actually did what also depended on how elaborate the establishment was, how much servant help was available and how involved the home was in the enterprise. Better-off women needed to understand housekeeping but not necessarily how to carry out specific tasks.

[. . .]

By mid century, genteel women in the wealthiest households would only have arranged flowers, done fancy embroidery, possibly being able to distil flower essence and make special confections. But the majority of middle-class women did a substantial portion of housework and childcare to reach the new standards, despite an increase in domestic servants.

Notes

1. E. Shore, *Journal of Emily Shore*, 1891, p 22.
2. A. Gilbert, *Autobiography and Other Memorials of Mrs Gilbert*, vol. 1, 1879, p. 68; F. Thompson, *Hampstead: Building a Borough 1650–1964*, 1974, p. 241.
3. M. Girouard, *Life in the English Country House: A social and architectural history*, New Haven: 1978.

4. H. Repton, 'View from my own cottage in Essex', in *Fragments on the Theory and Practice of Landscape Gardening,* 1816.
5. For the social implications see the novel, E. Eden, *The Semi-Detached House*, 1859.
6. J. Seabrook, 'Unpublished commonplace book' (*c.* 1830), by permission of Mary Mallawaratchi.
7. J. Stovin, *Journals of a Methodist Farmer 1871–1875*, 1982, p. 182.
8. A. Harvey, *Britain in the Early 19th Century*, 1978.
9. Rev. C. Tayler, 'A merchant's wife', in *May You Like It*, 1823, p. 104.
10. C. Fox and J. Melville, unpublished typescript: 'Diary of a visit to Bingley Hall, Birmingham', 1819, BRL 669392, p. 20.
11. J. Bensusan-Butt, *The House that Boggis Built: A social history of the minories*, Colchester: 1972.
12. In the 1790s, James Oakes remodelled his Bury St Edmund's home when he turned to full-time banking and included a new bank parlour. J. Oakes, 'Unpublished diary', April 1790.
13. E. Marshall, *A Biographical Sketch*, 1900, p. 20.
14. Charity Commissioners, *Reports on Charities and Education of the Poor in England and Wales*, 1815–37, vol. xxxv.
15. Janet Gyford, personal communication.
16. A. Brown, *Essex at Work*, Chelmsford, 1969, p. 160.
17. W. Withering, *The Miscellaneous Tracts of William Withering M.D., F.R.S. to which is prefixed a memoir by his son*, 1822, p. 74.
18. L. Redstone, *Ipswich Through the Ages*, Ipswich, 1969, p. 125.
19. C. Marsh, *The Life of the Rev. William Marsh*, 1867.
20. H. Horton, *Birmingham: A poem in two parts*, Birmingham: 1851, p. 87.
21. *Edgbaston Directory and Guide*, Birmingham: 1853.
22. G. Yates, *An Historical and Descriptive Sketch of Birmingham*, Birmingham, 1830, p. 247.
23. D. Cannadine, *Lords and Landlords: The aristocracy and the towns 1774–1967*, Leicester: 1980, p. 214.
24. *Edgbaston Directory*, introduction.
25. J. Burnett, *A History of the Cost of Living*, Harmondsworth: Penguin, 1969, p. 112.
26. ABG, (23 August 1830).
27. J. Oakes, 1789, op. cit.
28. J. Loudon, *The Suburban Gardener and Villa Companion*, 1838, p. 680.
29. L. Davidoff, 'The rationalization of housework', in D. Barker and S. Allen, eds, *Dependency and Exploitation in Work and Marriage*, London: Longman, 1976; J. Bunce, *Birmingham Life Sixty Years Ago*, articles for the *Birmingham Weekly Post*, Birmingham, 1899. See particularly the article dated 15 April 1899.
30. A. Biddell, in G. Ewart Evans, *The Horse in the Furrow*, 1960, p. 93.
31. M. Girouard, op. cit.
32. A. Gilbert, vol. 1, op. cit., p. 23.
33. J. Bunce, 25 March 1899; for a more commodious but similarly integrated house and enterprise see the merchant house described in an advertisement in ABG, 2 February 1804.
34. L. Redstone, op. cit., p. 125.
35. M. Cadbury, 'Ms book of childhood reminiscences: The happy days of our childhood', BRL Cadbury. Collection, 466/344.
36. E. Shore, op. cit., pp. 216–17.
37. In advice on building new farm houses, a parlour was urged as an 'absolute necessity'. T. Stone, *An Essay on Agriculture with a View to Inform Gentlemen of Landed Property Whether Their Estates are Managed to their Greatest Advantage*, Lynn, 1785, p. 243.
38. A. Gilbert, vol. 1, op. cit., p. 52.
39. J. Thirsk and J. Imray, *Suffolk Farming in the Nineteenth Century*, Suffolk Records Society, 1958, p. 129.

40. J. Priestley, 'Inventory of house and goods destroyed during the riots, 1791', BRL 174683; W. Hutton, 'Inventory to household goods etc. at High Street and Bennetts' Hill, destroyed in the riots 1791', BRL 145428.
41. J. Pudney, 'Unpublished diary of a farmer near Kelvedon, 1757–1823', ERO T/P 116/62.
42. Mahogany imported from the Empire had replaced the darker, heavier indigenous oak of the seventeenth century. Estate of Simcox as described in ABG, 15 March 1836; Estate of William Marsh, ABG, 27 July 1840; *Sale Catalogue of the Neat Household Furniture of the Late Bernard Barton*, 26 July 1849.
43. J. Burnett, *A Social History of Housing 1815–1970*, London: Methuen, 1980, J. Taylor, 'The life of a looking glass', *Contributions of QQ*, 1845.
44. Coal gas was used primarily for public lighting in streets and shops and was not available for domestic use until after mid century.
45. Anon., *Passages In the Life of a Young Housekeeper Edited by Herself*, 1862.
46. G. Mingay, *Arthur Young and His Times*, 1975.
47. L. Cryer, *A History of Rochford*, 1978, p. 29; for the struggle over water supplies and drainage in Colchester, see A. Phillips, *Ten Men and Colchester*, Chelmsford, 1985, pp. 23–31.
48. L. Wright, *Clean and Decent*, 1940.
49. C. Fox and J. Melville.
50. R. Rawlinson, *The Public Health Act: Report of Birmingham*, 1849, pp. 26–31.
51. J. Glyde, *The Moral, Social and Religious Condition of Ipswich in the Middle of the 19th Century*, 1971, p. 47.
52. G. Rosen, 'Disease, debility and death', in M. Wolf and H. Dyos, eds, *The Victorian City: Images and realities*, vol 2, 1974.
53. G. Young, *Victorian England: Portrait of an age*, Oxford, 1966, p. 7.
54. J. Austen, *Pride and Prejudice*, Oxford, 1980, p. 58.
55. H. Martineau, *Deerbrook*, 2nd edn, 1983.
56. M. Young, 'Account books 1818–1819'.
57. A. Vernon, *Three Generations: The fortunes of a Yorkshire family*, 1966, p. 101.
58. C. Davidson, *Womans's Work is Never Done: A history of housework in the British Isles 1650–1950*, London: Chatto and Windus, 1981; for a detailed description of goffering a baby's cap see E. Forster, *Marianne Thorton: A domestic biography 1797–1887*, 1956, p. 179.
59. L. N. Mutton ed., 'An engineer at work in the West Midlands. The diary of John Urpeth Raistick for 1820', *Journal of West Midlands Regional Studies*, special publication, no. 1, Wolverhampton, 1969.
60. Shaw Letters, BUL *passim*.

5.2 □ *Judy Attfield*

In this essay, Judy Attfield presents an oral history account of women who moved to a post-war new town. She records their memories of how it felt to live in Harlow during its pioneer days, and focuses on household decoration and furnishing practices – contrasting her interviewees' words with the discourses of official design institutions.

Inside Pram Town: a case study of Harlow house interiors, 1951–61

Harlow had its 40th birthday in 1987. In the early 1950s it was like a frontier town, with unpaved roads, few amenities, one street-light and no history of its own. No one felt the disorientation of newness more than the first young women who moved into Harlow in its pioneer days, when the roads were 'nothing but mud, mud, mud . . .'[1] and so 'choc-a-block with prams' that they called it Pram Town.[2] They didn't see the move away from London as a cosy retreat to a rural setting, although most of them came from overcrowded living conditions in rented rooms, small flats or shared family houses. The familiar areas they knew as home only offered them uncomfortable living conditions after the war. So, leaving the security of extended families and the communities of inner London to brave the discomforts of a new town was the only way they could secure a new house of their own.

At first many women suffered from a form of depression often referred to in the vernacular as 'New Town Blues'. In one town the number of women admitted to hospital with a diagnosis of neurosis was 50 per cent above the national average.[3] Critics who advocated a denser, more urban type of planning than the low-density 'prairie planning'[4] used in Harlow were quick to cite prairie planning as a contributing factor, suggesting that it led to isolation caused by the great distances between neighbourhoods and the centres for services and amenities.[5]

> I knew a lot of women that moved down here . . . we all moved together and some of them suffered terribly with depression and loneliness, although there was a better sense of community then than there is now . . . We had to start our foundation again . . . we were the ones, the women were the ones that was left to cope and adjust, harder than any of the men . . .[6]

Having children helped many of the young women of Harlow feel more at home. It was motherhood which brought them out of the isolation of their houses and into contact with each other as they tramped over the mud fields pushing their large prams to the shops and the baby clinics before the roads were made up.

> I don't think I can honestly remember that anybody didn't like Harlow for any other reason than mostly missing their family and it was nearly always Mum. 'Cause you must remember that we were all quite young. It wasn't the same for the men. There was the pub just down the lane at Glebelands called The Greyhound and quite a few men went down there and had a game of darts and a pint.[7]

In looking at the impact of design on the lives of women in the new towns, two important debates can be identified. The first centres around the control of space and how, through planning and the design of the house, it placed women in the home. The second, most easily discernible in the way tenants furnished the interiors of their houses, centres around the conflict between popular taste and the establishment's official 'good design' values, which it sought to impose on the public. Much to their consternation, architects found that their intentions for tenants' furnishings, in accordance with the rules of functional modern design, which disallowed traditional period styles or ornament, were totally ignored.

The plan for Harlow was based on the picturesque rural English tradition,[8] which considered architecture one of the aesthetic ingredients in the natural landscape. The New Town Movement, from which it stemmed, had originated with the concept of the garden city, formulated by Ebenezer Howard in 1898.[9] This attempted to embody a synthesis of political, moral and economic ideals based on the principles of nationalisation of land, decentralisation and community. Harlow was just one of a number of satellite towns planned to provide for overspill from London after the Second World War. The model for the ideal 'community' was the pre-industrial settlement or village.[10] Harlow's equivalent was the residential neighbourhood, which, unlike the medieval village, deliberately separated the public male domain of work – industry, trade and commerce – from the private female domestic world. Women's place in Harlow was unquestionably in the home. In spite of precedents in housing design to accommodate communal domestic work, such as kitchenless houses with cooperative housekeeping units,[11] there is no evidence that any such arrangements were ever envisaged here.

The reconstruction period launched a whole series of government reports and plans for the design of post-war Britain and took advantage of the austerity conditions of war to control the design of furniture and textiles through the Utility scheme. This was first implemented in 1943 in the hope that it could impose 'good design' ideals on the public by regulating the use of scarce materials and labour through rationing and statutory designs. The establishment's view is evident in Jeffrey Daniel's heroic description of the principles of Utility:

> The Utility scheme, although born out of necessity, was inspired by ideals of social justice based on a fervent belief in the perfectibility of man in society that is Neo-classicism's chief philosophic legacy, and its creators thought of it in those terms.[12]

Without an understanding of dominant cultural values it is not possible to explain why the dictates of 'good design', which designers thought would solve the social problems of housing, had nothing to do with how women related to the design of Harlow – its layout and their houses – nor why they furnished and designed their homes so differently.

The conflict between popular taste and the official 'good design' movement is usually characterised in conventional design history as the 'failure of Modernism', in which the professional design establishment blames itself, as it did in the fifties, for failing to educate the public to 'raise its standards' of taste and choose good/modern design.[13] More recently, since post-Modernism, the attack has been levelled at Modernism itself, for failing to incorporate vital human values or to fulfil its promise of effecting social reforms. But blaming the designers and planners or the modern aesthetic itself fails to take account of differences – in ways of looking, speaking or in the design process – from any position other than that of the professional design establishment.

'Back to front and inside out'[14]

The design concept, introduced in post-war housing, of placing the working area of the house in the front was, significantly, advocated by a woman – Elizabeth Denby,[15] an influential adviser on working-class housing:

> . . . workers and children have a surfeit of communal life during the day. Not so the women. While the living room should face west or south on to garden or balcony, with utmost obtainable privacy from being overlooked or overheard by others, the kitchen, the workshop, should look on to the street, so that the woman can join, however indirectly, in the life of the neighbourhood . . .[16]

This revolutionary design idea broke the traditional correlation of 'front' with public display of status, which placed the non-working, leisure area of the parlour or front room, with its window drapery and ornaments, on show to the street. It is a good example of the climate among post-war designers who favoured rational principles and innovation as a means of doing away with social pretensions. But they did not acknowledge anything problematic about a captive housewife marooned in her kitchen, passively catching glimpses of the outside world from the strategically designed windows but unable to participate actively in it. This isolation, however, was very real to women in Harlow, who, at home on their own during the day, looked out through their windows only to see blank expanses of landscape, devoid of familiar landmarks or human activity.

> When I used to look out of the window, I couldn't see a thing . . . I thought I was the only person on earth . . . It took me years before I classed this as a home. I loved the house and I was proud of it, but if ever I thought of going to Walthamstow, I was always going home, 'cause that's where my roots are, was . . . I was always going 'up home' to see Mum and Dad . . . It made us feel very emotional, we felt very much alone. I felt as if I'd been thrown right out of a nest, although I was 28 when I came here. It took a great deal of time to accept it, although I loved it and common sense told me I'd done the right thing.[17]

Most Harlow houses contained an open-plan 'larger living-room', often running from front to back, rather than the two separate reception rooms (dining and lounge) typical of the inter-war, middle-class, spec-built, suburban semis so disliked by Modernist architects. Some of the earlier houses, such as those built on the Chippingfield estate, combined kitchen with dining-room [. . .] but none of them had parlours or front rooms of the type found in the nineteenth century in London terraced houses familiar to Harlow tenants. Much confusion was caused by the disappearance of the wall separating the front room, traditionally kept for best, from the more private, everyday back of the house. The sense of dislocation was reinforced in estates like Chippingfield, where the 'back' or service door was positioned next to the 'front' door on the public façade facing the street.

To young women negotiating the newness of unfamiliar surroundings, traditional values embodied in the metaphor of 'front' must have had a significance totally different to those held by the young architects and designers trying to create a new concept in living.

> I had this cretonne and I made them [the curtains] myself. The front had to match, didn't matter too much about the back. This was going back to my mother's day, of course. The front of the house always had to be matched upstairs and downstairs. And [for] the front door's one, I crocheted lacy curtains.[18]

The parlour and all its trappings symbolised for the designers of the new society all that was anathema to the modern view. The rather abstract concept of space was considered crucial in the fifties, as *Design*, the magazine produced by the Council of Industrial Design, reported:

> Focus on space, a key word, space that gives freedom. Destroy the distinction between rooms. The home is subservient to life in the home. Banish the cold formality of front parlours that attempt to impress callers – then stand unused, to collect dust . . . Push back the wall, bring the kitchen in, dissolve divisions that separate life into compartments . . . Allow freedom to change and space to move.[19]

A censorious account of 'mistakes' made by tenants appeared in a 1957 review of 'Furnishing in the new towns' by *Design* magazine.

> They fight shy of open-plan living . . . there is a strong tendency to shelter behind net curtains. Large windows are obscured by elaborate drapes and heavy pelmets, by dressing table mirrors and large settees. Corners are cut off by diagonally placed wardrobes and sideboards. By careful arranging and draping, the open plan houses are being closed up again, light rooms are darkened and a feeling of spaciousness is reduced to cosy clutter . . . in achieving cosiness they are completely at variance with the architects' achievements in giving them light and space.[20]

From fairly early on, net curtains appear to have been a bone of contention between tenants and architects. The pages of the *Harlow Citizen* feature complaints from architects about 'windows heavily shrouded in net curtains' and from tenants that 'privacy is one of the things held in low regard in the town from the planners' point of view'. It reported the advice given by a doctor to a woman he diagnosed as suffering from

Harlowitis: 'Buy yourself net curtaining for every window in the house, shut yourself in for a week and forget the place ever existed. It will do you a power of good.'[21]

In the Harlow houses with an open-plan living-room, the stairs appeared to become the separating agent between private and public (display) areas, as Mr V. H., a former supervisor for the Sheraton group, which opened the first furniture shop in Harlow, in the Stow shopping precinct, noted:

> There wasn't much money about in those days . . . They always bought for the bottom half of the house and didn't matter so much about the top half . . . they had a nice new home and they wanted to impress their friends, who didn't necessarily go upstairs . . . the bedroom was last.[22]

To [. . .] Erving Goffman, 'front', or external façade, is a metaphor for display to an audience, so that 'back', or interior, becomes the less formal area where the individual can seek refuge, relaxation and 'drop *his* front' (my emphasis).[23] It is the separation, or boundary, which gives the two areas their definition. But what we also have here is a quite specifically male point of view. This is only made clear when we read critical feminist accounts of literature on the home, such as discussions in Davidoff et al. of these meanings using a gendered perspective:

> The underlying imagery is the unacknowledged master of the household looking *in*, so to speak, at the household . . .[24]

Mrs D. S. made a similar point. Having described how she finally felt 'this is my domain now' about her house in Harlow after many years of adjusting to her move from Walthamstow in 1951, she described how her husband felt about the house:

> 'As long you're behind the door, I'm at work all day so it doesn't make any difference to me where I am as long as I've got a comfortable place to come home to.'[25]

[. . .] For women it was their place of work – their view was from the inside.[26] Was the Harlow house in the 1950s really perceived by its inhabitants as a public statement of status, and if so in what ways was this class- and gender-specific? Much of contemporary literature on housing, based on Functionalism, dismissed the parlour as outdated and 'difficult to use',[27] a result of ill-considered design. [. . .]

Raymond Unwin's opinion that emulation of the middle class was the sole factor governing the popular preference for the parlour in 1918[28] was generally still held by the designers of the 1950s. However, recent feminist history of housing uncovers a different reason for the importance accorded to the parlour in the First World War reconstruction period. It shows that as a result of women's attempts to have their views taken into account on the design of housing, the government set up a Women's Housing Subcommittee in 1918 to report on the 'housewife's needs'. The conclusions were based on interviewing working-class women and on an intimate knowledge of their living conditions. They included a recommendation for a parlour, because of the need for women to have a room where they could relax and escape from unfinished work.[29]

The practical nature of women's views on housing design was confirmed by my interviews with women in Harlow, particularly those who moved into Harlow in the early 1950s. Mrs C. S.,[30] for example, liked the stairs in her new two-storey house because 'you could put the children to bed [knowing] they were away from the noise and we knew they would have a good night's sleep'. Another woman commented on the large size of the hall because it was big enough to fit the pram, while Mrs C. E.,[31] one of the first people to move into the Chippingfield estate in 1950, saw no objection whatsoever to having the 'back' door next to the front door. It was noticeable that it was in fact a man who attributed what was probably his own dislike of the working and main entrance doors being side by side to 'the housewife'.[32] In Mrs V. T.'s case, her husband's preference prompted them to move to an estate with the more conventional gabled roof and 'proper' back door.[33] This does not necessarily prove anything; and it is more than likely that functional reasons are given for preferences which are just as motivated by symbolic needs. Nevertheless, it is significant that the responses I received from women whose opinions I sought on what they valued most about their houses were weighted on the side of use. Yet there was also a strong element of display, which can't be reconciled with the separation that is usually made between function and display.

It is understandable that Harlow's first residents were uncritical of their new houses because they were such a change for the better, compared with the cramped conditions they had had to endure during the war – living with family or in rented rooms, in small flats over shops or converted requisitioned property, sharing bathrooms and toilets with other families. Many of them felt they had 'come up in the world with these houses'. Mrs C. E., who had lived in a Nissen hut, compared the difference 'moving from purgatory to heaven . . .'.[34] This is not to say there were no difficulties in adapting to the unconventional open plan, or any of the other design innovations introduced into people's lives by the new town concept. Mrs D. S.,[35] whose poignant account of her loneliness and sense of isolation is quoted earlier, explained her greatest problem rather incredulously: 'Funnily enough I couldn't get used to the *newness* of things.' This in a time, just after the war, when there was a craving for new things after a long period of having to 'make do and mend'.

Although most Harlow houses were designed along the lines of open plan, there was an awareness on the part of the architects of the preference for separating the dining area from the rest of the living-room, and provision was usually made for the fitting of folding doors or curtains between the two spaces. Some of the later developments, such as Hookfield (1966), actually provided two separate rooms.[36] From a lifetime's experience working for Harlow Corporation Architects Department, Mr A. M. was well placed to see both the way open plan was received by the tenants and the way architects reacted to tenants' ideas of interior decoration.

> Every architect thought that after his house had been built . . . it should be furnished as he thought it should be . . . Of course, that didn't happen. At one time we used to be very conscious of the interior decoration. We'd pick the wall colours, the ceiling colours, the colour of the doors . . . fairly early on we came to the realisation that we were utterly wasting our time because no matter what we put on the walls . . . no sooner had people gone in, they couldn't even wait for a year to pass . . . they'd paper them direct with some of the most awful wallpapers. And you'd throw your hands up in horror. Then you'd get the house where there was the do-it-yourself handyman who'd put up all these sort of

shelves and divisioning walls and change doors . . . despite the fact that they were renting housing . . . Right from the beginning people did things themselves . . . They wouldn't be allowed to change fireplaces and things like that but a lot of them did it surreptitiously . . . Architects, especially if you're working in mass housing, have got to try and design a basic framework in which people can do their own thing, because they're going to do it anyhow.[37]

[. . .]

Pride, polish and screw-on legs

The furnishing and equipping of the house played a vital role in the transformation of house into home. In the early fifties the most important factors determining choice, apart from differing tastes, were cost restraints and availability of goods. Rationing of furniture ended in 1948, but the Utility scheme continued to operate until 1952, with more freedom in the design allowed as long as certain specifications and cost limits were adhered to. Even with fewer restrictions, though, most Harlow inhabitants had little choice. There were still severe shortages, which made it difficult to obtain new furniture even when the money was available. Houses were often furnished with a mixture of pieces inherited from families and bought second hand as well as new. Hire-purchase schemes offered by retail furnishing shops made it easier to buy new, though it didn't allow much choice either. Mr V. H., the Sheraton supervisor, said:

> You didn't have to sell furniture, it was just a matter of being able to supply it . . . We used to do hire purchase and cash but the vast majority of our business was hire purchase . . . we worked everything out over a two-year period, with something like a 10 per cent deposit . . . They bought a suite for 39 guineas and paid ten shillings a week or whatever it was. They bought what was going in the shop at a price they could afford . . . It's difficult to realise today how hard it was for families then to maintain a front room with a three-piece suite, dining-set and television, all on hire purchase.[38]

Under the circumstances it was impossible to produce the kind of interior which architects would have approved of – even had Harlow residents had the same values – as Mr A. M., the Harlow corporation architect, remarks:

> I've seen houses of young couples where there was a genuine interest . . . in modern stuff but it wasn't necessarily integrated. You'd probably find one or two nicer pieces of furniture that were quite modern and then on the floor you'd find the most awful blooming design of carpet which would ruin the whole thing.[39]

The lighter, more 'contemporary' style of furniture was taking over by the 1950s but the traditional matching suites or sets continued to be sold, in spite of attempts by designers to introduce the modular 'unit' furniture advocated by the Modern Movement: pieces that could be bought singly and built up into groups. When the Utility scheme was discontinued in 1952, cost and quality controls were lifted. Much of the industry adapted its production to cater for the lower-income market, to the detriment of quality and design. The smaller, lighter style of contemporary design was used to economise on material. The Harlow branch of Sheraton's consistently made the record sales figures for the group, but without any particular effort to improve standards. In fact, the make of furniture a shop chose to sell was often determined by the manufacturer who gave the best discounts.

Many women I interviewed were able to recall in great detail the acquisition of their first pieces of furniture and equipment. The three-piece suite was accorded great importance. Mrs C. S. bought her Utility suite in 1945:

> It was a beautiful suite . . . solid and very, very comfortable. I'll always remember, it was green, uncut moquette with a sort of Alexandra rose pattern on it in beige.[40]

Mrs D. S. still has her french-polished walnut bedroom suite, consisting of two wardrobes, a chest of drawers and dressing-table. Purchased in 1951, it was her first piece of non-Utility furniture. She paid £50 for it, having earned 'fantastic money' making gliders during the war, and the price must have included the luxury purchase tax in force at the time.[41]

Another tenant recalled the colour scheme of her hall and living-room and the arrival of her first fridge, acquired in 1957:

> We had a blood-red wallpaper on one wall and grey up the stairs. That was the height of fashion. When we managed to save up, we bought this long carpet . . . grey with red and black dashes all over it . . . Nobody else had a refrigerator round here . . . I felt sick with the excitement of it. I had refrigerator coming! And there it was – splendid in its packaging and ice-blue inside. It looked beautiful. I'd really arrived.[42]

The beauty she exclaims over had little to do with the official 'good design' rules, although for all we know the fridge in question may have been a model on show at the Design Centre. Opened in 1956, the Centre exhibited to the public the Council of Industrial Design's approved selection of designed products – provided the manufacturer agreed to pay for the privilege.

The observation made by one of Harlow's architects that the ways people furnished their houses 'were not expressions of taste but pride of ownership', perfectly illustrates the elitist criterion which requires taste to be value-free. It is sustained by the assumption that someone with taste is in command of specialised knowledge about how to discern beauty from abstract form, and therefore how to put together a scheme so that the elements make a cohesive or integrated whole. This concept can afford to disallow any association of beauty with so-called vulgar materialism because it speaks from a privileged position. Pierre Bourdieu uses this definition in his critical analysis of taste,[43] showing how it works as a vehicle for class distinctions: it separates the I-know-what-I-likes from the I-know-what-to-likes.

Bourdieu's class analysis of taste helps to put the design establishment's criteria into a social context which allows criticism of dominant cultural values that are not normally questioned. This type of analysis can show how all tastes fit within a hierarchical framework with 'high' taste as dominant and therefore the measure by which the others are judged. It can be applied to the front/back debate and explains why the tenants' choice to use net curtains caused so much official disapproval and appeared at the time to be so transgressional. But how does this help to acknowledge women's work as a contribution towards the design of the home?

[. . .]

> One of the things about the Harlow houses was that people took great pride in them. They may not have had much but what they had they looked after . . . the women spent years giving the furniture a high polish.[44]

> We were the homeworkers . . . We had to get on and make the best of everything that we could. That was taking pride in what you'd got. Everything was polished.[45]

'Pride' and 'polish' cropped up in tandem time and time again during interviews. They seemed to go together particularly in the fifties, when people still expected to buy things to last a lifetime. Women's pride in their work to maintain their homes through the care and arrangement of its furnishings appeared to be associated with a sense of pleasure which, though associated with display, was also intimately connected with work. Therefore it is necessary to consider the way in which the interiors were used, to get away from the static concept of taste as something that recognises only features which are supposedly inherent in the form of the object.

[. . .]

While both furniture and money were in short supply among Harlow residents in the early fifties, pride and polish were used to construct meanings. But by the beginning of the sixties the consumer society was in full swing and second-generation Harlow tenants like Mr and Mrs T., who set up house in 1961, were less traditional than their parents, more affluent and very fashion conscious:

> I can remember the three-piece suite – it was uncut moquette, grey and mustard . . . we had a purple carpet . . . an orange wall . . . it was very modern. Mum and Dad didn't think it was up to much. I think it's awful now – some of those things we had . . . my father-in-law made us a cocktail bar . . . with white quilting on the front, and it had sort of Formica marble contact stuff on top . . . And everything had those screw-on legs. We bought a Pye radiogram and that had black screw-on legs as well . . . Once we couldn't afford any wallpaper so George painted the wall white and we got saucepan lids, even the dustbin lid, and with a black pen he drew circles and triangles all over this white wall. That looked fantastic and everyone said, 'Oh God, he's so artistic'. He's a butcher! We used to sit down and think up all these ideas . . . We loved furniture . . . that's all we used to do, walk around looking at furniture . . .[46]

There is little doubt that display as well as function played a part in the way Harlow tenants furnished and cared for their houses. They were making the places their own through the use of design. The way many chose to take possession, metaphorically speaking – because at the time housing was still rented from the Corporation – was to invest their own values, often knowingly in contravention of the approved official line. This involved replacing permanent fixtures, such as fireplaces, with models of their own choice, closing off open-plan areas and furnishing in reproduction style in spite of propaganda to throw away 'bulky white elephants'. Windows designed by architects to let in light were veiled behind Venetian blinds and layers of curtains, topped with double pelmets and an array of ornaments. Through the appropriation of privacy by the concealment of the interior from the uninvited gaze, people took control of their own interior space and at the same time made a public declaration of their variance from the architects' design.

[. . .]

This study of Harlow has been an attempt to record a part of its history which gives credit to the women pioneers who helped to make it into a home and a community, and transformed New Town into Pram Town – a place they could call their own.

Notes

1. This quotation, like others used here, comes from a series of taped interviews with residents and persons involved in the early days of Harlow. The interviews were carried out in 1982 and 1986 and are now housed in the New Town Record Centre.
2. The term 'pram town' was first used by the national press in 1952, when 35 live births per 1,000 population were recorded in Harlow, twice the national average.
3. J. Nicholson, 'Two generations of new towns', *Social Science Quarterly*, Winter issue, 1967/8.
4. J. Maude Richards, 'Failure of the new towns', *Architectural Review*, July 1953. In this article Richards attacked the new towns for their lack of urbanity: 'the Reith Committee, on whose report the New Towns Act was based, had in mind a picture of a scattered garden-suburb type of town . . . If by urbanity we mean the sense of being part of a built-up community, then noone standing in a typical neighbourhood of a new town, taking in the vast deserts of roadway verges and pavements rimmed with little houses dwindling acre by acre into the far distance, can say that the new towns . . . are, as attempts to create new urban communities, anything except a failure.' For an account of the architecture of the modern welfare state, see K. Frampton, *A Critical History of Modern Architecture*, London: Thames and Hudson, 1980, pp. 262–8.
5. J. Nicholson, op. cit.
6. Interview with Mrs D. S.
7. Interview with Mrs V. T.
8. N. Pevsner, *The Englishness of English Art*, Harmondsworth: Penguin, 1984, pp. 173–92.
9. E. Howard, *Garden Cities of Tomorrow*, London: Faber and Faber, 1946.
10. L. Davidoff, J. L'Esperance and H. Newby, 'Landscape with figures: Home and community in English society', in J. Mitchell and A. Oakley, *The Rights and Wrongs of Women*, Harmondsworth: Penguin, 1976.
11. In 1909, Ebenezer Howard constructed 'Homesgarth', 32 kitchenless apartments in a co-operative quadrangle at Letchworth. See D. Hayden, *The Grand Domestic Revolution: A history of feminist designs for American homes, neighborhoods and cities*, Cambridge, MA: MIT Press, 1981.
12. 'Utility furniture and fashion, 1914–1951', Exhibition catalogue, Geffrye Museum, 1974; see also G. Russell, *How To Buy Furniture*, Council of Industrial Design, 1947.
13. F. MacCarthy, *A History of British Design, 1830–1970*, London: Allen and Unwin, 1972, p. 93.
14. The quotation is taken from a report in the *Harlow Citizen*, 1 February 1957, on a discussion at the St Paul's Women's Fellowship in which the 'benefits and drawbacks of Harlow' were discussed. 'Benefits . . . were good, clean homes and healthy atmosphere for their

children. The main drawback, they all agreed, was the architecture of the houses. Those were described as being "back to front and inside out" but none of the women wanted to leave Harlow.'

15. E. Denby, 'Plan the Home', *Picture Post*, 4 January 1941, p. 21.
16. Ibid.
17. Interview with Mrs D. S.
18. Interview with Mrs V. T.
19. 'Focus on British design', *Design*, 121, 1959, p. 33.
20. 'Furnishing in the new towns', *Design*, 98, 1957, p. 43.
21. *Harlow Citizen*, 15 and 22 July 1955.
22. Interview with Mr V. H.
23. E. Goffman, *The Presentation of Self in Everyday Life*, Harmondsworth: Penguin, 1980.
24. L. Davidoff, J. L'Esperance and H. Newby, op. cit., p. 154
25. Interview with Mrs D. S.
26. See A. Ravetz, 'A view from the interior', in J. Attfield and P. Kirkham, eds, *A View from the Interior: Feminism, women and design*, London: The Women's Press, 1989.
27. D. Chapman, *The Home and Social Status*, London: Routledge and Kegan Paul, 1955, p. 58.
28. Quoted in Matrix, ed., *Making Space: Women and the man-made environment*, London: Pluto Press, 1984, p. 29.
29. Ibid.
30. Interview with Mrs C. S.
31. Interview with Mrs C. E.
32. Interview with Mr J. D.
33. Interview with Mrs V. T.
34. Interview with Mrs C. E.
35. Interview with Mrs D. S.
36. Interview with Mr A. M.
37. Ibid.
38. Interview with Mr V. H.
39. Interview with Mr A. M.
40. Interview with Mrs C. S.
41. Interview with Mrs D. S.
42. Interview with Mrs V. T.
43. P. Bourdieu, *Distinction: A social critique of the judgement of taste*, London: Routledge and Kegan Paul, 1984, pp. 11–96.
44. Interview with Mr V. H.
45. Interview with Mrs V. T.
46. Interview with Mrs B. T.

5.3 □ *Pauline Hunt*

Pauline Hunt examines the numerous ways in which a sense of home is actively constructed – from the choice of decor to the physical labour involved. She looks at dimensions of both class and gender in the transformation of houses into homes. In addition, her piece discusses contradictions between the home as a public statement of taste and as a private locus of comfort, as a place of women's work and men's leisure.

Gender and the construction of home life

In England for cultural, and possibly climatic, reasons most interpersonal relationships take place behind closed doors. Domestic life is not readily available for investigation. What really goes on in most people's homes remains a mystery, an intriguing and frustrating mystery:

> There is hardly a garden in England which is not surrounded by wall or hedge or railing, the obscurer the better . . . There is hardly a window in any family house which is not curtained effectively to obscure the view of the inquisitive passer-by. And as a consequence there is no play or book or film so successful as that which deals with the intimacies of family life, which, except in one family – his or her own – are a complete mystery to the ordinary man or woman.[1]

As a consequence the would-be investigator is at a loss even to devise pertinent questions. Some years ago in an attempt to grapple with this situation I supplied five professional middle-class households and five manual working-class households with instamatic cameras. I requested them to photograph aspects of their home environment that they particularly valued. The first round of interviews were based on these photographs, which had the merit that the subjects of the research formulated the initial agenda. They, not I, decided the topics of conversation. At a later stage I took some photographs myself and conducted interviews along more systematic and orthodox lines. Much of what follows draws on the experiences of these ten households.

Gender expectations and core-concerns

Men and women confront different social expectations and realities in the performance of their role as husband or wife. It is still the prevailing expectation that men will provide the main financial contribution to their family; and in practice this expectation becomes a moral requirement that the individual man may experience painfully if circumstances, such as unemployment, prevent its fulfilment. Furthermore his self-definition and conception are usually directly related to his occupation and to his ability to provide financial support to his family.

Social expectations for married women, especially mothers, centre on their domestic contribution. They are expected to exercise home-making skills and nurture their young. Husbands may well 'help' with this, but the main responsibility resides with the person being helped. Furthermore even when her financial contribution equals, surpasses or replaces that of her husband, her self-definition and conception usually remain anchored in her domestic role.

This different social perspective for men and women permeates domestic practice. Several men in my enquiry worked regularly in the garden. They did so by choice. The separation of their socially obligatory work from their domestic life had the effect of highlighting the home as an arena of freedom wherein work is transformed into play. [. . .]

Repair and maintenance jobs may confront men as a chore, but in contrast to the woman's daily round of repetitive domestic work they tend to be one-off or irregular jobs. When his wife is absent or ill he may take on some of 'her' work-load, yet the responsibility remains hers, for almost any work a male breadwinner does at home is beyond the call of duty, that is beyond the requirements of his social role. No social compulsion is involved.

Domestic coercion

For most breadwinners paid work is the direct opposite of home life. His toil in industry is rarely experienced as productive leisure, primarily because his paid work seems to be as unavoidable for him as his wife's domestic work seems to be unavoidable for her.

The unavoidability of the breadwinner's paid work is not simply an economic matter; it is experienced as a duty because his standing in the eyes of his family, and the community, is conventionally measured in terms of his ability to provide his family with economic security. The home-maker's domestic work is similarly experienced by her as an inescapable duty. At first glance a houseworker, especially a full-time houseworker, would seem to be largely free of social pressure in the performance of her highly privatised job. The main influence on her performance would seem to come from the recipients of her labours – her own family members. Certainly a large part of her job is geared to the accommodation of her family's needs and desires. Yet the wider community makes itself felt, and not only through the pressure of expectations exerted upon her by neighbours, her husband's kin and work associates, and the parents of her children's school friends and their adult associates. There is also a more general pressure resulting from her perception of her domestic role in society, which tends to be reinforced through cultural images and messages relating to domestic practice. [. . .]

The wishes of her own family constrain the houseworker's freedom to set her own standards. The most frequently encountered family preference concerns a desire for a relaxed attitude towards order and spruceness. Sometimes this is seen in terms of masculine authority:

> *Mr Scott*:   Have you ever been in a home where you have a house proud woman? Where the husband, and usually they are little men, you know hen-pecked, they sit on a chair and they daren't move . . . in case the wife gets on to them, either about not sitting properly, or putting the paper down. Things like that. It wouldn't do me. There would be more bothers than enough if she started that. But there are houses like that. I know quite a lot.

This sounds as though Mrs Scott has to conform or else. Yet Mrs Scott, like the other women I talked with, genuinely felt that it was undesirable that family members should constantly feel the need to be on their best behaviour. This would contradict the basic notion of what being at home meant. In the main, houseworkers would rather tidy up disorder than establish the kind of regime that would inhibit disorder being created in the first place.

This was the message of the interviews. It was not the message of the photographs, which illustrated the houseworkers' concern with the second, the publicly oriented, source of constraint. Most of the women respondents went out of their way to clean and tidy before taking, or permitting others to take, photographs of their home. Similarly some of the homes were put in order for my visits. So the homes in the photographs, and as I saw them, appeared to be particularly well-kept.

The contradiction between the visual and verbal sources of information point in my view to a contradiction between family (private) norms, and what are seen to be the social (public) norms which define the houseworker's job. She wants her home to be seen (publicly scrutinised) as clean and tidy, and at the same time she wants it to be experienced (privately appreciated) as free and easy. The houseworker's practice tries to reconcile these contradictory objectives. When family members are home she does not veto their disorder-creating behaviour but she constantly re-establishes order since, as Mrs Carter said: 'You never know who may come.' If someone should call and see the disorder, she has no doubt which family member will be held to have fallen short of her duty.

In the privacy of her own home she is sensitive to potential public scrutiny. Since she decides how to translate this sensitivity into domestic practice the standards she sets seem to be of her own making. It is as though she makes a rod for her own back. If the work gets her down she seems to have only herself to blame. The impression that her duties are self-imposed results from the privatised nature of domestic work. In fact the houseworker's duties in the home are a socially ascribed role which bind her in the same way as her husband is bound by his labour market duties.

Services provided

The home-maker's skills are directed towards others – towards meeting the needs of family members. This means that when the recipients of her labour are away from home, at work or at school, the home may be far from homely. In winter it may be cold if the homeworker is economising on fuel bills. Wet washing may be around, furniture may be out of place while cleaning is in process, hot meals are unlikely to be cooked 'just' for the houseworker on her own either now or in the past.[2] A transformation occurs when the recipients of her labour return; the house is warm, welcoming and in order, and a hot meal will shortly be served. This transformation may be taken for granted or expected.[3]

Thus much of the work of providing home comforts remains hidden from the recipients of those comforts. This is less true if the homeworker is employed full-time outside the home, in which case the weekend, far from presenting an opportunity to relax, represents an opportunity to catch up on domestic chores. Even for the full-time houseworker the family's presence at weekends leads to an increase in some chores, notably cooking and tidying.

A full-time houseworker is likely to organise her home to fit in with her husband's work timetable, and her children's school routines. If she does take on a paid job she will try to ensure that it is compatible with the externally imposed timetables of family members. She will, in other words, seek a job that fits in with her domestic duties.[4] The hallmark of a houseworker's relationship to her husband and children is her availability. She puts herself at their disposal. Her time is tailored to their needs. This is why, as Oakley has said, the image of someone waiting epitomises the social situation of a housewife and mother.[5] She waits for her husband's arrival to serve the meal, she waits on the family at table, she waits by the swings and at the school gate, she waits for the baby to fall asleep. And all this waiting expresses subordination, for it is those with most power who command the time of others.[6]

Class factors will enter into this picture, in relation for example to child-rearing practices:

> A woman wants to be a good mother and aims at giving herself to her children selflessly, providing them with concentrated attention, generous care, a lively mind quick to offer stimulus of an appropriate kind, perfectly balanced and delicious meals, unlimited time, and unstinted love. . . But the constructive play turns into a litter of cardboard boxes all over the kitchen, tacky flour and water paste in the coconut matting, and finger paints on the curtains. The carefully prepared food is rejected with noises of disgust from the older child and is simply expelled from the baby's mouth as a great glob of goo.[7]

The working-class mother is likely to be saved this frustrating lack of co-operation since her investment of time is unlikely to take the form of planning for and consciously extending the range of her offspring's experiences. The time she devotes to her children is best expressed by the phrase 'being on call'. She puts herself at their disposal.

Class differences are also observable at mealtimes. James Littlejohn found for example that upper-class housewives control the distribution of food, whereas the working-class wife 'performs a servant-like role during the meal'.[8] She manages to consume her food in between the interruptions required in order to meet her family's requirements.

Self-identity

The houseworker's occupation is so geared to meeting the needs of her family that the identification of her own needs, separate from theirs, becomes blurred. This is apparent in relation to the use of domestic space. Children and husbands usually have a territory of their own within the home. Children have their own rooms, or, if they share a room, their own part of a room; their own desk or cupboard. Husbands may have a shed or garage to work or relax in, a hobbies room in the house, or the garden may be seen as their particular domain. Now that the days of handbag-carrying women have largely drawn to a close, houseworkers rarely have a clearly marked-out personal territory – although for some the dressing-table may be a non-transportable handbag equivalent. The kitchen is frequently seen as the woman's room and yet, particularly if meals are consumed in the kitchen, it remains a family room which is not comparable to the husband's den.

Why is it desirable to have personal territory? Two obvious answers spring to mind: in order to have a place where it is possible to engage in personal activities relatively undisturbed; and a place where personal possessions may be stored. Neither of these obvious answers was obvious to the houseworkers I talked with. Most of them interpreted questions about the need to have a place to be on their own as questions about feeling depressed. Then the response was in terms of going into the bedroom for a good cry, or taking a long hot bath. Frequently they found questions about personal territory baffling: 'I'm on my own a lot here in the daytime when the children are at school'.

Similarly few houseworkers had personal items of property – clothing and jewellery apart – distinct from general household goods. The strong identification between the houseworker as a person and her home is reflected in the type of gifts she receives. Household items, or items that will be enjoyed collectively in a family setting, are frequently seen as appropriate gifts for the housewife. Ornaments, rugs, table-ware, domestic utensils, pot plants, etc. would almost always be given as gifts to the woman of the house – not the man. For him it is more appropriate to give gifts that he will enjoy consuming individually, or that fit in with his particular interests, tobacco, drink, an item of sports equipment, or a book, for example. As a result the need for personal territory seems remote to many houseworkers:

Pauline: Do you ever feel the need to have somewhere to put your own things?
Mrs Holland: These are my own things. (*Her hand sweeps round indicating all the furnishings in the house.*)
Pauline: And you don't feel the need for a room like Peter's [Mr Holland's]?
Mrs Holland: No. Like Peter has got his own personal things, not private, but things he's had before and since he's been married, upstairs. I haven't. Like this is my room, the house sort of thing.

In this situation the objects that houseworkers cherish most are 'signs of ties that bind the family together'.[9] A china cabinet often expresses close ties between the home-maker and her family, and is valued by her precisely for this reason – *Mrs Scott*: 'I like the whole thing, because that cabinet it's got something from everyone in the family, plus friends and relations, that has'.

The lack of personal territory and property, and the lack of a felt need for such, is expressive of the extent to which the houseworker's self-identity becomes submerged in the job of caring for others. She may remain fairly contented with her lot so long as the cared-for others constitute an appreciative audience for her labours. Yet the arrival of children often brings about a polarisation of gender roles within the house-hold, and the interests and lifestyle of the husband and wife begin to diverge. Over time such divergence can lead the breadwinner to regard the home-maker's efforts with indifference. In these circumstances when the offspring leave home the homeworker is left without an audience, and the meaning goes out of the home-making task.

Csikszentmihalyi and Rochberg-Halton noted the importance of the husband's interest in domestic matters.

> In those families where the husband expressed positive affect towards the home, 73 per cent of the wives also did; in those where the husband was neutral, only 46 per cent of the wives were positive; and of the ten families without husbands, in only one did the wife have a positive view of the home.[10]

Occasionally the houseworker may relish the scope for unilateral control that her husband's indifference affords her: *Mrs Poskier*: 'I run the home. If I say no, it's no!' Yet Mrs Poskier's home-making skills were not without an audience, for her teenage children were still living at home at the time of the interviews. When they leave to establish homes of their own, her domestic management skills may well be experienced as less satisfying and more meaningless. Then, like Mrs Scott, most of her satisfaction may come from visiting her children in their own homes. Yet this is an inadequate substi-tute in a world of nuclear families where homes are seen as the domain of the married couple, and where they operate as separate establishments.[11] Since Mrs Scott is not the focal point of her children's households, and her own house lacks an appreciative audience, she comes close to being emotionally homeless.

Domestic autonomy

Despite confronting the houseworker as a social necessity home-making contains emotional rewards and fulfilments. Planning is a central feature of the job. Home-makers spend a lot of time planning meals and ensuring that favourite items appear on the menu. They store up treats for the children, and activities for them to do on a rainy day. They organise the switch from summer to winter clothing; putting away and bringing out items as the season requires, and they check that each family member has a suitable range of clothes and footwear.

These organising activities reach a peak as special occasions approach. House-workers anticipate the holiday needs of each family member. Birthday festivities are painstakingly prepared, and purchases and preparations for Christmas begin months before Advent, even a whole year before if the houseworker is a member of a Christmas club. All this is work, but work tinged with a joyful anticipation of the pleasure that will be the result. [. . .]

Decisions concerning the purchase of food items give the home-maker further influence over family members. Also in her relationship with her children she has the power to make them happy or otherwise. Her position of influence may well find expression in her aesthetic preferences. So, for example, Mrs Holland values a framed print of a crying boy. There are several versions of crying boy pictures on sale in High Street shops and market stalls. Mrs Holland's picture, like most of them, shows a boy with tears on his cheeks set against a plain indeterminate background. His clothes do not give a precise clue as to either date or place. His head is lit from above, and his hands reach out inviting comfort; an invitation Mrs Holland responds to: 'I always want to pick up the child and love it because it's crying.'

Given the gender division of labour that characterises our society it is usually the mother who would comfort a child, and the possession of the ability to comfort is a source of pleasure. In other relationships one's intervention does not have such a direct or intense effect. Indeed many of the circumstances surrounding Mrs Holland's life are quite outside her control. The power of mothering is an isolated and confined power but Mrs Holland can relive it every time she looks at this picture.

It does not seem all that surprising that this ability directly to influence the lives of family members should be jealously guarded, although in 1939 Margery Spring Rice did find it surprising:

> Indeed a curious phenomenon in the position of women is that those who most need some measure of freedom from the restrictions of family duties, are often the first to resist the legislation which might give it to them. They are passionately jealous of any usurpation or delegation of their own authority.
>
> Examples of this are provided in the great difficulty which occurs in persuading women to go into hospital for their confinements. Although trained home helps can be provided to look after father and children the mother shows an inherent disinclination to entrust her home even temporarily to the care of someone else.[12]

Although the home-maker can experience great pleasure in the caring role she exercises in relation to her own family, the privatised nature of the household can mean that caring stops there. If she and other family members turn their concern and protectiveness inwards towards their own household, this may represent a simultaneous turning away from the welfare of the wider community, as Barrett and McIntosh[13] have argued. Conversely though, Csikszentmihalyi and Rochberg-Halton have found that it is the recipients of the loving care of family-oriented women who become most involved in community activities.[14]

Domestic artistic expression

The arrangement of domestic furnishings and the style of the home represent a form of artistic expression created by the homeworker. If several young children are at home, or when a mother attempts to combine paid work with running a home, the effort to keep the house in order can be experienced as a desperate struggle against dirt and chaos, rather than as the creative process of renewal described by Bachelard:

> A house that shines from the care it receives appears to have been rebuilt from the inside; it is as though it were new inside. In the intimate harmony of walls and furniture, it may be said that we become conscious of a house that is built by women, since men only know how to build a house from the outside, and they know little or nothing of the wax civilisation. . . And what a great life it would be if, every morning, every object in the house could be made anew by our hands, could 'issue', from our hands.[15]

Yet as soon as the pressure of keeping household mess in check eases, the creative process of home-making comes to the fore. Bachelard's 'wax civilisation' may be more applicable to professional middle-class homes containing furniture that will mellow rather than become shoddy with age. Even so, in working-class homes the composition of the home, the colour scheme, the arrangement and selection of ornaments and furnishings, the use of light and shade and space combine to express the artistic skills of the home-maker. Most of the interviews I conducted took place in settings bulging with visual evidence of the home-maker's deep aesthetic involvement in the domestic environment.

Jean E. Hess[16] in her study of domestic interiors in Northern New Mexico found a well established set of aesthetic practices and values. The women

> believe that the 'neutral' furnishings (couches, curtains, etc.) should always match. Women carefully plan the purchase of these larger items, leaving little to chance. Against the background of an emphasised color scheme, touches of brighter color are scattered. . . 'Brightness' is a word recurring often. . . But an article is 'bright' and 'shining' only if it is clean. Women devote as much time as possible to dusting, sweeping and straightening their homes. . . Women often purchase or make decorations in twos or threes so that they can be arranged symmetrically . . . The balancing and clustering of objects seem to help control clutter, imposing order on potential chaos . . . doilies and cloths serve to mediate between objects, protecting one object (a table or cabinet) from another (a plant or lamp). The theme of mediation or protection is in turn elaborated into a theme of covering. Lacework may cover whole shelves, small rugs or serapes cover furniture which is already upholstered, and a large carpet is protected by smaller ones, placed where people are most apt to walk.[17]

I have found similar aesthetic practices employed in the creation of working-class homes, which were characterised by ornamentation, warm textures and sometimes warm bright colours. The emphasis on warmth extended to clothing and food. The working-class definition of a main meal continued to be a hot substantial dish. The provision of this, and a warm house to welcome incoming family members, constituted the core of the houseworker's home-making duty.

There was also a preference for modern and new materials, so that the environment and its contents were changed every few years, involving much redecorating and the purchase of new furniture and furnishings. I found that curtains and cushion covers were likely to be changed even more frequently. There was a readiness to use artificial materials which resembled, but did not masquerade as, their non-artificial equivalent. Thus plastic flowers and wallpaper resembling stones or wood were frequently encountered in working-class homes. There was a tendency to cover and decorate, so that lavatory seats and stands were often surrounded by fluffy mats; flowerpots and paper-handkerchief boxes were covered in decorative material; frills or bobbles were often added to lampshades or curtains.

Contrasting class cultures

In an afterword to Hess's article on domestic interiors in New Mexico the editors suggest that the care and skill employed in the creation of such environments should be studied as a form of process art.[18] I think this is clearly so, but would add that cultural and especially class factors should be taken into account in the study of domestic process art. In my own enquiry I found that professional homes exhibit opposite traits from those identified above. The basic decor and furnishings were not frequently changed. There was a preference for furniture that would age well, and could therefore be kept for long periods, and possibly be handed on to future generations. I found a preference for plain and subdued colours, unadorned surfaces, simplicity of design and uncluttered space. Synthetic materials, particularly plastic products, were abhorred when used as substitute materials; thus plastic combs were acceptable but not plastic vases or flowers.

I think that when households are short of money this contrasting aesthetic approach is accentuated. For example, if a household of students from professional homes could not afford the kind of picture frame they wanted, which would probably be plain wood or metal, they would be far more likely to display their pictures unframed than to buy a cheap substitute frame. If 'nice' ashtrays could not be afforded tin-cans may be provided, or as Anna Coote reported, a carved wooden spoon stuck in a bottle may serve as an ornament.[19] Such improvisations have clearly cost nothing. They demonstrate an unwillingness to purchase cheap but 'nasty' substitutes for expensive goods, and by so doing they commemorate the good taste of the owner who, it seems, prefers to go without rather than to buy something which is not worth having.

Poor working-class households are much more likely to resort to cheaper versions of the desired product. The difference between what they purchase and what they wanted will not be primarily one of design and colour but of the material from which the product is made. So, for example, both prosperous and poor working-class homes may favour ornate gold picture frames, but in the former households the frames will be painted carved wood, and in the latter they will be moulded plastic that has been spray painted.

When cheaper substitute materials are employed in working-class homes this is rarely with an intention to fool anyone. Such households are not trying to appear to be other than they are. The substitutes merely enable household members to approach the effect they desired at a price they can afford. Furthermore, since in all probability the furnishings and decor will be changed within a few years, it makes little sense to use very costly materials.

I think that when trying to understand the basis of such class-related aesthetic preferences it is useful to ask from what the groups in question are trying to distance themselves. In the case of manual workers the first answer is obviously cold weather. The work of many working-class men takes place either out of doors or in cold uncomfortable circumstances, and warmth as expressed in texture, colour, covering, heat and food will continue to be prized so long as this is the case.

Secondly, economic want, and the more remote prospect of homelessness and destitution, continue to cast a shadow of insecurity over working-class lives. Although the stark and austere image of the workhouse, and the powerlessness inflicted upon inmates, is now a relic of the past, emotionally it symbolises the quality of life from which working-class people distance themselves when they make their homes. The right to be free of restrictions within the privacy of the home, the velvet-embossed wallpaper, the thick pile carpet, the up-to-date furnishings, the radiant fire (albeit a gas or an electric fire with an open grate façade), the substantial steak-and-kidney pie in the oven, the decorative ornaments and bright colours combine to clothe and protect, and to demonstrate that one is protected, from the cold winters of want, and the power of external authorities. The use of such blanketing as an insurance policy against destitution, that can be stripped off layer by layer in times of hardship is graphically illustrated by Hogarth in *A Harlot's Progress*, and tellingly described by Elizabeth Gaskell in *Mary Barton*.

It is usual in works of sociology to see the upper social ranks as setting cultural trends which are emulated by the ranks below them. Young and Willmott's study *The Symmetrical Family*[20] may serve as an example of this approach. But if one is less concerned with fashion and more concerned with identifying cultural ideologies, it may be wiser to look in the other direction and ask from what or whom are people trying to distance themselves. When this perspective is applied to professional middle-class groups it can be seen that the trend setter, in inverted form, is the working class. Professional middle-class decor is the opposite of working-class decor because the former are concerned to distinguish themselves from the latter. This is why consumer-durables long since rejected by the working class in favour of the protective aura surrounding modern goods are sometimes reclaimed by the professional middle class. Not only have such objects, given their age, acquired a scarcity value, they also represent objects that no longer grace working-class homes.

Ownership

I looked at the photograph Mr Carter had taken of his wife outside their house. Through her efforts their house was experienced as a home. That was her achievement. The house was also her place of confinement. In the photograph she is shown outside the house but within its jurisdiction. That represented her life situation. She is turned towards her husband who is taking the photograph. Her gaze is downwards. Subjectively she was totally within the situation. Mr Carter has photographed his wife leaning on the gate he had stripped down ready to paint. She is at the entrance of the house he has paid for. She stands in front of the car he uses every day to drive to and from work, in order to earn the money to support himself and his family in their home. That was his achievement.

As owners and consumers they had secured a degree of control over their lives; they could make choices. Of course through its privatised nature this form of self-expression is very limited, especially so for the home-maker who has few other means of self-expression available to her. 'It is unfair that she should receive feedback to her own self mainly from the restricted circle of the family, whereas her husband and children, fortified by her attention, can turn to the wider arena of public life to reap rewards and confirmation of their skills.'[21] The editors of Hess's article on domestic interiors feel the same way:

> The home was our only kingdom. . . If we want our energy and strength to go into other channels, we have to work at a transitional solution which may deprive us of a personal world altogether . . . we have to cope with our deep-seated, deeply instilled sense of responsibility. That means finding a more creative way of love and collaboration, of educating our children, or caring for a house, and we have to convince those we love that there are other ways of accomplishing these things.[22]

Families have a huge emotional stake in the status quo, and unless the 'more creative way' is clearly defined and looks achievable little is likely to change. In working-class homes in particular the domestic interior expresses being on the receiving end of a mother's love. While the emotional rewards for the mother herself are limited to the feedback she gets from her own family, she was in the past a recipient of the caring environment created by her own mother. Thus the emotional roots of the home she creates reach back into her own childhood. Perhaps this enables her to relive her childhood in a way that is not so readily available to most men.

[. . .]

Commitment to the status quo is fuelled by the fact that within the confines of private ownership the houseworker and her family can give expression to their lives, relatively free of interference. As Stuart Hall has said, 'At least you aren't required to tug your forelock and look "deserving" as you approach the till.'[23] As an owner and consumer within the jealously guarded privacy of the home one is largely free from the potentially damaging scrutiny of external authorities. Too often for working-class people the receipt of benefits and allowance has been tied to a paternalistic inspection of, and intrusion into, the household's domestic practice. Small wonder that there has been a tendency to keep the world at bay behind hedges, gates and curtains. The ability to decide one's own practice within the hard-won privacy of the home was emphasised by the housewives interviewed by Oakley: 'many used this phrase "you're your own boss" to describe the housewife's feelings of being in control'.[24]

In modern capitalist society property ownership confers the right to be in control. Anthony D. King in his study of *The Bungalow*[25] quotes a study of old people's homes in Britain[26] which concluded that it was not the design of facilities to which residents objected but the fact that they did not have exclusive (property) rights over their use.

As property owners people can exercise a direct, if marginalised, control over their lives. The margins of this control can be widened by redefining the rights of owners and users on a community-wide basis, as in the community architecture movement.[27]

And the margins of control within the cherished territory of the private household can be re-defined. One household that I studied was based on an outstandingly egalitarian relationship. It was a two-woman household. The ownership of personal property, notably books and records, was strictly delineated. Each had her own private space within the house, and the organisation, arrangement and use of joint space was extensively discussed between them:

> *Delia*: I quite often come across Pat reading, and I quite often say 'Do you mind if I sit and either half chatter to you or just be around while you are reading?' I mean we actually ask each other, and she will say 'yes' or 'no'.

In most other households the presence of family members in communal rooms passed without comment. Indeed it seems to be usual for little or no thought to be given to the way adult family members interact with one another and utilise the home environment. When thought is given it tends to be after the event, when someone is displeased by the way things have worked out. By and large established patterns of behaviour between adult family members are taken for granted; that is to say a large chunk of domestic practice confronts the individual as part of the given world. By contrast Pat and Delia exercise considerable control over their environment. Almost all changes and forms of association are consciously explored with a view to arriving at a mutually acceptable practice. They are both aware that their consciously evolved domestic practice is the outgrowth of their political involvement; and in turn their creation of a cherished domestic territory strengthens their capacity to be involved in community politics.

Inequalities between men and women, and between adults and children, characterise most households; inequalities concerning access to financial resources; inequalities in the use of space; in the use of time; in the development of personal interests and pursuits. These inequalities create barriers to the conscious use of the home as a means of extending control over the domestic environment. The rights of property owners and users are not individual rights in any but single-person households. In so far as egalitarian domestic practices can be evolved a basis for collective control of the household is thereby created that may well have an impact on the practice of family members in the wider community.

Notes

1. M. Spring Rice, *Working Class Wives*, London: Virago, 1981.
2. M. Roberts, 'Private kitchens, public cooking', in Matrix, ed., *Making Space: Women and the man-made environment*, London: Pluto Press, 1984.
3. N. Dennis, F. Henriques and C. Slaughter, *Coal is Our Life*, London: Tavistock, 1969.
4. C. Adams and R. Laurikietis, *Education and Work: The gender trap*. London: Virago, 1976.

5. A. Oakley, *Becoming a Mother*, Oxford: Martin Robertson, 1979, p. 11.
6. R. Frankenburg, 'Time for the subject? Time of the subject? Time in the subject?: Medical anthropology and clinical medicine disentangled', Keele University: Centre for Medical Social Anthropology, 1986.
7. S. Kitzinger, *Women as Mothers*, London: Fontana, 1978, p. 43.
8. J. Littlejohn, *Westrigg: The sociology of a Cheviot parish*, London: Routledge and Kegan Paul, 1963, pp. 127–9.
9. M. Csikszentmihalyi and E. Rochberg-Halton, *The Meaning of Things: Domestic symbols and the self*, Cambridge: Cambridge University Press, 1981.
10. Ibid., p. 133.
11. E. Shorter, *The Making of the Modern Family*, London: Fontana, 1979.
12. M. Spring Rice, op. cit., p. 14.
13. M. Barrett and M. McIntosh, *The Anti-Social Family*, London: Verso, 1982.
14. M. Csikszentmihalyi and E. Rochberg-Halton, op. cit., pp. 146–55.
15. G. Bachelard, *The Poetics of Space*, Boston: Beacon Press, 1969, pp. 68–9.
16. J. E. Hess, 'Domestic interiors in Northern New Mexico', *Heresies*, 3: 30–3, 1981.
17. Ibid., pp. 31 –2.
18. Ibid., p. 32.
19. *The Guardian*, 19 May 1977.
20. M. Young and P. Wilmott, *The Symmetrical Family*, Harmondsworth: Penguin, 1975.
21. M. Csikszentmihalyi and E. Rochberg-Halton, op. cit., p. 168.
22. J. E. Hess, op. cit., p. 33.
23. S. Hall, 'The culture gap', *Marxism Today*, 28: 18–21, 1984, p. 19.
24. A. Oakley, *The Sociology of Housework*, Oxford: Martin Robertson, 1974, p. 42.
25. A. D. King. *The Bungalow*, London: Routledge and Kegan Paul, 1984.
26. S. Peace, 'The balance of residential life: A study of 100 old people's homes', Paper to the British Sociological Association Conference on Sociology and the Environment, 1982.
27. C. Knevitt and N. Wates, *Community Architecture*, Harmondsworth: Penguin, 1987.

5.4 □ *Ondina Fachel Leal*

Ondina Fachel Leal deals here with different systems of appropriation and display which are in evidence in urban Brazilian households. She starts with a detailed inter-pretation of artefacts in a working-class home – where an entourage of decorative objects accompanies the television set – and goes on to compare this setting with the layout that is typically found in middle-class domestic interiors.

Popular taste and erudite repertoire: the place and space of television in Brazil

I will discuss the notion of beauty as it is represented through various material objects, the television set being one of them, in the houses of people from two different social classes in Brazil.

Culture is understood here as signifying practice, as structures of socially signifi-cant meaning. I am concerned with the logic of everyday life, and the way cultural forms – such as taste – find their articulations in situations of daily life.

The data I will be referring to here are parts of the ethnographic research I conducted in Porto Alegre, Brazil [. . .].[1] In that work I sought to reconstruct how a single mass-media message is watched, understood and re-elaborated by structurally differentiated individuals. [. . .] I analyzed the role of the television, the television set as an object, one soap opera and the viewer's perception and retelling of the soap opera narratives.

I worked with two groups of families; one from the professional upper middle class and the other from the working class (blue-collar workers). Each group occupies a struc-turally different position in a very hierarchical social context. [. . .] I concluded that the matrix of meanings of a mass-media text was not the message itself but the concrete experiences of the people, their life histories, their life projects, their class position, and their social contextualization.

[. . .]

The main argument of this paper is that the place of the TV set in people's lives, and

314

the place of the TV set in their home in Brazil (probably as everywhere else), are intimately related.

[. . .]

The place of things

While doing my fieldwork, I realized that there was something very important that I had been taking for granted all along. To illustrate this let me relate to you a field anecdote. In one of the suburban working-class houses where I was doing my work, the living room was being renovated. Among the changes was the relocation of the front door. With the change in the door position, the family relocated the place of the TV set in the room. The explanation given to me was that they had to change it because the new door would not allow the TV set to be seen. In fact, the door would not hide the TV screen from those who were watching TV inside the room. What was important was that the new door position would not allow the TV set to be seen from outside the house, that is from the street.

Significantly all the decorative objects that were displayed close to the TV were moved along with it to the other corner of the room: they followed it as an *entourage*, as interconnected pieces of one coherent set. The accidental fact of my presence during the moving of the TV set revealed that the place of the TV and the place of all decorative objects are not arbitrary. They confer upon each other, as parts of a system, relational properties and significance.

The choice of arrangement of these knickknacks illustrates the fact that objects are not ontologically meaningful in themselves, but human action is inherently symbolic. In social life we are actors defining cultural constituents, building up meanings, transforming material objects into cultural objects. [. . .]

A system of meanings

The objects around the TV set in the home that I just mentioned (where the objects were rearranged when the door was moved) were typical of a working-class neighborhood in Brazil, and the analysis is generalizable. These objects conform to an aesthetic and ethical standard, in the sense of referring to a specific ethos. They constitute a matrix of significations particular to them and their arrangement reveals a symbolic strategy. This TV *entourage* includes plastic flowers, a religious picture, a false gold vase, family photographs, a broken laboratory glass and an old broken radio.

Such decorative objects are recurrent facts and thus, in Geertz's sense, fundamental and should be treated as a sociological problematic.[2] These things are also of the same order as what Malinowski[3] called the 'imponderabilia' of social life. Now, I will try to analyze each of those elements and show how they conform to a system of meanings.

The people I interviewed classified their objects as belonging to two orders: the aesthetic order – 'the ones that serve only to decorate' (the vase, the plastic flowers); and the utilitarian order – 'the ones that we use, or that can be useful for something' (the TV, the cracked laboratory glass and the radio that does not work). The religious painting and the photographs transcend this distinction between utilitarian and decorative functions: 'they are pretty, and good for something'. As this matter was considered by both (the observer and the observed) during the interview, we realized that all of the objects correspond to both planes of reference. The vase and flowers are decorations, and decorative objects are useful. The TV, the radio, and pictures are made to be watched, i.e. they are useful, but they are also 'pretty'.

Let me now describe ethnographically each of the components of this TV *entourage*. I will start by the cracked laboratory flask in this house; although it is uncommon, I am taking it exactly because it is an extreme example: it is a stereotype of scientificity and the scientific is particularly rich in meaning for people such as these who, one generation ago, were rural peasants. Even though it is cracked, it preserves the image of rationality (albeit a cracked rationality), of 'modern', 'urban' and 'scientific stuff'. Its non-use as laboratory equipment, because it is not in a lab and is broken, is just a circumstantial fate. The glass is decorating the house because 'scientific stuff' has a magical appeal, and it is the magical appeal that makes the lab glass a beautiful thing.

The plastic flowers in gold-colored vases are interesting because they are found even in houses that have real flowers planted in the courtyard. Most of these suburban houses are owned by people who immigrated from rural areas, and they continue to grow plants, even in very small yards. Regarding plastic flowers, they say: 'they last forever and are always pretty'. It seems that they control the production of plants in the yard, or planted in the empty cooking oil cans. But it is the plastic flower that is the main protagonist here, and there is no direct control over the production of plastic flowers: the things whose fabrication escapes their control have, *hau*, a mystique, an enchanting magic.[4] They are what anthropologists call fetishes, syntheses of symbolic meanings. They are also what political economists call commodity fetishes: they cannot be produced inside the domestic space, they must be bought, they are commodities. In order to buy them, one needs money, another fetish, that in all of its symbolic dimensions is above all an attribute of social legitimacy, prestige and power in an urban capitalist society. The commodity nature of these knickknacks is concealed through the transformation of money into objects – nobody would decorate their houses with coins – this mystique that accompanies the objects is what makes them 'pretty'.

The repertoire of objects in a house in a working-class neighborhood is strategically located in the most evident corner, next to the television, as a point of magical contagion. There is a common quality among all of its elements – that of fetish: from the non-control over their production, from their nature as commodities, and because they reify knowledge of another order and are thus cultural capital from another social class.[5] In other words, the things do not reflect their qualities as things, but rather their social qualities, precisely in the sense Marx employed the notion of commodity fetishism. Classical anthropology teaches us that the mystique of objects being exchanged is that the exchanged objects function not only in a system of obligations of giving and receiving as affective and mystical cement, but the objects are also, in themselves, syntheses provided by and for symbolic thought.

On the wall, next to the TV set, there is a family picture with several smaller photographs in the frame corners. In these working-class houses, photographs are rare, expensive and made to be displayed. Here the fetish dimension is linked with alien technology, the event of capturing these feelings and images of relatives that have died or did not come to the city. Small snapshots from ID cards ('identities') are placed on top of the family picture, within the borders of its frame. These 'identities' qualify individuals to function in the urban institutional order (they must be shown in order to receive medical treatment, to attend school, to find a job, or to vote). The framed pictures are a bricolage of lost kinship webs through another magical technique – that of freezing images. The social system that broke these kinship webs is reproduced in the symbolic system within the photograph frames – the large pictures are of the *lost* relatives (dead or still in the country): the small IDs are the modern, urban relatives who have made the transition.

Religious pictures are also common in working-class homes. In this case, we have a brightly colored religious image of Noah building the Ark with his family, which is in itself a myth, and recognized as such. The caption, written in capital letters, THE ARK OF GOD ANNOUNCING THE FLOOD, strengthens the relation of the two myths – that of Noah's family and of the family-photograph image – because both refer to origins. Written words in illiterate households are like the family pictures and the laboratory-glass artifacts of distant origins; they are a discourse on divine things – things of another world and from an imprecise time. The written words are a wise speech about the unintelligible.

The TV is the most important element among the set of objects in a home of the working-class group. The TV set sits on its own small table, with the importance of a monument, and it is typically decorated with a crocheted doily. The TV, on or off, represents the owner's search for the social recognition of TV ownership which is why it has to be visible from the street. The old radio, next to the television, has already lost its charisma but is still there, documenting the earlier form of this status attribute. The television as an object is a vehicle of a knowledgeable and modern speech, it is rationality in the domestic universe, where the rational order is paradoxically sacralized as mystic. 'We like TV a lot because we find out about things, the fashions, the news, and on the Fantástico (a popular TV Sunday variety show) they even show some experiments that the scientists are doing.' The TV object here is a fetish in the sense that it is infused with an ethereal magical meaning (that for which there is no rational explanation or over which there is no control); even when it is turned off and when no one is watching it, it is potential cultural capital, consecration of legitimate knowledge.

All these objects in working-class houses are strategically placed in the most obvious corner of the house's front room. They are arranged around the TV set and they have a common quality: 'modernity'. They are seen as urban rationality inside the domestic space, and as an ethos and cultural capital of another class. They are meant to be seen from the street by those capable of recognizing this social code, which is also an aesthetic code.

In the working-class neighborhood the boundaries between house and street are imprecise. The doors are always open, in order to enlarge the space of the front room, and in many cases the door is the only opening in the room. The television and decorative objects seen from outside have a demonstrative role as indicators and as social attributes prized by those initiated into that status code. The tenuous demarcation of space between the house and the street is the veranda, or porch, the liminal space of the domestic sphere, the place of mediation and contagion, where the system of exposed objects is also a system of socially significant signifiers. The liminal space is ritualistically preserved as such. The external antenna, as an attribute of the television, could in part fulfill the function of indicating the household possessions to the neighborhood, but the liminal space where the body-to-body, face-to-face contact occurs – the immediacy of the mediation – is fundamental in this social relation.

The plastic rose in the 'golden' vase, the photographs, the religious image, the laboratory flask, and most of all the television set and the spaces they occupy in the domestic order are meanings that comprise a cultural rationale. That is, a symbolic system, including an ethos of modernity, that is itself a part of a larger symbolic universe that has as its principal locus of significance the city and industry. This system of meanings seeks to 'conquer' the urban power space (that of capitalistic relations), while insistently trying to differentiate and delimit urban cultural space from the rural space that is still very close to the actors, by manipulating signs that are shared by their group as indicators of social prestige.

Erudite repertoire

The popular taste of working-class people is expressed in objects which they think are elements of the elite's cosmology. Paradoxically, upper-class members identify those items as low-class and tasteless.

[. . .] In upper-class houses there is enough space for many things, while in small, working-class houses, turning the TV set on influences the dynamics of the entire home and mobilizes its occupants. In the day-to-day lives of the upper class (and in their life histories) there are many alternatives and possibilities and plenty of capital (in all its forms) that allow them access to a whole universe of commodities. In the lives of working-class people, watching TV is one of the few possibilities for leisure. This activity takes place during the scarce, non-working hours and it is understood as a form of participation, although marginal, in the universe of the other class.

The upper class does not consider watching soap operas to be a legitimate activity for members of their class. The identification of watching soap operas with lower-class taste implies, or could imply, that a person who watches TV regularly and readily admits to doing so lacks full participation in an elite system of values, which is associated with dominant positions in the social structure. The lack of participation in the elite's world view might also indicate in such a person a lack of aptitude for playing the dominant role.

The houses of upper-class families have many rooms and the TV set is never near the front door. Usually, the living room is very spacious and the TV set will be almost hidden inside it. TV tables with wheels are considered 'ugly' and in 'very poor taste'. In apartments that have smaller living rooms, the TV set is usually confined to the bedroom. In many cases, there is a specific room just for watching TV, so that it will not interfere with the other activities in the house. In contrast to working-class houses, those of the upper class have distinct rooms for each activity and the separation is strictly maintained. The notions of *privacy*, *self*, and *individuality* are important parts of this world view and wealth allows these notions to be made concrete in commodities, space, objects, possessions. There is a place for each thing and one of everything for everybody. Frequently, there is more than one TV set, one for the children, one for the maids, and another for the other adults of the house.

There is no positive aesthetic value associated with the TV set. In all forms and shapes it is considered a utilitarian object; it is not decorated, nor is it considered a decorative object.

Just as the lower classes value the TV as representing sophisticated technology, the upper classes prize their expensive sound systems which only they can afford to own. They seem to associate with them an analogous aesthetic value because the superlative stereo technique indicates prestigious erudition.

Decorative objects in upper-class houses can be classified according to three categories – *folk art*, *art*, and *antiques* – each category representing a search for originality, uniqueness, and possessions as indicators of privilege. Folk and 'native' handicrafts, such as weaving and pottery, are considered beautiful because of their uniqueness, and because they are not industrially mass-produced. Associated with folk and indigenous art is the idea of primitive exoticism. In fact, this is only possible because of the great social distance between the upper class and these 'primitive' and 'folk' artifacts. The distance is such that the consumption of these objects entails no risk for them of confusion with a lower-class identity. This practice, and the values associated with it, is an inversion of the role of plastic flowers in working-class homes. For the upper class, aesthetic and social taste is expressed in hand-made rural folk objects, for the working class it is the manufactured, urban object that carries meanings associated with prestige.

In contrast to working-class spaces, upper-class houses and apartments have a foyer or entrance hall that prevents contiguity of the house and the street. This is a space that establishes distant and formal relations. Before penetrating the most intimate interior rooms there are many spaces to traverse: the telephone, intercom, the foyer, the hall, and the sitting room. Such houses have more than one entrance – the social and the *de serviço* (tradesman's entrance). It is the entrances that classify those who come to the house as either subalterns or social equals; visitors classify themselves and know which entrance they should use. The service and work sphere is associated with the kitchen and 'social' life with the living room.

The notions of space, division of space, and empty spaces are aesthetic elements and crucial values in the upper-class group. Aesthetic conceptions of taste, beauty, and ugliness are socially produced. They are defined according to expectations of one group toward the other. In a class society, taste situates its generative locus of significance in the dominant culture or the representations that the other social groups make about what the dominant culture is. Thus, the working class imitates what it takes to be the aesthetic elements of the upper class, while the upper class studiously appropriates and labels as 'folk' and 'art' handicrafts, everyday items, and sacred objects from the others, and reconstructs them as exotic other. They become art only after their manipulation and their classification as such by the upper class. Also they become 'beautiful' only when lifted out of their original context and displayed together with 'fine art' and 'antiques', conveying an aura of erudite taste.

Taste, which is often considered to be a very subjective and individual notion, is in fact a social standard that takes for prestigious the established power relations.

[. . .]

Notes

1. O. Fachel Leal and R. Oliven, 'Class interpretation of soap opera narrative: The case of the Brazilian "Novela summer sun"', *Theory, Culture and Society*, 5: 81–91, 1988.
2. C. Geertz, *The Interpretation of Cultures*, New York: Basic Books, 1973.
3. B. Malinowski, *Argonauts of the Western Pacific*, New York: Dutton, 1961.
4. M. Mauss, *A General Theory of Magic*, London: Routledge and Kegan Paul, 1972.
5. P. Bourdieu, *Distinction: A social critique of the judgement of taste*, London: Routledge and Kegan Paul, 1984.

5.5 □ *Marianne Gullestad*

For the most part, Marianne Gullestad's contribution is concerned with the ongoing creation of homes by so-called ordinary people living in Bergen. Her work details the use of domestic space in these Norwegian households and reflects on the ways in which home and family are articulated to gender and class relations.

Home decoration as popular culture: constructing homes, genders and classes in Norway[1]

[. . .]

I want to approach constructions of gender and class through an examination of some of the cultural practices of the house.

[. . .]

The house as a key symbol for modern intimacy

[. . .] Western family-households have not only lost several functions in the process of modernization, they have also taken on new functions. The most important, in my view, is to provide a setting for modern intimacy. This function is so central that the modern family-household can be described primarily as a moral community. Intimacy is created and expressed by the way [. . .] household activities are performed. It is simultaneously a household function and an intrinsic part of family relations.

[. . .] Norwegians do not only have houses, they have homes. The word *hjem* (home) brings together in one notion both the idea of a place and the idea of a social togetherness associated with this place. The notion has both material and less tangible social, emotional, moral and spiritual connotations.

[. . .] I will argue that Norwegian culture is home-centred, and that the symbolic value of the concrete and physical aspects of the home is in the process of becoming more important. [. . .] Through the arrangements of their homes, Norwegians express

321

themselves as gendered human beings belonging to specific social classes and reference groups. Home decoration and home improvement is thus a part of the construction and reconstruction of social groups. Simultaneously the home is both highly gendered and highly shared as a cultural symbol and a focus of attention for women and men.

[. . .]

Homes in Norway

To Norwegians, the home is [. . .] a setting for interactions both within the family and with relatives, and extending outside of the family, with friends. There is not much of a pub or restaurant culture in Scandinavia and in the neighbourhoods there are few neutral and informal settings for meeting other people. Becoming friends often means being allowed to pass through the doorway. In many neighbourhoods, a line is drawn between the people one visits (*går inn til*) and others.

The most important opposition inherent in the form and use of the home is that between the home itself and the outside world (*hjemme/ute*). The doorway is the main boundary between the inside and the outside. The front door, locks, name-plate, door mat and door bell can be seen as practical and symbolic markings of this important boundary. The doorway can be seen as both a protection of the values of the home and a barrier against the outside world.

In the opposition between the home and the outside (*hjemme/ute*), 'home' stands for warmth, security, cosiness (and perhaps a little boredom). 'Out' stands for excitement but also some danger. [. . .]

[. . .] Within each house there are rooms which are more or less private. The hall and the living room are the most public rooms. The parents' bedroom is considered the most private room for outsiders. This is often expressed when someone shows off a new apartment or a new house. Guests walk into most of the rooms except the master bedroom where they often stand at the threshold just peeking in respectfully. [. . .]

The boundary between *the public and the private* does not only vary with place but also with time. Some parts of the day are more suitable for visits than others, and then the living room is more public than at other parts of the day or night.

[. . .]

'Ordinary people' in Bergen

My ideas about the Norwegian home derive from fieldwork [. . .] conducted among young urban working-class families with small children.[2] [. . .] A few glimpses from it will provide an empirical foundation for the discussion which follows. The husbands had jobs as labourers, craftsmen, salesmen and lower-level clerks. All of them were wage-workers, although one, a hairdresser, was planning to set up his own business.

The wives worked as self-employed childminders (*dagmammaer*), as cleaning assistants, shop assistants and office personnel. Husbands and wives alike had relatively little education beyond the nine years of obligatory schooling. They used the expression 'ordinary people' (*vanlige folk*) as a designation for themselves.

The couples were young, at a stage in the life cycle where they had little money and many needs. Most lived in three-room apartments with a kitchen and a bathroom. The apartments were located in large co-operative housing estates in different satellite towns of Bergen. This meant that the home-making activities were mainly concentrated upon the interiors of the houses. In addition, the car was, as we shall see, an object of improvement and decoration.

The young couples were also at a stage of life where home-making is important. At any one point in time, most had a project planned. 'Last year we did the bathroom and next year we plan to panel the hall', was a typical refrain. Within the apartment, the different rooms were decorated according to different rules. The living room is the main room for display and has a higher priority than all the other rooms. It is the most public room, where guests are received, as well as the room where the family 'relaxes' in the evenings. To 'relax' (*slappe av*) and to have a good time (*kose seg*) means to sit idly, maybe watching television, chatting and eating some snacks.

Since the living room is a room of display, it usually contains the best furniture, lamps, pictures and ornaments. The arrangement of objects shows a desire for a polished and almost sumptuous comfort. This impression was created by shining surfaces, for example leather, glass, painted wood and an abundance of plants and ornaments made of glass, porcelain, brass, alabaster and onyx, and by maintaining a spotless order.

Furniture was dark and voluminous, and together with lamps, plants, pictures and ornaments, arranged in a set of compositions or zones. The couch ensemble with soft chairs and a coffee table, often close to the TV and the wall unit is one zone. Other zones may be a dining table, a bar, or a stereo unit. Some people have a dining table and chairs, but many prefer instead to create an extra zone around the TV by adding a couple of soft comfortable chairs and a coffee table. This kind of furniture fits well with serving cream cakes and open-faced sandwiches. If guests are invited for dinner, it is also served on the coffee table. In this way, a balance is ideally struck between a polished and spotless display and a soft and easy comfort.

Few old things are found in these homes. The young couples see no charm in buying furniture at a flea market as many students do. Neither is it relevant to obtain a prestige-filled past by going to auctions as many well-off, educated people do. They would rather be modern and follow the fashions in the furniture catalogues which arrive in the mail. The young women are the consumer experts, study the pictures and comment upon who in their circle of friends already has this bedroom set or that living room set. This explicit interest for novelty and fashion appears to have some connection with a childhood in which they lived in close quarters and could not afford things: old things are associated with a past one wants to leave behind, not with a past one looks back on with nostalgia.

The furniture making up the different zones is co-ordinated with lamps, pictures and ornaments. The wall unit, preferably with glass doors, is the frame for several of the decorations (*pynte-tingene*). Having baby Vaseline or similar items of use in the wall unit is quite clearly not right – such things just do not belong there. In some cases, the decorations are bought from the wife's earnings, to symbolize her paid work in a special way. 'I buy one ornament every month when I get my wages', a young woman says, 'just to know that I am working.' Such ornaments may be grouped in twos and threes in the wall unit, on the TV set or on the window sills. The principle behind each of these smaller compositions is some kind of likeness of, for instance, colour and material, combined with an interesting contrast of shape. Sometimes small crocheted doilies, placed underneath an object or a group of objects, mediate between the different small compositions. The principle behind the total arrangement of decorations seems to be symmetry: each little ornament or group of ornaments is placed at a fair distance from the others.

In this way, smaller compositions make up larger compositions or zones which again make up the 'wholeness' (*helheten*) or 'style' (*stilen*) of the living room. In the desire to be able to display a spotless and shining living room 'in case someone should drop by', we can sense a certain continuity with the parlours of earlier peasant and working-class generations. Signs of activity, for example children's toys on the carpet or newspapers on the coffee table, damage the general representative impression. In order to keep the living room spotless, small children are seldom allowed to play there. They play in their own room (the smallest of the two bedrooms), in the kitchen and in the narrow hallway. The door to the living room is very often locked in the morning, being first unlocked to the children for the daily ritual of children's evening television and for the time that parents and children spend there together. Then the parents are also present and make sure the children do not break anything.

The kitchens of these apartments are generally rather small and narrow, and from the functionalist middle-class architect's point of view, apparently intended just for cooking and doing the dishes. The young families, however, turn it into a much more central, multi-purpose room. The family takes most of the daily meals around a small Formica table in the kitchen. Often the young women have their purses sitting in a regular place in the kitchen. Many families also have important papers, such as bills and bank books, in the kitchen, which therefore also functions as an office.

In one of the drawers, cosmetics, hair brushes and combs are found. There is a mirror on one of the counters which is brought out when needed. Women often sit in the kitchen when they make themselves up and do their hair. In other words, nature is converted to culture in the kitchen, not only through the preparation of food, but also to a certain degree through the decoration of the human body.

In addition, the kitchen is a second room for receiving guests. It is the more intimate, smaller stage of the apartment. Close women friends who come for a visit in the morning are invited into the kitchen for a cup of coffee. Then they sit around the kitchen table and chat while the children play.[3] In the afternoons and evenings, when the husband is at home, the kitchen is an extra place to be. If a woman comes to visit, the two women can gather in the kitchen while the husband watches television in the living room; or he can listen to the sports news in the kitchen while they occupy the living room. If a couple come for a visit, the women often go together to the kitchen to prepare food or drinks. Those sitting in the living room may note the door to the kitchen being closed carefully: the conversation behind the kitchen door is then confidential.

Being shown into the living room can be either a way of honouring the guest or a way of creating distance. There is a degree of creative ambiguity in this. With two places to choose between, there is a greater opportunity for juggling the definition of the situation. When many people choose not to have a kitchen which opens directly into the living room, it is not only because they dislike the cooking odours, but also because a separate kitchen offers the opportunity of having two separate rooms for social interaction.

Even if the kitchens are small and narrow, the inhabitants carry on more activities there than the planners of the estates had intended. This use has its roots back in the farm kitchen where, for example, one had a barber's mirror and a wash-basin. While the planners intended a separation of functions (applying make-up in the bathroom/bedroom, playing in the children's room, receiving guests in the living room, etc.), their inhabitants thus put some of these activities back together in more complex ways.

The picture the inhabitants hold of a good kitchen is neither the functionalist laboratory nor the romanticized farm kitchen with a lot of cooking smells and tastes. The working-class town kitchen is the pivotal place in the house. It is similar to the farm kitchen by virtue of the many functions that are collected there, but different from the romanticized notion of the farm kitchen which parts of the Norwegian middle class now entertain.

While the living room is the most public and most representative room, the bedrooms are considered the most private rooms. The rules for their decoration are therefore less strict. At this stage of young family life, the living rooms had been renovated, but not all the bedrooms. Most used the bedrooms just as the architect had imagined: the big bedroom for the parents and the little one for the children.

In principle, the home as a whole is a gender-neutral universe. In practice, it is largely a female universe. Especially for husbands engaged in physical work, there may be a contrast between the living room's ideal polished comfort and their own appearance. There is a somewhat greater contrast between men and women in this social class than, for instance, in much of the Norwegian academic middle class. A 'real man' is strongly built and handy when it comes to building things and making repairs. Parts of the home are associated more with one gender than with the other. To a large degree, the kitchen is the domain of women, while the men have the cellar, the garage, or the car. But as these apartments do not have cellars, garages or other typical masculine places, the men turn to the car as the most masculine place to be and to do things. The car is, so to speak, the apartment's male annexe. Small wonder, then, that the cars in these social circles are in very good condition.

That the home is very much the woman's domain is discursively expressed in many ways. When talking about their parental home, young adults say 'at my mother's' (*hos min mor og de*). Also, the young women commonly used the expression 'my carpets' and 'my floors' in discussions about housework with women friends. Having the main responsibility for housework gives a degree of control over the placing of people and objects. These observations say something about both the women's creative activity as well as their controlling influence in the small and close contexts of the home. This influence, however, is often paired with a corresponding impotence in other social contexts.

[. . .]

Home decoration as a continuous project

Norwegian men and women have for several generations prioritized a good house (or apartment) over other kinds of consumption, such as visits to cafés, restaurants and bars. This may be related to the cold climate and to an underlying value of religious pietism that explains the relative dearth of public meeting places. However, there are today some striking new tendencies which require analysis. Over the last generation, many kinds of home production have been reduced, while one kind has become considerably more important. There is an increasing emphasis placed upon renovating and furnishing the home. Most people use less time on such things as making juice and jams and sewing their own clothes, while at the same time they spend more time, money and love on decorating their homes.

Beate's and Nils' home is a good illustration of how home decoration has become an ongoing concern. These are people admired by friends and acquaintances for their nice home. As soon as they moved in, they started decorating their apartment. When they completed decoration, they started all over again, so parts of the apartment were decorated more than once during the two years of my fieldwork. First they did the living room and the hall. The living room has two different wallpapers in patterned red and green, and contains a dark leather couch ensemble, dark brown tables and a white cupboard with drawers and shelves. There is a white bench for the stereo equipment, brown velvet curtains, and an abundance of lamps and ornaments. An old kerosene lamp from the husband's childhood home at a farm near Bergen, with a pot of green plants where the kerosene used to be, hangs over the coffee table. An Italian reproduction of a crying boy hangs over the couch, in addition to a 'real painting', made in Japan from a photograph of Beate's son (obtained from a door-to-door salesman who came to everybody in the block).

When the living room was done, the kitchen was redecorated. Walls and cupboards were panelled with different kinds of laminated panelling; every cupboard and drawer was covered and framed by wooden mouldings and given new knobs. A dish-washer was installed, and the room was equipped with new curtains and a new dining table. Then the bathroom walls were covered with Formica, and a new mirror, hooks and towel-racks were installed. The walls and ceiling in the toilet were painted. In the boy's room they put up two kinds of 'boyish' wallpaper (with cars and airplanes), as well as curtains, shelves, a table and a bed. Lastly they did up their own bedroom. They sold the beds that Beate's father, a carpenter, had made for them (nobody in the family wanted them) and bought new fashionable beds. New wallpaper and a soft wall-to-wall carpet was installed. In all the rooms in the apartment they had installed new covering on the floors, either carpet made of artificial materials or vinyl.

In the meantime, the furniture in the living room was rearranged many times. Beate's father made them an original bar in the form of a small open wagon arranged as a man lying over a woman. The bar-wagon is about 1½m long and stands on the floor with glasses and bottles. They bought stereo equipment in a vertical rack, acquired second-hand from someone who needed the money. The stereo bench they had before was given to Beate's brother: since her father had made it, she did not like the idea of selling it to him.

Beate lost her liking for the dark patterned wallpaper in the hall and she wanted lighter colours which became more fashionable in 1980–1. They plastered and textured the walls in white, and changed the frames around the doors, the door sills and the floor covering to a dark-brown shade. The fashion was inspired by the architecture of holiday hotels in Spain. They also changed the floor covering to imitation tiles to go with the white walls and dark brown frames. The next project was to treat one of the walls in the living room with the same white plaster. There, too, Beate became tired of the two dark, patterned wallpapers. But she did not want more than two white walls; four white walls would have been too uniform in her opinion. They subsequently changed the couch ensemble to a still more fashionable one, covered with oxblood-coloured leather and filling the whole corner.

Whenever I asked Beate about the division of work between her and her husband Nils, she answered, 'We do it together. We share it.' After a while I learned what this means: that it is a joint project, not that there is no division of tasks. For heavy reconstruction work 'doing it together' meant that she helps Nils, for instance by holding something, or handing tools to him if he works alone. She may also help him by making a good meal, and keeping him company while he works. He is an especially handy man, having been brought up on a farm close to Bergen. Beate, on the other hand, is a 'typical urban girl', and does not identify with rough kinds of work. She knows how to sew and knit, even though she does not practise this very much. She is proud of several silk lampshades that she has made for herself and for others. Both of them, and especially Nils, get help cheaply from relatives and friends. Because of his job, as a repairman in an automobile repair shop, Nils is able to offer other services in return. They may also occasionally use hired craftsmen, but that is uncommon. He often (alone or together with male friends) puts up the wallpaper or the panel, but she is responsible for choosing the equipment and often for finding the best buys and paying the bills. For larger items they always go shopping together. Both want to have a say and agree on what to buy, but she plans and directs most of the aesthetic and economic aspects of home-making, whereas he plans and carries out the more technical aspects. As she explains, 'He does not care whether there are one or ten pots of plants in the window. To me it means a lot.' She plans, but needs his consent and co-operation. 'Beate has such good taste', other women say, 'and she is so determined.'

In their social circles, this couple is particularly successful in the way they manage to equip and decorate their apartment. There are several reasons why Beate and Nils are so successful at this stage of their marital life, where many other families have economic problems. They receive income from two full-time jobs. In addition, he often works overtime and together they have a job of a few hours of cleaning every week in the neighbourhood. Because of his job, Nils is able to offer services to many friends and acquaintances and to get their services and help in return. There is much work and a complex economy behind their success.

Home improvement has generally become more important not only for working-class people, but also for other groups, and not only for the very young, but also for their parents who are now in their fifties, and not only for urban people, but also for people in the rural areas. Holtedahl,[4] for instance, describes the 'suburbanization' of patterns of life in northern Norway, while Thorsen,[5] in her study of three generations of farmer women in inland Norway, describes how the family and the home have become more important. All over Norway, Norwegians are thus buying furniture and gluing wallpaper like never before. Renovating and furnishing have in many ways become a continuous project. Home furnishing is not something done and finished with only to be redone when something wears out. Things are renewed for the sake of change.

[. . .]

Middle-class professionals seem to lament what they see as a waste of time and money. Their understanding of why people restructure the interiors of their houses and apartments is generally somewhat condescending: money to burn, psychological obsolescence, compensatory consumption, hunting for status, privatizing, materialism, egotism and manipulation by advertisers. Since the home is a rich and multi-faceted phenomenon, there may be something to several of these explanations. For example, when more time, money, love and care are put into the house, there may be less time, money and strength left for other things. Home improvement activities can therefore have unintended consequences. However, there is also evidence that house-building and home improvement are embedded in a social network exchange of goods and services.[6]

The usual ways of looking at the phenomenon are in my view one-sided and negative. Before we have listened to the people themselves and participated in their daily rounds of life, we have not really understood why secularized Norwegians invest so much of their time and money this way.

[. . .]

Home decoration as creativity

Norwegians do not only use more time for renovating and furnishing the home. These activities have also received a new significance. 'The home' is also a creative and expressive statement and it is my theory that this has come more into the foreground. The advantage of the analysis that follows is that it takes into consideration the reasons people themselves give.

In order to develop this argument, let me first point out some striking contrasts between the outsides and the insides of co-operative estates. Planners are responsible for the outsides of apartment estates and residential areas, reflecting the functionalist architectural view. [. . .] The outsides of the houses are, therefore, often lacking in decorations, detail and any visual stimuli. These houses are, so to speak, almost 'mute' on the outside. They 'talk' very little and the message that emanates from them is relatively monotonous and dull.[7] By contrast, the *inside* of the houses is a great display of objects and ornaments. The interiors are decorated to what is almost an extreme.[8] These interiors 'talk' by constituting very rich and flexible representational forms.

When Norwegians receive visitors for the first time, they often say something like: 'Well, we do not care about how other people decorate their homes. We have chosen to do it our way.' First and foremost these utterances demonstrate the importance of independence and self-sufficiency as cultural values in Norway. But implied in such statements is also a request that each home be considered personal and unique. True, seen from a superficial point of view, such statements can appear to be a little off the mark as one home is usually not that much different from other homes in the same social group. But the fact that people themselves emphasize the unique and exceptional qualities of their homes is an important piece of information. Why do they do this?

One of the answers is that home improvement is a way to be creative. Many elements are involved in this creative process, including gifts, furniture bought at a store and self-made bookshelves. The decoration of the home is, therefore, a result of inheritance, exchange in social networks, tangible home productions and creative consumption. The objects are given new meanings through recontextualization, actively interpreted and arranged in new compositions. These compositions follow established patterns, but they are also in a certain sense unique. Each person or family creates its own representational form. [. . .]

The activities involved in interpreting and recontextualizing mass-produced goods are not necessarily less creative than the interpretation and recontextualization of objects of fine arts. [. . .] The meanings [. . .] do not derive from the objects in isolation, but from the relationship between persons and objects. Wallpaper, furniture and other elements are creatively selected and combined in compositions which can give subtle messages with many nuances, since the elements which make up these compositions are also involved in other contexts of meaning.

In this way, the interior of the home has not merely large utility value but also large symbolic value. Since the supply of mass-produced goods, and therefore the possibilities of choice, are greater than ever before, the expressive aspect has become more prominent and the home become more of an expressive manifestation. [. . .]

The home as an expressive statement

What values and ideas are made manifest through the home? One answer is that people create themselves as individuals and as families through the processes of objectification involved in creating a home. The home is a rich, flexible and ambiguous symbol;

it can simultaneously signify individual identity, family solidarity and a whole range of other values. The following lists some elements in the symbolic value of a home: personal identity; the identity of the family; marital, filial and parental love; closeness (*nærhet*), sharing and togetherness (*deling og fellesskap*); a sense of wholeness (*helhet*), integration and unity in life; independence and self-sufficiency; safety, security (*tryg-ghet*), control, order, 'peace and quiet', cosiness (*kos*) and comfort (*hygge*), and decency (*være skikkelig*); practical sense and a realistic outlook; control and mastering; direction in life; and social reference groups.

The connotations of the expression 'a good home' (*et godt hjem*) are moral, while the connotations of the expression 'a nice home' (*et pent hjem*) are of an aesthetic kind. However, through aesthetics a vision of a moral order is created and expressed. One of the worst things one can say about somebody's home is that it is impersonal (*uper-sonlig*) and without ambience (*uten atmosfære*). Impersonal interiors give off the conno-tations of institutions or public waiting rooms, and do not really qualify as homes. The centrality of the home in Norwegian culture is thus complemented by a fear of insti-tutions.[9] A nice home should literally and figuratively be warm. The figurative mean-ings of warmth (*varme, lunhet, hygge, kos*) are, among other things, achieved through the arrangement of and care for objects. A home should be decorated (*pyntet, utsmykket*) in order not to give off an impression of impersonal emptiness. In addi-tion, a nice home should, of course, be relatively clean and tidy, and thus bear witness that the inhabitants are decent (*skikkelige, ordens*) people.

[. . .]

When interviewing people about their house, one quickly discovers that talking about houses often involves telling a life story. The individual's life cycle and the family's development cycle are closely connected to moving house or forming and reforming a house. Improving the home is a lifetime project which gives meaning to life.

[. . .]

Constructing genders

Until now I have emphasized some of the shared aspects to the cultural categories underlying the continuous home decoration project in Norway. Both women and men of different social categories create themselves as individuals and as families through their homes. I now want to problematize this analysis by discussing first gender and then social class. The home is a joint project for a husband and a wife, but they have different roles and are also differently located in relation to the division between the home and the outside.

I begin the discussion by spelling out some meanings of the shared cultural notion of 'a female hand' (*en kvinnelig hånd*), closely associated to notions such as good taste, *hygge* (comfort), *kos* (cosiness), *nærhet* (closeness) and care (*omsorg*). A female hand is needed to turn the house into a home: to create a good emotional ambience, to arrange the objects, as well as to clean, polish, tend and keep order. Even though particular men may be good home-makers, as they are defined in contemporary Norway, these abilities and activities are to a great extent a part of femininity. Men are expected to be handy and clever at construction work and repairs, while women are aesthetic and emotional specialists. [. . .]

This means that the healing potential of the home is to a large extent something wives provide for their husbands. Since women embody the home values of love (*være glad i*) as against the abstract and impersonal values of the outside, husbands are dependent on their wives to find wholeness and a point of balance in relation to their paid jobs. Wives [. . .] have been dependent on their husbands for economic provisioning for themselves and the children. The interesting question is what happens to these dependencies when women take up paid work and it is no longer legitimate to be an authoritarian husband or father.

On the face of it, there is a contradiction between women's paid work and home improvement becoming more (and not less) important as a creative and expressive activity. Actually, there is no contradiction. These different trends are related in several ways of which I will explore a few.

Even if women continue to be left with the main responsibilities for cleaning, nurturing and care, and even if they mainly work part-time, women are now allowed legitimately to leave their homes. The general trend is that Norwegian women no longer have to justify all their actions away from home in terms of the needs of their families. However, as married women engage in paid work, they also have the daily strain of reconciling quite different fields of activity. The opportunities to leave the home give women a less direct and more sentimental relationship to the home than before. Like their husbands, they also need a 'point of balance' and a place of 'wholeness', and this is part of the background for the home as a shared sentimental concern.

There are other interconnections. The new ideals of 'sharing' (*deling*) and 'togetherness' (*fellesskap*) among family members are created and maintained through the kinds of co-operation they are able to achieve, and these feelings are objectified in the composition and arrangement of objects in space. As the household is a moral community, producing and reproducing human beings, *how* decisions are made and tasks are allocated is very important.

The new ideologies of sharing, togetherness and equality defined as sameness between spouses in marriage, imply that the division of tasks can no longer be taken for granted, but constantly has to be negotiated and renegotiated. Because many factors other than ideologies shape the division of tasks, ideological changes have relatively little impact. Yet there are some important changes, both direct and indirect. Men do more child-care and housework than before. But, by tradition, different tasks have accumulated symbolic value as belonging to one gender or the other, and this makes changing the division of tasks much more than simply a practical and organizational matter. Playing with the children does not threaten masculinity as much as, for instance, changing soiled diapers or cleaning the floors. Sports, overtime at the job, repairing the car and redecorating the home are some of the alternatives men prefer, and throw into the negotiations. Of these alternatives, home decoration is, for many reasons, most attractive to the wife. Husbands, when negotiating division of tasks, may trade installing new wallpaper for cleaning the floors, and thus expand some of the masculine tasks within the household.

This pattern of exchange seems to prevail in many different forms of organizing work. In my [. . .] study in Bergen, for instance, I found interesting differences between working-class families where both spouses had grown up in the countryside and families where both had grown up in the city. The rural men had fewer buddies than the urban men, and the rural women were less opposed to doing rough work than urban women. For these and other reasons, rural couples in the city acted more as a team compared with urban couples who were engaged in gender-segregated social networks for performing household tasks. There are also differences between these social circles and career-oriented couples who may be inclined to use hired help for some of the tasks. The heavy reconstruction work may therefore be done by the husband alone, by husband and wife as a team, by the husband and his buddies, or by paid craftsmen.[10]

In spite of such differences, making home improvements in most families is a joint creative project, with the husband fulfilling a male role and the wife fulfilling a female role – in a transformed traditional sense. Making home improvements is in a special way an expression of a man's love for his wife. He is doing something for her and shows her that he gives her and the family a high priority in relation to other activities outside the family. For couples, home decoration can therefore be said to be a project of love.

[. . .]

Constructing classes

[. . .]

Most Norwegians want to have a 'nice home', but different social classes have somewhat different ideas about what 'a nice home' should look like, and differential economic and other means to realize their ideas. The concrete ideas of a carpenter in a rural community differ from those of an architect in the capital. Young people do not have the same ideas as middle-aged and old people. Their particular objectives may differ, as well as the ways of organizing the tasks to be done. The variation is associated with a diverse set of factors: (a) way of life, associated with occupation, education, region, religion, age and generation; (b) type of ownership of the housing unit; (c) financial means; (d) knowledge and interest in doing things for oneself; (e) participation in exchanges of goods and services in social networks; and (f) alternatives for using one's time.

[. . .]

The pattern underlying the decoration and use of working-class homes around 1980 was closer to that underlying the homes of the old or middle-aged business upper middle class than to the homes of younger academics. The established upper middle class (my informants called them 'directors' [*direktører*] and 'fine people' [*fine folk*]) also want a comfortable and representative living room where everything is spotless. Their homes also give off an impression of polished comfort and fashion. Moreover, tradition is more important here than in the satellite towns. The most important contrast is thus not the overall pattern, but the price and quality of the buildings and objects. For example, whereas one type of home is equipped with wall-to-wall nylon carpets, the other has pure new wool or parquet. Where one home has a store picture of a rococo lady, the other home has paintings signed by known artists, though in both cases they may be in gold frames. The objects vary, but their arrangement is not so different.

In these respects, there is more of a contrast between my informants and the younger part of the educated middle class. In the 1960s and 1970s, many of those who bene-fited from the 'educational explosion' after World War II found their livelihood in the service of the expanding welfare state, as social planners, social workers, teachers on all levels, and so on. There are obviously many differences concerning income, working conditions and lifestyle within such a broad category. There is, however, a common ethos in this part of the educated middle class. [. . .]

In these families, the husband may be interested in aesthetics as much as his wife, but often he is not. The husband will generally have a job with more autonomy and influence than the working-class man. His wife may have a similar job, but since she often works part-time, there will be some difference in power and prestige between them.

Around 1980, the homes of many young educated people displayed a typical Scan-dinavian mixture of modernism (*funksjonalisme*) and a transformed rustic peasant tradi-tion (*almuestil*). Walls were often painted white or covered with pine wood; floors were made of wood or covered with cork. Furniture was made of pine wood, with wool covering the couch ensemble. Instead of the wall unit, one would find simpler book-shelves filled with paperbacks and original graphic arts or posters on the walls. This representational form objectified a political vision, containing ideas about being close to nature by using 'natural' products, ecological awareness, a sense of quality, and so on. The rustic theme was evident from the natural materials and craftsman-ship. The living room did not necessarily have to be spotless: signs of activities (the 'right' pedagogical toys, musical instruments, periodicals, books) bore witness to an 'active' prestigious life. Tradition did not mean polished mahogany, but rather antiques from Norwegian farms and objects from other parts of the world – such as India and Afghanistan.

When choosing ornaments, these people favour the authenticity and exclusivity of hand-made objects as opposed to what they consider cheap, mass-produced goods. Young educated people like to think of themselves as uninterested in fashion and 'status symbols'. While the satellite town families I studied would rather have the latest colour television, many academics demonstrated that they did not 'sit and passively watch television all the time', by having only a black and white television set. In such ways, by setting up a contrast to the 'passiveness' of uneducated people, the educated middle class usually construct themselves as 'active'. They implicitly present themselves as

The Cultural Construction of Home

always eager to move on, in terms of social status as well as in terms of personal development.

At the time of my fieldwork, young educated people interpreted the polished and sumptuous living rooms of my informants in terms of notions such as 'passive', 'petty bourgeois', 'tasteless'. When my informants, on the other hand, interpreted the signs of multiple activities and the rustic quality of the living rooms of these young educated people, they applied notions such as 'shabby', 'disorderly', 'unfashionable'. Both tend to formulate an awareness of cultural class differences in moral terms. Since middle-class people define themselves in contrast to the working class, the working class to some extent influence what the middle class will or will not adopt. For instance, working-class people were the first to adopt video-recorders in Norway, while the middle class vigorously opposed it. But now, slowly, the meanings of video-recorders are reinterpreted from 'passive' to 'active'.[11]

Conclusion

[. . .] I have attempted discursively to spell out some of the very rich, flexible and ambiguous meanings of the Norwegian home as a representational form in Norway. The particular concern for the material and physical aspects of the home [is] connected to immaterial values and ideas. Or, to put it more precisely, values and identities are created and objectified in home decoration. Through explicating the meanings of cultural categories such as 'wholeness' and 'style' and their associated activities, I have demonstrated that the creative recontextualization of consumption[12] is not only a question of a period of time following the purchase, but a question of a very complex interplay of ideas and practices. It is crucial to the development of modern, creative mass-consumption that individuals are organized in family-households, based on modern feelings of romantic love and intimacy, and with a gender-specific division of tasks.

[. . .]

The home objectifies both individual identity and family solidarity. It is a shared concern for the spouses, as well as a female domain. It ties together the social classes, as well as being instrumental in the construction of the differences between them. These many contradictions constitute a span of ambiguity which demonstrates the very ambiguous and powerful location of the home in contemporary Norwegian culture: the home is privately central and publicly marginalized by being taken for granted. The values of the home are privately important and publicly neglected. And, to the extent that women are tied to the home, they may be privately strong and publicly powerless.

Because the modern desire for intimacy is particularly anchored in the home, it is possible to 'feel the pulse', so to speak, of modern Western civilization through an analysis of homes in Norway. The most seemingly trivial social fields may turn out to hold the greatest potential for cultural analysis.

Notes

1. The ethnographic material in this chapter is taken from M. Gullestad, *Kitchen Table Society: A case study of the family life and friendships of young working class mothers*, Oslo: Universitetsforlaget, and Oxford: Oxford University Press, 1984. See also M. Gullestad, *Livet i en Gammel Bydel* (Life in an Old Part of Town), Oslo: Aschehoug, 1979; M. Gullestad, *The Art of Social Relations: Essays on culture, social action and everyday life in modern Norway*, Oslo: Universitetsforlaget, and Oxford: Oxford University Press, 1992. The full version of this article was originally published in *The Art of Social Relations*, op. cit.
2. The term 'working class' is used as a shorthand and not as an analytical category.
3. This typical scene gave the book based on this fieldwork its title. *Kitchen Table Society*, op. cit.
4. L. Holtedahl, *Hva Mutter Gjør er Alltid Viktig*, Oslo: Universitetsforlaget, 1986.
5. L. Thorsen, 'Det Fleksible Kjønn: Mentalitetsendringer i Tre Generasjoner Bondekvinner', Unpublished Doctoral Dissertation, University of Oslo, 1989.
6. M. Gullestad, 'Arbeidsdeling, Forvaltning av Lønnsinntekter og Makt i Familien', *Tiddskrift for Samfunnsforskning*, Bind, 19: 415–30, 1978; M. Gullestad, 1979, op. cit.; M. Gullestad, *Livsstil og Likhet*, Oslo: Universitetsforlaget, 1985. In a study of council housing in England, Miller concludes that there is a link between people who seem lonely, depressed and isolated and a lack of decorative development. See D. Miller, 'Appropriating the state on the council estate', *Man*, 23: 353–72, 1988, p. 368.
7. The exception to this are a few owners of single homes who have not only decorated inside the house, but also the outside, with, for example, painted wheels, twisted roots, statues, running water and the like. In recent years, prefabricated houses have also become less functional, for example, the so-called Tyrol houses. In other words, there has been an expansion of decorating from inside to outside.
8. To many Americans, a typical Norwegian home appears as if an auction were about to take place, because of the staggering amount of furniture and decorations. However, both Americans and Norwegians have homes as opposed to just houses.
9. This is especially visible in childcare. Norway has fewer kindergartens and other daycare institutions than other welfare states.
10. M. Gullestad, 1978, op. cit.
11. In the years following my fieldwork, the fashions in both classes have changed. Educated middle-class homes have become either more sumptuous and polished or more high-tech; but with a slightly different vocabulary of objects, the mutual construction of contrasts is maintained.
12. D. Miller, *Material Culture and Mass Consumption*, Oxford: Blackwell, 1987.

□ *Sources and Acknowledgements*

1.1 Christine Delphy, 'Sharing the Same Table: Consumption and the Family', from *Close to Home: A Materialist Analysis of Women's Oppression*, translated and edited by Diana Leonard, London: Hutchinson, 1984. Reprinted with permission of the author, translator and Unwin Hyman/ITPS.

1.2 Ann Whitehead, '"I'm Hungry, Mum": The Politics of Domestic Budgeting', from Kate Young, Carol Wolkowitz and Roslyn McCullagh, eds, *Of Marriage and the Market: Women's Subordination in International Perspective*, London: CSE Books, 1981. Reprinted with permission of Routledge/ITPS.

1.3 Jan Pahl, 'Household Spending, Personal Spending and the Control of Money in Marriage', from *Sociology*, 24(1): 119–38, 1990. Reprinted with permission of the author and BSA Publications Ltd.

1.4 Gail Wilson, 'Money: Patterns of Responsibility and Irresponsibility in Marriage', from Julia Brannen and Gail Wilson, eds, *Give and Take in Families: Studies in Resource Distribution*, London: Unwin Hyman, 1987. Reprinted with permission of Routledge.

1.5 Sallie Westwood, 'Money, Money, Money', from Chapter 8 of *All Day, Every Day: Factory and Family in Women's Lives*, London: Pluto Press, 1984. Reprinted with permission of Pluto Press.

2.1 Anne Murcott, '"It's a Pleasure to Cook for Him": Food, Mealtimes and Gender in Some South Wales Households', from Eva Gamarnikow, David Morgan, June Purvis and Daphne Taylorson, eds, *The Public and the Private*, London: Heinemann Educational Books, 1983. Reprinted with permission of the author, the British Sociological Association and Ashgate Publishing Ltd.

2.2 Nickie Charles, 'Food and Family Ideology', from C. C. Harris, ed., *Family, Economy and Community*, Cardiff: University of Wales Press, 1990. Reprinted with permission of the author and University of Wales Press.

2.3 Peter Corrigan, 'Gender and the Gift: The Case of the Family Clothing Economy', from *Sociology*, 23 (4): 513–34, 1989. Reprinted with permission of the author and BSA Publications Ltd.

3.1 Rosemary Deem, 'Leisure and the Household', from Chapter 5 of *All Work and No Play?: The Sociology of Women and Leisure*, Milton Keynes: Open University Press, 1986. Reprinted with permission of Open University Press.

3.2 Dorothy Hobson, 'Housewives and the Mass Media', from Stuart Hall, Dorothy

Hobson, Andrew Lowe and Paul Willis, eds, *Culture, Media, Language: Working Papers in Cultural Studies, 1972–79*, London: Hutchinson, 1980. Reprinted with permission of the author and Routledge.

3.3 Janice Radway, 'The Act of Reading the Romance: Escape and Instruction', from Chapter 3 of *Reading the Romance: Women, Patriarchy and Popular Literature*, Chapel Hill: University of North Carolina Press, 1984, and London: Verso, 1987. Reprinted with permission of the author, University of North Carolina Press and Verso.

3.4 David Morley, 'The Gendered Framework of Family Viewing', from Chapter 6 of *Television, Audiences and Cultural Studies*, London: Routledge, 1992. Reprinted with permission of the author and Routledge.

3.5 Marie Gillespie, 'Technology and Tradition: Audio-Visual Culture Among South Asian Families in West London', from *Cultural Studies*, 3 (2): 226–39, 1989. Reprinted with permission of the author and Routledge.

3.6 Derek Wynne, 'Leisure, Lifestyle and the Construction of Social Position', from *Leisure Studies*, 9(1): 21–34, 1990. Published by E. & F. N. Spon, reprinted with permission of Chapman and Hall Ltd.

4.1 Cynthia Cockburn, 'Black and Decker Versus Moulinex', from Chapter 7 of *Machinery of Dominance: Women, Men and Technical Know-How*, London: Pluto Press, 1985. Reprinted with permission of Pluto Press.

4.2 Judy Wajcman, 'Domestic Technology: Labour-Saving or Enslaving?', from Chapter 4 of *Feminism Confronts Technology*, Cambridge: Polity, 1991. Reprinted with permission of Blackwell Publishers.

4.3 Ann Gray, 'Technology in the Domestic Environment', from Chapter 5 of *Video Playtime: The Gendering of a Leisure Technology*, London: Routledge, 1992. Reprinted with permission of the author and Routledge.

4.4 Graham Murdock, Paul Hartmann and Peggy Gray, 'Contextualizing Home Computing: Resources and Practices', from Roger Silverstone and Eric Hirsch, eds, *Consuming Technologies: Media and Information in Domestic Spaces*, London: Routledge, 1992. Reprinted with permission of the authors and Routledge.

4.5 Ann Moyal, 'The Gendered Use of the Telephone: An Australian Case Study', from *Media, Culture and Society*, 14(1): 51–72, 1992. Reprinted with permission of Sage Publications Ltd.

5.1 Leonore Davidoff and Catherine Hall, '"My Own Fireside": The Creation of the Middle Class Home', from Chapter 8 of *Family Fortunes: Men and Women of the English Middle Class, 1780–1850*, London: Hutchinson, 1987. Reprinted with permission of the authors and Routledge/ITPS.

5.2 Judy Attfield, 'Inside Pram Town: A Case Study of Harlow House Interiors, 1951–61', from Judy Attfield and Pat Kirkham, eds, *A View from the Interior: Feminism, Women and Design*, London: The Women's Press, 1989. This material, first published by The Women's Press Ltd, 34 Great Sutton Street, London, reprinted on pages 290–300, is used by permission of The Women's Press Ltd.

5.3 Pauline Hunt, 'Gender and the Construction of Home Life', from Graham Allan and Graham Crow, eds, *Home and Family: Creating the Domestic Sphere*, Basingstoke: Macmillan, 1989. Reprinted with permission of Macmillan Ltd. © Graham Allan and Graham Crow 1989. All rights reserved. No reproduction, copy or transmission of this publication may be made without written permission.

5.4 Ondina Fachel Leal, 'Popular Taste and Erudite Repertoire: The Place and Space of Television in Brazil', from *Cultural Studies*, 4(1): 19–29, 1990. Reprinted with permission of the author and Routledge.

5.5 Marianne Gullestad, 'Home Decoration as Popular Culture: Constructing Homes, Genders and Classes in Norway', from Teresa Del Valle, ed., *Gendered Anthropology*, London: Routledge, 1993. Reprinted with permission of the author and Routledge.

Index

Notes
1. Most references imply household or family, which are therefore generally omitted as qualifiers
2. Most references are to Britain, except where other countries are specified
3. Names in the Notes have been omitted, except where they are quoted

Aborigines 259
Africa
    and budgeting, politics of 39–46, 51
    and food 33, 60
    see also Ghana
aged people see elderly
agriculture see farmers
alcohol
    expenditure 58–9
    farmers and peasants 29, 30, 31, 33, 42
    and leisure 200, 201–3, 204, 208, 291
allowance
    for housekeeping 39, 46–9, 54, 83, 84
        see also budgeting; expenditure
    for pocket money see personal spending
    see also finances
alternatives to individualized housework 223–4
altruism 34, 45, 49, 101
    see also sharing
Anderson, B. 197
Andrews, W. and D. 230
Ang, I. 176
Arnheim, R. 159–60
Aronson, S. 261
artistic expression, domestic 307–9
Asia 60, 256
Asian people in Britain 4, 83–4, 148
    see also audio-visual culture
Attfield, J.: on Harlow house interiors 14, 290–300
audio-visual culture in South Asian families in London 10, 13, 186–98
    context of domestic viewing 188–9

fantasy and realism 194–5
genre 191–2
India, representation of 189–91
narrative 192–4
social and cultural uses of viewing experience 295–7
talking about and during 188, 196–7
Austen, J. 286
Australia 182, 217
    telephone use in 13, 258–73
authors of romance books 169
autonomy of women 306–7
    see also privacy

Bachelard, G. 308
Barrett, M. 100, 307
Barton, B. 283–4
Batstone, E. 93
BBC (British Broadcasting Corporation) 179
    computers 251–2
    programmes 155
    research 139
    see also radio
beauty of objects, perceived see Brazil
Bebel, F.A. 224
Beeton, I.M. 102
Bell, C. 208
Berk, R. and S. 143
Berthoud, R. 68
Bettelheim, B. 170
Biddell, A. 282
bills, major, payment of 59, 68, 72
Birds Eye Housekeeping Monitor 60
Birmingham: construction of home 279–83, 285, 287
birthdays
    gifts 119, 120, 123, 124, 125, 127, 132
    planning for 306
Bittmann, M. 223
black box, household as 54–5, 65
'Bombay' films see audio-visual culture
books see reading

Index